HANDBOOKS

P9-BBQ-554

FOUR CORNERS

JULIAN SMITH

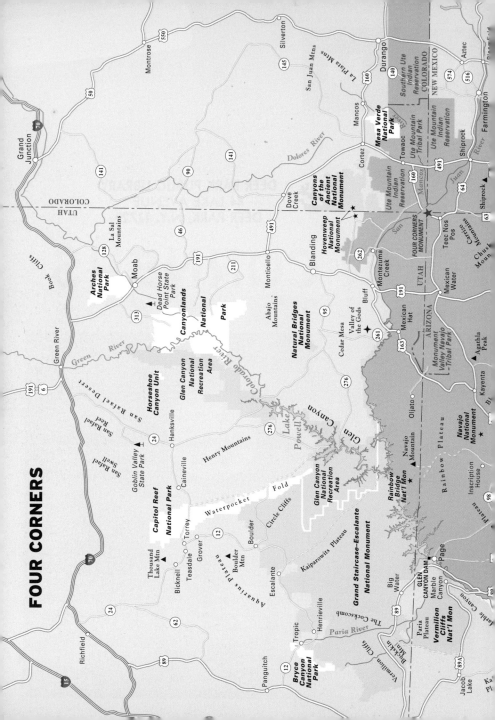

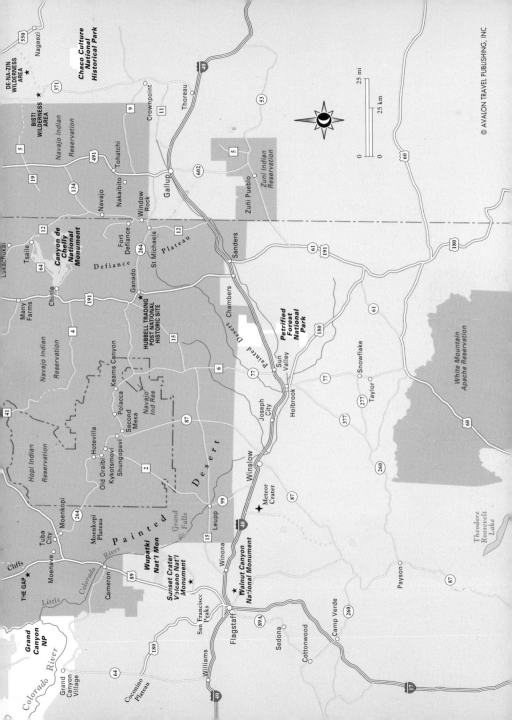

DISCOVER
THE FOUR CORNERS

I'm not sure when I realized the Four Corners was my favorite place on earth. It might have been during a summer monsoon over the canyon country, dark anvil clouds opening in a biblical torrent that in an hour was gone into the sand. A few pieces probably fell into place during a sunset from Muley Point, watching the sparks from a juniper campfire sweep out into the deepening darkness. The crazy thrill of paddling a dime-store raft across the Colorado River, hearing the thunder of rapids just around the bend, probably had a bit to do with it. Some sort of realization may also have dawned in a slot canyon in the Escalante, wading through muddy, ice-cold water with camera and pants held overhead, although that might just have been hypothermia coming on. Or maybe it's all thanks to Romeo, the old Navajo man I picked up hitchhiking near Page, who told me about his herds of horses and then just smiled and said, "I am happy."

Goblin Valley State Park

In any case, there is nowhere else I have ever been that is even remotely like the high, windswept, sun-punished heart of the Southwest. It's a landscape that exhausts the vocabulary, has you reaching for the thesaurus and tossing it aside in frustration. Wallace Stegner called it "a country that calls for wings," and spending an hour watching ravens play above a valley strewn with thousand-foot mesas will have you aching to join them. Over it all stretches the endless, indescribable bowl of sky, the "brilliant blue world of stinging air and moving cloud" that Willa Cather described in *Death Comes for the Archbishop:* "Everywhere the sky is the roof of the world; but here the earth was the floor of the sky. The landscape one longed for when one was far away, the thing all about one, the world one actually lived in, was the sky, the sky!"

The Four Corners is a region steeped in history, with villages centuries older than the country they eventually became part of. A crossroads of Native American, Spanish, and American cultures, this area lets you interact with tribes on two of the country's largest reservations and explore the ruins of peoples far older. Gazing up

blooming prickly pear cactus

© JULIAN SMITH

at huge, wraithlike figures painted in Old Testament times, it's hard not to marvel at a culture that prospered in this merciless setting, yet evaporated in less than a century, leaving countless ruins and artwork behind. The Navajo, Hopi, and Ute tribes weathered the influx of Anglo settlers and all they brought with them, and have emerged with their pride and many of their traditions intact. Here you can eat a taco next to a Navajo matron dressed in her best turquoise and silver, watch a feathered god dance in the plaza of a Hopi village, and enjoy a good-humored bargaining session over a rug that took months to weave by hand. Sometimes the adjustment is a shock, but the reward – being able to see your own culture through the lens of another – is well worth it.

If you're never happier than when you are careening down a single-track on a mountain bike, paddling raging white water, riding a horse through an aspen meadow, or sleeping under the stars, then you're also in luck. As outdoor recreation goes, the only thing the Four Corners lacks is a good surfing beach – though Moab does have a water park, and Lake Powell has plenty of shoreline. Pick a sport

Horses graze along Highway 12 in southern Utah.

for each season – hike in the spring, raft in the summer, bike in the fall, and ski in the winter – and you'll still have plenty to spare, from llama packing and hot-air ballooning to rock climbing and trout fishing. There are even a few activities special to the area, such as riding the narrow-gauge rail line out of Durango or heading down a slot canyon so narrow you have to scoot through sideways. It's possible to get good and truly lost out here, and to have a heck of a lot of fun doing it. For those addicted to solitude, there is nowhere else in the lower 48 where it's as easy to lose the crowds, or anyone else at all, for that matter.

The true enchantment of the place, though, is impossible to put into words, although many have tried. "I am drunk with the fiery elixir of beauty," wrote Everett Ruess, the vagabond artist who disappeared into a Utah canyon at the age of 20. "I have seen almost more beauty than I can bear." Edward Abbey, one of the most famous voices of the western deserts, told of the "huge vibration of light and stillness and solitude" that "shapes itself in the form of hovering wings spread out across the sky from the world's rim to the world's end."

Native American pottery

© JULIAN SMITH

In the end, though, it's futile – the spirit of the Southwest, cli-ché as the term has become, is beyond description, and has to be experienced in person. "It is a mystery," said Steinbeck in *Travels with Charlie,* "something concealed and waiting." With that, though, comes the possibility of discovery, and the fact that you're reading this far is a good start.

When you take the next step, you'll come to understand how extraordinary this place really is, and why it inspires such reverence among residents and even casual visitors. Spend some time, and you will appreciate the words of the Blessing Way, a ceremonial chant the Navajo use to restore *hozho,* the sacred harmony that gives focus and purpose to life:

In beauty I walk
With beauty before me I walk
With beauty behind me I walk
With beauty above me I walk
With beauty around me I walk
It has become beauty again

pictographs, Canyonlands National Park

Contents

MAP CONTENTS

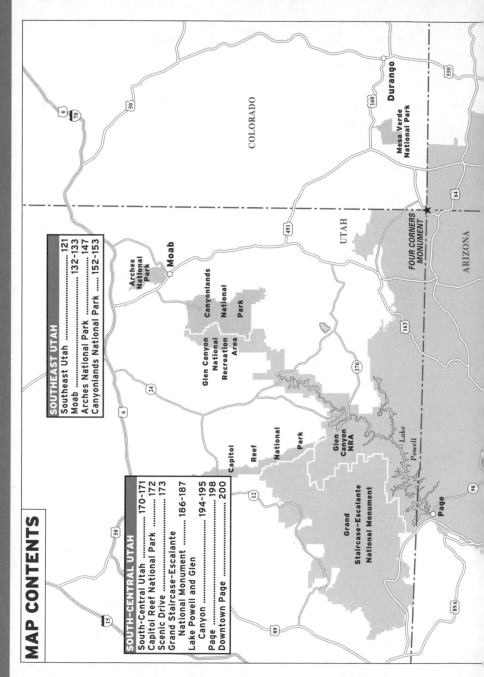

COLORADO

UTAH

ARIZONA

Durango

Mesa Verde
National Park

Moab

Arches
National
Park

Canyonlands
National
Park

Glen Canyon
National
Recreation
Area

Capitol
Reef
National
Park

Glen
Canyon
NRA

Grand
Staircase–Escalante
National Monument

Lake Powell

Page

FOUR CORNERS
MONUMENT

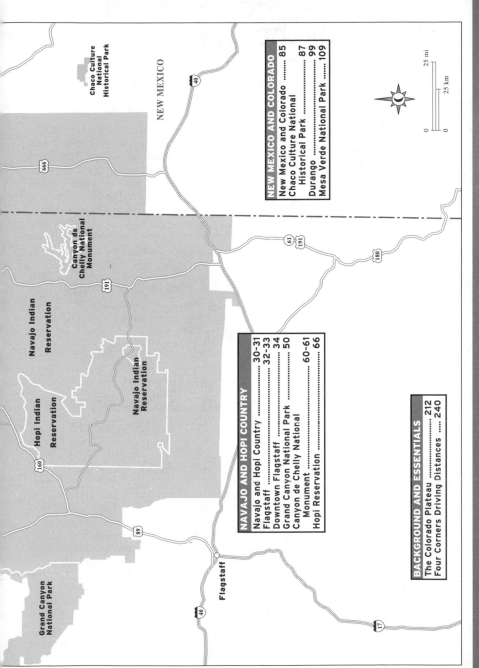

The Lay of the Land

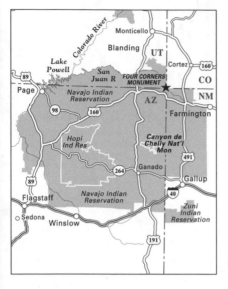

NAVAJO AND HOPI COUNTRY

Arizona's northeast corner contrasts the geologic wedding cake of the Grand Canyon with the snowy crests of the San Francisco Peaks. Flagstaff, the region's tourist hub, is an active city with enviable outdoor offerings, an outstanding cultural museum, and a lively college scene. Only a short hop away are the sublime expanses of the Navajo and Hopi reservations, ranging from the lush river bottom of Canyon de Chelly to the airy reaches of the Hopi mesas. There are few places on earth where you can hike into one of the Natural Wonders of the World one day, explore thousand-year-old ruins the next, and bargain with native artisans over handwoven rugs or finely wrought jewelry the day after that—this is one of the them.

NEW MEXICO AND COLORADO

The United States' archaeological heartland covers the northwest corner of New Mexico and the southwest corner of Colorado. It's anchored by two world-class historic sites: Mesa Verde National Park, with its famed "cliff palaces," and Chaco Culture National Historical Park, whose vast ruins sit open to the desert sky. Other outstanding ruins in the area include Hovenweep and Aztec Ruins national monuments and Salmon Ruins in Bloomfield, and you can learn all about them at the Anasazi Heritage Center or the Crow Canyon Archaeological Center near Cortez. Durango is the most entertaining city in southern Colorado, with hiking, skiing, mountain biking, and camping galore, as well as one end of the old-timey mountain train to Silverton.

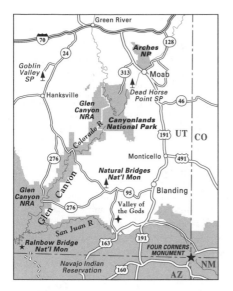

SOUTHEAST UTAH

It's easy to feel small in Southeast Utah, whether you're standing on the edge of a thousand-foot precipice or gazing up at a red stone arch that could hold an office building. **Canyonlands** and **Arches national parks** are both wonderlands of geology and less than an hour from the adventure-sports hotbed of **Moab**. Take a mountain bike ride on the famous **Slickrock Trail**, climb a desert tower, raft the **Colorado River**, or watch the sun set from Grandview Point on the **Island in the Sky**—whatever your preference, here you'll find yourself humbled and uplifted at the same time.

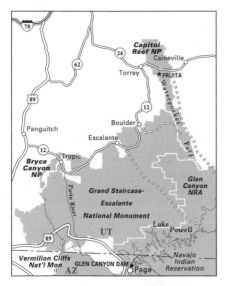

SOUTH-CENTRAL UTAH

It takes a little more driving to explore the U.S. version of Australia's hinterland, but for every slot canyon you negotiate, rock art panel you see, and apple you pick in **Fruita's desert orchards,** you'll give thanks you did. This part of the Four Corners is also the wettest, with houseboats and personal watercraft plying **Lake Powell's** hallucinatory blue expanse. There really aren't any tourist centers out here, and that's part of the point. **Escalante** and **Boulder** offer access to the canyons of the gigantic **Grand Staircase-Escalante National Monument,** and **Page** is tucked neatly between the Navajo Reservation and **Glen Canyon Dam,** but beyond that you're more or less on your own—and happier for it.

Planning Your Trip

The Four Corners is a sprawling, roughly defined, rugged, and all-around exotic place to travel, and there are as many ways to go about visiting as there are people who come. Some want nothing more than to drive their RV to the edge of the Grand Canyon and gaze into the abyss (and vice versa). Others point their dusty vans down the farthest dirt road and vanish for weeks on foot, bike, or raft. College students pile out of hostels and buses to explore national parks, families pore over jewelry at roadside stands on Native American reservations, and archaeology buffs poke around the crumbling ruins of long-gone cultures. But that is part of the fun: You can approach this region any way you choose, and rest assured that it will satisfy just about anything you have on your to-do list—as long as you arm yourself with the right information and take a few simple precautions.

With so many different destinations to choose from—not to mention a road map that looks like a spiderweb after a high wind—it can be a little overwhelming planning a trip around the Four Corners. A little guidance is therefore in order. The routes suggested later in this chapter are organized by type of activity, but they all follow roughly the same pattern. Starting at Flagstaff, the first three each describe a clockwise loop (following the layout of this book), touching New Mexico, Colorado, and stopping in Moab, Utah, before heading back south to Arizona. This way you can start or stop in either Flagstaff, Durango, or Moab, the three main tourist cities in the Four Corners, and switch from one route to another along the way. Each will take 2–3 weeks, depending on how quick you are. They all assume you have your own vehicle, and they don't include everything in the book—just the most outstanding sights in each category. Happy planning!

WHEN TO GO

In terms of weather, the best times to visit the Four Corners are in spring and fall. Warm days give way to cool nights, and the skies are mostly crystal-clear. Summer is hotter, making a venture into the backcountry (especially the Grand Canyon, the Escalante, and Utah's canyonlands) an exercise in getting from one water source to the next as much as anything else. Summer also brings the monsoon season, with mornings of cloud buildup relieved by brief downpours (which don't always make it all the way to the ground). Increased rainfall turns many dirt roads into mud bogs. It's still possible to have a great time here in summer. Most locals head into the hills, where temperatures are cooler and running water more abundant.

Winter brings out a whole new side of the Four Corners. The place is mostly deserted, for starters, and many local businesses are closed. As a result, you'll have just about everything to yourself, whether it's the snow-dusted hoodoos in Bryce Canyon or Mesa Verde's ruins soaking up the brief sunshine. Like rain, melting snow can make dirt roads impassable. The desert in winter is a weird, wonderful thing. Skiing is a great way to get around, whether it's cross-country into a park, backcountry in the La Sals near Moab (be careful of avalanches), or at resorts near Flagstaff and Durango.

WHAT TO TAKE

Water, water, water. Except for when it's actually raining on your head, you really should never be without a water bottle in your hand in the Southwest. Backpack hydration systems like those made by Camelback are very handy. Sun protection is just as important: light, long-sleeved shirts, pants, sunglasses, and a hat with a wide brim are ideal. Otherwise, slather on the sunscreen (at least SPF 30). Some companies make special "desert" hats, basically baseball caps with long flaps in the back to protect your neck. A warm layer such as a light fleece jacket or sweater comes in handy for cool evenings. When packing clothing, try to avoid cotton, as it can chafe when it gets damp; synthetic fabrics are light, breathe well, and dry almost instantly.

TOURISM INFORMATION

Along with the various local chambers of commerce, convention and visitors bureaus, and travel councils listed in the text, a number of state and regional tourism departments and governmental agencies are there to answer your travel-related questions.

ARIZONA OFFICE OF TOURISM
866/275-5816
www.arizonaguide.com

NEW MEXICO DEPARTMENT OF TOURISM
800/733-6396, ext. 0643
www.newmexico.org

SOUTHWEST COLORADO TRAVEL REGION
800/933-4340
www.swcolotravel.org

UTAH TRAVEL COUNCIL
800/200-1160
www.utah.com

NAVAJO NATION TOURISM DEPARTMENT
520/871-6659 or 520/871-6436
www.discovernavajo.com

GRAND CIRCLE ASSOCIATION
888/254-7263
info@grandcircle.org
www.grandcircle.org

BUREAU OF LAND MANAGEMENT
National Office: 202/452-5125
Arizona: 602/417-9200
Colorado: 303/239-3600

New Mexico: 505/438-7400
Utah: 801/539-4001
www.blm.gov

NATIONAL PARK SERVICE, INTERMOUNTAIN REGION
303/969-2500
www.nps.gov

ARIZONA STATE PARKS
602/542-4174
www.pr.state.az.us

COLORADO STATE PARKS
303/866-3437
http://parks.state.co.us

NEW MEXICO STATE PARKS
888/667-2757
nmparks@state.nm.us
www.emnrd.state.nm.us/nmparks

UTAH STATE PARKS & RECREATION
801/538-7220
parkcomment@utah.gov
www.stateparks.utah.gov

NAVAJO PARKS & RECREATION DEPARTMENT
928/871-6647
info@navajonationparks.org
www.navajonationparks.org

Bring a swimsuit if you want to take a dip in a river or your hotel pool.

If you plan on doing any hiking, bring a light pair of boots or sneakers, and consider a walking stick or a pair of trekking poles. Sports sandals such as Tevas or Chacos are comfortable for everything but hard-core hiking. They're particularly good in situations where your feet are getting wet constantly, such as rafting.

Camping brings its own gear list. For the desert, I often bring just a tarp (or nothing at all) instead of a heavy tent. Remember that you'll have to carry more water than you're probably used to for extended hikes and backpacking trips, so bring bottles or bladders enough to carry at least a gallon, and perhaps more. The rest is standard gear: compass, sleeping bag and pad, cook set and stove, and the like.

Don't forget your camera, and a lens hood to prevent sunlight flares. (Digitals are better than film for many reasons, including film's tendency to react poorly to high temperatures.)

In your car you should always have a good map and a few extra gallons of water.

Explore the Four Corners

THE BEST OF THE FOUR CORNERS

Even if you only have two weeks to explore this huge expanse, and no particular interest to sculpt your itinerary, it's still possible to see most of the highlights before you have to head home. Like the rest of these itineraries, this one starts and finishes in Flagstaff, the closest city to a major airport (Phoenix) in the region.

DAY 1

Visit the **Museum of Northern Arizona** for an overview of the Four Corners' art, history, and native cultures, and the **Arboretum at Flagstaff** for an interdiction to its plants. If possible, attend an evening viewing program at **Lowell Observatory.** Sleep at the Weatherford Hotel or the Hotel Monte Vista.

DAY 2

Head north on Highway 89, stopping at **Wupatki** and **Sunset Crater national monuments** en route. Have lunch in **Cameron,** and continue on to spend the night in **Page.**

DAY 3

Spend the day either hiking some of Page's famous slot canyons, including **Antelope** and **Canyon X,** or houseboating or kayaking (or both) on **Lake Powell.** Sleep in Page again.

DAY 4

Continue east from Page on Highway 98, a good introduction to the backcountry of the **Navajo Reservation.** Keep going on Highway 160 to Kayenta, stopping briefly at **Navajo National Monument** if you like. North of Kayenta is **Monument Valley,** which you should reach by sunset. (Don't miss sunrise either, if you can help it.) Either camp here or sleep at **Goulding's Lodge.**

DAY 5

Head north into Utah on Highway 163, where you'll pick up Highway 261 and climb onto

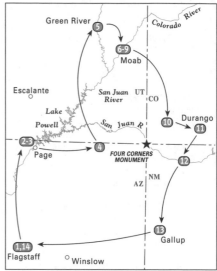

Cedar Mesa. Where the road meets Highway 95, stop at **Natural Bridges National Monument,** good for a few hours' hike. Keep going west across the upper reaches of Lake Powell and the Burr Desert. If you're camping, sleep among the weird formations at **Goblin Valley** or near the trailhead into **Horseshoe Canyon,** a detached portion of Canyonlands' Maze District. If not, continue on to the interstate and **Green River,** stopping if time permits.

DAY 6

In Green River, visit the **John Wesley Powell Museum** before turning back south toward

Moab on Highway 191. Spend the night in Moab, catching sunset from Grandview Point in the Island in the Sky district of Canyonlands National Park if you can.

DAY 7

Explore Arches National Park, which can easily take a full day if you do some of the hiking trails. Sleep in Moab.

DAYS 8-9

Moab and its environs are well worth a few days' exploring. Take your pick from a short raft trip on the Colorado River, a ride on one of the many mountain bike trails nearby, or a hike in the Needles District of Canyonlands, an hour south. Sleep in Moab.

DAY 10

Head south on Highway 191 to Monticello, where you should turn east onto Highway 491 toward Colorado. Get a hotel room or campsite in Cortez. If you have time, see the Four Corners Monument or the stone towers of Hovenweep National Monument.

DAY 11

Spend the day touring Mesa Verde National Park. Spend the night in Durango, ideally at the Strater or General Palmer hotels.

DAY 12

Head south from Durango to Aztec, a neat

little town near two more good sets of ruins: Aztec Ruins National Monument and Salmon Ruins in Bloomfield. Sleep in Aztec or Farmington.

DAY 13

Continue west to Shiprock, near the monolith of the same name, and south on Highway 491 across the eastern edge of the Navajo Reservation to Gallup, where you should stay at the El Rancho Hotel and do some trading-post browsing.

DAY 14

For your last day you have two route choices. One is to stick to I-40, stopping off at the many interesting sights along the way: Petrified Forest National Park, La Posada and the "Standin' on the Corner Park" in Winslow, and Meteor Crater to the west. Otherwise, for a final dose of native culture, head west from Gallup on Highway 3 to Highway 264 through Window Rock to Ganado, where you can see the Hubbell Trading Post National Historic Site. Continue on Highway 264 across the mesa-top villages of the Hopi Reservation, eventually reaching Highway 160 at Tuba City, where more great trading posts await. Turn south on Highway 89 soon after. Either way, you'll be back in Flagstaff before you know it.

NATIONAL PARKS AND SCENERY TOUR

This route is for those who don't plan on venturing far from the pavement, but still want to maximize their oohing and ahhing opportunities.

DAY 1

From **Flagstaff,** head east on I-40, stopping off at the **Meteor Crater.** Take the scenic drive through **Petrified Forest National Park** and spend the night in **Holbrook.** (Try to have lunch or dinner at La Posada's Turquoise Room in Williams.)

DAY 2

Head up Highway 191 though Ganado to **Canyon de Chelly National Park.** You can tour this one your own, or descend into the canyon itself on a guided tour. Spend the night here camping or at the Thunderbird Lodge.

DAY 3

Take Highway 191 to Highways 160 and 163 to get to **Monument Valley** on the Arizona-Utah border. To make sure you catch sunset and sunrise, spend the night here camping or at Goulding's Lodge.

DAY 4

Keep going north into Southeast Utah, stopping for a peek at the **Goosenecks of the San Juan** near Mexican Hat. Climb the precipitous Moki Dugway (Highway 261) up onto **Cedar Mesa,** and don't miss the views from Muley Point at the top. Stop off at **Natural Bridges National Monument** and return to Highway 191 via Highway 95, the "Trail of the Ancients," through the giant gash in Comb Ridge. Spend the night in **Bluff, Blanding,** or, ideally, **Monticello.**

DAYS 5-7

Colorado is a short distance east on Highway 491, and offers the cliff palaces of **Mesa Verde National Park** near Cortez. This is worth at least a full day or more, as is the **San Juan Skyway** that loops in the mountains north of **Durango.** Spend a few nights in the area, then head back west toward Moab.

DAYS 8-9

Use **Moab** as a home base to visit **Arches National Park** and **Canyonlands National Park,** whose Island in the Sky District offers the quickest visual bang for the buck. Sleep in Moab.

DAY 10

Continue north on Highway 191 to I-70 and head west through Green River to reach the turnoff for Highway 24 south to **Hanksville.** Here the surroundings get downright weird, from the sawtooth bulwarks of the **San Rafael Swell** to the melting mudstone of **Goblin Valley State Park.** Make it to **Torrey** by nightfall.

DAY 11

In nearby **Capitol Reef National Park,** a

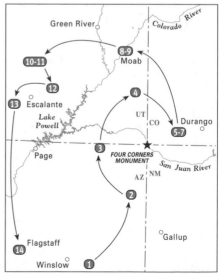

short scenic drive gives access to a surprising chunk of the park's stupendous sights. Spend a day touring and spend another night in Torrey.

DAY 12

Turn south onto **Highway 12,** one of the most spectacular drives in the country. It winds up onto Boulder Mountain for amazing views before descending into the slickrock wildness of the northern **Grand Staircase-Escalante National Monument.** Depending on how much time you need, spend a night or two en route, ideally at the Boulder Mountain Ranch in Boulder.

DAYS 13-14

Keep going on Highway 12 to **Bryce Canyon National Park,** whose wonders can be absorbed in a day from the rim. Take Highway 89 south to Kanab, where you should hop south across the border to Fredonia (as many fugitive polygamists have over the years) and take Highway 89A up onto the Kaibab Plateau, with the option of a detour to the **North Rim of the Grand Canyon.** Highway 89A continues east along the base of the Vermilion Cliffs to **Marble Canyon** and the impressive twin spans of **Navajo Bridge** (leave time to drive down to the river at **Lees Ferry**).

Eventually you'll find yourself back on Highway 89 heading south toward Flagstaff. You can take Highway 64 west from Cameron to visit the **South Rim of the Grand Canyon,** or else continue south to Flagstaff to finish the loop.

OUTDOORS AND BACKCOUNTRY TOUR

If a beautiful view makes you want nothing more than to run out and disappear into it for as long as possible, this route is for you. Make sure to stock up on water and gasoline, and if you have a chance, take a four-wheel-drive.

DAY 1

From Flagstaff, drive east on I-40 to the **Petrified Forest National Park,** where you can grab a free permit to camp in the **Painted Desert** portion north of the interstate.

DAY 2

Head north on Highway 191 to Chinle and the **Canyon de Chelly National Park.** One trail lets you hike to the bottom without a permit; otherwise, sign up for a guided hike among the Navajo farms and orchards at the bottom of this gorgeous canyon system. The park campground is free.

DAY 3

The detour east to **Farmington** is not as easy as it looks – Highways 12, 134/32, 491, and 64 are probably the fastest way – but south of the city are two little-visited spots that are perfect for finding solitude. The **Bisti** and **De-Na-Zin wilderness areas** are full of otherworldly rock formations, and the badlands surrounding **Angel Peak** are amazing at sunset and sunrise.

DAY 4

Rest and recuperate in **Durango,** less than an hour north of Farmington in the foothills of the trail-packed San Juan National Forest.

DAYS 5-6

Head north until you're on Highway 191 in Southeast Utah, which you've probably

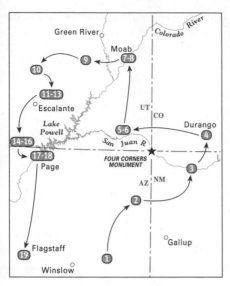

Green River

Colorado River

Moab

9

7-8

10

11-13

Escalante

UT | CO

Lake Powell

5-6

Durango

4

14-16

San Juan R.

17-18

Page

FOUR CORNERS MONUMENT

3

AZ | NM

2

Flagstaff

Gallup

19

1

Winslow

Canyon, a detached part of the Maze district of Canyonlands National Park.

DAY 10

Highway 24 continues west to **Capitol Reef National Park,** with more slot canyons slicing through the **Waterpocket Fold,** accessed via the rough **Notom-Bullfrog Road.** Spend the night under the stars or in **Torrey** or **Boulder.**

DAYS 11-13

Highway 12 heads south from Torrey into the backcountry smorgasbord of the gigantic **Grand Staircase–Escalante National Monument.** Warm up on the short hike to Calf Creek Falls, or perhaps Box-Death Hollow or the Boulder Mail Trail near the town of Boulder, before taking the **Hole-in-the-Rock Road** south from Escalante into the heart of the monument. The canyon trails off this route are good for at least a couple of days' exploring, from narrow slots to the wide, easy flow of the Escalante River itself.

DAYS 14-16

Make an end run around the western end of the monument along Highways 12 and 89 through Kanab. East of the city is the **Paria Plateau,** bisected by an outstanding multi-day hike through the Paria River canyons. (Pressed for time? Get a taste at the upper end of the canyon, called **Buckskin Gulch.**) Highway 89 gives access to the trailheads, as well as to water sports on **Lake Powell** and the famous slot hike through **Antelope Canyon** near Page.

DAYS 17-19

Instead of Highway 89 to Page you can choose to take the Highway 89A spur around the south side of the plateau, if you'd like to hit the (relatively) cool and less-crowded **North Rim of the Grand Canyon.** The canyon's **South Rim** awaits on Highway 64 west of Cameron. By now you're probably bushed, and ready to straggle back south to Flagstaff.

been waiting for from the beginning of the trip. If it's the right time of year, and you have the time to spare, consider the quick, easy raft trip on the **San Juan River** from Bluff to Mexican Hat, or a hike down into **Grand Gulch** (or the less-traveled Owl and Fish Creek canyons) up on **Cedar Mesa.** Spend the nights en route wherever you end up.

DAYS 7-8

Highway 191 continues north to **Moab,** the epicenter of the outdoor playground that is southern Utah. Take one of the dozens of **mountain bike trails** that made the town famous, including the famous Slickrock Trail, or backpack among the spires of the Needles district of **Canyonlands National Park.** This area also has the highest concentration of **rock climbing** in the region. Spend the nights camping or in Moab.

DAY 9

Continue north to Green River on I-70 and back south down Highway 24, where the slot canyons of the **San Rafael Swell** await, across the road from the excellent short hike to the stunning pictographs in **Horseshoe**

HISTORY AND ARCHAEOLOGY TOUR

The past is everywhere you turn in the Four Corners, from ancient ruins to trading posts and museums. If history is your forte, try this itinerary.

DAY 1

Start your journey before leaving Flagstaff at the excellent **Museum of Northern Arizona,** followed by the ruins at **Wupatki** and **Walnut Canyon national monuments.** Spend a night in town.

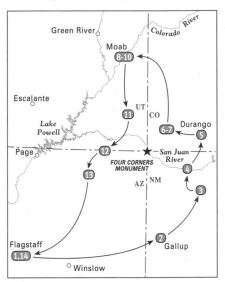

DAY 2

Heading east on I-40 are two **classic hotels** of very different character: the Wigwam Motel in Winslow and La Posada in Holbrook. Continue up Highway 191 onto the Navajo Reservation to the **Hubbell Trading Post National Historic Site** in Ganado. Take Highway 3/264 east to Gallup, and spend the night at El Rancho Hotel.

DAY 3

Your next destination is just a stone's throw away, but without four-wheel-drive, you'll have to go all the way up to Farmington, over to Bloomfield on Highway 64, and down Highway 550 to reach the turnoff to **Chaco Canyon National Historical Park,** the center of one of the Southwest's greatest prehistoric cultures. Spend the night camping at the Park or at the Inn at the Post B&B in Nageezi.

DAY 4

Chaco's ruins are on such a monumental scale that you may understandably be a bit underwhelmed by those you'll hit today: **Aztec** and **Salmon ruins,** near the cities of Aztec and Bloomfield, respectively. That's not an excuse to miss them, however, as each is outstanding in its own way. Sleep in Aztec or Farmington.

DAY 5

Take Highway 550 north from Aztec to **Durango,** where you can return to the present

for a breather. Spend a day and night here, grabbing a cocktail at the Strater Hotel's Diamond Belle Saloon and sleeping there (the hotel, not the saloon) or at the equally antique General Palmer.

DAYS 6-7

West of Durango on Highway 160 is a place that will have you awestruck all over again: **Mesa Verde National Park,** whose cliff dwellings have to be seen to be believed. The area around Cortez and the Four Corners itself is rich in archaeology, including the boulder-perched towers of **Hovenweep National Monument,** the sprawling **Canyons of the Ancients National Monument,** and the **Anasazi Heritage Center** near Dolores. Spend two nights in Mesa Verde or Cortez.

DAYS 8-9

Continue west on Highway 491 into Southeast

Utah at Monticello. On your way toward Moab to the north, you'll pass the turnoff for the Needles District of **Canyonlands National Park,** rich in rock art and ruins. Don't miss **Newspaper Rock** on the way there. More petroglyphs line roads near Moab, where you should spend a couple of nights (if you're not camping).

DAY 10

The full-day trip via Green River to the **Horseshoe Canyon** portion of Canyonlands' Maze District (and back) rewards you with one of the most impressive walls of pictographs you'll ever see. This is Butch Cassidy Country, too, so keep your eyes peeled for outlaws. Spend the night in Moab again.

DAY 11

Back down Highway 191 from Moab is the **Edge of the Cedars State Park** in Blanding, full to the rafters with artifacts, and you can probably guess what the **Dinosaur Museum** is filled with. Take an afternoon detour west onto Cedar Mesa to visit some ruins along Highway 95. Spend the night in Blanding or Bluff.

DAY 12

Keep going south along Highway 191, which becomes Highway 163 as it enters Arizona at **Monument Valley,** backdrop for innumerable Westerns. Nearby are two **trading posts** not to be missed – Goulding's and Oljato, the first a museum and the second one of the most authentic left in the Southwest. Spend the night in Monument Valley, camping or at Goulding's Lodge.

DAYS 13-14

Kayenta is south on Highway 163, and near it is **Navajo National Monument,** where you can see more cliff palaces either from the road or after a long one-day or overnight hike. More trading posts await as you return on Highways 160 and 89 to Flagstaff, including **Old Red Lake, Tuba City,** and **Van's** in Tuba City, and **Cameron** on Highway 89. Finish up in Flagstaff.

NATIVE CULTURES TOUR

The Four Corners' three largest Native American tribes—Navajo, Hopi, and Ute—each have their own reservation (the Ute actually have two), and you can visit each without going far out of Arizona. This route can be done in as little as a week, and since it strays somewhat from the circular paths presented above, your route-finding and time-planning is a little more flexible.

DAY 1

Starting in **Flagstaff** with an orientation visit to the Museum of Northern Arizona, head north on Highway 89 to **Tuba City,** where you can grab a Navajo taco at the Tuba City Truck Stop Cafe and peruse the wares at Van's and the Tuba City Trading Post. If you're here on a Friday, visit the flea market for an undiluted dose of life on the "Res."

DAY 2

On Day 2, take Highway 264 east from Tuba City across the **Hopi Reservation,** surrounded by the larger Navajo Reservation. If you time it right, you can watch a traditional Hopi festival in a timeless stone village perched on one of three long mesas. The road continues east to Ganado, where a detour north on Highway 191 brings you to the **Canyon de Chelly National Park,** a time bubble of agrarian life little changed in centuries. Another side trip heads east to **Crownpoint,** where a rug auction is held on the third Friday of every month. Spend the night camping or at the Thunderbird Lodge.

DAY 3
Back on Highway 264/3 is **Window Rock,** the administrative center of the Navajo Nation, and **Gallup,** its commercial hub. The latter teems with trading posts and galleries full of crafts made by tribes from across the Southwest, and has the classic El Rancho Hotel at which to spend your third night.

DAYS 4-5
Head north on Highway 491 to the town of **Shiprock,** stopping off at the Two Gray Hills Trading Post along the way, and consider a detour up into Colorado to visit the ruins in the **Ute Mountain Tribal Park,** similar to those at Mesa Verde but not reconstructed. Leave the soaring shape of Shiprock in your rearview as you drive west on Highway 64 to Teec Nos Pos and the Carrizo Mountains, where it becomes Highway 160 and passes Mexican Water before reaching **Kayenta.** This is a good long day of driving (more if you detour to the Ute tribal park), so you'll be glad to reach Monument Valley, where you can camp or

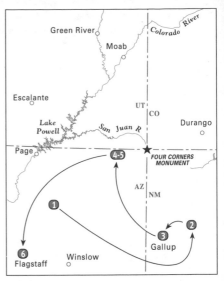

stay at the historic Goudling's Lodge, John Wayne's home-away-from-home while filming classic Westerns. **Monument Valley** itself stands on the northern horizon, its looming mesas sacred to the Navajo and famous worldwide thanks to Western movies and car commercials.

DAY 6
From here, continue down Highway 160 to Tuba City, catching anything here you missed the first time through, and take Highway 89 south back to Flagstaff.

NAVAJO AND HOPI COUNTRY

The high tablelands of northeastern Arizona, northwestern New Mexico, and southernmost Utah encompass two of the country's largest Native American reservations, as well as one of the Four Corner's most vibrant cities (Flagstaff) near one of the country's most incredible natural sights (the Grand Canyon). These are some of the loneliest yet most extraordinary acres of the Colorado Plateau, averaging between 5,000 and 7,000 feet elevation. The wide-open country is a textbook of geology: buttes, washes, mesas, volcanic plugs, and dikes break the otherwise flat expanse, but all pale next to the biggest gorge of them all, northwest of Flagstaff. Sagebrush, yucca, and desert grasses march to the rim of deep canyons, and the heights of Navajo Mountain, Black Mesa, and the Chuska Mountains on the Arizona–New Mexico border are dusted with snow in winter. The largest ponderosa pine forest in the world spreads to both rims of the Grand Canyon, and virtually every hill in sight in the 1,800-square-mile San Francisco Volcanic Field is or was a volcano, some of which have erupted within the past 1,000 years.

But it is the indigenous cultures that truly define this part of the Four Corners. Anasazi cliff dwellings are scattered throughout the region, with those at Navajo National Monument rivaling anything in Colorado or Utah. The Navajo and Hopi tribes have maintained their traditions into the 21st century in the face of almost overwhelming odds. Farming, ranching, herding, and tourism provide an income for many, while mining and logging

© JULIAN SMITH

HIGHLIGHTS

◖ **Museum of Northern Arizona:** An extensive collection, clearly presented, makes this Flagstaff museum a must-see (page 30).

◖ **Oak Creek Canyon:** When you're ready for a break from psychic readings or mountain biking in the red-rock sanctuary of Sedona, this water-filled canyon between Flagstaff and Sedona is a great place to beat the summer heat (page 46).

◖ **The North Rim:** Less visited and cooler in the summer, the Grand Canyon's northern rim seems a world apart from its southern one (page 49).

◖ **Monument Valley:** Towering mesas and buttes make up one of America's best known vistas (page 57).

◖ **Canyon de Chelly National Monument:** A gorgeous canyon system preserves a timeless slice of Navajo life (page 58).

LOOK FOR ◖ TO FIND RECOMMENDED SIGHTS, ACTIVITIES, DINING, AND LODGING.

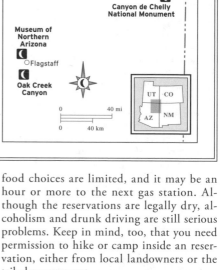

enrich a few. With the exception of Flagstaff, the larger cities on or near the reservations, including Tuba City, Kayenta, Window Rock, and Gallup, are not very big, and the surrounding poverty can make them as much sobering as inviting. But there is still much to do: shopping at the many native galleries in Flagstaff and Gallup; taking in breath-stopping views of Canyon de Chelly National Park, Monument Valley, or the Grand Canyon; walking the creaking floors of the Hubbell Trading Post in Ganado; and watching dances in the timeless villages of the Hopi Reservation. Flagstaff alone can keep visitors occupied for weeks, with three national monuments, some of the Southwest's best museums, a ski resort, and trails galore amid the 600-plus volcanic peaks that dot the skyline.

Outside Gallup and Flagstaff, tourist services are few and far between. Most of the towns on the reservations have hotels, but food choices are limited, and it may be an hour or more to the next gas station. Although the reservations are legally dry, alcoholism and drunk driving are still serious problems. Keep in mind, too, that you need permission to hike or camp inside an reservation, either from local landowners or the tribal government.

PLANNING YOUR TIME

Flagstaff is the most obvious staging point for an exploration of Northern Arizona's Native American country. This piney college town is an appealing place to spend 2–3 days, including at least part of one perusing the collection of the outstanding **Museum of Northern Arizona.** You'll want to take at least a day to visit **Grand Canyon National Park,** although for anything more than the view from the edge you'll need gear, permits, and some strong legs. **Sedona,** down lovely Oak Creek

Canyon, is worth another day or two if you plan on soaking up more than just a bit of the groovy local energy.

The Navajo Reservation has impressive gorges of its own, led by the **Canyon de Chelly National Monument,** whose sandy bottoms are still inhabited after centuries. **Monument Valley** is a visual cliché for good reason: the stone monoliths rising from the flat desert is one of the most amazing sights in the American West.

The railroad towns of Flagstaff, Winslow, and Holbrook are along I-40, which parallels the southern border of the Navajo Reservation. The interstate passes the gaudy palettes of the Painted Desert and Petrified Forest National Park as well, as it continues east to New Mexico and west to California, and I-17 heads south from Flagstaff to Phoenix. Highway 89 runs north from Flagstaff, splitting off Highway 89A before reaching Page and the Utah border (covered in the *South-Central Utah* chapter).

Highway 491 (formerly, and infamously, named Highway 666) cuts across the northern border of the Navajo Reservation from Tuba City to Shiprock via Kayenta—actually Highway 64 from Tec Nos Pos. Highway 89 runs north from Flagstaff to Page along the western edge. Crossing the reservation, you have two main choices: Highway 191 up the center, through Ganado and Chinle to Mexi-

can Water, Utah (paralleled by Highway 12 north of Window Rock), and the east–west Highway 264/3, from Tuba City across the Hopi mesas to Ganado, Window Rock, and Gallup. Countless dirt roads reach much of the rest of the reservations, but a large portion remains inaccessible. These tracks can be very rough, particularly in bad weather, and they are seldom marked; the AAA *Indian Country* map (see *Information and Services* in the *Essentials* chapter) is your best weapon against getting lost.

Guided Tours

For tours of the reservation, try **Largo Navajoland Tours** (505/863-0050 or 888/726-9084, jlargo@navajolandtours.com), run by tribe members John and Brenda Largo. They cover all the major sites on and near the reservation, from Monument Valley and Canyon de Chelly to the Grand Canyon and Chaco Canyon. They also run a traditional Navajo hogan bed-and-breakfast, and do horseback, hiking, and rafting trips. Will Tsosie runs **Coyote Pass Hospitality** (928/724-3383, coyotepass@excite.com, http://navajocentral.org/cp-page.htm), offering B&B accommodations ($85 pp) in traditional Navajo hogans in Tsaile, Lukachukai, and the Chuska Mountains as well as private tours in your own four-wheel-drive vehicle for $20 per hour.

Flagstaff and Vicinity

"Flag" (pop. 65,000) is and has always been a railroad town—an average of 135 trains still roar through every 24 hours, sounding their whistles by law and dividing the city frustratingly in two for up to half an hour. It's also a city very aware of its heritage, from the historical markers on downtown buildings to the great old neon motel signs on Route 66 out of town. With 20,000 students in residence at Northern Arizona University (NAU), the music, art, and outdoors scenes are all thriv-

ing. The pointed San Francisco Peaks tower directly over the city, covered with snow a good part of the year. It may be hard to believe as the heat waves shimmer up off the flat desert below, but at 7,000 feet, Flagstaff is actually the second-snowiest metropolitan area in the country after Syracuse, New York, with an average of 108 inches of snow yearly.

In terms of tourist attractions, there is very little that Flagstaff lacks: skiing the Arizona Snowbowl, hiking the Grand Canyon, visiting the outstanding Museum of Northern Arizona and Lowell Observatory, or taking a day trip to Sedona or a nearby Native American reservation. Three national monuments are within half an hour of the city, making a great loop day trip in themselves.

HISTORY
The Sinagua, less-advanced cultural cousins of the Anasazi, were living in pit houses and canyon-edge dwellings in the foothills of the San Francisco Mountains when major eruptions in 1064 and 1065 covered 800 square miles of the surrounding countryside with lava and ash. They returned soon after to build Anasazi-style pueblos and farm the newly enriched soil, but moved on around the same time the Anasazi did, perhaps for similar reasons.

The area was explored by four separate military surveys before Flagstaff itself came into being. In 1876, a group of settlers arrived from Boston, and on July 4 they raised an American flag on a peeled pine tree in what is now Antelope Park. The early settlement didn't last, but the flagpole did, and travelers heading west were told to keep an eye out for the good campsite it marked. Some of these settlers eventually stayed, and the name stuck. The first post office and the railroad both arrived in 1881, and by 1886 Flagstaff was the biggest city on the railroad line between Albuquerque and the Pacific Ocean. The Arizona Lumber and Timber Company made a fortune from the abundant forests, shipping logs out cheaply by rail. Sheep and cattle ranches provided more jobs.

Coconino County, established in 1891, was soon the second largest in the country. Three years later the Lowell Observatory was built, and in 1930 Dr. Percival Lowell discovered the planet Pluto in Flagstaff's crystal skies. Route 66 and its attendant traffic arrived in the 1920s, allowing more and more visitors to discover the wonders of the Grand Canyon and the Native American reservations nearby.

SIGHTS
◖ Museum of Northern Arizona
Founded in 1928, this outstanding museum

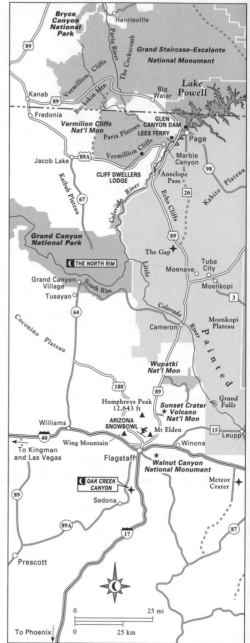

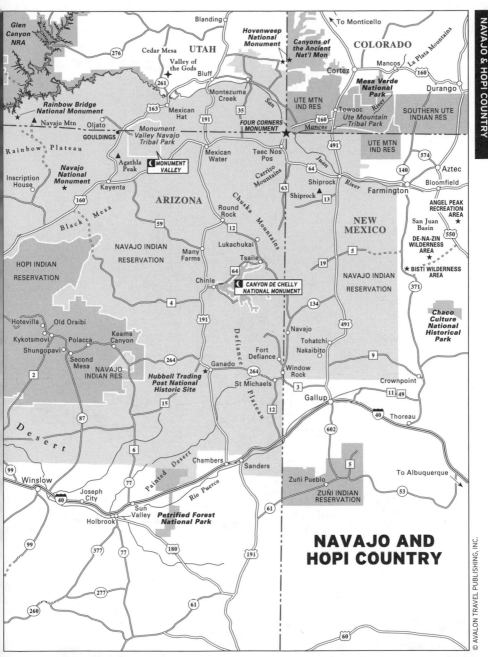

NAVAJO AND HOPI COUNTRY

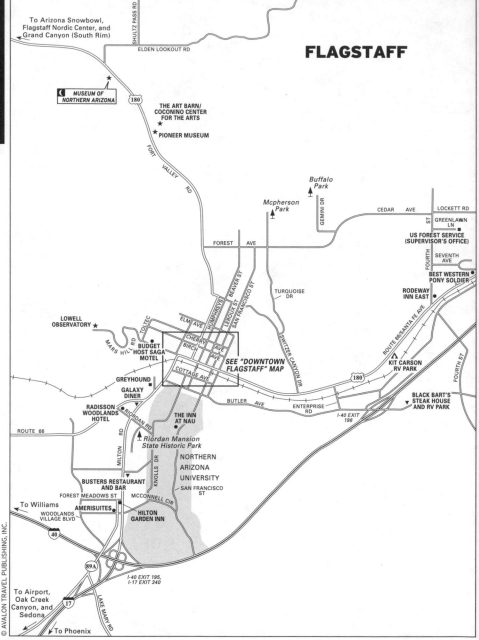

FLAGSTAFF

To Arizona Snowbowl,
Flagstaff Nordic Center, and
Grand Canyon (South Rim)

SHULTZ PASS RD

ELDEN LOOKOUT RD

MUSEUM OF
NORTHERN ARIZONA

180

THE ART BARN/
COCONINO CENTER
FOR THE ARTS

PIONEER MUSEUM

FORT VALLEY RD

Buffalo
Park

Mcpherson
Park

GEMINI DR

CEDAR   AVE   LOCKETT RD

ST

GREENLAWN
LN

FOREST   AVE

US FOREST SERVICE
(SUPERVISOR'S OFFICE)

FOURTH

SEVENTH
AVE

BEST WESTERN
PONY SOLDIER

TURQUOISE
DR

RODEWAY
INN EAST

LOWELL
OBSERVATORY

BEAVER ST

LEROUX ST

SAN FRANCISCO ST

HUMPHREYS

ELMI AVE

TOLTEC

MARS HILL RD

CHERRY

BIRCH

AVE

AVE

BUDGET
HOST SAGA
MOTEL

SWITZER CANYON DR

ROUTE 66/SANTA FE AVE

KIT CARSON
RV PARK

SEE "DOWNTOWN
FLAGSTAFF" MAP

COTTAGE AVE

180

FOURTH ST

GREYHOUND

GALAXY
DINER

RADISSON
WOODLANDS
HOTEL

RIORDAN RD

BUTLER   AVE

ENTERPRISE
RD

BLACK BART'S
STEAK HOUSE
AND RV PARK

ROUTE 66

THE INN
AT NAU

I-40 EXIT
198

MILTON   RD

Riordan Mansion
State Historic Park

KNOLLS DR

NORTHERN

ARIZONA

UNIVERSITY

BUSTERS RESTAURANT
AND BAR

SAN FRANCISCO
ST

FOREST MEADOWS ST

MCCONNELL CIR

To Williams

WOODLANDS
VILLAGE BLVD

AMERISUITES

HILTON
GARDEN INN

40

89A

I-40 EXIT 195,
I-17 EXIT 340

To Airport,
Oak Creek
Canyon, and
Sedona

17

LAKE MARY RD

To Phoenix

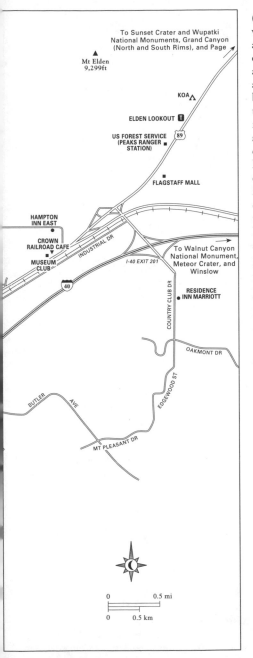

To Sunset Crater and Wupatki National Monuments, Grand Canyon (North and South Rims), and Page

▲
Mt Elden
9,299ft

KOA▲

ELDEN LOOKOUT 🛈

US FOREST SERVICE (PEAKS RANGER STATION) ⬛ 89

■ FLAGSTAFF MALL

HAMPTON INN EAST
●

CROWN RAILROAD CAFE
■ ▼
MUSEUM
CLUB ■

INDUSTRIAL DR

I-40 EXIT 201

To Walnut Canyon National Monument, Meteor Crater, and Winslow

40

COUNTRY CLUB DR

RESIDENCE INN MARRIOTT ●

OAKMONT DR

EDGEWOOD ST

BUTLER
AVE

MT PLEASANT DR

0   0.5 mi

0   0.5 km

(3101 N. Fort Valley Rd., 928/774-5213, www.musnaz.org, 9 A.M.–5 P.M. daily, $5 adults, $2 children) has evolved into the best of its kind in the Four Corners. Displays on anthropology, biology, geology, and fine art are clearly laid out and comprehensive without being exhausting, even though they have more than 600,000 artifacts cataloged. The histories of the Colorado Plateau's tribes are clearly spelled out, and exquisite examples of crafts are on display, including weavings, kachinas, baskets, pottery, and jewelry. Changing exhibits examine topics such as the role of Native Americans in Westerns. The museum's Kiva Gallery contains a mock-up of a Hopi kiva with a beautiful mural by Michael Kabotie and Delbridge Honanie, covering everything from Buddha and Hopi spirits to the Internet and modern problems of drugs and diabetes. Special collection tours ($10 pp) are offered on the third Friday of every month. Ideally you'd start your visit to the Colorado Plateau here, on North Fort Valley Road (Highway 180) three miles northwest of downtown Flagstaff.

Pioneer Museum

The 1908 Coconino County Hospital for the Indigent was converted to a boardinghouse and then a museum in 1963. Today, the northern division of the Arizona Historical Society administers the building as a museum (928/774-6272, 9 A.M.–5 P.M. Mon.–Sat., free) on North Fort Valley Road on the way to the Museum of Northern Arizona. The collection includes more than 10,000 bits of Flagstaff's past, from an old iron lung to farm gear and clothing. Nearby are a 1910 barn, a 1912 steam locomotive, and a historic cabin that was moved here from the east side of the San Francisco Mountains. In the blacksmith shop behind the museum, the sweaty craft is demonstrated Thursday–Saturday in summer.

The Art Barn

Behind the Pioneer Museum is Flagstaff's Art Barn (928/774-0822, 10 A.M.–5 P.M. Tues.–Sat.), a large gallery operated by local artists and their patrons. The work leans

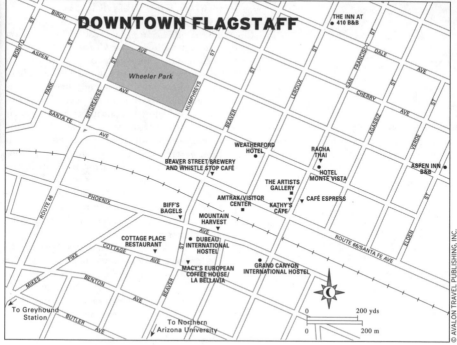

DOWNTOWN FLAGSTAFF

© AVALON TRAVEL PUBLISHING, INC.

strongly in the Native American and Southwest directions, and prices, direct from the artists, are low. You'll find paintings, rugs, pottery, jewelry, and many other things for sale. They also organize workshops and offer a bronze foundry and matting services. Music, theater, and dance performances are held in the 200-seat theater of the adjacent **Coconino Center for the Arts** (928/779-2300).

Lowell Observatory

Boston aristocrat-turned-astronomer Percival Lowell founded this observatory (1400 W. Mars Hill Rd., 928/774-3358, www.lowell.edu, 9 A.M.–5 P.M. daily, from noon Nov.–Mar., $5 adults, $2 children) in 1894. He spent 15 years gazing at Mars through the 24-inch refractor telescope, convinced that he was looking at the remains of canals built by an intelligent race. On that matter he was way off, but his hunch about "Planet X" orbiting beyond Ura-

nus proved correct: 14 years after his death in 1916, Pluto was discovered by Clyde Tombaugh, and Lowell is given most of the credit. Today the privately owned observatory sits at 7,260 feet in the clear mountain air above Flagstaff, and is still used for serious research. The Steele Visitor Center offers tours of the original telescope inside historic Clark Dome, built of native ponderosa pine in the days before power tools, as well as the spectrograph used to prove the universe is expanding, and plates with the first images of Pluto. Evening viewing programs are offered from 8 P.M. Mon.–Sat. June–Aug. and from 7:30 P.M. Wed., Fri., and Sat. Sept.–May., weather permitting.

Riordan Mansion State Historic Park

Prominent local businessmen Timothy and Michael Riordan were responsible for the success of the Arizona Lumber and Timber Company near the turn of the 20th century. They each married one of the Metz sisters, cousins of the famous traders the Babbitt Brothers, and in 1904 commissioned the architect of the Grand Canyon's El Tovar Hotel to build them a monumental home of logs and volcanic stone. The mansion (409 Riordan Rd., 928/779-4395, www.pr.state.az.us/parkhtml/riordan.html, 8:30 A.M.–5 P.M. daily, from 10:30 A.M. Nov.–Apr., $6 adults, $2.50 children) is actually two separate homes joined by a common area, and has 40 rooms totaling 13,000 square feet. Timothy's side of what the brothers dubbed *Kinlichi* ("Red House" in Navajo) is open for tours. Original fixtures and hand-carved American Craftsman–style furniture give a taste of life at the high end in early Flagstaff. Reservations are a good idea for the guided tours, offered every hour in the summer.

The Arboretum at Flagstaff

More than 2,500 species of high-elevation plants thrive at the country's highest research botanical garden (4001 S. Woody Moun-

tain Rd., 928/774-1442, www.thearb.org, 9 A.M.–5 P.M. daily Apr.–Dec., $5 adults, $2 children). The arboretum is at 7,150 feet, which gives it only a 75-day growing season, but they still do an amazing job of raising plants from across the Colorado Plateau. Some 2,500 species are cultivated here, half of which are native to the Four Corners. The collection includes the largest herb garden in the Southwest. Wildflowers are particularly impressive during the summer monsoon season, the best time to visit. Several miles of trails wind through the garden's 200 acres, and hour-long guided tours are given daily at 11 A.M. and 1 P.M.

ENTERTAINMENT AND EVENTS
Nightlife

Built in 1931, **The Museum Club** (3404 E. Rte. 66, 928/526-9434) has evolved into the best country-music roadhouse in Arizona and one of the most outstanding in the United States, according to both *Country America Magazine* and *Car and Driver*. Enter through the ponderosa

© JULIAN SMITH

Flagstaff's Museum Club is one of the country's classic roadhouses.

FLAGSTAFF CLIMATE

MONTH	AVG. HIGH	AVG. LOW	MEAN	AVG. PRECIP.
Jan.	43°F	16°F	30°F	2.18 in.
Feb.	46°F	19°F	32°F	2.56 in.
Mar.	50°F	23°F	37°F	2.62 in.
Apr.	58°F	27°F	43°F	1.29 in.
May	68°F	34°F	51°F	0.80 in.
June	79°F	41°F	60°F	0.43 in.
July	82°F	50°F	66°F	2.40 in.
Aug.	80°F	49°F	64°F	2.89 in.
Sept.	74°F	42°F	58°F	2.12 in.
Oct.	63°F	31°F	47°F	1.93 in.
Nov.	51°F	22°F	37°F	1.86 in.
Dec.	44°F	17°F	30°F	1.83 in.

pine archway onto the state's largest wooden dance floor. Five more ponderosas support the A-frame roof, and the mahogany bar in the back dates to the 1880s. Live blues, country, rock, and reggae have included national acts like Willie Nelson and John Lee Hooker.

For more live music, **The Alley** (22 E. Rte. 66, 928/774-7929) is probably your best bet, with pool tables, a bar, and a stage in back. A block away is **Joe's Place** (102 E. Rte. 66, 928/774-6281), another good bar with pool tables. If these don't fit the bill, try the **Mogollon Brewing Company** (15 N. Agassiz St., 928/773-8950), a 100-year old place with live music on weekends. In 2005, they opened the Arizona High Spirits Distillery on-site, producing prickly pear–flavored vodka and other Southwest-themed spirits in a custom-made still.

The Arts

NAU's **Richard E. Beasley Gallery** (928/523-3549, 11 A.M.–3 P.M. Mon.–Fri.) displays rotating exhibits of contemporary art by students and faculty on the second floor of the Fine and Performing Arts Building. Eighteenth-century furniture, glassware, silver, and art fill the **Marguerite Hettel Weiss Collection** on the third floor of the Old Main Building. These galleries are both under the auspices of the **Old Main Art Gallery and Museum** (928/523-3471, www.nau.edu/artgallery, 10 A.M.–4:30 P.M. Mon.–Fri., 10 A.M.–3 P.M. Sat.) on the northern end of campus, whose varied collection is open to the public.

The **Flagstaff Symphony Orchestra** (928/774-5107, www.flagstaffsymphony.org) has been entertaining northern Arizona audiences since 1949. Performances are held in NAU's Ardrey Auditorium September–April, and tickets are available online.

Events

Flagstaff's **Winterfest** in February rolls together more than 100 snow-themed events, including skiing and sled-dog competitions. May brings the beginning of the Museum of Northern Arizona's **Heritage Program,** which highlights the food, music, dance, arts, and traditions of the Colorado Plateau's diverse cultures all summer long. This includes the **Festival of Hispanic Arts and Crafts** in late May, the **Hopi Marketplace** in early July, the **Navajo Marketplace** in early August, the **Zuni Marketplace** in late August, and the **Festival of Pai Arts** (including the Havasupai, Hualapai, Yavapai, and Paiute nations) in late September.

June is full of events, from the **Gem and Mineral Show** and the **Great Fiesta del Barrio and Fajita Cook-off** to the **Pine Country Pro Rodeo and Parade.** The founding of the city and its country are celebrated during the **Fabulous Fourth Festivities,** which serve as a prelude to the **Flagstaff Summer Fest** the first weekend in August, with artists from across the Southwest. The **Coconino Country Fair** and the **Arts and Crafts Festival** both occur over Labor Day weekend, and the **Flagstaff Festival of Science** (www.scifest.org) comes in late September.

SHOPPING

It makes sense that Flagstaff, surrounded by mountains, deserts, canyons, and rivers, has plenty of good sporting-goods stores. Try **Aspen Sports** (15 N. San Francisco, 928/779-1935), **Babbitt's Backcountry Outfitters** (12 E. Aspen Ave., 928/774-4775), or **Mountain Sports** (928/226-2885, 24 N. San Francisco St.). **Peace Surplus** (14 W. Rte. 66, 928/779-4521) stocks climbing, fishing, skiing, and backpacking gear.

The Artists Gallery (17 N. San Francisco St., 928/773-0958) collects the works of more than 40 local contemporary artists under one roof, ranging from blown glass and painting to sculpture and furniture. Herbs, jewelry, kachina dolls, and baskets are on sale at the **Winter Sun Trading Company** (107 N. San Francisco St., 928/774-2884). For more Native American crafts, try **Puchteca Indian Crafts** (20 N. San Francisco St., 928/774-2414).

RECREATION
Hiking
Beyond the 22-mile **Flagstaff Urban Trails System,** hikers and bikers have to look no

farther than the San Francisco Peaks to find some of the best trails this close to a city in Arizona. Many of them are in the **Mt. Elden/ Dry Lake Hills Trail System** and start from the **Mount Elden trailhead,** near the National Forest Service's **Peaks Ranger Station** (5075 N. Hwy. 89, 928/526-0866). Take Rte. 66 east out of town until it becomes Highway 89, and look across from the Flagstaff Mall. The trails climb up through boulders and huge junipers and piñon pines. The two-mile **Fatman's Loop** overlooks the city and is named as a warning—you have to be at least somewhat fit to tackle this one. A steep, three-mile trail climbs 2,400 feet leads to the **Elden Lookout Tower** at 9,300 feet, with views as good as you'd expect.

Buffalo Park on the north side of town serves as a trailhead for the **Oldham Trail,** leading 5.5 miles through aspen, spruce, pines, and fir trees to views over Oak Creek Canyon, Sunset Crater, and the Painted Desert. To get there, take San Francisco Street north, take a right on Forest Avenue, which becomes Cedar, and then a left on Gemini; the park is at the end of the road. The Arizona Snowbowl (see *Around Flagstaff*) offers access to a number of trails as well. For more information, pick up a copy of Cosmic Ray's *Favorite Hikes Flagstaff & Sedona,* available locally.

Mountain Biking
Cyclists can tackle the 19.6-mile **Mount Elden Loop,** which circles the mountains clockwise by connecting the Schultz Creek, Little Elden, Pipeline, Oldham, and Rocky Ridge trails. This is a great all-day ride, and most of it is moderately difficult single-track. The trailhead is 3.2 miles north of town on Highway 180; turn right onto Schultz Pass Road (FR 557), then park at the intersection with Mount Elden Road (FR 420) and head north on the Schultz Creek Trail. The **Elden Lookout Road** is another good ride, and one of many in the national forests near town—just make sure to stay out of the wilderness area. For more information on roads among the San Francisco Peaks, see *Around Flagstaff.*

Absolute Bikes (18 N. San Francisco St., 928/779-5969) rents full-suspension mountain bikes and cruisers. **Single Track Bikes** (575 W. Riordan Rd., 928/773-1862) is another good source of local riding info, gear, and service.

Rafting and Kayaking

As the closest city to the Grand Canyon proper, Flagstaff is often the base of choice for river-runners out to tackle the rapids of the Colorado River and other waterways nearby. **Canyoneers** (928/526-0924 or 800/525-0924, answers@canyoneers.com, www.canyoneers.com) traces its origins to 1936, when Norman Nevills first guided a trip down the San Juan River. Their Grand Canyon offerings range from weeklong trips on powered boats ($1,575 pp) to 12-day excursions on oar boats for $2,700 per person.

Tim and Pam Whitney have been running the Grand Canyon since 1973, and in 1986 they founded **Rivers and Oceans** (928/526-4575 or 800/473-4576, info@rivers-oceans.com, www.rivers-oceans.com). Their guided trips include the Grand Canyon and rivers in southern Utah and Idaho. **Arizona Raft Adventures** (800/786-7238, info@azraft.com, www.azraft.com) also offers Grand Canyon raft trips. **Canyon Rio Rafting** (800/272-3353, www.canyonrio.com, inquiries@canyonrio.com) offers family raft trips on rivers in central Arizona, the San Juan, and the Chama River in northern New Mexico. These range from two hours to all day ($100 adults, $80 children), and they also have gear rentals and kayak instruction.

Skiing

For information on downhill skiing at the Arizona Snowbowl in the San Francisco Mountains, see *Around Flagstaff.* The **Flagstaff Nordic Center** (928/220-0550, www.flagstaffnordiccenter.com, 9 A.M.–4 P.M. daily Dec.–Mar.) offers over 20 miles of groomed trails ($10 pp) in the National Forest, and well as gear rentals ($15–20 pp), refreshments, and instruction ($35 pp including rentals and ski

pass). It's 16 miles north of town on Highway 180. Other popular cross-country skiing trails are on Wing Mountain, northwest of Flagstaff via Highway 180 and Forest Road 222B, and Hart Prairie, 9.5 miles northwest via Highway 180 and Forest Road. 151.

Other Activities

Four Season Outfitters & Guides (107 W. Phoenix Ave., 877/272-5032, info@fsoutfitters.com, www.fsoutfitters.com) organize hiking, backpacking, climbing, and rafting tours throughout the Four Corners. Day hikes into the Grand Canyon are $145, including transport, food, and park admission, and can be lengthened up to a week and more. Three days in the Escalante canyons are $675 per person. They have a rental/retail shop on the premises, and rent gear, too.

Maxis and Frank Davies have been guiding horseback trail rides into the San Francisco Peaks from their **Flying Heart Ranch** (928/526-2788) for 50 years. They're located next to the Horsemen Lodge about 20 minutes north of downtown on Highway 89, and their rides last from 90 minutes to all day.

ACCOMMODATIONS

As northern Arizona's main tourist center, it's no surprise that Flagstaff has an abundance of lodging options. Rates fall by as much as half in the off-season, and many inexpensive chain motels (some with great old neon signs) line the Route 66 "strip" on its way out of town.

Under $50

The popular **Grand Canyon International Hostel** (19 S. San Francisco St., 928/779-9421 or 888/442-2696, fax 928/774-6047, info@grandcanyonhostel.com, www.grandcanyonhostel.com) has dorm rooms ($16–18) and five private rooms ($32–39). They organize trips to Sedona ($25 pp) and the Grand Canyon ($50 pp), and offer Internet access, a cable TV/VCR room, and laundry services. The same couple owns and operates the nearby **Dubeau International Hostel** (19 W. Phoenix Ave., 928/774-6731 or 800/398-7112, fax 928/774-6047, www.dubeauhostel.com, info@dubeauhostel.com) with dorm rooms for the same price and eight private rooms ($34–41). Breakfast is included at both places, and it's a good idea to book private rooms a few weeks or even a month in advance, especially in the summer.

On Route 66, the **Budget Host Saga Motel** (820 W. Rte. 66, 928/779-3631) has rooms for under $50 as well.

$50-100

On January 1, 1900, John W. Weatherford opened a hotel in the dusty frontier town of Flagstaff that still bears his name. The (**Weatherford Hotel** (23 N. Leroux St., 928/779-1919, fax 928/773-8951, information@weatherfordhotel.com, www .weatherfordhotel.com, $60–65) has gone through various incarnations since then—billiard hall, theater, and radio station, to name a few—but after two decades of work it has been restored to its pioneer peak, when Zane Gray wrote *Call of the Canyon* while staying here. Period touches include a 19-foot lobby ceiling, the wraparound third-floor balcony, and a huge wooden bar in the ballroom, built for a Tombstone saloon over a century ago. **Charly's Pub & Grill** offers sandwiches ($8–9), Southwest specialties ($9–10) and dinner entrées for $16–20, as well as live music on weekends.

The (**Hotel Monte Vista** (100 N. San Francisco St., 928/779-6971 or 800/545-3068, fax 928/779-2904, montev@infomagic.net, www.hotelmontevista.com, $55–85) is Flagstaff's other historical (and, purportedly, haunted) lodge downtown. It has hosted presidents and Hollywood stars since it was built in 1927, including John Wayne, who reported a friendly ghost in his room. Most of the 50 rooms on four floors have good views, and all are named after famous guests. There is a day spa on-site, and the cool **Monte Vista Lounge** downstairs has live bands Thursday–Saturday, and the original 1927 bar.

A number of chain hotels on Route 66 fall into this price category, including the **Rodeway Inn East** (2650 E. Rte. 66, tel./fax 928/526-2200), and the **Best Western Pony Soldier**

(3030 E. Rte. 66, 928/526-2388, fax 928/527-8329). Students at NAU's School of Hotel and Restaurant Management run **The Inn at NAU** (928/523-1616, fax 928/523-1625, theinn-p@ jan.ucc.nau.edu, www.inn.nau.edu, $80–85) on campus. Room rates include breakfast at the Garden Terrace Restaurant, also run by the program. **Amerisuites** (2455 S. Beulah Blvd., 928/774-8042, fax 928/774-5524, $95) has efficiencies with high-speed Internet access

$100-150

C. B. Wilson, cousin to Wyatt Earp, built the graceful 1912 home three blocks from downtown that has been turned into the **Aspen Inn Bed & Breakfast** (218 N. Elden St., 928/773-0295 or 888/999-4110, fax 928/226-7312, info@flagstaffbedbreakfast.com, www.flagstaffbedbreakfast.com, $100–110).

The **Hilton Garden Inn** (350 W. Forest Meadows St., 928/226-8888, fax 928/556-9059, $70–150) is also in this price range.

$150 and Up

Some of the nine rooms at (**The Inn at 410 Bed & Breakfast** (410 N. Leroux St., 928/774-0088 or 800/774-2008, www.inn410.com, info@inn410.com, $150–210) have fireplaces and/or whirlpool tubs. The owners of the 1894 Craftsman home, which was at one time the home of NAU's Sigma Nu fraternity, offer gourmet breakfasts and can arrange two-night packages, including a tour of the Grand Canyon, starting at $480 double. They've repeatedly won awards as one of the best B&Bs in the state.

The **Residence Inn Marriott** (3440 N. Country Club Dr., 928/526-5555, fax 928/527-0328, $80–170) has one-bedroom units with kitchens, and the **Hampton Inn East** (3501 E. Lockett Rd., 928/526-1885, fax 928/526-9885, $70–180) offers a heated indoor pool, spa, and complimentary breakfast. Not to be outdone, the **Radisson Woodlands Hotel** (1175 W. Rte. 66, 928/773-8888, fax 928/773-1827, $90–180) offers a heated outdoor pool, the Sakura Japanese restaurant (see the *Food* section), and a café.

Campgrounds

All of the following are open year-round. **Black Bart's RV Park** (2760 E. Butler Ave., 928/774-1912) has 174 wooded sites for $20–22 near I-40 exit 198. They also have a saloon, an antiques store, and host a musical revue in the steak house (see the *Food* section). The **Flagstaff KOA** (5803 N. Hwy. 89, 928/526-9926 or 800/KOA-FLAG, 800/562-3524) offers both campsites ($24–33) and cabins ($42), five miles northeast of town near I-40 exit 201.

You can camp just about anywhere in the national forest that surrounds Flagstaff; just make sure you're not on private land (signs, fences, and houses are good clues), and be very careful with fires in this tinderbox woodland. In the Coconino National Forest, the **Bonito Campground** is on the loop road near Sunset Crater Volcano National Monument, with 43 sites open April–October for $15. Turn left (west) at the Sunset Crater turnoff from Highway 89 onto Forest Road 552 and keep follow the signs to the **Lockett Meadow Campground,** which has 17 sites at 8,600 feet for $8, open May–October. Call 928/526-0866 for information on both of these.

FOOD

Flagstaff has an amazing variety of places to eat, with plenty of inexpensive options priced for student budgets.

Historic Downtown Area

Many restaurants are south of the train tracks on Beaver Street, close to NAU. **La Bellavia** (18 S. Beaver St., 928/774-8301, breakfast and lunch daily) is a comfy spot that has earned Flagstaff's "best breakfast" title many times since they opened in 1976. Try their signature Swedish oat pancakes. The smell of fresh-roasted coffee permeates **Macy's European Coffee House, Bakery and Vegetarian Restaurant** (14 S. Beaver St., 928/774-2243, all meals daily) thanks to the big red roaster by the tables. Their creative menu includes many vegetarian and vegan selections, with soups, salads, and sandwiches for $5–6.

A few blocks away is **Biff's Bagels** (1 S. Beaver St., 928/226-0424, 7 A.M.–3 P.M. Mon.–Sat., 8 A.M.–2 P.M. Sun.) serves breakfast, coffees, and bagels, with sandwiches in the $4–5 range. They also have Internet access. Stop by the **Beaver Street Brewery and Whistle Stop Café** (11S. Beaver St., 928/779-0079, lunch and dinner daily) for catfish platters and wood-fired pizzas ($8 and up), or enjoy one of their home-brewed ales on the outdoor patio. There's a billiard room for after dinner, too.

Occupying a restored 1909 bungalow, the **Cottage Place Restaurant** (126 W. Cottage Ave., 928/774-8431, dinner Tues.–Sun.) may just be Flagstaff's best restaurant. This intimate spot, built in 1909, serves appetizer such as charbroiled ahi for $6–13 and a wonderful two-person tenderloin for $63 (à la carte entrées are $21 and up). Their wine list has earned *Wine Spectator* magazine's "Award of Excellence" six times. Reservations are recommended. **Mountain Harvest** (6 W. Phoenix Ave, 928/779-9456, 8 A.M.–8 P.M. Mon.–Sat., 9 A.M.–6 P.M. Sun.) a natural market offering organic produce and a deli. Sandwiches and other wholesome bites are $5 and up.

Heading north of the train tracks, an excellent Asian option is **Racha Thai** (104 N. San Francisco St., 928/774-3003, lunch and dinner Tues.–Sat., dinner Sun.), with candlelit tables and many vegetarian choices. Dinner entrées run $8–12, but they offer lunch specials for $6–7. Homemade vegetarian plates are a specialty of **Cafe Espress** (16 N. San Francisco St., 928/774-0541, breakfast and lunch daily, dinner Wed.–Sat.) along with coffees and fresh-baked treats. It's also a gallery that exhibits local artists' works. **Kathy's Cafe** (7 N. San Francisco St., 928/774-1951, lunch and dinner daily) offers no pretense, just good smoothies and sandwiches ($4–6).

Route 66

Sixty-six omelets fill the menu at the **Crown Railroad Cafe** (3300 E. Rte. 66, 928/522-9237, 6 A.M.–9 P.M. daily) next to Museum Club. Lunch and breakfast specials are $4, and they have northern Arizona's largest electric train running around the restaurant. (It's one of two in town.) Meat loaf sandwiches, malts, movie posters, and waitresses in Hawaiian shirts sum up the **Galaxy Diner** (931 W. Rte. 66, 928/774-2466, all meals daily) a neon-and-silver faux–Route 66 diner (it's only eight years old) that does American road staples for $5–9. The burgers are good, and they serve breakfast all day.

Elsewhere in Town

Busters Restaurant and Bar (1800 S. Milton Rd., 928/774-5155, lunch and dinner daily) is an animated place with steaks, seafood, and chicken dishes for lunch ($5–10) and dinner ($10–18). Northern Arizona's finest sushi bar is probably **Sakura,** in the Radisson Woodland Hotel (928/773-9118, lunch Mon.–Sat., dinner daily). They also serve teppanyaki, with entrées starting at $5 for lunch and $11 for dinner.

If you like music with your prime rib, head to **Black Bart's Steak House and Musical Revue** (2760 E. Butler Ave., 928/779-3142, dinner daily), a Western-theme place abutting an RV park where students in NAU's voice program serenade diners over oak-broiled steaks and chicken.

INFORMATION

The **Flagstaff Convention and Visitor's Bureau** (928/774-9541 or 800/842-7293, cvb@ci.flagstaff.az.us, www.flagstaffarizona.org) runs a **visitors center** in the old train station at 1 EastRoute 66 (8 A.M.–5 P.M. daily). Find information on the surrounding mountain country, including maps and brochures, at the **Coconino National Forest supervisor's office** (1824 S. Thompson St., 928/527-3600, www.fs.fed.us/r3/coconino, 7:30 A.M.–4:30 P.M. Mon.–Fri.). behind the shopping center. They also operate the **Peaks Ranger Station** (5075 N. Hwy. 89, 928/526-0866), open similar hours.

TRANSPORTATION

Flagstaff's local **Mountain Line** bus service, (928/779-6624) runs three routes through the city Mon.–Fri., and two on Saturday. **Greyhound** (399 S. Malpais Ln., 928/774-4573) takes advantage of the city's location on I-40 with service to major cities to the east and west. **Amtrak** (1 E. Rte. 66, 928/774-8679) has tickets to Los Angeles and Albuquerque daily. **Open Road Tours & Transportation** (800/766-7117, www.openroadtours.com) offers daily bus shuttle service to Phoenix ($40 one-way, $70 round-trip) and the South Rim of the Grand Canyon ($25 pp), stopping in Williams. From April to October, **Backpacker Bus** (info@backpackerbus.com, www.backpackerbus.com) stops by Flagstaff's hostels at 8 A.M. on Wednesday and Saturday on its way between Las Vegas and Big Bear Lake, California; each leg is $35 per person. Their laid-back bus routes connect hostels throughout the Southwest and California, and you can get on and off whenever and wherever you like.

From Pulliam Field, five miles south of town, **America West** (800/235-9292) flies daily to Phoenix. (It's usually cheaper to fly to Phoenix and take a bus from there, or vice versa.)

AROUND FLAGSTAFF
Walnut Canyon National Monument

This steep, lush canyon south of Flagstaff was home to at least 100 members of the Sinagua ("without water") culture in the 12th and 13th centuries, who built homes in shallow alcoves on the steep walls. The sandstone gorge itself is a wonder, with abundant vegetation and wildlife nourished by Walnut Creek. Residents raised corn, beans, and squash in fields among the pine forests on the canyon rim, above limestone ledges in the upper canyon dotted with marine fossils. Eventually they moved on; today, some Hopi clans trace their ancestry to Walnut Canyon.

Six miles of the 20-mile canyon are protected today, including more than 300 masonry ruins. The **visitors center** (928/526-3367, www.nps.gov/waca, 8 A.M.–6 P.M. daily June–Aug., 9 A.M.–5 P.M. Dec.–Feb., otherwise

8 A.M.–5 P.M., $5 pp) sits on the edge of the 400-foot-deep ravine, and holds exhibits on the Sinagua culture, a bookstore, and information on ranger-guided hikes given in summer (backcountry hiking on your own is not allowed). The self-guided, mile-long **Island Trail** climbs down into the canyon past the ruins of 25 cliff dwellings. The trail's steepness and the altitude (6,700 feet) make it harder than you'd think. Another short trail leads along the rim past viewing points, a pit house, and a small pueblo.

Keep your eyes peeled for the canyon's varied wildlife, which inhabit several overlapping ecological communities. About 70 species of mammals in the area include coyotes, mule deer, elk, mountain lions, black bears, pronghorn antelopes, and a host of smaller critters. Canyon wrens, Cooper's hawks, prairie falcons, and great gray owls are some of the 121 resident bird species.

To get there, take exit 204 off I-40 and drive south three miles to the visitors center.

A **local passport** to Walnut Canyon, Sunset Crater and Wupatki costs $25, and is good for one vehicle for a year.

Grand Falls of the Little Colorado

A tongue of lava from Merriam Crater created this 185-foot cascade about 100,000 years ago. It's only worth coming in the spring and after summer thunderstorms, when meltwater roars over the edge. The falls, which are higher than Niagara, are just over the border of the Navajo Reservation, about 30 miles northeast of Flagstaff. To get there, take exit 245 off I-40 east of Flagstaff, and take Route-99 north to Leupp. From there take Route-15 west to a sign reading "Grand Falls Bible Church," where you'll turn right onto a rough road that ends at the river. A quarter-mile trail heads to the overlook. The dirt roads can be muddy and impassible in bad weather.

Sunset Crater National Monument

In about A.D. 1064, the youngest of more than

600 volcanoes in the San Francisco Volcanic Field started to blow its top. Flowing lava and forest fires lighted the night sky, and residents fled as firebombs rained down and earthquakes shook the ground. The eruptions subsided around A.D. 1180, but by then people had already begun moving back into the newly fertile area north of the new black peak.

The dramatic cinder cone volcano is 1,000 feet high and nearly a mile wide at its base. Surrounded by deep cinders and lava flows, it is far from the most hospitable-looking landscape, but trees, shrubs, and flowers have begun slowly recolonizing the scorched habitat. The name comes from multicolored mineral deposits on the crater rim that seem to light up at sunset.

A 36-mile **loop road** off Highway 89 north of Flagstaff connects Sunset Crater (8,029 feet), the Strawberry Crater Wilderness (in the Coconino National Forest), and Wupatki National Monument. It's a lovely drive through a landscape of black- and rust-colored volcanic debris, sagebrush, and juniper. Sunset Crater Volcano is on the southern end of the loop; turn right 12 miles north of Flagstaff and go two more miles to the newly renovated **visitors center** (928/526-0502, www.nps.gov/sucr, 8 A.M.–6 P.M. daily June–Aug., 9 A.M.–6 P.M. Dec.–Feb., otherwise 8 A.M.–5 P.M., $5 pp), where you can find a bookstore, picnic tables, and information on daily guided walks and evening programs. The entrance fee is good for a week both here and at Wupatki. Across the road is the U.S. Forest Service's (USFS) **Bonito Campground** (928/526-0866, May–mid-Oct., $15). One of the monument's two trails begins a mile east of the visitors center. The steep **Lenox Crater Trail** goes half a mile to the top of a cinder cone, and will have the less fit gasping for air by the end. Another half mile down the loop road is the beginning of the **Lava Flow Trail,** a mile-long loop past sharp lava flows, spatter cones, lava tubes, and cinder drifts like black snow. There is also a quarter-mile paved wheelchair-accessible trail through this landscape.

A **local passport** to Walnut Canyon, Sunset Crater, and Wupatki costs $25, and is good for one vehicle for a year.

Other Crater Hiking

Just east of the Sunset Crater visitors center is the road leading to the O'Leary Group Campground and the seven-mile round-trip trail to the fire tower on top of **O'Leary Peak** (8,965 feet). This lava-dome volcano offers excellent views of the Painted Desert and the San Francisco Volcanic Field, including Sunset Crater.

Farther north up the loop road is the 10,141-acre **Strawberry Crater Wilderness,** centered on yet another cinder cone and its accompanying lava flow. It's much older the Sunset Crater, formed between 50,000 and 100,000 years ago, and the wilderness area is full of prehistoric ruins. Indigenous residents used volcanic cinders as a sort of mulch to hold water, to make up for the area's dry location in the rain shadow of the San Francisco Peaks. (Only about seven inches of precipitation fall here every year.)

The easiest access to the area is from Highway 89. About 16 miles north of the Flagstaff Mall, take Forest Roads 546 and 779 east to the wilderness boundary, where an unmarked trail leads to the summit. You can also enter the wilderness area from the loop road to the east.

Wupatki National Monument

The only place in the Southwest where at least three separate cultures overlapped, Wupatki preserves four multistory pueblos, including the largest in the Flagstaff area. They rose during the 12th century A.D., when residents returning after the eruption of Sunset Crater Volcano found the soil much improved by the water-retaining ash and cinders. The Wupatki Basin bears the distinct signs of the Sinauga, Cohonina, and Kayenta Anasazi cultures, which arrived during a period of general population rise throughout the Southwest. By the mid-13th century, however, they had moved on to the north, east, and south,

where they were assimilated into the cultures of those areas.

The Wupatki **visitors center** (928/679-2365, www.nps.gov/wupa, 8 A.M.–6 P.M. daily, June–Aug., 9 A.M.–5 P.M. daily Dec.–Feb., $5 pp) is 14 miles from the northern end of the loop drive. There's a picnic area, vending machines, and a bookstore available, and exhibits inside on the various cultures that met and coexisted more or less peacefully here. A reconstructed pueblo room gives you an idea of life in the distant past. Entrance is good for a week both here and at Sunset Crater. Ask about orientation programs and guided hikes, given occasionally in summer and more often in spring and fall.

A short self-guided trail leads to the multistory **Wupatki Pueblo** on a side branch of Deadman Wash. This 100-room structure is built from red stone that contrasts with the black lava and green vegetation. The trail circles the pueblo, passing rooms on the far side that were once used to house rangers. Nearby are a reconstructed Mexican-style ball court—

© JULIAN SMITH

Lomaki Pueblo, Wupatki National Monument

the northernmost one yet found—and a blowhole, a small opening to an underground chamber that expels or draws in air depending on barometric pressure.

A side branch from the loop road leads 2.5 miles to **Wukoki Pueblo,** which once houses two or three families and is the monument's best-preserved pueblo. Farther north on the loop road are three smaller pueblos. The 30-room **Citadel Pueblo** stands like a castle on a small butte, near **Nalakihu Pueblo,** about half as big. **Lomaki Pueblo** sits on the edge of a small box canyon, and had nine rooms between two stories.

A **local passport** to Walnut Canyon, Sunset Crater, and Wupatki costs $25, and is good for one vehicle for a year.

San Francisco Mountains

The most distinctive features of Flagstaff's skyline were named by Franciscan monks after St. Francis of Assisi, the founder of their order, as they went about their holy business on the Hopi Reservation. The Navajo consider them *Doko'oosliid,* ("Abalone Shell Mountain"), the Sacred Mountain of the West. The Hopi call them *Nubat-i-kyan-bi* ("Place of the Snow Peaks"), and believe their kachina spirits live among the summits for part of every year, before flying to the Hopi mesas in the form of nourishing rain clouds. The play of light over the amazingly symmetrical peaks makes it easy to see why they Hopis revere them—the 1930s Works Progress Administration (WPA) guide to Arizona wrote, "At sunrise they appeal gold; at noon they are Carrara marble against a turquoise sky, at sunset they are polished copper, ruby, coral, and finally amethyst."

The range tops out at **Humphrey's Peak,** Arizona's highest point at 12,633 feet, and is home to a ski resort and miles upon miles of trails. Many of these are inside the 18,960-acre **Kachina Peaks Wilderness,** which encloses most of the highest peaks north of Mt. Elden. A huge caldera formed during the mountain's most recent eruption (about two million years ago) forms an inner basin filled

with aspens, pines, and firs. As you can imagine, the views from up here are fabulous, from flower-covered meadows all the way down to the Painted Desert and, if it's a clear day, the Grand Canyon.

The easiest way to get into the heart of the hills is the road to the **Arizona Snowbowl** (928/779-1951, info@arizonasnowbowl.com, www.arizonasnowbowl.com), which leaves Highway 180 seven miles north of downtown and climbs another seven uphill. In the winter, 32 mostly intermediate runs are served by four lifts and a towrope. All-day lift tickets are $42 adult, $24 children 8–12, and instruction and rentals are also available.

In summer, the chairlift (10 A.M.–4 P.M. daily, $10 pp) still runs to the 11,500-foot peak. It operates from late June to Labor Day, and Friday–Sunday under mid-October. The Agassiz Lodge Restaurant offers a deli-style menu for lunch and live music on Saturday afternoons. Two excellent trails leave from the lower parking lot; the five-mile **Kachina Trail** is a good, moderate hike south to Schultz Pass, and the six-mile **Humphrey's Peak Trail** leads above tree line to Humphrey's Peak. (Note that hiking is not allowed off trails above 11,400 feet to protect the fragile tundra vegetation.) The **Schultz Pass Road** is a gravel route connecting Highways 180 and 89 between Mt. Elden and the wilderness area. This 26-mile drive traverses ponderosa forests, open glades, and streams perfect for an afternoon picnic. It's open April–November, weather permitting, and offers access to the **Weatherford Trail,** built by hand in 1926 and popular with families for its gentle grade and views. This trail crosses the Fremont Saddle (11,354 feet) before connecting with the Humphrey's Peak Trail from the Arizona Snowbowl. The western end of the Schultz Pass Road joins Highway 180 just north of the Museum of Northern Arizona. It begins as Forest Road 420, and heads left (north) where the Elden Lookout Road heads right (east).

Another good drive through the mountains is the **Around the Peaks Loop,** a 44-mile gravel route around Humphrey's Peak that's also open April–November, weather permitting. Like the Schultz Pass Road, it is particularly pretty in autumn when the aspens are turning gold. To do the loop counterclockwise, drive 14 miles north of Flagstaff on Highway 89 to Forest Road 418, go west 12 miles to Forest Road 151, and then south 8 miles to Highway 180, 9.5 miles north of Flagstaff.

Cameron Trading Post and Gallery

In 1911, a suspension bridge was built over the Little Colorado River about 50 miles north of Flagstaff. Five years later, Hubert and C. D. Richardson established a trading post where the Navajo and Hopi exchanged wool, blankets, and livestock for dry goods. Today the Cameron Trading Post and Gallery (800/338-7385, fax 928/679-2501, info@camerontradingpost.com, www.camerontradingpost.com) is owned by Joe Atkinson, grand nephew of the Richardsons, who has remodeled the old place into a beautiful enclave that's the perfect home base for a Grand Canyon visit.

About a mile north of the intersection of Highways 89 and 64, the Cameron Trading Post has a lodge with 66 rooms ($90) featuring hand-carved furniture and balcony views of the Little Colorado Gorge. Many rooms are arranged around the hotel's exquisite gardens, where Chinese elms, fruit trees, and rosebushes were originally planted by Hubert's wife Mabel. A large stone fireplace, pressed-tin ceiling, and native crafts from throughout the Southwest decorate the dining room, serving all meals daily.

There's a food market, gas station, RV park ($15), and post office elsewhere in the complex, and an active trading post where locals buy craft supplies and sundries and sell wool and piñon nuts. Make sure you don't miss the gallery, which has an outstanding collection of antique and contemporary native art Rugs, concho belts, pottery, kachinas, baskets, and Old West memorabilia fill the place from wooden floor to wide-beamed ceiling. More pieces are on display upstairs, in a series of rooms restored to look like living quarters.

© JULIAN SMITH

Cameron Trading Post and Gallery

Sedona

South of Flagstaff on Highway 89A is one of Arizona's more famous and unique destinations. Part art center, part resort retreat, and part New Age nexus, Sedona (pop. 10,000) is blessed with unearthly red-rock scenery, a moderate climate at 4,500 feet, and (according to many) seven spiritual energy "vortexes" scattered among the stones. With more hypnotherapists, masseuses, yoga teachers, spirit guides, life coaches, and artists per capita than any other place in the West, if not the country—not to mention spas and luxury accommodations galore—Sedona makes for a fascinating and wonderfully scenic day trip from Flagstaff.

Getting there is half the fun. Highway 89A follows Oak Creek Canyon most of the 30 miles from Flagstaff to Sedona, an amazing drive past rock monoliths, swimming holes, viewing points, and secluded resort lodges. It gets very crowded on summer weekends, so consider coming at some other time if you can. The same applies to Sedona itself; it's definitely not off the beaten track, with some four million people making the pilgrimage every year.

History

The Hohokam people were the first to live in this arid area, which they improved for cultivation by digging irrigation canals, from roughly 300 B.C. to about A.D. 1450, when they left abruptly and mysteriously. Small groups of Maricopa and Pima Indians arrived later to the banks of the Salt and Gila rivers.

Sedona's first Anglo settler was J. J. Thompson, who homesteaded across from what is today the Indian Gardens Store in 1876. More settlers followed with cattle and horses, digging irrigation ditches to water crops and raise orchards. The homestead of Frank Pendley is now Slide Rock State Park in Oak Creek Canyon, and his original irrigation system still works. Author Zane Grey helped popularize the landscape with his novel *The Call of the Canyon,* and Smithsonian Institution scientists explored local cliff dwellings near the turn of the 20th century. The remote ranching and farming settlement was finally named after the wife of settler T. C. Schnebly, who chose his spouse's name while establishing the town's first post office out of love and the fact that it was short enough to fit on a cancellation stamp.

Hollywood arrived in the 1940s and 1950s, and in the ensuing decades a new cadre of visitors was drawn by the town's stunning location. Artists, tourists, and retirees came for the scenery and stayed for a variety of reasons, and Sedona gradually became one of the top destinations in the Southwest. The New Age movement of the 1980s brought a new influx of seekers. The city was incorporated in 1988, and half of the 19-square-mile city still belongs to the government in the form of the Coconino National Forest. High-end tourism has begun to replace the desert-love-in vibe of Sedona's early years, but spirituality is still the name of the game.

Sedona is roughly divided into two parts along Highway 89A: "West Sedona," a quieter, residential section, and the more touristy "uptown," to the east where 89A meets Highway 179.

SIGHTS
Chapel of the Holy Cross

Sedona's famous Chapel of the Holy Cross (780 Chapel Rd., 928/282-4069) seems to be anchored into the red rock itself, 200 feet above the valley, by a huge cross. The Catholic chapel is open to people of all faiths, who come for the views (especially at sunset) and the spiritual energy that seems to pervade the place. From "uptown," take Highway 179 south toward the village of Oak Creek for three miles, then turn left on Chapel Road.

◖ Oak Creek Canyon

Oak Creek Canyon is said to be Arizona's second-most-popular attraction, and it's easy to see why. Multicolored stone cliffs and pine forests above lush riparian habitat make it one of the most inviting spots in this dry state. Take a dip in Oak Creek at **Slide Rock State Park** (928/282-3034, 8 A.M.–7 P.M. daily in summer, $10 per car, $2 on foot or bicycle), where you can, of course, slide down smooth rocks and hike on three short trials. The park is 10 miles north of Sedona. A bit farther north, **Red Rock State Park** (928/282-6907, 8 A.M.–8 P.M. daily in summer, visitors center 9 A.M.–6 P.M., $3 per car, $2 on foot or bicycle) has a five-mile network of trails along the creek, with ranger-led interpretive hikes and an herbarium. There are six Forest Service campgrounds in the canyon as well as numerous picnic areas.

EVENTS

In early March is the **Sedona International Film Festival** (www.sedonafilmfestival.com), a three-day event with workshops and independent movies. **Sedona Jazz on the Rocks** (www.sedonajazz.com) brings great music and master classes in September, the same month that the **Sedona Ecofest** (www.sedonaecofest.com), the state's largest ecological performing arts festival, come to town. Bela Fleck, B. B. King, and Blues Travelers have all performed at past events.

SHOPPING AND SERVICES

Sedona is chock-full of art galleries and shops selling everything from T-shirts to fine art. A good place to start is the **Tlaquepaque Arts & Crafts Village** (336 Hwy. 179, 928/282-4838, www.tlaq.com), an imitation Mexican village with more than 40 galleries and shops as well as four restaurants with outdoor dining. Many galleries are concentrated along Highway 179, including **Exposures International Gallery of Fine Art** (561 Hwy. 179, 928/282-1125 or 800/526-7668) and **Arte-Misia** (617 Hwy. 179, Suite BST-4, 928/282-3686), with contemporary originals. Stock up on all things spiritual at the **Sedona Crystal Vortex** (271 N. Hwy. 89A, 928/282-3543), where you can have a psychic reading or a massage.

Sedona's **Center for the New Age** (928/282-2085, info@sedonanewagecenter.com, www .sedonanewagecenter.com) is on Highway 179 across from the Tlaquepaque shopping plaza, where they offer guided vortex tours, psychic readings, and massage therapy. Not to be outdone, the **Healing Center of Arizona** (25 Wilson Canyon Rd., 877/723-2811, johnpaul@sedonahealingcenter.com, www.sedonahealingcenter.com) occupies a geodesic dome on the north end of town, where guests can enjoy outdoor whirlpool tubs, saunas, herbology acupressure, yoga, and tai chi. Vegetarian meals and lodging are also available; dorm rooms are $30 per person, private rooms are $75 double.

RECREATION
Hiking

On a more earthly plane, Sedona is outstanding in the outdoors department. Dozens of hiking trails wind among the red-rock formations. Two great options are accessed off Dry Creek Road (Forest Service Road 152), which leaves Highway 89A 3.1 miles west of the Y. To reach **Devil's Bridge,** a two-mile out-and-back stroll to one of Sedona's many natural arches, turn right onto the dirt Forest Service Road 152, two miles from Highway 89A and go 1.3 miles to the marked trailhead. Keep going another 2.5 miles on Dry Creek Road to the dirt Boynton Pass Road on your left, which you take another 1.2 miles to the trailhead to **Doe Mountain,** a 3.6-mile out-and-back climb up a mesa with great views.

If it's an energy vortex you're after, head to **Boyton Canyon** by turning right instead of left toward Boynton Pass. The trailhead is near the private Enchantment Resort. The entire canyon is said to be an energy hot spot, but Boynton Spires, reached by the Vista Trail on the right shortly after starting the hike, is a particular spiritual hot spot. In any case, it's all beautiful. **Cathedral Rock** is said to be another vortex, and is a fun slickrock scramble/climb around regardless. (Agoraphobes should think twice.) Head south on Highway 179 from the Y intersection for 0.6 mile to the trailhead. For more information on Sedona's great hiking, pick up a copy of Cosmic Ray's *Favorite Hikes Flagstaff & Sedona,* available locally.

Biking

Mountain bikers should head to **Absolute Bikes** (6101 Hwy. 179, Suite C, 928/284-1242, www.absolutebikes.net/sedona) for rentals ($30–50 per day), sales, and service as well as trail information. Mountain Bike Heaven (1695 W. Hwy. 89A, 928/282-1312, www.mountainbikeheaven.com) leads tours on the area's 200 or so miles of trails.

Other Activities

If you'd rather experience the countryside from horseback, **Trail Horse Adventures** (165 Mockingbird L., 928/282-7252 or 800/723-3538) leads guided rides in the Coconino National Forest. Prefer motorized adventure? Try **Sedona Red Rock Jeep Tours** (270 N. Hwy. 89A, 928/282-6826 or 800/848-7728, www.redrockjeep.com), whose four-wheel-drive tours start at $40 per person for 1.5 hours.

ACCOMMODATIONS

In this luxury resort town, you can choose from dozens of outstanding B&Bs. The **(Canyon Villa Inn** (125 Canyon Circle Dr., 800/453-1166, canvilla@sedona.net, www.canyonvilla.com, $190–300) is probably the best, with rooms designed around their peerless views of Bell Rock and Courthouse Butte, an outdoor heated pool, and gourmet breakfasts, as well as afternoon hors d'oeuvres. The **Casa Sedona B&B Inn** (55 Hozoni Dr., 800/525-3756, casa@sedona.net, www.casasedona.com, $185–290) is another AAA four-diamond option, with more of a cowboy/Western flavor.

If your budget permits, you can opt for a place like the **Enchantment Resort** (800/826-4180, info@enchantmentresort.com, www.enchantmentresort.com, $300 and up) with a spa, athletic facilities, and restaurants at the mouth of Boynton Canyon. If it doesn't, there's always the **Village Lodge** (78 Bell Rock Blvd., 928/284-3626, $50–60) or the fun-to-say **Lo Lo Mai Lodge** (50 Willow Way., 928/282-2835, $60–95).

FOOD

Sedona's food choices are as varied as its lodging options, with a local twist; even the Mc-

Donald's here forgoes the usual golden arches in favor of a mellower, pastel green "M" on a pink stucco wall. The **Oaxaca Restaurant** (321 N. Hwy. 89A, 928/282-4179, all meals daily), offers the appeal and food of Sonora Mexico and a rooftop cantina to boot. Mexican entrées are $7–12 for lunch and $10–17 for dinner, and there are more than 50 varieties of tequila at the bar.

The innovative American cuisine of **The Heartline Cafe** (1610 W. Hwy. 89A, 928/282-0785, lunch Thurs.–Mon., dinner daily) has earned it repeat best-restaurant honors. The feel is casual but the food is anything but; entrées run $8–12 for lunch and $15 and up for dinner. The **Blue Moon Cafe** (6101 Hwy. 179, Suite B, 928/284-1831, all meals daily) is a breakfast-all-day kind of place, with hand-tossed pizzas and great Philly cheesesteaks.

An elegant dining spot hidden in an upscale shopping plaza, chef/owner Walter Paulson's **Rene at Tlaquepaque** (336 Hwy. 179, Suite 118, 928/282-9225, lunch and dinner daily) has an extensive wine list and tempting continental selections. Entrées are $8–13 for lunch, $18–28 for dinner. Buffalo and rattlesnake are both on the menu at the southwestern-themed **Cowboy Club** (241 N. Hwy. 89A, 928/282-4200, lunch and dinner daily), a lively spot that occupies one of Sedona's oldest buildings.

The award for Sedona's classiest dining spot goes to **(L'Auberge de Sedona** (301 L'Auberge Ln., 928/282-1661 or 800/272-6777, all meals daily), one of the Southwest's premiere fine dining restaurants, serving elegant French dishes inside or more relaxed bistro fare on the outdoor Terrace on the Creek (April–October). Five-course prix fixe meals are one option ($65–85), or à la carte entrées for $25 and up.

INFORMATION

For more information on Sedona and the surrounding area, contact the **Sedona-Oak Creek Canyon Chamber of Commerce** (1 Forest Rd., 928/282-7722 or 800/288-7336, fax 928/204-1064, info@sedonachamber.com, www.visitsedona.com).

Grand Canyon National Park

Northwest of Flagstaff stretches one of the world's natural wonders, a mile-deep chasm carved into the high desert by the relentless force of flowing water. Over tens of millions of years, the Colorado River has eaten away the surface of the Colorado Plateau, leaving the canyon to end all canyons: 277 miles long and up to 18 miles wide, with countless side gorges each of which could be a national park in itself. It's one of the country's greatest tourist draws, and justifiably so. The view from the edge is something you'll never forget, and a trip to the bottom—particularly a raft voyage through the famous Colorado River rapids—is almost beyond words.

THE SOUTH RIM

Most visitors approach the canyon from this side, which offers the quickest access from major cities (Flagstaff and Phoenix). As a result, the South Rim has more tourist amenities than the more remote North Rim.

Grand Canyon Village

Highway 64 runs north from Williams on I-40 to Grand Canyon Village, the largest settlement in the park. Here you'll find **park headquarters** (928/638-7888, www.nps.gov/grca, $20 per vehicle for one week), a post office, a bank, medical services, numerous stores and gift shops, and the **Canyon View Information Plaza** at Mather Point (8 A.M.–5 P.M. daily).

The Rim Trail offers access to many excellent viewing points over the vastness of the canyon and its tributaries. Highway 64 runs east from Grand Canyon Village for 25 miles along the edge of the canyon, where it's called East Rim Drive inside the park. Along the way are ruins, viewing points, and the **Desert View Watchtower,** a stone structure designed by Mary Colter for the Fred Harvey Company in 1932 and lined with Hopi murals. Highway 64 continues east to Cameron.

Accommodations and Food

Six national park lodges offer accommodations, including the grand old **El Tovar,** built in 1905. Rooms range $55–300, depending on season. For reservations, contact Xanterra Parks & Resorts (303/297-2757 or 888/297-2757, fax 303/297-3175, www.grandcanyonlodges.com). Most of the lodges have restaurants, and you can camp at the **Mather Campground** (800/365-2267, http://reservations.nps.gov, $15, year-round) and its attached **Trailer Village** ($25) in Grand Canyon Village, or else the **Desert View Campground** (May–Oct., $10), 26 miles east.

More tourist services are available at **Tusayan,** on Highway 64 outside the park boundary.

Getting There

Open Road Tours (800/766-7117, www.openroadtours.com) runs a daily shuttle from Flagstaff to Grand Canyon Village and Tusayan for $25 per person each way, not including park entry fee. Otherwise, to get from Tusayan to Grand Canyon Village, you'll have to drive or call a taxi. From Williams, you can take the charming **Grand Canyon Railway** (800/843-8724, www.thetrain.com), which has been chugging along since 1901. The 2.25-hour ride includes roving musicians, a bar car, and a train robbery. Various packages including lodging at the Grand Canyon Railway Hotel Williams are available, but the ride itself is $60–155 per person.

For a view from above, take a ride with **Maverick Helicopters** (702/261-0007 or 888/261-4414, www.maverickhelicopter.com), whose flights from the South Rim start at $330 per person.

THE NORTH RIM

Though only about 10 miles from the South Rim as the raven flies, the less-developed North Rim is more than 200 miles away by road, so it sees far fewer visitors. You can still depend on the same stupendous views and

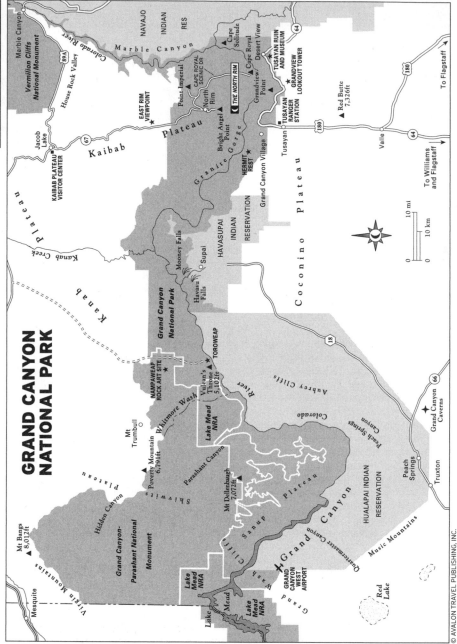

GRAND CANYON NATIONAL PARK

the same precipitous trails—you'll just have several thousand fewer people to share them with. Plus, since it's over 1,000 feet higher, it's significantly cooler in summer.

Sights and Hikes

Your first stop, after you've tasted the view, should be the **North Rim Visitors Center** (8 A.M.–6 P.M. daily May–Oct.).

A 23-mile **scenic drive** leads to the overlook at **Point Royal,** passing half a dozen more viewing points along the way, many with picnic areas and short trails.

Day hike choices include the half-mile paved Bright Angel Point Trail, the three-mile Transept Trail from the lodge to the campground, and the five-mile Uncle Jim trail to another overlook.

Accommodations and Food

Built in 1928, the log-beam **◖ Grand Canyon Lodge** boasts two porches and an octagonal sunroom with huge windows to take advantage of the panorama. Rooms and cabins range $87–112 per night, and it's a good idea to make reservations as far ahead of time as possible (through Xanterra, above, or the website www.grandcanyon-northrim.com). The same goes for the restaurant, which serves all meals, as well as the **North Rim Campground** (800/365-2267, http://reservations.nps.gov) with sites for $15–20, showers, laundry facilities, a grocery, and a camping store.

The Kaibab Plateau

Highway 89A climbs into the cool evergreen forests of the Kaibab Plateau, and at almost 8,000 feet hits Jacob Lake, where it joins with Highway 67 toward the northern edge of the abyss. The **Jacob Lake Inn** (928/643-7232, jacob@jacoblake.com, www.jacoblake.com) has a restaurant and year-round rooms ($91–93) and cabins ($72–86). It's also where you'll find the **Kaibab Plateau Visitor Center** (928/643-7298, 8 A.M.–5 P.M. daily May–Oct.). Across the road, **Allen's Outfitters** (801/644-8150) organizes horseback trips into the Kaibab National Forest, and the USFS Jacob Lake Campground has primitive sites for $12. A quarter mile south is the Kaibab Camper Village (928/643-7804,

$15–30) with full hookup sites open May–October. From here, Highway 67 reaches almost 9,000 feet as it winds through the parklike meadows and pine-clad hills of the Kaibab National Forest, one of the prettiest in the Lower 48. Buried by snow in winter, the road is open mid-May–mid-October, weather permitting.

Tuweep

For the slightly more adventurous, this "back door" to the North Rim of the Grand Canyon offers something that may seem unbelievable if you've ever been to the South Rim in tour-bus season: solitude. To get there you'll have to negotiate about 60 miles of dirt roads; turn off onto BLM Road 109 (the "Sunshine Route") from Arizona Highway 389 about seven miles west of Fredonia, and don't try it with a low-slung car or when it's wet. There aren't any tourist facilities (or water), just a lonely ranger station, but you can drive literally to the edge of the canyon—which looks more like a gorge here rather than a mountain range seen from above—and camp for free, often with only a handful of other people around. It's a whole other way to experience the Grand Canyon.

The 1.5-mile **Lava Falls Trail** offers the shortest route to the Colorado River from the rim in the entire park. It's steep and rough

Tuweep Overlook, Grand Canyon

going over lava, but at the bottom you can watch rafters tackling Lava Falls, the meanest in the park. Eleven primitive campsites (first-come, first-served) are available near the rim, with picnic tables, fire grates, and composting toilets. Contact the North Rim of the park or the park website (www.nps.gov/grca/grandcanyon/tuweep/) for more information.

THE INNER CANYON

First, the warnings: Since it gets hotter as you descend into the gorge, and it typically takes twice as much time, energy, and water to climb back out, *and* it can hit over 100°F down there in summer, you should carry at least one gallon of water per person per day from spring to fall. And don't go unprepared, gear- and fitness-wise. Park rangers have countless horror stories about businessmen with briefcases and mothers with baby carriages trundling down the Bright Angel Trail. The best times to venture into the canyon are in spring and fall; March, April, October, and November are ideal. From May to September, temperatures at the rim can be in the 90°F, and in the canyon can climb to over 100°F.

Permits are necessary for overnight camping in the backcountry ($10 plus $5 pp per night). These can be requested in person, by fax, or by mail, but be warned that the park receives about 30,000 requests every year and only grants 13,000, so file early—up to four months ahead, on the first of the month. See the park's backcountry website (www.nps.gov/grca/backcountry/) for more details.

Hiking

From the South Rim, the **Bright Angel Trail** heads 9.3 miles downhill to **Phantom Ranch** at the river. Dorm rooms here (segregated by sex) are $27, and meals are also available. An overnight permit is not required at the ranch; reserve rooms through Xanterra, above. A wealth of other trails lead down into the gorge. One popular hike is the **Grandview Trail** from Grandview Point to Horseshoe Mesa, an old Native American route improved by miners (six miles round-trip).

From the North Rim, you can take the **North Kaibab Trail** 15 miles from **Bright Angel Point** to Phantom Ranch. The steeper **Bill Hall** trail also goes all the way to the river, 10 miles and 5,200 feet down. Near the bottom it passes **Thunder River,** which gushes out of a sheer limestone cliff before flowing right into the Colorado, making it by some estimates the shortest in the world.

Rafting the Canyon

Riding the rapids of the Colorado River ranks high up on the list of Things You Should Do Before You Die. Follow in the footsteps of daring explorers as you explore side canyons, float the placid stretches, shrink in significance next to billions of years of geology, and—here the footsteps end—enjoy gourmet meals and the luxury of sleeping bags on a sandbar beneath the stars. Companies in Page, Flagstaff, and other cities in Utah and Arizona offer many different options for running the river, which is a good thing, considering the waiting list for private permits is over a decade long. Choose from motorboats or the classic oar-powered dories, and either the full 226 miles from Lees Ferry to Diamond Creek or a partial trip. The full journey takes 11–19 days by oar or 6–8 days with a motor, or you can join or leave a trip at Phantom Ranch, cutting your travel time considerably.

For more information, see the appropriate listings under *Page* and *Flagstaff* or see the website of the **Grand Canyon River Outfitters Association** (www.gcroa.org).

Tours and Activities

Besides boot leather, another classic way to enter the canyon is on a **mule ride,** which have been lumbering on for over a century. These start at $133 per person for a day trip to Plateau Point on the South Rim, and you can go to Phantom Ranch and back for $360 per person, including food and accommodations. Contact Xanterra, above, for reservations and information.

The **Grand Canyon Field Institute** (928/638-2485 or 866/471-4435, gcfi@grandcanyon.org, www.grandcanyon.org/fieldinstitute/) organize a wealth of guided, educational overnight trips into the canyon March–November.

Navajo Reservation

TUBA CITY AND VICINITY

One of the Navajo Reservation's most diverse communities, Tuba City (pop. 8,250) sits off Highway 89 between Flagstaff and Page. It was named by early Mormon settlers after a Hopi called Tuuvi, chief of the Water and Corn Clans at Orabi. Tuuvi was the first Hopi to meet Brigham Young, and after converting to the Mormon faith in Salt Lake City, he donated a plot of land to the church on the condition that Mormon settlers would protect the Hopi from Navajo and Paiute raiders. Jacob Hamblin, the "Buckskin Missionary," helped establish a settlement at a well-watered area called Moenave at the foot of a cliff to the north. Mormons heading south along a trail blazed by Hamblin to the Little Colorado River valley often stopped here to rest and re-supply. (The trail became known as the Honeymoon Trail, since young Mormon couples had to travel all the way back to St. George, Utah, to have their wedding vows officially solemnized by the church.) The last Latter-Day Saint left Moenave near the turn of the 20th century, when the area was added to the Navajo Reservation.

Although predominantly Navajo, Tuba City has many residents who belong to the Hopi and other tribes, as well as Anglos. The Basha's grocery store serves as the unofficial community gathering place. Although most travelers zip past on their way to the North Rim of the Grand Canyon without a second glance, Tuba City is worth a detour for its shopping and its Navajo tacos.

Sights

Tuba City sits on a mesa north of Highway 160 in one of the most striking expanses of the **Painted Desert** (see the sidebar *The Painted Desert*). About two miles east on Highway 160 from Highway 89, a dirt turnoff leads to the top of a small hill, a great place to take photos and enjoy the view.

Three more miles bring you to another turnoff marked by a hand-lettered sign for **Moenave,** the site of the original Mormon settlement. Near the turnoff are a set of **dinosaur tracks** laid down by the nine-foot Dilophosaurus in the late Triassic mud. Navajo children are usually on hand to give you a short tour (a small tip is expected), and will point out the three-toed footprints, petrified eggs, and even an embedded claw. The settlement of Moenave itself, at the base of Hamblin's Ridge, is a green oasis fed by springs. John D. Lee, of Lees Ferry,

THE PAINTED DESERT

The Navajo call it *halchíítah,* meaning "among the colors." The arid badlands of the late-Triassic Chinle Formation are famous for their psychedelic scenery, heavily eroded and dotted with buttes and mesas of nearly every color imaginable. Pastel pinks, reds, yellows, greens, and grays stain the barren hillsides, and crazy eroded shapes make up a surrealist landscape that is almost unbelievable at sunrise and sunset.

The Painted Desert extends in a narrow arc for about 160 miles from Cameron to the Petrified Forest, between the Little Colorado River and the Hopi tablelands. Most of the soils were laid down as silt and volcanic ash, and are marked by clays that shrink and swell so much as they get wet and dry that hardly anything can grow. A few different factors have dictated which colors ended up where. Reds, oranges, and pinks come from iron and aluminum oxides concentrated in slowly deposited sediments, while blues, grays, and purples are the results of rapid events, such as floods, that removed oxygen from the soils.

NAVAJO CRAFTS

The Diné tell how Spider Woman taught their ancestors to weave on looms built by her husband. The introduction of curly-horned Churro sheep by the Spanish in the 17th century, along with the embracing of pueblo-style looms and a more sedentary lifestyle, allowed the tribe to become expert weavers. Today their **rugs** can hold their own among the world's finest handmade textiles. Women traditionally own the sheep and weave the rugs, which can take months to make. (The Churro sheep was almost extinct by the 1970s, and is being pulled back from the brink through careful breeding.)

Navajo rugs combine Mexican stylistic influences with geometric designs and representations of natural phenomena. At the advice of early Anglo traders, the weavers expanded their repertoire to include brighter colors and more intricate patterns, as well as synthetic yarns. True Navajo rugs, however, are woven from sheep wool, and a quick sniff will reveal an earthy aroma. Other things to look for in a quality rug include symmetry, straight edges, even coloration, and a tight, flat weave. You'll often find a "spirit line" running to the border in older rugs, included to keep the weaver's spirit from being trapped inside the pattern.

Patterns include the geometric Two Grey Hills, made of natural white, gray, and brown wool; the warm pastels of the Burnt Water style; the elaborately banded Wide Ruins; and the self-explanatory Eye Dazzlers and Pictorials. Sometimes rug patterns are dictated by the color of their background, from Dinnebito (black) to Ganado (red) and Klagetoh (gray). Yei rugs depict the Holy People, and Yeibichai illustrate ceremonies in which the Holy People are impersonated by human dancers. Prices range from the low hundreds to well into the thousands, with a quality 3-by-5-foot rug going for about $500-750. This is an exacting art, and sadly, a dying one, since fewer young weavers are learning the old techniques. For this reason, a quality rug will hold its price well and probably even climb in value. Good rugs will also last for years – some old ones have endured over a century of boot traffic.

The Navajo originally learned the technique of **silversmithing** from Mexicans in the 1850s, before taking it to new levels. They don't have to melt down silver coins any more, but today's silver jewelry is just as impressive: chunky bracelets, elaborately detailed concha belts, rings and watchbands inlaid with turquoise and coral, and gorgeous squash-blossom necklaces that make your neck ache just to look at them. Silver jewelry is usually sand-cast and then polished to a bright luster, and die-stamped with decorative details. You'll often see Navajo matriarchs decked out in their best necklaces and bracelets, with enough turquoise to ransom a princess, and men wear the *ketoh*, or "bow guard," a wide forearm band that is now purely decorative. Turquoise is the most common inlay material, but new techniques have seen the addition of gold and other precious minerals.

Navajo **sandpaintings** re-create the ceremonial designs drawn on hogan floors by medicine men, which are gathered and scattered to the winds when the ritual is finished. The paintings are drawn with glue on plywood or particleboard, then sprinkled with minerals gathered and ground on the reservation. Look for precise workmanship, and know that you're not getting a true religious artifact – small details are changed in the paintings to avoid offending the Holy People. Other types of **paintings** in oils and acrylics depict life on the reservation, and are sometimes quite abstract.

One of the most widely recognized type of basket made in the Southwest is the Navajo **ceremonial basket,** a wide, shallow dish woven of sumac and mahogany fibers. These are made using a concentric coil technique, and have geometric designs in muted colors. They're most commonly used in traditional weddings. Tribe members make many other types of crafts as well, including their own versions of Hopi **kachinas, wood carvings,** ceramic and alabaster **sculpture,** and **"folk art,"** a generic term for figurines carved from wood or fashioned from clay.

hid out here for a while before being tracked down and executed for his role in the Mountain Meadows Massacre.

Shopping and Events

A huge red building on Highway 160 at the base of the mesa houses **Van's Trading Company** (928/283-5343) which is half supermarket and half general-goods store. The pawn department, open daily 9 A.M.–6 P.M., has lots of jewelry and rugs. Dead pawn is auctioned off on the 15th of every month. Up in Tuba City proper is the **Tuba Trading Post** (928/283-5441, 8 A.M.–6 P.M. Mon.–Fri., 8 A.M.–5 P.M. Sat., 9 A.M.–5 P.M. Sun.), built in 1870 out of local blue limestone and logs from the San Francisco Peaks. Teddy Roosevelt stayed here in 1913 on his way back from hunting mountain lions on the North Rim of the Grand Canyon, and Zane Gray also stopped by. Today the two-story octagonal showroom holds a wealth of quality crafts, particularly jewelry.

Every Friday the **Tuba City Flea Market** coalesces behind the Community Center. A little bit of everything is for sale—car parts, used clothing, medicinal herbs, turquoise jewelry—and you can listen to the lilting sounds of the Navajo language over a bowl of mutton stew and frybread when you need a breather. The **Western Navajo Fair** is held in the Rodeo and Fair Grounds every October, on the first weekend after Columbus Day.

Accommodations and Food

Next to the Tuba Trading Post, the **Quality Inn** (928/283-4545, fax 928/283-4144) has rooms for around $100, a restaurant serving all meals, and an RV park with six tent sites. Students at the Greyhills Academy High School run the 32-room **Greyhills Inn** (928/283-6271, ext. 142, $42), as part of a training program in hotel management. Back at the intersection of Highways 160 and 264, the **Tuba City Truck Stop Cafe** (928/283-4975) is a must-eat for road-food gourmands. They boast the "Best Navajo taco in the Southwest," and the messy, heaping concoction of beans, lettuce, tomatoes, and cheese on top of frybread is hard to beat. Navajo matriarchs decked out in their best jewelry munch quietly beneath signed photos of various celebrities who have stopped in for a bite.

KAYENTA AND VICINITY

The largest city in the northern part of the Navajo Reservation (pop. 5,000) takes its name, loosely, from the Navajo word *teehindeeh*, meaning "bog hole" or "natural game pit," after the gluelike soil around a nearby spring that mired livestock. In truth, it's not the most inviting place, with little of interest besides a few motels, inexpensive restaurants, and a shopping center at the intersection of Highways 160 and 163. It's a dusty town of pickup trucks and cowboy hats, home to miners and farmers. (The Navajo also call it *Tódíneeshzheé*, meaning "water spreading out like fingers" and referring to nearby springs.)

Shopping and Events

Crafts, Western wear, and craft supplies are sold at the **Navajo Arts and Crafts Enterprises** outlet (928/697-8611, 9 A.M.–6 P.M. Mon.–Fri., in summer, 8 A.M.–4 P.M. Sat., 10 A.M.–4 P.M. Sun.) near the main intersection. The Fourth of July brings the **Todineeshzee Fourth of July Rodeo and Fair** to Kayenta.

Accommodations and Food

Kayenta has only a few chain hotels, all near the main intersection. In the $100–150 range are a **Best Western Wetherill Inn** (928/697-3231, fax 928/697-3233), the **Hampton Inn** (928/697-3170, fax 928/697-3189), and the **Holiday Inn** (928/697-3221, fax 928/697-3349).

Back at the main intersection, the **Blue Coffee Pot** (928/697-3396, 6 A.M.–9 P.M. Mon.–Fri.) is a local favorite. Named after a type of container that was once common on the reservation, it serves good steaks, Mexican, and Navajo dishes for $4–8. The Basha's supermarket complex contains a hardware store, movie theater, a Wendy's, a Blimpie's, and a Burger King, with an interesting

THE OWL, THE SNAKE, AND THE PILE OF WOOL

Monument Valley is just the beginning of the fascinating geology near Kayenta. Just north of Kayenta on Highway 163, **Agathla Peak** (6,096 feet) is a jagged volcanic neck with the same blackened, ominous look as Shiprock. This is believed to be the center of the Navajo world, set in place by the Holy People to prop up the sky. In Navajo, *'aghaa'lá* means "much wool," and preserves the legend of a huge snake that made its home at the base of the rock. His wife, an owl, lived nearby – look for distinctive **Owl Rock** (6,547 feet) across the road, formed of Wingate Sandstone. The snake grew fat on the plentiful local antelope, and tossed so much leftover hair outside his home that the name stuck. Kit Carson later renamed the peak El Capitan, and the classic Western *Stagecoach* was filmed here in 1938.

Half Dome, which stands closer to Kayenta near **Church Rock** (5,580 feet), looms west of the town on Highway 160. Heading south along Highway 160 toward Tuba City, you'll pass along the south side of the **Organ Rock Monocline,** also called Skeleton Mesa. Huge sandstone teeth point northwest in the remains of this geologic uplift, raised 75-80 million years ago. **Marsh Pass** (6,750 feet) brings you to **Tsegi Canyon,** home to the Anasazi Inn. This beautiful canyon, coming in from the north, was carved by Laguna Creek and is relatively lush, with many Anasazi sites and fields of Navajo corn in summer. Highway 160 continues southwest through **Long House Canyon** to the turnoff for Navajo National Monument. An electric coal train passes over the road here, leading south to **Black Mesa** and the Peabody coal mines.

exhibit on the Navajo code talkers (see the sidebar *Navajo Code Talkers* in the *Essentials* chapter). You can buy food at the Kayenta Trading Post, a supermarket down the hill behind the Best Western.

NAVAJO NATIONAL MONUMENT

Twenty miles south of Kayenta, Highway 564 leads north to this small monument that protects three of the most impressive and intact Anasazi ruins in the Four Corners. Start at the **visitors center** (928/672-2700, www.nps.gov/nava, 8 A.M.–7 P.M. daily, free) on the Shonto Plateau nine miles north of Highway 160. It contains a craft shop and museum, and next door is a **campground** with 16 sites open April–September, also free.

Sights and Hikes

Two short, easy trails lead to overlooks above the **Betatakin** cliff dwellings, but to really experience the monument, you should really take a ranger-led tour, which are offered Memorial Day–Labor Day. This is a little more of an undertaking—the trails are steep and

sandy, and you'll need a permit—but both are well worth it.

Betatakin is a five-mile hike, and **Keet Seel** is 17 miles from the visitors center, meaning you can stay the night or do the whole thing in an epic, one-day push. Either way, you can follow a ranger through this 100-room settlement tucked under a cliff overhang. The inhabitants kept their stored food safe from rodents in ingeniously sealed storage chambers. Stone slabs fit perfectly into small doorways, and were held in place by poles slid through wooden loops set into the masonry on either side. Betatakin sits in a 435-foot high alcove, which has dropped so much sandstone lately that tours now stop outside instead of entering.

Accommodations and Food

The closest lodgings to the monument are in Tsegi Canyon, about five miles northeast on Highway 160. Here the **Anasazi Inn Tsegi Canyon** (928/697-3793, fax 928/697-8249, info@anasaziinn.com, www.anasaziinn.com) has 57 rooms ($50) and a small café serving all meals daily. It's nothing special, room-wise, but you can't beat the setting in the pink sandstone gorge.

◖ MONUMENT VALLEY

Driving north of Kayenta on Highway 163 toward the Utah border, and it's easy to feel like you just entered a Western movie sunset just as the credits started to roll. Rising from the flat plain like the gods' own rock garden, the stone monoliths of Monument Valley are the unmistakable symbol of the American West, imbedded in the imagination of the world by countless movies, photos, and car commercials.

The Navajo consider all of *Tsébii' nidzisgai* (the "Valley Within the Rocks") to be one huge hogan, with the traditional east-facing door situated near the visitors center. Tribe members sought refuge here during Kit Carson's campaign in the 1860s, and many still live and farm here. Despite the valley's near-mythic status, visitation is limited to a single loop road and permitted tours. (Rock climbing is forbidden, despite what you saw in *The Eiger Sanction* or *Vertical Limit*.) More prosaically, the buttes of Monument Valley are formed of Cedar Mesa Sandstone on top of sloping bases of Halgaito Shale. Over the millennia, the softer shale has eroded more quickly, causing the sandstone to fracture vertically into the towering formations. Many are capped by ledges of red Organ Rock Shale.

Visitors Center and Tours

At an intersection on the state line, a short road leads east to the **Monument Valley Navajo Tribal Park visitors center** (435/727-5870, www.navajonationparks.org, 6 A.M.–8 P.M. daily, 8 A.M.–5 P.M. Oct.–Apr., $5 pp). Here you'll find a snack shop, gift shop, and a restaurant upstairs. There's a desk where you can sign up for a tour, and dozens of local operators have set up booths in the parking lot, offering trail rides, hikes, and vehicle tours through the monument. One of them, **Sacred Monument Tours** (435/727-3218 or 928/380-4527, smtours@ citlink.net, www.monumentvalley.net), has daily offerings starting at $45, with an all-day horseback riding tour for $268 per person. Longer tours leave the loop road for obscure petroglyphs and ruins. **Roland's Navajoland Tours**

(928/697-3524) out of Kayenta also does Monument Valley tours.

The visitors center is perched on the edge of the sandy valley filled with massive square buttes, including the Totem Pole, Castle Rock, the Stage Coach, and the famous Mittens. There are 100 campsites in the **Mitten View Campground**—sites 24 and 25 have the best views, making it well worth getting up for sunrise. Group, tent, and RV sites are available ($10), along with coin-operated showers open in season. From here the 17-mile **loop road** descends into the valley, past many Navajo homes and a viewing point named for John Ford, who brought this place to the attention of the world in his films. Allow at least two hours for the dirt road, which is good enough for most two-wheel-drive vehicles and closes shortly before sundown. It's also a great mountain bike ride.

For the classic road-trip shot of Monument Valley—the place where Forrest Gump finally stopped running—approach from the north on Highway 191, which changes to Highway 163 in Arizona. A little over 13 miles north of the Utah border there's a small hill, with the

West Mitten Butte, Monument Valley

© JULIN SMITH

highway heading straight as an arrow toward the valley below. Trust me—you'll recognize the view.

Goulding's Lodge and Trading Post

Opposite the valley at the state-line intersection is a complex centered around a trading post opened in the 1920s by Harry Goulding and his wife "Mike" in a 10-person tent. Harry, called *Dibé Nééz* ("Tall Sheep") by the Navajo, purchased 640 acres at the base of Black Door Mesa in 1937 for $320. Goulding bought local crafts, settled disputes, and acted as a liaison between the Navajo and the government. He also persuaded director John Ford that the local scenery would make an ideal movie backdrop, hoping to bring jobs to the area during the Great Depression. The rest is celluloid history. The valley has been used as the backdrop for countless movies, including the classic Westerns *Stagecoach, My Darling Clementine,* and *Fort Apache.* As Hollywood started to arrive, the Gouldings opened a lodge that became a second home to stars like John Wayne. Movie memorabilia and trading-post artifacts fill the original trading post, which has been turned into a museum (open daily year-round). A suggested donation of $2 is put toward scholarships for local children.

The immaculate modern **lodge** (435/727-3231, gouldings@gouldings.com, www.gouldings.com) has 62 rooms ($118–170 in season) and the Stagecoach Dining Room, built for the filming of *She Wore a Yellow Ribbon.* There's a VCR in each room where you can watch the many Westerns available for rent—or just look out from your balcony for the real thing. A modern **campground** has view of the valley as well, along with a heated indoor pool, coin laundry, hot showers, and a grocery store. It's also open year-round, with sites for tents ($18) and RVs ($28–32). Sign up at the lodge for Navajo-guided **tours** to nearby ruins, petroglyphs, crafts demonstrations, and movie locations.

Oljato

Eight miles past Goulding's is one of the most

THE LAUGHING PARTY

Part of Navajo tradition is the *Chi Dlo Dil,* or Laughing Party, held for newborns. At first, babies are considered to be in the "soft world," and are kept away from hard objects for fear they will adopt "hard" qualities. About six weeks after birth, relatives gather to eat and play with the baby. The first person to make the baby laugh, it is thought, will play an important role in the child's life.

---

authentic trading posts left on the reservation, and one of my personal favorites. The **Oljato Trading Post & Museum** (435/727-3210, oljatotp@hotmail.com, http://a-aa.com/monumentvalley), was built in 1921, making it one of the oldest in existence. In 2005 they were closed "for now," but the owners still offer trail rides of the area. (Call first.) The drive out here is still worth it for the scenery and the external ambiance alone. If you find them open, step past the rusting gas pumps into the U-shaped "bullpen" for everything from hose clamps to ice cream sandwiches. In the back are museum pieces and old photo albums.

◖ CANYON DE CHELLY NATIONAL MONUMENT

Joseph Campbell, international guru of mythology, once called this canyon system in northeast Arizona "the most sacred place on earth." There is definitely something special about this place that makes it stand out even among the Four Corners' scenic and historical marvels. Covering 130 square miles of precipitous gorges and fertile canyon bottoms, Canyon de Chelly (de-SHAY) has the ageless quality of a place inhabited for thousands of years, as Navajo families farm and tend orchards and herds of animals beneath soaring stone monoliths. It's almost as if a pane of glass had been laid across the cliff tops, preserving a way of life that once came dangerously close to extinction. The Navajo still own the land that comprises the monument, which is administered by the National Park Service. Roads run along the canyon's north and south rim, with sweeping overlooks that take in rock spires, Anasazi ruins, and farmland. Aside from one trail to the bottom, the only other way to break the glass floor is to join a Navajo-led tour.

The monument comprises three ravines— Monument Canyon, Canyon del Muerto, and Canyon de Chelly—whose rims range 5,000–7,000 feet in elevation. Down the center runs the Rio de Chelly, from its beginnings in the Chuska Mountains in the east to the mouth of Canyon de Chelly near the town of Chinle, "the place where the water flows out." The glowing red sandstone walls are over 1,000 feet high in places, and as sheer as the side of a skyscraper. Temperatures range from well below 0°F in winter to over 100°F in summer, but the river-deposited sediments and reliable water supply make the canyon bottom excellent for farming. Side streams dry up in summer and rage with flash floods during the summer rainy seasons and spring snowmelt. Quicksand is often a concern in wet, sandy spots.

History

People have lived in this sheltered canyon system for millennia, starting with the Basketmaker-phase Anasazi, who left some 700 ruins here between about A.D. 350 and 1300. They pecked hand and foot trails in the stone faces and progressed from pit houses to apartment-style stone dwellings in alcoves, similar to those at Navajo National Monument, but on a smaller scale. Plentiful rainfall from A.D. 1050 to 1150 let the population grow significantly, with as many as 800 people living in the main canyon. This bounty was short-lived, though—a regional drought during the 1200s lowered the water table and dried up the canyon's streams, forcing the Puebloans to move on.

The Hopi tribe occupied the Canyon de Chelly sporadically thereafter, but by 1700 the Navajo had taken over. They named the place Tséyi', meaning "rock canyon," but it is the Spanish mispronunciation of the word

that has stuck. From the Hopi, the Navajo acquired dry-farming techniques (peacefully) and women and food (by force), and from the Spanish they stole livestock and horses. Members of many tribes fled here after the Pueblo Revolt of 1680, but it was the Navajo who suffered most during Kit Carson's merciless campaign against them in 1863. Carson's men swept the length of the canyon, laying waste to the orchards and slaughtering livestock. After a brave but futile resistance, the survivors were forced on the "Long Walk" to eastern New Mexico. Carson signed a peace treaty with the tribe in 1864 on the present site of the National Monument headquarters.

The canyons were declared a national monument in 1931, under a rare arrangement in which management is shared by the tribe and the National Park Service. The Navajo still grow melons, corn, beans, and squash on the fertile canyon bottom, where sheep and goats wander among cottonwoods and peach orchards.

Visiting Canyon de Chelly

Just east of the town of Chinle, a seasonal wash of the same name marks the beginning of the canyon system. You can only descend the rough road leading down into the canyons if you're on a guided tour or if you're a resident. At the **visitors center** (928/674-5500, www.nps.gov/cach, 8 A.M.–6 P.M. daily, to 5 P.M. Oct.–Apr.), three miles west of Chinle, are exhibits on the area's history and geology, as well as restrooms, pay phones, and drinking water. Entrance to the monument is free, as is a spot at the pleasant **Cottonwood Campground,** open year-round. (There is also a privately owned campground on the South Rim Drive.) Nearby is the beautiful **Thunderbird Lodge** (928/674-5841 or 800/679-2473, fax 928/674-5844, tbirdlodge@frontiernet.net, www.tbirdlodge.com), which began as a trading post built by Sam Day in 1902. The original post building is now the cafeteria, decorated with Navajo rugs. Frybread, chili stew, and other tasty bites are available for all meals daily. The lodge is open year-round, with 73 rooms for $100–145, and a gift shop with

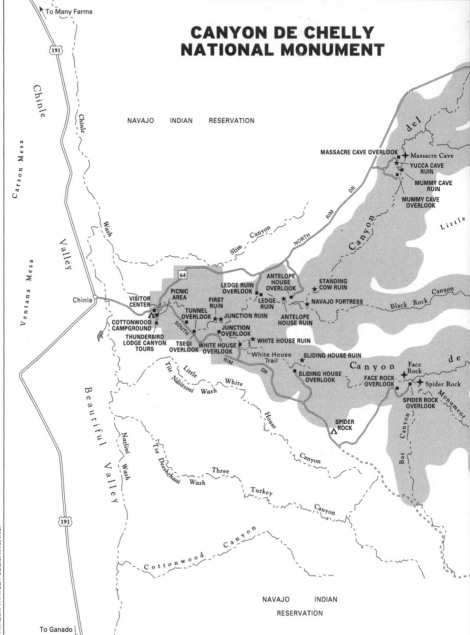

CANYON DE CHELLY NATIONAL MONUMENT

NAVAJO   INDIAN   RESERVATION

To Many Farms

191

Chinle

Carson Mesa

Chinle Wash

Valley

Ventana Mesa

Chinle

MASSACRE CAVE OVERLOOK — Massacre Cave

YUCCA CAVE RUIN

MUMMY CAVE RUIN

MUMMY CAVE OVERLOOK

del

Canyon

Little

Slim Canyon

NORTH RIM DR

VISITOR CENTER

PICNIC AREA

64

ANTELOPE HOUSE OVERLOOK

LEDGE RUIN OVERLOOK

STANDING COW RUIN

FIRST RUIN

TUNNEL OVERLOOK

LEDGE RUIN

NAVAJO FORTRESS

Black Rock Canyon

JUNCTION RUIN

ANTELOPE HOUSE RUIN

COTTONWOOD CAMPGROUND

SOUTH

JUNCTION OVERLOOK

THUNDERBIRD LODGE CANYON TOURS

TSEGI OVERLOOK

WHITE HOUSE OVERLOOK

WHITE HOUSE RUIN

White House Trail

SLIDING HOUSE RUIN

Canyon de

RIM DR

SLIDING HOUSE OVERLOOK

FACE ROCK OVERLOOK

Face Rock

Spider Rock

SPIDER ROCK OVERLOOK

Monument

SPIDER ROCK

Tlis Nditsooi Wash

Little White Wash

House

Beautiful Valley

Nazlini Wash

Tse Deeshchaai Wash

Three Wash

Turkey Canyon

Canyon

Bat Canyon

191

Cottonwood Canyon

NAVAJO   INDIAN

RESERVATION

To Ganado

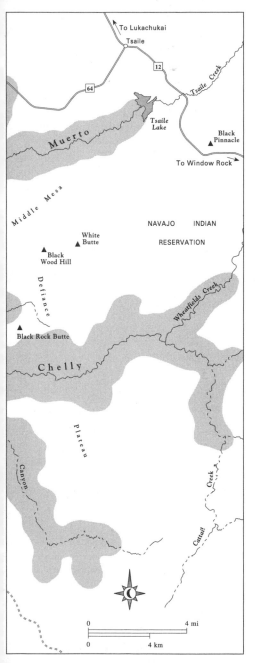

a selection that would make Day proud. They also offer tours of the canyon.

Canyon de Chelly consists of four main gorges, and many side canyons, slicing generally eastward into the Defiance Plateau. From a car you can only access the northern and southern edges, but the fantastic views almost make up for the limitations. Short trails lead to the cliff edges. Be careful at the overlooks, not only for the sharp drop-offs, but also for highly skilled and incredibly fast car thieves. Break-ins have been a serious problem in the past; ask at the visitors center for an update. You definitely don't want to leave anything of value in plain view. The two rim drives would make an excellent bicycle ride, except for the complete lack of anything approaching a bike lane.

North Rim Drive

Also called Highway 64, this road runs along the Canyon del Muerto, connecting Chinle to the Dine College and Tsaile on Highway 12. The canyon was named the "Canyon of the Dead" in Spanish by a Smithsonian anthropologist who excavated many buried bodies among its ruins. Just over five miles from the visitors center is the **Ledge Ruin Overlook,** looking down on a ruin dated to the 11th and 12th centuries. Two more miles brings you to the **Antelope House Overlook,** above a ruin named for pictographs of running antelopes painted by a Navajo artist around 1830. The ruins themselves, and artwork left by the Anasazi, are over than a thousand years older. Directly across the canyon, above the junction of the Canyon del Muerto and Black Rock Canyon to the south, is the **Navajo Fortress,** an aerie where Navajo warriors hid from Kit Carson, sneaking down at night for water and food. Carson waited below, enduring showers of stones, until the starving Navajo surrendered. Just upcanyon is **Standing Cow Ruin,** where Navajo pictographs show a blue-and-white cow and a priest accompanying a Spanish cavalry unit.

The next turnoff is 18 miles from the visitors center. Take a right at the fork for **Mummy Cave Overlook,** named for two bodies found in the ruins that fill two caves, thought to be occupied between A.D. 300 and 1300. A right at the fork will bring you to **Massacre Cave Overlook.** When the Spanish sent Lieutenant Antonio de Narbona into the canyon in 1805 to quell Navajo raids, they found a group of women, children, and elders hiding there while the men were off hunting deer in the Lukachukai Mountains. In two days, Spanish riflemen killed 115 of the Navajo by bouncing bullets off the canyon ceiling from the rim above, and took 33 prisoners. The bones of the victims remain in the cave untouched, per Navajo custom.

South Rim Drive

Although not a through road, the South Rim Drive offers even more impressive views than the northern route. You'll pass the **Tunnel Overlook** and the **Tsegi Overlook** over the upper canyon before reaching the **Junction Overlook** where the Canyon del Muerto joins the Canyon de Chelly. **First Ruin** and **Junction Ruin** are both visible from here. Six

© JULIAN SMITH

White House Ruin, Canyon de Chelly

miles from the visitors center is the turnoff for the **White House Overlook** which offers not only a great view but also the only way to reach the canyon bottom without a guide. The trail down to **White House Ruin,** dated to about A.D. 1200, is just over one mile from the canyon edge 500 feet down to the canyon floor and across it. The steep, rocky trail passes through a few short tunnels, a farm, and an orchard before crossing the stream in front of the well-preserved ruins (bring water). You'll find restrooms and tribe members selling jewelry nearby. Don't wander off the trail without a guide.

Farther down the rim drive is the turnoff for the overlook above **Sliding House Ruin** and the **Spider Rock Campground** (928/674-8261 or 877/910-CAMP, spiderrock@earthlink.net, home.earthlink.net/~spiderrock). Owned by tribe member Howard Smith (no relation), this place has tent sites for $10 and RV sites for $15, as well as solar-heated showers ($2) and two authentic hogans starting at $25. The South Rim Drive continues southeast as Route 7 (unpaved), but follow the pavement northeast back into the monument to the **Spider Rock Overlook,** the park's most outstanding viewing point. An 800-foot rock tower thrusts from the canyon bottom where three canyons come together. The monolith is understandably special to the Navajo, who call it *Tse' Na' ashjé'ii* and tell of the supernatural being who lives on top. Spider Woman teaches weaving on a loom whose warp is the rays of the sun. Navajo mothers once warned their children to behave or else Spider Woman would carry them to her perch, which is now white with bones.

Tours

Canyon De Chelly Unimog Tours (928/674-5433, leonskyhorse@yahoo.com, www.canyondechellytours.com) offers tours of the canyon bottom in jeeps; the military-looking, natural-gas powered Unimog; or your own vehicle starting at $50 for half a day. The **Tseyi Guide Association** also offers vehicle tours for $15 per hour, and hiking tours (15 people maximum) for the same price. Ask at the visitors center for details. Vehicle tours booked at the Thunderbird lodge run $40 per person for a half day and $65 for a full day, and go all the way to Spider Rock and back.

Chinle

There isn't much in the town of Chinle itself aside from a **Best Western** (928/674-5875, fax 928/674-3715), with 100 rooms for $100–120, and a **Holiday Inn** (928/674-5000, fax 928/674-8264, $110). Both have heated pools and restaurants open daily for all meals. The Chinle Comprehensive Health Care Facility is one of the best hospitals on the reservation, and combines traditional Navajo healing practices with modern medicine; it even includes a hogan for ceremonies. Look for labels in Navajo on products in Basha's Grocery Store, and for souvenirs try **Navajo Arts & Crafts Enterprises** (928/674-5338) at the main intersection.

Many Farms

North of Chinle at the intersection of High-ways 59 and 191 is a settlement called *Dá'ák'ehaláni* by the Navajo. Several hundred small farms are cultivated in the area. The **Many Farms Inn** (928/781-6363, mfhsinn@manyfarms.bia.edu), behind the Many Farms High School, is run by Navajo students studying hotel management and tourism. Rooms in a school dormitory with shared bathrooms are $30 per night, and there's a TV lounge, a gym, and basketball courts.

HUBBELL TRADING POST NATIONAL HISTORIC SITE

The oldest continuously operating trading post on the Navajo Reservation was built on the bank of Ganado Wash in 1871. Clerk and interpreter John Lorenzo Hubbell bought the place seven years later, and it stayed in his family until the National Park Service took over in 1967. Hubbell quickly turned the post into one of the most successful in the Southwest, buying out and opening other posts throughout the Four Corners and earning the nickname

NAVAJO & HOPI COUNTRY

© JULIAN SMITH

The old Hubbell Trading Post, opened on the Navajo Reservation in 1871, is still open for business.

WHERE TO SHOP

There are two main options when it comes to purchasing indigenous crafts (well, three, if you count paying five times as much at a boutique back home): buy directly from the artists themselves, or buying from a trading post or gallery. Buying from the creator, either in his or her home or at a roadside or flea market stand, adds not only the personal touch but also the opportunity to get the best price. It helps to know what you're looking for in this situation, and to have an idea of how to judge quality and a fair price. To be honest, a good bit of the merchandise for sale at tourist spots like Monument Valley are, for lack of better words, cheap trinkets. This kind of stuff is relatively easy to spot, however.

Trading posts and galleries have higher prices, but at the better ones you can be assured that you're getting a quality product, with the reputation of the store behind it. Employees are happy to let you browse and to lend their expert advice if necessary, and can pack up and ship your purchases back home. Many also have pawn departments where people leave goods as collateral for cash loans and often don't return for them ("dead pawn"). Pawnshops are also common. This is a great way to get a deal on crafts, especially jewelry. Dead pawn is sometimes auctioned off on a monthly basis.

You'll find the best selection and quality at places like the Tuba City Trading Post, Noteh Dineh in Cortez, Toh-Atin in Durango, Twin Rocks in Bluff, Fifth Generation in Farmington, and Blair's Dinnebito in Page. For atmosphere, don't miss Hatch Brothers near Farmington, Goulding's and Oljato in Monument Valley, Cow Canyon in Bluff, and the Hubbell Trading Post National Historic Site west of Window Rock. Richardson's Trading Company in Gallup can hold its own in both categories.

Wherever you buy a piece, try to find out where and when it was made, and ask for a **certificate of authenticity**, or else a receipt with the name and contact information of the artist or gallery, the artist's name and tribal affiliation, and the price, including the original price if you received a discount.

SHOPPING RESOURCES

Many trading posts and galleries have their own websites, that are continually updated as goods are bought and sold; these are listed in the various sections of the guide. The **Southwest Indian Foundation** (800/504-2723, swif@cia-g.com, www.southwestindian.com) is a nonprofit organization with an extensive mail-order catalog of arts and crafts. Profits go to help native communities by supporting schools, providing food during holidays, and setting up homes for battered women. The nonprofit **Indian Arts and Crafts Association** (505/265-9149, fax 505/265-8251, info@iaca .com, www.iaca.com) offers consumer tips and lots of other information on their website.

The **Indian Arts and Crafts Act of 1990** prohibits the misrepresentation of Native American arts and crafts (defined as a tribe member or artisan certified by a tribe) produced after 1935. For more information, contact the Indian Arts & Crafts Board of the U.S. Department of the Interior (888/ART-FAKE, 888/278-3253, fax 202/208-5196, iacb@ios .doi.gov, www.doi.gov/iacb).

Some of the many books on Southwest Indian crafts are listed in the *Suggested Reading* section in the *Resources* chapter. The Southwest Parks and Monuments Association puts out the pocket-size *A Guide to Navajo Rugs*, available at many bookstores and gift shops in the Four Corners.

"Don" Lorenzo, a Spanish term of respect, for his fair trading and hospitality.

A true friend of the Navajo, Hubbell spoke their language fluently and advised weavers on which designs would fetch the best prices. (The handsome Ganado pattern, with its deep red wool and cross motif, is still woven.) He brought a silversmith from Mexico to teach his art, and treated Navajo struck down by smallpox. The Hubbells—Lorenzo, his wife Una Rubi, and their four children—amassed one of the largest art collections in the Southwest in their home next to the post.

Today the original 160-acre homestead, one mile west of Ganado on Highway 264, is administered by the National Park Service (928/755-3475, www.nps.gov/hutr, daily 8 A.M.–6 P.M., until 5 P.M. in winter, free). The old trading post is run by the Western National Parks Association (www.spma.org). They still buy and sell crafts, food, and supplies, though most sales now are to tourists, and stock a king's ransom in Navajo rugs in the rug room. Demonstrations and auctions of Native American crafts are held throughout the year, and daily tours take visitors into the Hubbell home ($2 pp), which retains all its original furnishings (except for the rugs). The ceiling in the main hallway is covered with dozens of woven baskets, and works by artists who visited the family adorn the walls, including many of E. A. Burbank's portraits, mostly of Native Americans, done with red conte crayon.

Lorenzo Hubbell also helped start the **Ganado Mission,** the largest Presbyterian mission to the Navajo, in 1903. The mission concentrated on education and health care early on, and was transferred to the Navajo Nation Health Foundation in 1974. On its grounds, across Highway 264 from the trading post, you'll find the **Cafe Sage** (928/755-3411, ext. 292, 7 A.M.–7 P.M. Mon.–Fri., 9 A.M.–2 P.M. Sat.) serving inexpensive cafeteria fare.

Hopi Reservation

A cultural island within the larger Navajo Reservation, the Hopi Reservation centers around 12 ancient villages on three fingerlike mesas that rise to 7,200 feet. First, Second, and Third Mesa were named from east to west, since early explorers arrived from the east, and are strung together by Highway 264 between Tuba City and Ganado. A few of the Hopi villages have been inhabited for over eight centuries. This is a quiet, isolated place, whose main draw is the almost tangible sense of tradition that hangs in the clear air.

The boundaries of the Hopis' ancestral lands, or *Tutsqua,* extended from Canyon de Chelly and the Four Corners to the San Francisco Peaks, and from Navajo Mountain to the Zuni Reservation near Gallup. The 600-foot-high Hopi mesas are dotted with homes made from adobe, cinder block, and stone, standing alongside trailers, pickup trucks, and the shells of unfinished or abandoned buildings. Ladders poke out of kivas, both above and below ground level, and scattered outhouses indicate which of the traditional villages do not have plumbing. Most of the Hopi are farmers or artisans and highly respectful of tradition, although more and more live in modern towns in between the older villages perched atop the steep-walled mesas.

The Hopi welcome visitors; they just expect you to behave yourself. The tribe guards its privacy and traditions even more than the Navajo, so photography, videotaping, sketching, and any other methods of recording are *strictly* prohibited—no exceptions. Accept the fact that this is one part of your vacation you'll have to recall from memory, because if you're caught breaking this rule, you will be asked to leave.

Most social dances are open to non-Hopi—some require a personal invitation from a tribe member—but many kachina dances and all snake dances and flute ceremonies are closed to visitors. If you want to watch a ceremony, be aware that you will be considered a part of the collective spiritual effort, so you should act and dress respectfully. This means no shorts, short skirts, or T-shirts, no loud talking, and no striding across the plaza to get a closer look at someone's headdress. Many residents sell crafts and food from their homes, and advertise with signs out front—try some traditional, wafer-thin *piiki* bread, made with blue-corn flour. Don't wander far down back

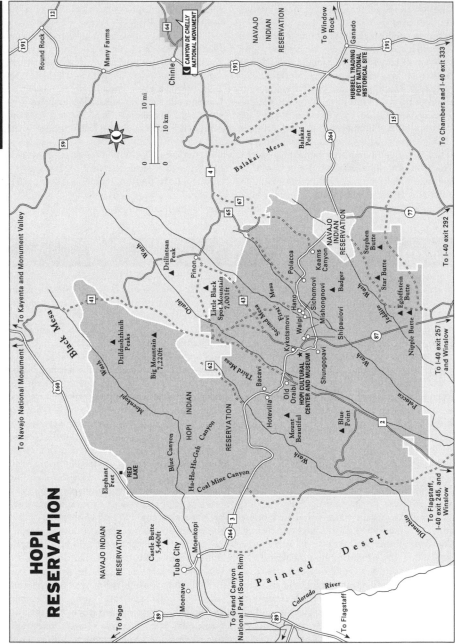

© AVALON TRAVEL PUBLISHING, INC.

alleys, though, particularly during ceremonies, and get permission from a village leader if you plan on spending more than a few hours in any village.

Visitors are prohibited from certain culturally sensitive areas on the reservation; check with the Hopi Cultural Center on Second Mesa for a list of these sites, and a schedule of religious ceremonies open to the public. A number of tribal members offer guided cultural and archaeological tours of the area. Try **Gary Tso** (928/734-2567, lhhunter58@hotmail.com) or **Bertram Tsavadawa** (928/734-9544 or 928/306-7849, ancientpathways2004@yahoo.com). Professional anthropologist **Micah Loma'omvaya** (928/734-0230 or 928/734-9549, info@hopitours.com or hopianthro@yahoo.com) offers archaeological tours to ruins and other sites on the reservation, starting at $65 per person for a half day.

The information in this section is listed from east to west, following Highway 264 from Ganado to Tuba City.

EAST OF FIRST MESA

The natural oasis of **Keams Canyon,** called *Pongsikya* by the Hopi, was originally known to Anglo settlers as Peach Orchard Springs. Englishman Thomas Keam, once a trooper under Colonel Kit Carson (whose own 1863 signature is inscribed in the canyon wall), opened a trading post here in 1869. Keams married a Hopi woman and quarreled strongly with the Bureau of Indian Affairs (BIA) superintendent, who demanded that the Hopi stop their ceremonial dances and send their children to the nearby BIA boarding school under threat of force. The superintendent was eventually dismissed.

Today, Keams Canyon is a U.S. government town with a hospital, post office, and **Keam's Canyon Shopping Center.** McGee's Indian Art Gallery (928/738-2295, www.hopiart.com) is inside, centered around Keam's original trading post, and selling an excellent selection of local crafts, particularly kachinas. They have added a grocery store, a coin laundry, and a small café. They also offer lodgings; call for details. Follow the road up Keams Wash 1.5

miles to a shelter on the west (left), marking an inscription left by Kit Carson.

At the southern tip of Antelope Mesa are the ruins of **Awat'ovi** (ah-WAHT-oh-vee), which has a sad and bloody history. A Franciscan church built in this Hopi village in 1629 was destroyed by the tribe and residents of other pueblos who feared the friars' influence. When Awat'ovi's residents allowed the missionaries back in two decades later, however, the other Hopi villages took drastic steps. Almost all of the village's men were killed, and its women and children scattered among other villages. The area is closed to the public.

FIRST MESA

At the base of First Mesa is **Polacca** (po-LAH-kah), founded in 1890 by a resident of Hano. The BIA tried to convince Hopi in the older villages up above to move here, but to this day most of Polacca's residents still consider themselves to be from Walpi or Sichomovi. In Polcaa is the turnoff for the road to the top of First Mesa, a steep and narrow paved road just over a mile long. (Larger vehicles must be parked at the bottom.)

The first traditional village on the mesa is **Hano,** which was founded by Tewa Indians from the Rio Grande near Albuquerque. Fleeing the Spanish after the Pueblo Revolt of 1680, the Tewa were allowed to settle here by the Hopi if they agreed to guard access to the mesa. This was the home of the famous Hopi potter Nampeyo, born in 1860, who based her work on the ancient techniques used in pottery shards dug up by anthropologists. Thanks to the efforts of Fred Harvey, who had her display her work at the Grand Canyon, she eventually became famous and traveled around the country demonstrating her craft. She eventually became blind, but was able to teach her daughters her techniques. Her legacy continues in various homes selling pottery; look for signs.

Sichomovi (see-CHO-mo-vi), just beyond Hano, was founded in 1750 by residents of **Walpi** (WAHL-pee), which perches on the narrow southernmost tip of the mesa. Walpi, meaning "the gap," refers to the narrow neck of stone that isolates the tiny village almost completely from the rest of the mesa—and, it seems, from the modern age as well. Walpi lacks running water and electricity, and is exceedingly traditional. Along with its setting, the village is known for its crafts and its ceremonies, which are unfortunately closed to the public. With nothing by sky and stone in every direction, Walpi offers a striking panorama that has hardly changed in centuries. Arrange a guided walking tour at Ponsi Hall (928/737-2262, $8 pp) in Sichomovi, or else contact the village of Walpi directly, ideally in advance (928/737-9556, $5 pp).

Walpi sits above the original settlement of Old Walpi, which was inhabited since the 13th century and abandoned for this more secure location after the Pueblo Revolt. The ruins of an old Spanish mission are also visible (although closed to visitors), as are prehistoric foot trails up the mesa and stone depressions used to catch rainwater.

SECOND MESA

Highway 264 is joined by Highway 87 at the foot of Second Mesa. Near the intersection are a **post office**, the **Sekakuku supermarket**, offering deli takeout food, and **LKD's Diner** (928/737-2717), serving a small menu for breakfast and lunch Monday–Saturday in season (Monday–Friday otherwise). Al Sakakuku's **Hopi Fine Arts** has a good selection of crafts.

Villages

Two routes take Highway 264 to the top of Second Mesa. They split half a mile west of the Highway 87 intersection, where you'll find a **gas station** and the **Honani Crafts Gallery** (928/737-2238), which has an excellent array of jewelry behind four stained-glass windows depicting kachinas. From here, a steep, twisting track—more of a loading ramp than a road—leads up to two traditional villages. **Shipaulovi** (shih-PAW-loh-vee) has little more than an old abandoned trading post and a few homes. The name means "place of the mosquitoes." **Mishongnovi** (mi-SHONG-no-vee) is at the very top of mesa, with not a yard to spare between the building walls and the cliff edges.

The other route takes you past the turnoff for **Shungopavi** (shon-GO-pah-vee), meaning "sand grass spring place." Its story is similar to Walpi—an older village at the base of the mesa was abandoned for a more secure spot after the Pueblo Revolt. A number of galleries sell jewelry and other crafts, and you can grab a bite here at HildaBurger.

Hopi Cultural Center and Vicinity

This small complex (928/734-2401, fax 928/734-6651, info@hopiculturalcenter.com, www.hopiculturalcenter.com) serves as unofficial nexus of the reservation where the two routes rejoin on top of Second Mesa. It has a museum of Hopi crafts and cultural items (928/734-6650, 8 A.M.–5 P.M. daily, Mon.–Fri. only Nov.–Mar., $4 pp), as well as a motel with modest but clean rooms for $95–100 ($70–75 Oct.–Mar.) and a campground. A restaurant serves dishes ($5–7) such as burgers, blue-corn pancakes, and *nöqkwivi*, a traditional hominy-and-mutton stew for all meals daily. The **Hopi Arts and Crafts Silver Cooperative Guild** (928/734-2463), established in 1949, is nearby in a two-story pink building. Many trainees have gone on to start their own successful businesses.

A mostly dirt road (Highway 43) leaves from here north up Second Mesa, joining Highway 41 at Piñon, offering a scenic alternate way to reach Chinle and Canyon de Chelly. Other galleries are scattered along the roads on Second Mesa, including **Sewukiwma's Arts & Crafts** (928/734-0388) and Alph Secakuku's **Hopi Fine Arts** (Hwys. 264 and 87, 928/737-2222). One and a half miles east of the Cultural Center is Janice and Joseph Day's **Tsukurosovi** (928/734-2478), a fascinating store with a great selection of Hopi and Navajo work, including jewelry, kachinas, and baskets. The Days supply the Hopi with materials for their ceremonies, which explains all the turtle shells, furs, and herbs around, and are a font of information on the area.

THIRD MESA

Kykotsmovi (kee-KOOTS-moh-vee) was founded by residents of Old Oraibi near a spring at the base of Third Mesa. Today it's

HOPI CRAFTS

The Peaceful People are best known for two types of crafts. Hopi **silver jewelry** is more delicate than the Navajo style, and dates to the 1890s, when Sikyatala, the first Hopi silversmith, learned his craft from artisans at the Zuñi pueblo. Since World War II it has been done in an overlay style, in which a design is cut from a flat sheet of silver and set in front of another sheet that has been textured and oxidized until black. Hopi jewelry is marked with the artist's name, clan, or village, and the design may be pictorial or abstract. Gold and inlaid precious stones are sometimes incorporated into the design, which range from rings, bracelets, and bolo tie clasps to necklaces, belt buckles, and button covers.

Kachina (katsina) dolls were originally used to teach children about the spirit beings who live in the San Francisco Peaks and bring rain. These brightly painted figures are carved from the root of the cottonwood with an attached base, and can be amazingly detailed. They come in all sizes, and the quality of the carving and painting varies as widely as the price. Prime examples are true works of art, and justifiably fetch thousands of dollars. There are dozens of kachinas depicted as dolls, including Mongwa, the Great Horned Owl; Salako Mana and Salaka Taka, the male and female kachina leaders; and the humorous Koyemsi and Koshare clowns. Kachinas are some of the most distinctive souvenirs of the Southwest, and if they strike your fancy, it's well worth it to read up on the art and talk to carvers.

Hopi artisans also make **baskets** and **paintings** not too unlike those of the Navajo, as well as ground-fired **pottery.**

---

surrounded by fruit trees and is the home of the modern Hopi government. The **Hopi Tribe Cultural Preservation Office** (928/734-3612 or 928/734-3000) provides visitor information out of the Tribal Headquarters building, and the **Kykotsmovi Village Store** offers sandwiches, pizzas, and other deli items. Highway 2 heads south from here for I-15 at the town of Leupp ("loop"). This is the quickest way back to Flagstaff, and is a lovely, empty drive that's paved the entire way. At the turnoff is **Gentle Rain Designs** (928/734-9434 or 928/734-8535), a friendly place that sells clothing made from cotton, denim, and recycled-plastic "fleece," all decorated with Hopi motifs.

On the way up onto Third Mesa to Old Oraibi you'll pass **Pumpkin Seed Point,** a picnic area with a great view of the Hopi buttes to the south. Soon comes the turnoff for Old Oraibi, two miles west of Kykotsmovi, where you'll find the pink **Monongya Gallery** (928/734-2344), with a large selection of paintings, jewelry, pottery, and baskets made by various tribes. Their selection of kachinas is one of the largest around.

Inhabited since the mid 12th century, **Old Oraibi** (oh-RYE-bee) is arguably the oldest continually occupied community in the country. In 1906, this windswept collection of stone and cinder-block buildings was split by internal strife. The Bear clan, led by Tawaquaptewa, wanted to cooperate with the U.S. government's Indian Service, while the Skeleton clan, led by Youkeoma, refused. They settled the dispute with a pushing contest: a line was etched in the ground and the groups lined up on either side, with their respective leaders in front. At a signal each started shoving. When the dust cleared Tawaquaptewa's clan had won. Youkeoma led his people off to found Hotevilla, where they were labeled "hostiles" by the U.S. government. The event is commemorated by an inscription in the mesa, near the line itself, which reads:

Well it have to be this way not
pass me over this LINE
it will be DONE.
Sept. 8, 1906.

Wandering the streets of Old Oraibi is an experience in time travel. Notice the ruins of the old Mennonite church at the south end of the mesa, built in 1901 and destroyed by lightning (a second strike) in 1942, to the quiet delight of many of the town's traditional residents. A few homes sell crafts. Resident Bertram Tsavadawa offers guided walking tours.

A few miles west on Highway 264 are the villages of **Hotevilla** (HOAT-vih-lah), founded by Youkeoma's people, and **Bacavi** (BAH-kah-vee), founded three years later by another Oraibi splinter group. These are residential villages without much to see.

West of Third Mesa

Just over 30 miles west of Bacavi and Hotevilla is **Coal Mine Canyon,** a marvelous ravine that leads north to join Blue Canyon and, eventually, Moenkopi Wash toward Tuba City. Look for a dirt road between mile markers 336 and 337 leading to a windmill, beside the rodeo grounds. The Navajo call this serrated landscape *háåhonoojí,* or "jagged," and the Hopi tell of *Quayowuuti,* the Eagle Woman from Old Oraibi, who stepped from the edge of the canyon to her death. Her ghost is said to appear under the full moon.

Just east of Tuba City on Highway 264 is the town of **Moenkopi** (a small cultural island separated from the greater Hopi Reservation. "The place of running water" was founded in the 1870s by farmers from Oraibi, who would run to their fields and back—a distance of over 30 miles—several times a week. Like many Hopi villages, it is split into upper and lower sections.

East of Flagstaff

I-40 leaves the San Francisco Mountains for the high desert plains as it rolls east toward New Mexico. It follows the Little Colorado River upstream from Winslow to Holbrook, where it is joined by the Rio Puerco. Rugged hills dotted with buttes and junipers continue past the Petrified Forest and Painted Desert to the southern end of the Defiance Plateau at the state line.

METEOR CRATER

About 50,000 years ago, a meteorite 150 feet across slammed into the Arizona plain at upwards of 30,000 mph, igniting an explosion greater than 20 million tons of TNT. The impact threw 175 million tons of stone into the atmosphere, uplifted the bedrock by 150 feet, and turned graphite into diamond at pressures of over 20 million pounds per square inch—and it left a really, *really* big hole in the ground. You can fit 20 football fields into the crater, which is 2.5 miles in circumference and deeper than the Washington Monument. It was originally thought to be volcanic in origin, but the tireless research of Philadelphia mining engineer Daniel Barringer convinced the world otherwise, even though his efforts to find the meteorite itself didn't pan out.

The crater (800/289-5898, info@meteorcrater.com, www.meteorcrater.com, 8 A.M.–5 P.M. daily, $12 adults, $6 children) is five miles south of I-40 exit 233. The "first proved and best preserved meteorite crater in the world" is privately owned, and has a well-done museum on its edge with exhibits on astrogeology and space travel. A computer simulation of a meteor impact offers the perverse pleasure of seeing how big and fast you can make your imaginary comet before it vaporizes the earth. There's a gift shop and snack bar, and guided walks a third of a mile around the rim trail are included in admission. On the crater floor, a dummy figure in a space suit provides a sense of scale; Apollo astronauts trained here before going to the moon. On the way there from the interstate you'll pass the **Meteor Crater RV Park** (800/478-4002) with 81 sites ($20–22), a gas station, showers, and laundry.

WINSLOW

This city was founded in 1882 as a railroad stop near Sunset Crossing, one of the few places to ford the sandy-bottomed Little Colorado River. Winslow hit its stride in the early 1900s, when cross-country traffic poured in off the new Route 66 and local ranchers shipped their stock out through the rail terminal. Fred Harvey opened La Posada, perhaps the prettiest of his Spanish-style hotels, and in 1930, Charles Lindberg flew to Winslow Airport, which he had designed as a stop between Chicago and Los Angeles.

The town slid toward the end of the 20th century, when traffic began to pass by on both the interstate and the railroad. Still, you've probably heard of Winslow if you've ever listened to pop radio: the Eagles sang about "Standing on a corner in Winslow, Arizona" in their hit "Take it Easy." Today, Winslow (pop. 9,500) has a south-of-the-border ambience, with lots of weathered adobe buildings. It's hoped that the restoration of La Posada will inject some much-needed vitality into the town, which has a number of interesting sights within day-trip distance.

The **Winslow Chamber of Commerce Visitor Center** (300 W. North Rd., 928/289-2434, winslowchamber@cybertrails.com, www.winslowarizona.org, 8 A.M.–5 P.M. Mon.–Fri.) is north of I-40 exit 253. If you're here in October, don't miss the **"Standin' On the Corner" Festival,** with music, arts, crafts, an auction, and a car show.

Sights

The actual corner that Jackson Browne and Glen Frey sang about is commemorated at the **Standin' on the Corner Park** at 2nd Street (Route 66) and Kinsley Avenue. You can have your photo taken next to the statue of one of the Eagles holding a guitar, or the "girl, my Lord, in a flatbed Ford" painted in a two-story mural on the facing wall. This part of downtown is starting to cash in on its Route 66 heritage, with shops offering souvenirs and memorabilia.

The Winslow corner made famous in the Eagles' song "Take it Easy" is commemorated by Ron Adamson's bronze statue and John Pugh's mural.

The quirky **Old Trails Museum** (212 Kinsley St., 928/289-5861, 1–5 P.M. Tues.–Sat. Apr.–Oct.; 1–5 P.M. Tues., Thurs., and Sat. Nov.–Mar., free) is housed in a 1921 bank building, nicknamed "Winslow's attic." An interesting collection includes dinosaur bones, Route 66 memorabilia, Anasazi artifacts, and the still of a local moonshiner, who lived to the age of 97 on a daily breakfast of black coffee, raw eggs, and a shot of his own firewater.

North of Winslow on the banks of the Little Colorado River is **Homolovi Ruins State Park** (928/289-4106, www.pr.state.az.us/parkhtml/homolovi.html, 8 A.M.–5 P.M. daily, $5 per car), opened in 1993. The site's four main pueblo ruins were inhabited in the 13th and 14th centuries by the ancestors of the Hopi, who eventually migrated north to the three Hopi mesas. Their name for the group archaeologists call the Anasazi (or today, the Ancestral Puebloans) is the *Hisat'sinom,* and the Hopi still consider this part of the ancestral homeland and make periodic pilgrimages. More than 300 archaeological sites have been uncovered here, and three of the four pueblos are open to the public. There's a visitors center and a 53-site campground ($10–20). To get there, take I-40 exit 257 to Highway 87, go north 1.3 miles to the entrance on the left, then proceed another two miles to the visitors center.

Shopping

The photogenically weathered Lorenzo Hubbell Co. Trading Post building is now home to the **Arizona Indian Artists Cooperative** (523 W. 2nd St., 928/289-3986, 9 A.M.–5 P.M. Mon.–Fri.). A good variety of crafts are offered at competitive prices, direct from the artisans. **Roadworks Gifts & Souvenirs** (101 W. 2nd St., 928/289-5423) is on the second floor overlooking the Corner Park. They stock every kind of Route 66 souvenir you can think of, plus a few hundred more: T-shirts, bumper stickers, books, magnets, postcards, and mugs. Don't miss Bob Waldemire's postcards and map-guide to Route 66. He used to run the Route 66 visitors center in Seligman, west of Flagstaff, and his detailed drawings are works of art.

Accommodations and Food

Architect Mary Coulter designed **☾ La Posada** (303 E. 2nd St., 928/289-4366, fax 928/289-3873, info@laposada.org, www.laposada.org, $90–130) for hotelier Fred Harvey in 1930, calling it her masterpiece. Built in the style of an old Spanish hacienda, the "Last Great Railroad Hotel" counted among its guests luminaries such as Albert Einstein, Howard Hughes, Dorothy Lamour, and the Crown Prince of Japan. All trains between Los Angeles stopped here, as did planes before better designs let them make the trip without stopping. It was closed for 40 years and nearly razed before it was rescued from the wrecking ball in the late 1990s and put on the historical preservation list.

Somewhere, Mary Coulter is smiling; thanks to the tireless efforts of owner Allan Affeldt and his wife, artist Tina Mion, the hotel is well on its way to recapturing its former glory. Suits of armor, religious icons, and Tina's large, intriguing paintings make up an eclectic art collection, and Amtrak trains still rumble past the cottonwoods and gardens out back. Decorated with Navajo rugs and artwork, the **☾ Turquoise Room Restaurant** (928/289-2888, all meals daily) serves wonderful contemporary Southwest cuisine including recipes from the Harvey heyday of the 1930s. Dishes ($16–25 for dinner) use local ingredients such as lamb and Colorado elk, and go well with a chili-pepper martini or prickly-pear cactus bread pudding for dessert. On either side of the restaurant are a martini lounge and the gift shop. This is a special place, well worth a stop if only for lunch.

Winslow has many inexpensive hotels, including a **Days Inn** (2035 W. Hwy. 66, 928/289-1010, fax 928/289-5778, $60–80), a **Motel 6** (520 W. Desmond St., 928/289-9581, fax 928/289-5642, $45–60), and an **Econo Lodge** (1706 N. Park Dr., 928/289-4687, fax 928/289-9377, $50–90). The **Best Western Adobe Inn** (1701 N. Park Dr., 928/289-4638, fax 928/289-5514, $85–95) has the family-oriented Adobe Inn restaurant (dinner daily, entrées $7–20) and a heated outdoor pool.

Family-owned for half a century, the **Casa Blanca Cafe** (1201 E. 2nd St., 928/289-4191, lunch and dinner daily) serves up authentic Mexican food every day of the week. Entrées are $5–10. Grab a burger or burrito at **BoJo's Grill & Sports Club** (117 W. 2nd St. 928/289-0616, lunch and dinner daily) and settle down to watch the Arizona Diamondbacks play. **The Seattle Grind** (106 E. 2nd St., 928/289-2859) is near the Corner Park, and has local art on display and live music to complement the java.

Transportation

Amtrak serves Winslow, but the station (next to La Posada on East 2nd Street) is unstaffed; call 800/872-7245 for information. **Greyhound** buses stop at the Super American Truck Stop (2201 N. Park Dr., 928/289-2171).

HOLBROOK

This ranching center was founded, as so many other southwestern cities were, with the arrival of the railroad in 1881. The second-largest ranch in the county, the Hashknife, was based nearby, where cowboys herded up to 60,000 cows and 2,000 horses across two million acres. This attracted rustlers, naturally, and for a time Holbrook was known as the "town too tough for women and children." Patrons at the Bucket of Blood Saloon tried to outdo each other in downing shots of whiskey "before they touched the bottom of the glass," and cowboys would gallop through town on payday with guns blazing, crying "Hide out, kids, the cowboys are in town!" In 1887, Sheriff Perry Owens (scoffed at on arrival as a bit of a dandy) single-handedly killed three members of the Cooper-Blevins gang in a gunfight, and wounded a fourth. Until 1914, Holbrook was known as the only county seat in the country without a church.

Today Holbrook (pop. 5,000) has the easiest access to the Petrified Forest National Park, and provides a rest stop along I-40.

Sights

Holbrook's 1898 county courthouse has been turned into the **Navajo County Museum** (100 E. Arizona St., 8 A.M.–5 P.M. daily, free), full to the rafters with local history. The collection focuses on Holbrook's colorful Wild West past, and the claustrophobic jail downstairs is decorated with prisoners' graffiti. The offices of the **Holbrook Chamber of Commerce** (928/524-6558 or 800/524-2459) are here as well.

Entertainment and Events

If you happen to arrive in Holbrook right after the holidays and have someone in Scottsdale you want to write to, you're in luck. Reenactors with the **Hashknife Pony Express** carry mail on horseback along the old express route every January. (Send your mail, marked "Via Pony Express" in the lower-left-hand corner, enclosed in another envelope addressed to "Postmaster, Holbrook, AZ, 86025.") Holbrook's **Old West Days** in mid-June bring more reenactors, music, crafts, dancing, and bike and foot races. In September, the **Navajo County Fair** arrives, and the **Christmas Parade of Lights** illuminates downtown the first Saturday in December.

Shopping

With all the petrified wood for sale in town, it's hard to believe there's any left in the park—but luckily the law dictates that anything offered for sale must be taken from private land. Polished specimens, geodes, turquoise, and other geological curiosities are offered at places like the **Rainbow Rock Shop** (101 Navajo Blvd., 928/524-2384), with huge green dinosaurs guarding its entrance near the train tracks. **McGee's Beyond Native Tradition Gallery** (2114 E. Navajo Blvd., 928/524-1977) is the best of Holbrook's many native crafts stores, stocking an excellent collection of rugs, kachinas, baskets, jewelry, and pottery.

Accommodations and Food

Fittingly, Hopi Drive and Navajo Boulevard are Holbrook's main commercial arteries, and are where you'll find most of the city's hotels and restaurants. Leading the least-expensive category by a wide margin is the ((**Wigwam Motel** (811 W. Hopi Dr., 928/524-3048, clewis97@cybertrails.com). It looks like a classic car collection parked among a forest of big fake tepees, and that's just what it is. It was built in the 1940s, and the wigwams still have their original furniture and all their Route 66 charm. Other options around $50 include the **Best Inn** (2211 E. Navajo Blvd., 928/524-2654, fax 928/524-1496) and the **Relax Inn** (2418 E. Navajo Blvd., 928/524-6815, fax 928/524-2328).

In the $50–100 category are a **Days Inn** (2601 Navajo Blvd., 928/524-6949, fax 928/524-6665) and a **Best Western Arizonian Inn** (2508 Navajo Blvd., 928/524-2611, fax 928/524-2253). The **A-OK RV Park** (1576 Roadrunner Rd., 928/524-3226) has 136 sites for $20–24. There's also a **KOA Kampground** (102 Hermosa Dr., 928/524-6689, $19–21) with 208 sites, plus all the usual KOA amenities.

Authentic diner fare befitting Holbrook's location on Old Route 66 is what makes **Joe & Aggie's Cafe** (120 W. Hopi Dr., 928/524-6540, all meals Mon.–Sat.) such a gem. From the honey bottles for the sopapillas to the cheesy joke books and chicken-fried steak platters, Holbrook's oldest restaurant (1946) does Mexican and American road food right. Sandwiches are $4–5, entrées $6–8, and breakfasts $4–7. They also cut hair. For steaks head to the Western-themed **Butterfield Stage Co. Steak House** (609 W. Hopi Dr., 928/524-3447, daily dinner), and for tasty Italian food try the **Mesa Italiana** (2318 E. Navajo Blvd., 928/524-6696, lunch Mon.–Fri., dinner daily), where traditional Mediterranean dishes are around $8 for lunch and $7–14 for dinner.

Transportation
The town **Greyhound** stop (928/524-3832), is at the Circle K at 101 Mission Lane and Navajo Boulevard.

PETRIFIED FOREST NATIONAL PARK
This park, extending both north and south of the interstate, protects one of the world's largest and best-preserved concentrations of petrified wood. The petrifaction process was so slow and exact that in some trees the original cell structure is still clearly visible. A wealth of late Triassic fossils and ruins and petroglyphs from 10,000 years of human habitation complete the picture. It's hard to believe that this area wasn't always valued for its historic significance, but the logs were once pulverized to make industrial grinding powder. The area was declared a national monument by President Theodore Roosevelt in 1906, and in 1962 it was made a park.

In the late Triassic Period, 225 million years ago, this part of Arizona crawled with giant reptiles and fish-eating amphibians. Some of the first dinosaurs plodded among cycads, ferns, and early conifers. Huge *Araucarioxylon arizonicum* trees, some up to 200 feet high, were uprooted by wind or old age and swept down into a vast floodplain and buried

© JULIAN SMITH

Wigwam Motel, Holbrook, Arizona

in silt and mud. Over the aeons, silica-bearing groundwater seeped through the wood and replaced it, cell by cell, with silica. Iron-rich minerals tinted the silica a rainbow of brilliant colors—hematite made red and pink; goethite caused yellow, orange, and brown; and manganese dioxide created purples and blues. Erosion eventually exposed the fossilized logs in the hillsides of the Painted Desert. (The native legend regarding the logs' origins is even more colorful: a weary tired goddess had killed a rabbit and tried to make a fire, but the logs were too wet, so in anger she cursed them to remain forever fireproof—as stone.)

Visiting the Park

A 28-mile drive is the park's backbone, arcing from I-40 exit 311 to Highway 180 east of Holbrook. Everything is on or near this road, which connects to seven short trails. Very few people venture off it, but backcountry camping is permitted (with a free permit) in the psychedelic Painted Desert Wilderness Area north of the interstate.

Warnings against stealing petrified wood are everywhere, but some people still do it, even though there is plenty for sale in Holbrook gathered from private lands (and thus legal). "Conscience wood" displays showcase pieces that guilt-ridden visitors have returned after taking them home, often after a rash of mysteriously bad luck. It doesn't need repeating, but I will anyway: Don't remove anything from the park, lest you become like the visitors then-ranger Edward Abbey would ask about smuggled wood at the park gate: "The driver would look me back straight in the eye, sincere and honest as only an American can be, and reply, 'No sir, we don't.' One of the kids in the back seat would say, 'But Daddy, what about that big log we put in the trunk?'"

Starting at the northern end, the **Painted Desert Visitor Center** (928/524-6228, www.nps.gov/pefo, 8 A.M.–5 P.M. daily,

7 A.M.–7 P.M. in summer, $10 per vehicle) has an introductory video, bookstore, restrooms, and general information on the park. A short distance farther, past viewing points over the Painted Desert, is the **Painted Desert Inn** (8 A.M.–5 P.M. daily), a historic Fred Harvey lodge decorated inside with murals by Hopi artist Fred Kabotie. Native American artists demonstrate crafts here during the summer, and rangers lead tours year-round.

Keep going past more viewing points and cross the interstate (no access) and the train tracks to reach the central portion of the park, where most of the prehistoric ruins and petroglyphs are found. The **Puerco Pueblo** ruins and **Newspaper Rock** are two of these, but **The Tepees** and **The Haystacks** are actually rock formations. (The pueblo is believed to have been occupied twice, A.D. 1100–1200 and 1300–1400.) A short side road leads to **Blue Mesa,** with panoramic viewing points and a mile-long interpretive loop trail. Farther down the main road, **Agate Bridge** is a large petrified log spanning an eroded gully.

The southern part of the park is where you'll find the best stone wood. A trail starting near the Rainbow Forest Museum leads to the popular **Long Logs Trail** and **Agate House,** a seven-room structure built by ancient inhabitants entirely out of petrified wood, which has been partially restored. The **Rainbow Forest Museum** (8 A.M.–5 P.M. daily) displays astounding fossils near a bookstore and information desk. Out back is the short **Giant Logs Trail,** true to its name—one stone trunk stands taller than a man. Across the road, **Fred Harvey's Rainbow Gift Shop and Fountain** sells souvenirs and snacks.

Just inside the scenic drive's southern entrance are two places not affiliated with the park: the **Petrified Forest Museum Gift Shop** (928/524-3470) and the **Crystal Forest Museum and Gift Shop** (928/524-3500). Both let you satisfy your acquisitive cravings with beautiful petrified wood for sale, and allow camping on their property.

Gallup and Vicinity

Although it's outside the reservation boundary, Gallup (pop. 20,000) is the Navajo Nation's most important commercial center. A plethora of arts-and-crafts shops and galleries, along with a good slice of turn-of-the-20th-century history and the country's premiere Native American gathering, await those who look past the city's weather-beaten facade. Surrounded by the Navajo and Zuni reservations (and within an hour of the Acoma, Laguna, and Jicarilla Apache reservations), unpretentious Gallup easily earns the title "Gateway to Indian Country."

History

Coal was discovered in the area near the middle of the 19th century, helping to insure that the Atlantic & Pacific Railroad chose a route the passed near this tiny stagecoach stop. The town itself was founded in 1881, named after a railroad paymaster, and quickly became a timber- and coal-mining hub. Between 1880 and 1948, more than 50 mines were in operation near Gallup, which stayed relatively quiet as Western cities went. In 1929 alone, 25,177 railroad cars full of coal left the city's freight station, averaging one 70-car train every day of the year. The coal boom drew people from around the world to Gallup's already diverse ethnic mix, which included members of the Navajo and Hopi tribes and the Acoma and Zuni Pueblos. Workers from Germany, Italy, Spain, Greece, China, Japan, Austria, Wales, Scotland, and Yugoslavia, among other countries, left descendents who still call the city home.

Gallup Today

A 30-car coal train still rumbles of out Gallup seven days a week, and the Santa Fe Railroad passes through town every 15 minutes, but the city has shifted its focus to tourism, particularly the rich arts-and-crafts traditions of the nearby Native American tribes. Making Gallup "Indian Capital of the World" has been a successful marketing strategy; the city now boasts more than 100 trading posts, shops, and galleries, along with a few good museums and some 2,000 hotel and motel rooms for the traffic from I-40.

A classic, neon-signed stretch of Old Route 66 serves as Gallup's Main Street, parallel to the train tracks. The 12-block downtown area, enclosed by Main Street, Hill Avenue, 1st Street, and 4th Street, contains most of Gallup's galleries and trading posts, along with a reassuring amount of public artwork, including a mural on the Navajo code talkers (see the sidebar *Navajo Code Talkers* in the *Background* chapter) on 2nd Street near Main Street. Motels and restaurants (mostly serving Mexican food) line Route 66/Main Street toward either end of town. Gritty pawnshops sidle up next to high-end craft boutiques, and Navajo cowboys share the sidewalks with tourists hopping off the interstate for a quite browse.

The scourge of drunk driving reaches a pinnacle in Gallup, so keep a sharp eye out behind the wheel, especially on weekend nights.

Sights

The 1916 Santa Fe Train Depot in the center of town was renovated in 1995 and turned into the **Gallup Cultural Center** (201 E. Hwy. 66, 505/863-4131, 8 A.M.–4 P.M. Mon.–Fri., free). A sculpture of Manuelito, the famous 19th-century Navajo chief, stands in front of the large blue-and-gray building. On the second floor is the Storyteller Museum, with dioramas and displays on trading posts and native crafts, illustrated with great old black-and-white photos, and the Ceremonial Gallery, filled with modern Native American art. Films are shows in the Navajo Cinema, and you can grab a bite at the El Navajo Cafe, serving an inexpensive breakfast and lunch, including organic espresso drinks, on a wood table and chairs carved by the owner (they're also for sale). Open Monday–Friday. The gift shop, run by the Southwest Indian Foundation, stocks a good variety of crafts.

The Gallup Historical Society runs the **Rex Museum** (300 W. Hwy. 66, 505/863-1363, 8 A.M.–3:30 P.M. Tues.–Sat. $2 pp). in what was once the Rex Hotel (circa 1900). Vestiges of Gallup's mining heyday are on display inside nowadays. The **Red Mesa Art Center** (105 W. Hill, 505/722-4209) is a nonprofit run by the Gallup Area Arts Council and dedicated to encouraging local artists. They hold a monthly artist lecture series; call for details.

The local Chamber of Commerce (see the *Information and Transportation* section) has brochures detailing a **walking tour** of historical Gallup. Some two dozen buildings downtown date to the turn of the 20th century or before, including the 1925 **Grand Hotel** (306 W. Coal Ave.); **Kitchen's Opera House** (218 W. Hwy. 66), built around 1890; and the ornate **El Morro Theater** (207 W. Coal Ave., 505/726-0050), built in 1928 in the Spanish Colonial Revival style and still in operation.

Events

All of Gallup's annual events are held at Red Rock State Park. The **Lion's Club Rodeo,** one of the state's best, arrives in June, but the biggest event of the year comes in August: the **Gallup Inter-Tribal Indian Ceremonial** (505/863-3896 or 800/233-4528). This event, called "The Greatest American Show" by none other than Will Rogers, has been held since 1922 and is one of the biggest of its kind. Members of more than 30 tribes come from as far away as Canada for four days of rodeos, dances, parades, and art displays. It's a good idea to get tickets ahead of time for this one: dances are $12–25, rodeos are $10, and to get on the grounds only will run you $3. The same goes for hotel reservations, which are booked solid months in advance.

Close to 200 hot-air balloons float skyward during the **Red Rock Balloon Rally** the first weekend in December. Free **Indian dances** are held for the public nightly from May–August at the Cultural Center.

Shopping

The real reason to spend time in Gallup is to browse the wares in the city's seemingly endless array of trading posts, art galleries, pawnshops, and gift stores. This is one of the Four Corners' top shopping destinations, and a stroll down Old Route 66 near the Santa Fe Train Depot is enough to burn a hole in the wallet of any devotee of southwestern arts and crafts. Of them all, **Richardson's Trading Company** (222 W. Hwy. 66, 505/722-4762, www.richardsontrading.com) is the most steeped in history—and around here, that's saying a lot. Opened in 1913, it stocks an overwhelming selection of crafts and goods from the wooden floor to the roof. At last count there were 2,000 rugs in the rug room, which is just behind the stuffed white buffalo (this one was bleached).

Tobe Turpen's Trading Post (1710 S. 2nd St., 505/722-3806, www.tobeturpens.com or www.pntrader.com) was started in 1939 by Tobe Sr., and is run today by Tobe Jr. with the help of Tobe III. They have tons of jewelry in the pawn vault, along with hundreds of pawned saddles. The Tanner family traces its trading history back to the arrival of Seth

Gallup sidewalks evoke a bygone era.

THE CROWNPOINT RUG AUCTION

On the third Friday of every month or thereabouts, the gymnasium of the Crownpoint Elementary School is filled with Navajo artisans, browsers, and visitors at one of the best shopping – and cultural – opportunities on the Rez. This isn't oriented to tourists, but a major local social event that brings out friends and families for a fun night. Previewing runs 4-6 P.M., and students set up tables with snacks and drinks around 5 P.M. Artisans display jewelry, pottery, and other crafts in the halls, but inside the gym the focus is on rugs. You can pick up and examine any one that strikes your fancy and talk directly to its creator. Not only are prices lower here than just about anywhere else, but it is also a major source of income for the weavers, who get the money directly. Rugs sell for under $100 and up into the thousands. The auction starts at 7 P.M., and lasts until around midnight.

The school is in Crownpoint, 56 miles northeast of Gallup on the way to Chaco Canyon. Head north from Thoreau (I-40 exit 53) for 25 miles on Highway 371, turn left (west) at the Crownpoint sign, then take a right at the second four-way stop. The school is on the right – look for all the cars. Admission is free, and they don't take credit cards for purchases. For more information and to double check the time and date, contact the **Crownpoint Rug Weavers Association** (505/786-7386, www .crownpointrugauction.com).

Tanner in the company of Brigham Young in the 19th century. Today, his fourth-generation descendants run some of Gallup's better stores: the **Ellis Tanner Trading Co.** (1980 Hwy. 602, 505/863-4434, www.etanner.com) stocks (among many other things) lots of pawned goods and paintings; and the **Shush Yaz Trading Co.** (1304 W. Lincoln, 505/722-0130, www.shushyaz.com) is named after Seth's son Don, nicknamed "Little Bear" by the Navajo. The **Kiva Gallery** (202 W. Hwy. 66, 505/722-5577 or 800/338-2140, www.kivagallery.com) specializes in original paintings, and **Yazzie's Indian Art** (236 W. Hwy. 66, 505/726-8272) has a selection of outstanding jewelry.

Recreation

Gallup has started marketing itself as an outdoor destination as well as a cultural one, and with good reason. There are many hiking and biking trails, and even some good rock climbing, in the immediate vicinity. Two good trails start at **Red Rock State Park** (505/722-3829), 640 acres of beautiful scarlet canyons about six miles east of town via Route 66. (Head north on Highway 566, take another left after half a mile and follow the signs.) The **Pyramid Rock Trail** is a three-mile round-trip loop that takes you up to 7,500 feet, and the **Church Rock Trail** (two miles round-trip) offers views over sandstone towers. The park also has a 103-site campground (505/863-9330, $10–14), a historical museum, and the 1888 Outlaw Trading Post.

The **Mentmore rock climbing area** features more than 80 bolted and top-climbs up to 45 feet high and 5.13 in difficulty. Find Mentmore Road by going half a mile west on Route 66 from I-40 exit 16, then turning north onto County Road 1, which becomes Mentmore when it turns sharply left (west). Follow this another 1.5 miles up and over a hill, and continue straight through an open gate where the road veers right.

Behind the Gallup Community Service Center at 410 Bataan Veterans Street is the trailhead of the **Northside bike trail,** an 18-mile technical single-track ride through the piñon-and-juniper desert. Another good trail network open to bikers and hikers is the High Desert Trail System, accessed from the east at the Gamerco trailhead; head north three miles on Highway 491, turn left onto Chino Road, and turn left again after about 300 yards at the first road. The Scoreboard bike shop (107 W. Coal Ave., 505/722-6077) has maps and info.

Accommodations

Gallup has no shortage of hotel rooms, although some of the cheaper ones along Route 66, advertising rates as low as $15 per night, are better off avoided. There is one place in town you should stay if at all possible, or at least peek inside: the **El Rancho Hotel** (1000 E. Hwy. 66, 505/863-9311 or 800/543-6351, fax 505/722-5917, www.elranchohotel.com). It was opened in 1937 by D. W. Griffith's brother, and became a second home to movie stars filming nearby during the 1940s, '50s, and '60s. Ronald Reagan, Spencer Tracy, Kirk Douglas, and Katherine Hepburn all stayed here, and their signed photos grace the hallways today. It's a proud shrine to Hollywood's golden age of Westerns, with a flamboyant balconied lobby full of Native American art, big fireplaces, animal heads, and dark-wood furniture. Armand Ortega's Indian Store sells quality crafts, and live music floats from the 49er Lounge. Plates named after Carmen Miranda and Anthony Quinn are served at the restaurant, open daily for all meals. Rooms are $76–85, but rooms at the attached motel start at only $35.

For about $50, you can find a dependably clean and secure place at the **Economy Inn** (1709 W. Hwy. 66, 505/863-9301, fax 505/722-9112) and the **Red Roof Inn** (3304 W. Hwy. 66, 505/772-7765, fax 505/772-4752). In the $50–100 price range you'll also find a **Best Western Inn & Suites** (3009 W. Hwy. 66, 505/722-2221, fax 505/722-7442) and a **Days Inn** (3201 W. Hwy. 66, tel./fax 505/863-6889). The only campground in town, aside from the one at Red Rock State Park, is the **USA RV Park** (2925 W. Hwy. 66, 505/863-5021, reservations@usarvpark.com, www.usarvpark.com), where tent sites are $20 and RV sites are $25–27. To get there, take exit 6 off I-40, then go a mile east on Highway 66; it's next to the Holiday Inn.

Food

The parking lot is always packed at lunch at **Don Diego's Restaurant and Lounge** (801 W. Hwy. 66, 505/722-5517, all meals Mon.–Sat.), which is a good sign that the Baca family is still cooking up the same great Mexican food they have been for decades. Dishes are $4–6 for breakfast, $6–8 for lunch, and $8–12 for dinner, including baby back ribs and carne adovada. There's a lounge with the "best margaritas in town," too. **Earl's Family Restaurant** (1400 E. Hwy. 66, 505/863-4201, all meals daily) is another local landmark, open since 1947. They serve inexpensive Mexican and American family fare.

For fine dining, the only game in town is **Chelles** (2201 W. Hwy. 66, 505/722-7698, dinner Mon.–Sat.). This place specializes in seafood, but they will also accommodate fans of Mexican cooking—a given this close to the border. They boast an extensive wine list and enticing desserts made in-house. **The Coffee House** (203 W. Coal Ave., 505/726-0291), next to the El Morro Theater, is open from 7 or 8 A.M. to 10 or 11 P.M. (Sunday 10 A.M.–4 P.M.). Live music, poetry readings, and local art on the walls make it a cozy neighborhood spot, serving snacks and the usual caffeinated beverages. Western BBQ and Navajo tacos have been on the menu of **The Ranch Kitchen** (3001 W. Hwy. 66, 505/722-2537, all meals daily), for four decades, and **PeeWee's Kitchen** (1644 S. 2nd St., 505/863-9039, breakfast and lunch Mon.–Sat.) serves "family fare, cooked with care"—particularly the breakfasts.

Information and Transportation

For more information on Gallup and the surrounding area, stop by the Gallup Chamber of Commerce's **visitors center** (103 W. Hwy. 66, 505/722-2228 or 800/380-4989, hwy66@cia-g.com, www.gallupchamber.com, 8:30 A.M.–5 P.M. Mon.–Fri.), which includes a small display on the Navajo code talkers. The **Gallup Convention & Visitors Bureau** (800/242-4282, www.gallupnm.org) is another good source. Gallup's **Greyhound** station is at 255 East Highway 66 (505/863-3761) and **Amtrak** is located at 201 East Highway 66 (505/863-3244).

WINDOW ROCK, ARIZONA

The administrative center of the Navajo Nation straddles the New Mexico/Arizona border 24 miles west of Gallup on Highway 264/3. It owes its importance to John Collier, commissioner of Indian Affairs in the 1930s, who brought the reservation's various offices together here as the Navajo Central Agency. He is remembered for his sympathetic ear in matters such as the tribe's education and health care, including the replacing of boarding schools with day schools for children.

Sights

The **Navajo Museum, Library, and Visitor Center** (928/871-6673, 8 A.M.–5 P.M. Mon., 8 A.M.–8 P.M. Tues.–Fri., 9 A.M.–5 P.M. Sat., free) is in the Navajo Arts and Crafts Enterprises building near the intersection of Highway 264/3 and 12. This large building houses a museum with sparse but well-done displays on tribal history, geology, and archaeology. Sharing the same parking lot are the **Navajo Parks & Recreation Department** (928/871-6636 or 871-6647, info@navajonationparks.org, www.navajonationparks.org, 8 A.M.–5 P.M.), where you can pick up permits for camping on the reservation, and the small **Navajo Zoological & Botanical Park** (928/871-6574, 8 A.M.–5 P.M. daily, free), which houses animals injured or otherwise unfit for the wild. The collection ranges from ducks and sheep to a cougar, black bears, bobcats, and one endlessly pacing wolf. (Pets are not allowed "for many reasons.")

The headquarters of the Navajo Tribal Government sit in front of **Window Rock Tribal Park** (928/871-6413, 8 A.M.–5 P.M. daily, free), centered around *Tségháhoodzání,* the "Perforated Rock," a natural window which figures in the Water Way ceremony. The park includes a sanctuary for healing and reflection with a sandstone fountain. The tribe's executive offices, council chamber, and police headquarters (for readers of Tony Hillerman's novels)

are all here. To find it, take a right half a mile north of the intersection of Highway 264/3 and 12.

Shopping

A big selection including concha belts, books, jewelry, and craft supplies awaits at the **Navajo Arts & Crafts Enterprises** outlet (928/871-4090, 9 A.M.–5 P.M. Mon.–Fri.) near the Navajo Nation Inn. It's one of four on the reservation, and shares an entrance with the **Horned Moon Apparel Company** (9 A.M.–6 P.M. Mon.–Fri., 9 A.M.–5 P.M. Sat.), which stocks Western wear. **Griswold's Inc** (1591A Hwy. 264, 928/371-5393) is between the KFC and the Napa Auto Parts Store a few hundred yards east of Arizona/New Mexico line. Although it's only been in business since 1988, the front room is laid out in the classic bull-pen design, and is full of locals cashing paychecks on Friday afternoons. They have a little of everything in stock, from cradle boards to saddles and pottery, as well as a few hundred rugs in the rug room.

Accommodations and Food

Most tourist activity in Window Rock centers around the **Quality Inn** (48 W. Hwy. 264, 928/871-4108, fax 928/871-5466, www.explorenavajo.com, $75–80), a modest place with 56 rooms near the main intersection. The hotel's **Dine Restaurant** (all meals daily) is also the local favorite, serving good food (plates $5–7) including a breakfast buffet, burgers, Navajo tacos (of course) and a good spicy roasted corn–chili soup. Other than that, your only choices are the Days Inn in St. Michaels and the bevy of fast-food outlets in Window Rock.

Information

The main office of the **Navajo Tourism** department (520/871-6659 or 520/871-6436, www.discovernavajo.com) is in the governmental complex at Window Rock, although it's not a visitors center setup.

ST. MICHAELS

Katharine Drexel, heiress to an investment banker's fortune, followed a higher calling instead and founded the Sisters of the Blessed Sacrament for Indians and Colored People, a Franciscan mission just west of Window Rock, in 1896. With the help of two priests from Ohio, the Reverend Mother turned the 440-acre spread into a successful mission, and named it after her childhood home in Pennsylvania. One of the Ohio priests was said to have written more than 3,000 letters to help the tribe increase the size of the reservation. Among their guests was Father Bernard Haile, who helped develop the written form of the Navajo language and published the first Navajo dictionary.

Turn south at the mustard-color trailer housing the St. Michaels post office to reach the mission, shaded by large old cottonwoods. Across from the church, a small stone building houses the **St. Michaels Historical Museum and Bookstore** (928/871-4171, 9 A.M.–5 P.M. daily Memorial Day–Labor Day) which still sells some of Father Haile's publications.

St. Michaels is also home to the **Navajoland Days Inn** (392 W. Hwy. 264 (928/871-5690, fax 928/871-5699, $80–90) with a heated indoor pool and fitness center.

NORTH OF GALLUP
Highway 491

The northeastern corner of the Navajo Reservation is a stark lesson in geology. Heading north from Gallup, Highway 491 parallels the Chuska Mountains on the Arizona border, rising darkly to almost 10,000 feet. About 40 miles north of Gallup, Highway 134 heads west from Sheep Springs. On its way to Window Rock it crosses Washington Pass, named (to the chagrin of locals) after a U.S. Army soldier. Ten miles farther north on Highway 491 is a side road at Newcomb that quickly turns to dirt and leads 6.5 miles to the **Two Gray Hills Trading Post** (505/789-3270, 8:30 A.M.–5:30 P.M. Mon.–Sat.). Les Wilson runs this timeless place, which was built in 1897 and gave its name to the distinctive white, black, and gray geometric rug pattern. Ask to see the small rug room in back, where he stocks a good selection made by local weavers.

The highway continues through a bizarre landscape of mesa, monoclines, and volcanic detritus. **Bennett Peak** and **Ford Butte**, on opposite sides of the highway near milepost 64, are both volcanic necks, left behind when softer outer layers eroded away, leaving the harder solid core behind. Dikes of hardened lava radiate from the necks like crazed bicycle spokes across the flat terrain.

To the north are **Rol-Hay Rock** to the west, sharp little **Barber Peak** and the **Hogback** monocline to the east, and then the main attraction, Shiprock.

Shiprock

There's not much to the town at the crossroads of Highways 64 and 491 of interest to tourists, aside from an impressive rock tower, a handful of fast-food restaurants, and a few good places to shop. The **Shiprock Trading Company** (505/368-4585 or 800/210-7847, www.shiprocktrading.com) has been operating at the same location since 1894, and is now run by Jed Foutz, the fifth-generation Foutz to own the business. Ask to see the back rooms full of dead pawn, crafts, and antiques, which were once the original post's rug rooms. The Foutz family, one of the oldest trading families on the reservation, also runs the **Foutz Trading Co.** (505/368-5790 or 800/383-0615, www.foutzrug.com) with a good selection of Navajo folk art, knives with embroidered sheaths, and Navajo kachinas. The store is also full of craft supplies, including a colorful wall of yarn, and has separate rooms for rugs and sandpaintings. (There's another Foutz Trading Co. on Highway 64 toward Farmington, across from a huge pile of scrap metal, but that one stocks mostly pawned goods.)

The town of Shiprock is also the home of the **Northern Navajo Fair** in early October, which brings a rodeo, powwow, traditional song and dance, a parade, and arts and crafts to the town fairgrounds. This colorful event has been going for almost a century, making it one of the oldest on the reservation.

The perfect impression of the inside of a volcano, **Shiprock** itself towers 1,700 feet above the desert, with a shape that explains why the Navajo call it *Tsé Bit´ A´´*, the "Rock with Wings." The name, however, actually comes from a legend that tells how the Navajos' ancestors, praying for deliverance from their enemies far to the north, felt the ground rise up beneath their feet and carry them here. Other stories tell how the Hero Twins, Monster Slayer and Child Born For Water, scaled Shiprock to kill a nest full of monstrous birds that were preying on their people. Shiprock was first climbed by Anglos in 1939, but is now off-limits as a sacred site. (The English name comes from early Anglo settlers who were reminded of the sails of a 19th-century clipper ship.)

NEW MEXICO AND COLORADO

Slashed by arroyos and backed by pine-covered peaks, the rolling plains of northwestern New Mexico and southwestern Colorado aren't as dazzling as, say, southern Utah, but more than make up for it in their archaeology and the lively mountain city of Durango. Most of this region is part of the San Juan Basin, a shallow bowl that encompasses 7,800 square miles of desert scrub and low, dun-colored hills. The region is one of the richest deposits of oil and natural gas in the country, and is also heavily grazed. More than 10,000 head of cattle graze among 20,000 wells, which pump 10 percent of the country's domestic supply of natural gas. (Thanks to this bonanza, New Mexico ranks fourth in oil reserves and second in gas reserves in the United States, and the industry contributes $1.3 billion to the state's economy every year.)

The region surrounding Cortez and Mesa Verde is considered the archaeological center of the United States, and for good reason. Start with the world-famous cliff dwellings of Mesa Verde National Park on the piney tablelands south of Cortez, which has been a protected site since the turn of the last century. The monumental ruins in Chaco Culture National Historical Park in New Mexico are equally impressive, albeit in a more subtle way, as the once-grand center of a civilization that built hundreds of miles of roads and traded as far away as Central America. Smaller archaeological sites like Aztec Ruins near Aztec, Salmon Ruins in Bloomfield, Hovenweep National Monument, the Canyons of the Ancients, and the Anasazi Heritage Center near Dolores, Colorado can each be easily explored in a day.

© JULIAN SMITH

HIGHLIGHTS

((Loop Road and Ruins: Explore the remote and enigmatic remains of the Four Corners' ancient cultural hub in Chaco Culture National Historical Park (page 88).

((Aztec Ruins National Monument: Influenced by the Chacoan culture, this smaller site is impressive in its own right (page 95).

((Durango & Silverton Narrow Gauge Railroad: An awe-inspiring tribute to the skill and determination of railroad engineering in the 1880s, still running today (page 98).

((Mesa Verde National Park: Apartment-size cliff dwellings in one of the world's archaeological jewels (page 108).

((Anasazi Heritage Center: Millions of artifacts, interactive computer displays, and real ruins out back make up this exceptional collection near Dolores (page 116).

((Four Corners Monument: Your chance to play interstate Twister ("Right foot Arizona ...") (page 117).

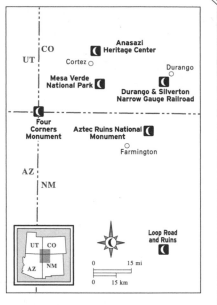

LOOK FOR ((TO FIND RECOMMENDED SIGHTS, ACTIVITIES, DINING, AND LODGING.

Durango, the largest city in southwest Colorado, is an energetic college town enviably close to great skiing, hiking, and biking in the San Juan Mountains. And for fans of places to visit just to say you did, the Four Corners Monument commemorates the only place in the country where four states meet at one remote, arbitrary point.

Gallup, New Mexico is covered at the end of the *Navajo and Hopi Country* chapter.

PLANNING YOUR TIME

Start your travels—ideally for to five days—in Durango, which merits a day or two with its upscale dining and lodging options and nearly limitless outdoor recreation options. A trip on the **Durango & Silverton Narrow Gauge Railroad** to Silverton will take the better part of a day. With a few more days you can visit the Ute Mountain Tribal Park or go rafting on the Animas River. If you prefer a mellower home base, start in Cortez or Aztec, which are close to the **Anasazi Heritage Center** and **Aztec Ruins,** respectively. **Mesa Verde National Park** requires at least a full day to tour, as does seeing the ruins along the **loop road in Chaco Culture National Historical Park**—each is worth two days if you have the time. Hovenweep is good for half a day of exploring, and while you're out there you can hit the **Four Corners Monument** as well.

Durango and Cortez are linked by Highway 160, which joins Highway 491 in the latter as it heads north to Monticello, Utah and south to Shiprock, New Mexico. Highway 550 connects Durango to Aztec, Bloomfield, and points southeast, while Highway 64 runs from west to east near the state line, stringing together Shiprock, Farmington, and Bloomfield.

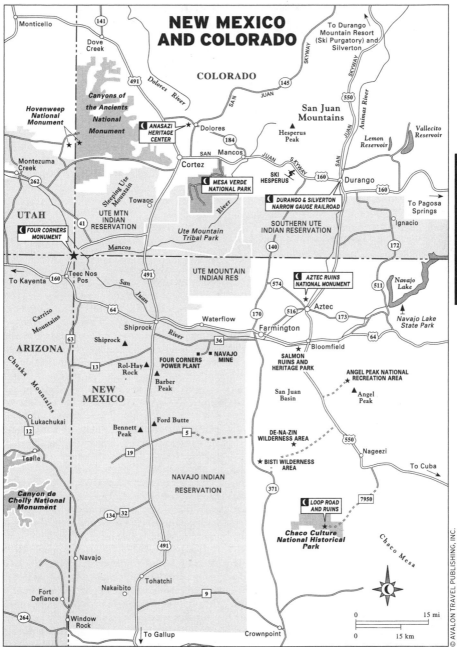

Chaco Culture National Historical Park

The road to Chaco Canyon is long, rough, and occasionally impossible in bad weather—putting you in the perfect frame of mind to experience one of the country's premiere cultural sites. The ceremonial and cultural hub of the Ancestral Puebloan world once teemed with as many as 5,000 inhabitants, who lived in a society as impressive as the great sites of Mexico. Today, this dry valley in the remote high desert of northern New Mexico isn't the easiest place to reach, but Chaco rewards anyone interested in the monumental remains of a vanished civilization.

About 4,000 ruins, roads, dams, and petroglyphs have been found in the park, which has been declared a UNESCO World Heritage Site. Many of these are the "great houses," huge stone complexes that were linked to each other, and many others "outliers" throughout the region, by an astounding system of roads (see the sidebar *All Roads Lead to Chaco*). Chaco flourished for almost 400 years, peaking in the 11th century, and its cultural repercussions lasted much longer. An abundance of enigmatic petroglyphs and trade items from far-off lands add to the aura of mystery that surrounds these isolated ruins. Overlooking Pueblo Bonito as the sun rises or sets, it's easy to imagine this windswept canyon full of the bustle of life, or haunted by the ghosts of the past.

THE SETTING

Chaco Wash is a wide, shallow canyon near the center of the San Juan Basin. It drains to the northwest and becomes the Chaco River, an intermittent tributary of the San Juan River. The landscape is dry and uninviting, with escarpments, mesas, and buttes breaking the drab monotony. If you're wondering the obvious—why here?—keep in mind the changing climate, and the skill of Chaco's builders in growing crops with hardly any rain. One theory holds that Chaco actually served as a buffer against the harsh, unpredictable environment. The erratic climate may have made it necessary to organize the agriculture of the entire San Juan Basin, and the cultural leaders at Chaco may have stored surplus food and redistributed it during bad harvest years.

HISTORY

Chaco was inhabited long before the beginning of the Christian era, but people began settling here more or less permanently in during the Basketmaker III Period (A.D. 450–750). Underground pit houses became multiroom, multistory surface dwellings and ceremonial rooms (kivas), and by A.D. 900 Chaco's heyday had begun.

This is when the characteristic **great houses** were first constructed. These massive, multistory structures were built using unique masonry techniques that, to a great extent, stand unaltered to this day. Containing hundreds of rooms and dozens of ceremonial kivas, the great houses were unlike anything that had been built before in the Southwest. They were planned in detail, oriented to the sun, moon, and stars and linked by line of sight to each other to insure direct communications with fires or reflectors. It's not clear what their exact purpose was; in this marginal land, they were too big to be simple farming villages. Their size might have served some greater ceremonial or symbolic purpose—perhaps, as much as anything, to demonstrate the power of their builders and to help unite the Pueblo world. If so, they might have been occupied only part of the time.

The great houses of Pueblo Bonito, Peñasco Blanco, Una Vida, Hungo Pavi, Pueblo Alto, and Chetro Ketl were erected in the 9th and 10th centuries. New masonry techniques (surrounding thick rubble cores with thin, intricate facing layers) allowed the builders to raise taller structures than anything that had been seen before. By the 11th century, Chaco was connected to more than 150 other great houses throughout the San Juan Basin. Population estimates range from 2,000 to 5,000 people, who lived in some 400 settlements in and near Chaco Canyon.

By now Chaco's importance as a ceremonial and cultural center matched its architecture, and most important social, religious, and commercial activity in the San Juan Basin passed through the valley at some point. A trading network that extended into northern Mexico brought tropical birds, copper, and seashells that were exchanged for distinctive black-on-white pottery, and turquoise mined nearby and processed into jewelry at Chaco. Black-and-white pottery was painted with detailed geometric designs using mineral or carbon paints.

The cultural zenith began to pass in the 12th century, when new construction stopped. By 1300 the place was almost completely deserted. The jury is still out on this massive, sudden emigration. Pressure from Athapascan tribes arriving from the north may also have been a factor, although without the horses the Spanish would bring, these tribes couldn't have done much damage. Some archaeologists think Chaco was a northern outpost of the Toltec Empire of Mexico, which fell around the same

time and took Chaco with it. The most evidence, however, points to the difficulties of sustaining high populations while farming in marginal areas. A prolonged drought hit the San Juan Basin between A.D. 1130 and 1180, and may have overcome the inhabitants' ingenious irrigation methods and diminished the food supply. By then the valley might already have been well on its way to being farmed out, having supported thousands of people for centuries. Social upheaval may have followed, and those who didn't fight with each other simply moved on to places with a more dependable water supply and joined with people at Hopi, Zuni, Acoma, and along the Rio Grande.

Chaco's influence was still felt into the 13th century to the north, west, and south, in places such as Aztec and Salmon Ruins, but its peak had passed. As the Mesa Verdean culture grew, Chaco faded, and its residents moved south and east, eventually metamorphosing into the Hopi and Rio Grande Pueblo cultures. These groups still trace a spiritual lineage to Chaco, and return from time to time to honor their spiritual

NEW MEXICO & COLORADO

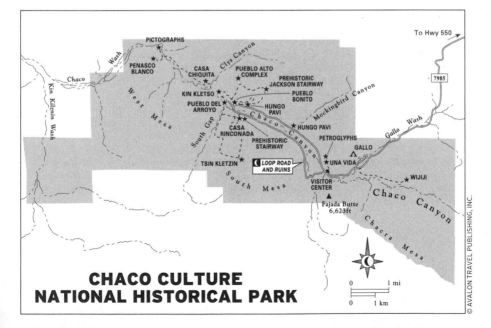

**CHACO CULTURE
NATIONAL HISTORICAL PARK**

© AVALON TRAVEL PUBLISHING, INC.

and biological ancestors. They remember the connection in songs and prayers and also participate in management decisions with the park. The Navajo moved into the canyon in the 1700s and lived there until 1948, and still trace the origins of certain clans to Chaco, which they call *Tse' biyahnii'a'ah,* "The Home of the Great Gambler." The word "Chaco" itself may be a Spanish corruption of the Navajo word *Ts,koh,* meaning "canyon," or **Tzak aik,** meaning "white string of rocks" (referring to the light-colored sandstone atop Chacra Mesa).

The ruins were discovered by Anglos in 1949, when the Washington Expedition under Lieutenant James Simpson surveyed the area. Further photographic expeditions led to excavations near the turn of the 20th century, including some by the cowboy/amateur archaeologist Richard Wetherill. The Hyde Expedition (1896–1900) from the American Museum of Natural History excavated Pueblo Bonito, and tree-ring dating by a National Geographic party the late 1920s pinpointed the ages of the sites. The area became a national monument in 1907, a national historical park in 1980, and a UNESCO World Heritage Site in 1987.

ACCESS

The most direct and easy way to drive to Chaco, relatively speaking, is the road from Highway 550. This route, which involves 16 miles of dirt road, can become impassable after bad weather, so call ahead first for conditions if it has been raining. Turn off Highway 550 onto Country Road 7900 at the sign at milepost 112.5, three miles southeast of Nageezi, and follow it to the park boundary after 21 miles.

Two other routes access Chaco to the southeast, from Highway 9 between Crownpoint and Cuba, but they are longer, rougher, and not recommended for casual visitors (and definitely not for RVs).

VISITORS CENTER AND VICINITY

The **Gallo Campground,** about 23 miles from Highway 550, is open year-round with 47 sites available on a first-come, first-served basis for $10 per night. A trail from the campground (also a good mountain bike ride) leads 1.5 miles to the pueblo of **Wijiji,** built in the early 1100s. This ruin is unusual in its symmetry and the fact that it seems to have been built in one go, rather than added to over the years. A Navajo legend tells that a Pueblo woman living near here taught the tribe how to weave.

A mile farther is the park **visitors center** (505/786-7014, ext. 221, www.nps.gov/chcu, 8 A.M.–5 P.M. daily). This houses a museum and bookstore as well as telephones, restrooms, and drinking water, which is it as far as amenities go. Pay the entrance fee ($4 pp, $8 per vehicle, good for one week) and check here for information on campfire talks and ranger-guided hikes. Pick up a free permit for longer trails here or at the trailhead. A short trail from the parking lot leads to the partially excavated **Una Vida** ruin, with five kivas, about 150 rooms, and great petroglyphs.

█ LOOP ROAD AND RUINS

The visitors center is at the beginning of a nine-mile paved loop drive that passes the park's major archaeological sites, or trailheads leading to them. Heading counterclockwise around the one-way loop, you'll first pass **Hungo Pavi,** an unexcavated ruin, before reaching the parking area for Pueblo Bonito and Chetro Ketl. **Chetro Ketl** was built in the 11th century and enlarged in the early 12th. It has about 500 rooms, 16 kivas, and a huge, elevated plaza. At the far end of the loop, **Pueblo Bonito** is the largest and best known of Chaco's great houses. This four-story, D-shaped complex was occupied from the 10th through the 13th century and was built in stages, ending up with about 600 rooms and 40 kivas. If you can, take the steep Pueblo Alto trail up the cliff behind Kin Kletso to overlook the massive structure. Pueblo Bonito is one of the most studied ruins in North America, and is a sacred place to native tribes. A leaning sandstone column known as Threatening Rock once loomed over the rear of the pueblo.

ALL ROADS LEAD TO CHACO

Archaeologists always knew it must have taken a sophisticated transportation system to link the scattered settlements of the Chacoan society, but it took the advent of aerial photography to reveal the amazing extent of the Chaco road system. More than 400 miles of ancient roadway have been identified, linking Chaco Canyon to some 75 surrounding communities. The longest of these reached all the way to Salmon and Aztec ruins, over 40 miles north, while others seemed to begin and end in the empty desert.

These were not just foot trails, either. Averaging 30 feet across, the roads were built on leveled beds that were raised above sloping terrain, with rock borders or masonry walls to keep the dirt fill in place. They were laid out in amazingly straight lines, and double and quadruple road segments were sometime built near the great houses. Settlements were spaced about a day's travel apart on the longer north-south routes.

The network must have taken an amazing amount of planning and effort to build and maintain, and it is thought that the roads were more than just ways to move goods and people. Most date to the 11th and 12th centuries, when Chaco's population was expanding, and the roads may have helped bind the burgeoning culture into a cohesive whole. By facilitating

communications and bringing spiritual pilgrims to Chaco, the roads may have helped spread the Chacoan religion across the inhospitable landscape and provide yet another way to reflect their worldview in earth and stone.

The Chacoans braced it with earth, timbers, and masonry, and the Park Service monitored its tilt carefully, but in January 1941 it finally made good its promise and fell, crushing about 30 excavated rooms. A short trail leads from Pueblo Bonito along the base of the cliffs to Chetro Ketl, passing many petroglyphs en route.

From the far end of the loop drive a short spur heads to **Pueblo del Arroyo,** a 280-room complex with some two dozen kivas, built in a short period about 1100. Near the Pueblo del Arroyo parking lots is the trailhead for the Pe-asco Blanco and Pueblo Alto trails. Both go to **Kin Kletso** a quarter mile down

Chaco Wash, which was built in two stages around 1130 and may have had three stories on one side.

The Pe-asco Blanco Trail continues to the **Casa Chiquita** ruins near the mouth of Clys Canyon, past numerous petroglyphs and pictographs including one that may depict a supernova in A.D. 1054, and arrives at **Pe-asco Blanco,** 3.6 miles from the trailhead. This is one of Chaco's oldest pueblos, begun along with Pueblo Bonito and Una Vida in the 10th century. The Pueblo Alto Trail heads east from Kin Kletso to **Pueblo Alto,** at the intersection of several ancient roads on top of a mesa. Great views and farming terraces and a prehistoric staircase are visible from the 5.4-mile loop.

As the loop road heads back to the visitors center, it passes **Casa Rinconada** on the south side of the canyon, with the largest-known "great kiva" in the park. From here the **South Mesa Trail** leads south to **Tsin Kletzin,** dating to the early 12th century. The 4.1-mile loop trail leads to several good viewing points and reconnects with the loop road at Casa Rinconada.

NEAR CHACO
Bisti and De-Na-Zin Wilderness Areas

South of Farmington, a dreamlike terrain of multicolored stone hoodoos spreads between Highways 371 and 550. The best of these are preserved within the 45,000 acres of the Bisti and De-Na-Zin wilderness areas. Both are equally acid-etched, like bad science-fiction movie sets, with strange tabletop formations set off against bands of earth the color of burgundy and charcoal. Barely 10,000 people visit per year, so chances are you'll have it mostly to yourself. "Bisti" means "large area of shale hills" in Navajo, and "De-Na-Zin" comes from the Navajo word for "cranes," since petroglyphs of cranes have been found just to the south. Many fossils from the late Cretaceous period, the end of the time of the dinosaurs, have also been found here.

To get there, turn east (right) off of Highway 371, 36.5 miles south of the San Juan River (46 miles north of Crownpoint) onto State Road 7297. Follow the gravel road two miles to a "T" intersection, head left, and continue just over a mile to a parking area on the right surrounded by boulders. For more information, contact the Bureau of Land Management's (BLM's) Farmington office (505/599-8900).

Angel Peak National Recreation Area

Twenty miles south of Bloomfield on Highway 550 is another small but striking area of badlands. The Angel Peak National Rec-

reation Area is presided over by a rock spire know to the Navajo as *Tsethi Gizhi,* the "Rock with Two Prongs on Top." It's easy to zip by the turnoff, but fans of striking scenery won't be disappointed. About eight miles down the dirt road are several overlooks taking in the colorful, eroded landscape and there are a few dozen primate campsites as well. Most of the time you'll have this place all to yourself. Again, contact the BLM's Farmington office for information.

At milepost 117 is the Nageezi Trading Post, home of **The Inn at the Post B&B** (505/632-3646). Opened as a trading post in 1939, this place added accommodations in 1990 under the guidance of postmaster Don Batchelor. They offer three rooms for $70–80, depending on whether you want a shared or private bathroom. A continental breakfast is included, and there's a kitchen guests can use, which is a good thing as there aren't any restaurants around. The inn is the closest lodging to Chaco Canyon that involves a bed, and they also sell groceries and gas.

Angel Peak badlands

© JULIAN SMITH

Farmington and Vicinity

At the northeastern corner of the Navajo Reservation, the La Plata and Animas rivers join the San Juan in a dusty landscape of bluffs and mesas called *Totah* ("The Place Where Rivers Meet") by the Navajo. Farmington (pop. 42,000), the urban hub of northwest New Mexico, is joined by smaller Bloomfield and Aztec. Across the reservation boundary to the west is Morgan Lake and its two industrial neighbors: the Navajo Mine, one of the largest open-pit coal mines in the world, and the Four Corners Power Plant that feeds on it. (The power plant keeps the waters of the lake at 75°F year-round, to the delight of local windsurfers.)

Farmington was founded in the late 19th century by white settlers drawn to the fertile riverside soils, who called their settlement Farmingtown. Its early years were lively. In 1883, when a drunken cowboy shot and wounded a Native American within the city limits, local tribes gathered and threatened to take the offenders by force. A war chief arrived just in time to prevent a fight. When the town's first preacher arrived two years later, cowboys shot at the floor around his feet after he refused to drink with them. (He survived and stayed on.) That same year, a prominent Native American named Largo Pete died after riding into a wire fence, and the local militia had to be called out to prevent another clash. More troublemaking cowboys blasted the screen during a stereopticon show in the schoolhouse, forcing the showman to leap out the window to save his skin.

Eventually the "w" was dropped from the name, and the small farming and ranching town took off in the 1950s when oil and gas deposits were discovered nearby. Uranium was eventually added to the list. Farmington is now home to San Juan College, with more than 6,000 students, as well as some of the best mountain biking in the Four Corners area. In the historic downtown area along Main Street and Broadway, boutiques and specialty stores are interspersed with galleries and restaurants.

SIGHTS

Main and Broadway run parallel through Farmington's historic downtown area, where you'll find a few classic old theaters. The Totah Theater, with its great neon sign on Main Street, was scheduled to reopen in 2005. Two and half miles east is the **Gateway Park Museum and Visitors Center** (3041 E. Main St., 505/599-1174, 8 A.M.–5 P.M. Mon.–Sat., $2 pp), a big glass-fronted building by the Animas River. The museum has exhibits on local history as well as lectures and art shows year-round. Animated dinosaurs screech and pressure valves hiss within the exhibit titled "From Dinosaurs to Drill Bits," which includes the Geovator, a simulated ride down an oil well that wouldn't be out of place at Disney World. At the end of an exhibit on the town's history is a replica of a pre-WWII trading post filled with items taken from real posts around the Four Corners.

Also in Animas Park are the **Riverside Nature Center** (9 A.M.–4 P.M. Sat., 1–4 P.M. Sun. in summer), with interpretive exhibits on riverine ecology, and the **Harvest Grove Farm & Orchards Exhibit Barn,** open Saturday mornings in summer, when a farmer's market is held. Kids might also like the **E-3 Children's Museum & Science Center** at 302 North Orchard (noon–5 P.M. Tues.–Sat., free).

ENTERTAINMENT AND EVENTS
Music and Theater

Theater performances are given at the James C. Henderson Fine Arts Center of **San Juan College** (505/326-3311, www.sanjuancollege.edu) on the north side of town. The college also has a planetarium (505/566-3430) which gives free shows for the public on Friday evenings. Ballet, musicals, and theater productions are held at the **Farmington Civic Center** (200

W. Arrington Ave., 505/599/1148 or 877/599-3331) including performances by the San Juan Symphony (www.sanjuansymphony.com). Occasional live music at K. B. Dillons (see the *Food* section) and the **Top Deck** (515 E. Main St., 505/327-7385) are about it for Farmington nightlife.

Events

In late May the **Farmington Invitational Balloon Festival** sees hot-air balloons launch from the shore of Farmington Lake at dawn on Saturday and Sunday. Also in late May, Farmington's **Riverfest** brings music, food, art, raft rides, and live entertainment to Animas Park. In late June the **Badlands Battle Mountain Bike Race** takes place on Piñon Mesa.

The **San Juan County Sheriff's Posse Rodeo**, the largest open rodeo in northern New Mexico, rides into the San Juan Rodeo Grounds on Highway 516 east of Farmington in June. Early August brings some of the county's best amateur baseball to Farmington during the **Connie Mack World Series** in Rickett's Park. Later that month is the **San Juan Country Fair,** the largest in the state, with livestock, live music, fiddlers, a parade, and more. It happens in McGee Park on Highway 64 between Farmington and Bloomfield.

The **Totah Festival** celebrates native cultures in the Farmington Civic Center over Labor Day weekend with a powwow, rug auction, and juried art show. In October the **Road Apple Rally** (www.roadapplerally.com) brings riders from all over the country to try their skill on the loop courses north of the city. This it the oldest continuously held mountain bike race in the United States, and is open to beginners and veterans alike.

SHOPPING

With the Navajo Reservation just on the edge of town, Farmington boasts a number of excellent places to shop for Native American crafts. Most are concentrated in the downtown area. The **Fifth Generation Trading Company** (232 W. Broadway, 505/326-3211) has been operating since 1875, and stocks rugs, kachinas, jewelry, alabaster sculptures, and one of the largest collections of sandpaintings in the Southwest. **Emerson Gallery** (121 W. Main St., 505/599-8597, www.emersongallery.com) displays the vivid paintings of Anthony Chee Emerson, as well as folk art by his mother and brother.

RECREATION
Mountain Biking

The high-desert landscape of rolling hills, river alleys, and piñon-juniper forests that surrounds Farmington is filled with great mountain biking trails. Many of these, including a network of dirt roads built to access petroleum deposits, are on public lands and within easy range of Farmington. Bike trails crisscross the mesa north of San Juan College, which offers everything from hilly jumps to sandy arroyos. The **Glade Run Trail** is an easy 3.4-mile loop, and there's also the longer **Road Apple Rally** loop, a 29-mile New Mexico classic with views of the San Juan Mountains and Shiprock. Both start from Lions Wilderness Park at the north end of College Avenue; to get there, take Piñon Hill Boulevard north from Main Street, then turn onto College Boulevard.

Other popular trails include two loops on **Piñon Mesa,** three miles north of Main Street on Highway 170 (look for a large cottonwood on the east side of the road for the trailhead), and **Kinsey's Ridge,** an eight-mile trail (one-way) through scrubby forests that starts at the end of Foothills Drive. A 5.6-mile loop circles **Lake Farmington** northeast of the city. The trail to Hart's Canyon near Aztec, supposed crash site of a UFO (see the sidebar *Aliens in Aztec*), is another good local ride.

For more riding information contact one of the local bike shops: **Cottonwood Cycles** (4370 E. Main St., 505/326-0429) or **Havens Bikes and Boards** (500 E. Main St., 505/327-1727).

Other Recreation

There's a public pool and waterslide at the **Farmington Aquatic Center** (1151 N. Sullivan, 505/599-1167, daily, $5 adults, $3.25 children). You can access a network of foot trails along the river from Fairview Road and Tucker Road south of Main Street.

For gamblers, the **SunRay Park and Casino** (505/566-1200) is one of the largest in the area, with 480 slot machines and live horse racing. It's between Farmington and Bloomfield on Highway 64. From late June to August, outdoor summer theater performances are held evenings in the natural amphitheater at Lions Wilderness Park, north of San Juan College, Wednesday–Saturday. Call 800/448-1240 for information.

ACCOMMODATIONS

For about $50 you can find at room at the **Knight's Inn** (701 Airport Dr., tel./fax 505/325-5061). A **Super 8** (1601 E. Broadway, tel./fax 505/325-1813) and a **Comfort Inn** (555 Scott Ave., 505/325-2626, fax 325-7675) both have rooms for under $100.

Much more distinctive are the Juniper and Cottonwood Rooms at the **Silver River Adobe Inn** (3151 W. Main St., 505/325-8219 or 800/382-9251, fax 505/325-5074, reservations@silveradobe.com, www.silveradobe.com) a B&B overlooking the San Juan and La Plata rivers. It's an adobe-and-wood place with a cozy library, a minispa, and organic breakfasts included with the rooms ($105–115) and the four-person suite ($175). The turnoff for the inn is at the La Plata bridge.

The **Casa Blanca Bed & Breakfast** (505 E. La Plata St., 505/327-6503 or 800/550-653, fax 505/327-5680, info@4cornersbandb.com, www.4cornersbandb.com, $125–145), has eight guest rooms and a cottage on a bluff overlooking downtown. One room has a hot tub right on the edge, and there's a fountain in the brick courtyard out back. It was completely remodeled in 2004–2005, and all rooms now feature cable TV, DSL Internet lines, and hand-carved Spanish colonial furniture. Several have whirlpool tubs and fireplaces. The owners have planted more than a thousand flowering bulbs outside.

Even more distinctive is **Kokopelli's Cave Bed & Breakfast** (206 W. 38th Ave., 505/325-7855, fax 505/325-9671, kokoscave@hotmail

.com, www.bbonline.com/nm/kokopelli), a 1,650-square-foot cave for rent that's been featured on *Oprah* and CNN. It was dug out in the 1980s, originally intended to be the office of a consulting geologist. A waterfall shower, a replica kiva in the den, and the steep descent to reach the front door complete the experience. Rates are $220 per night for two people, and $260 for up to four.

Campsites are available at **Mom & Pops RV Park** (901 Illinois, 505/327-3200) for $17 with hookups or $7 for tents, as well as at Navajo Lake State Park.

FOOD

If Farmington is your first foray into New Mexico and its cuisine, be prepared for some belt-tightening meals. All restaurants are open for lunch and dinner daily unless otherwise noted. **Los Hermanitos** (3501 E. Main, 505/326-5664) does New Mexico fare right, including green chili and carne adovada. It's run by native New Mexicans Sam and Cathy Gonzales in the Middle Fork Square. At **Jean's Cafe** (321 W. Main St., 505/324-5556) they make everything fresh—"Not Fast Food" says the sign—from the mutton stew to the best fry-bread in town. It's a local favorite with rugs on the wall and a red police light rotating in the window. Nothing is over $7; breakfast and lunch served Monday–Saturday.

The **Three Rivers Eatery and Brewhouse** (101 E. Main, 505/324-2187) occupies the 1912 Andrew Building downtown. It's decorated with artifacts from the building's former tenants: a drugstore and the *Farmington Times-Hustler* newspaper (now the *Daily Times*). It has an outdoor patio and the biggest collection of beer labels and coasters in the state. Burgers, steaks, pasta, and burritos are $6–15. Grab a burrito and a pint of stout at **Clancy's Irish Cantina** (2701 E. 20th St., 505/325-8176), a local favorite that even offers sushi 5–9 P.M. Tues.–Sat.

You can find a good cup of tea at the **Something Special Bakery and Tearoom** (116 N. Auburn, 505/325-8183, breakfast and lunch daily), and high-school kids chat over lattes at

NEW MEXICO & COLORADO

Andrea Kristina's Bookstore and Kafe (218 W. Main St., 505/327-3313), a friendly and colorful place whose restrooms are labeled "XX" and "XY." Head to **K. B. Dillons** (101 E. Broadway, 505/325-0222, lunch and dinner Mon.– Sat.) for cocktails at the dark bar, or steak, lobster, and other entrées starting at $15.

INFORMATION AND TRANSPORTATION

The **Farmington Convention & Visitors Bureau** (505/326-7602 or 800/448-1240, fmncvb@earthlink.net, www.farmingtonnm .org) operates a visitors center in the Gateway Park complex at 3041 East Main Street.

The **Four Corners Regional Airport** is west of downtown, north of Main Street. **Mesa Airlines** (800/637-22478, www.mesa-air.com), flies to Albuquerque, Phoenix, and Pueblo, Colorado; **Great Lakes Airlines** (800/554-5111, www.greatlakesav.com) offers flights to Denver; and **America West** (800/2FLY-AWA, 800/235-9292, www.americawest.com) flies to Phoenix. Farmington's **Greyhound** bus station is at 101 East Animas Street (505/325-1009).

© JULIAN SMITH

Farmington Convention & Visitors Bureau

WEST OF FARMINGTON
Waterflow

Cottonwoods rustle over fields, orchards, and herds of sheep along the banks of the San Juan River as it flows west of town. In Waterflow, 15 miles west, is the **Hogback Trading Company** (3221 Hwy. 64, 505/598-5154 or 505/598-9243). It was established in 1871 by owner Tom Wheeler's great-grandfather Joseph, and the two-story octagonal building has served as a bank, mercantile store, and livestock brokerage over the years. Rugs are the focus of the first floor, while upstairs is more of an art gallery, with alabaster sculptures, a wagon, and a mock hogan. The ruins of the original post is across the road at the foot of the Hogback. Nearby is **Bob French Navajo Rugs** (3459 Hwy. 64, 505/598-5621, www.bobfrenchs .com) where you should head for the back room piled high with rugs of all sizes, styles, and quality. If money is tight, ask to see the sale pile of rugs that haven't been sold in a while.

Fruitland

Southeast of Waterflow is Fruitland, an anomalous Mormon community founded in 1877. Here you'll find the **Hatch Brothers Trading Post** (36 Riverside Dr., 505/598-6226), a gem of a place in business since 1949, with an old-style bull-pen layout and just about everything from food to pawned items and rugs for sale. Venerable owner R. S. Hatch says he'll be here for another half century. To get there, take the turnoff from Highway 64 to Fruitland and pass the FINA gas station on your left. Go straight through the light (if the gas station comes up on your right, turn left instead) and bear right immediately onto a dirt road. Pass the boarded-up Fruitland Trading Co. and go another quarter of a mile to the riverbank.

AZTEC

Hilly streets lined with trees and historic homes make Aztec stand out from its neighbors, as do the signs at the edge of town:

Welcome to Aztec
Pop. 6,378
and Six Old Soreheads

The town began as a trading post on the bank of the Rio de las Animas, and was most likely named Aztec after the distant Mexican civilization that early inhabitants thought had built the ruins nearby. (The river itself may have been dubbed the "River of Spirits" in Spanish for the same reason.) A farming and ranching center, it shared in the 1950s oil and gas boom as well as the Cold War–era UFO fever (see the sidebar *Aliens in Aztec*). Today Aztec is a quiet and friendly community, misanthropes notwithstanding. The Soreheads are a tongue-in-cheek tradition whose honorees help raise funds for community projects.

(Aztec Ruins National Monument

Step back in time at this well-preserved site (505/334-6174, www.nps.gov/azru, 8 A.M.–6 P.M. daily, to 5 P.M. in winter, $4 pp) northwest of the center of town at the intersection of Highway 516 and Ruins Road. These ruins are unusual both in their size and the fact that they were inhabited for some two centuries, a relatively long time in the scheme of the prehistoric Southwest. The first inhabitants were either from Chaco or strongly influenced by that

culture. They started modifying the landscape around A.D. 1100 with dozens of small and large structures and earthworks. The largest structure, a great house known today as the West Ruin, is a three-story, 450-room structure that included more than two dozen ceremonial kivas, including the Great Kiva in the central plaza. The site was abandoned by the late 1200s.

Today you can take a short, self-guided walk through the West Ruin, and marvel at the intricate construction of the well-preserved walls—at least those that weren't dismantled by early Anglo settlers to build their own homes. Much of the masonry, ceilings, and timber are original. This abundance of original wood offers many opportunities for tree-ring dating. The Great Kiva was excavated in the 1920s and rebuilt by archaeologist Earl Morris in the 1930s, and is the only reconstructed great kiva in the Southwest. A museum in the visitors center presents some of the many artifacts recovered at the site.

Other Sights

Many buildings in Aztec's downtown area date to the 19th century, celebrated at the **Aztec Museum and Pioneer Village** (125 N. Main,

© JULIAN SMITH

kivas, Aztec Ruins National Monument

ALIENS IN AZTEC

"HUGE 'SAUCER' ARMADA JOLTS FARMING-TON," blared the headlines of the *Farmington Daily Times* on March 18, 1950. "Crafts Seen by Hundreds, Speed Estimated at 1000 mph, Altitude 20,000 feet." The Cold War was just gearing up, and the state that gave birth to the Nuclear Age was gripped by UFO fever. Whatever streaked through the New Mexican skies on those spring nights – residents reported up to 500 saucer-shaped objects visible for a number of nights – the story that stuck is that one of them crashed near Aztec on the night of March 25. The silver craft was said to be 100 feet in diameter and undamaged by its detour, but its inhabitants weren't so lucky. Sixteen humanoid bodies between three and four feet

tall, the story goes, were removed and spirited away to government labs.

Whether you buy it or not, Aztec's **UFO Crash Site** makes for a scenic side trip from town. To get there, drive four miles north on Highway 550 and turn right (east) at mile marker 164 onto Hart Canyon Road. (County Road 2770). Follow this six more miles and take a left to a parking area, following the "Crash Site" signs. Mountain bikers can ride the popular **Alien Run** trail through Hart Canyon, which makes a seven-mile single-track loop and starts about four miles earlier on Hart Canyon Road, before the large pump station (a race is held here every April). Find out more during the Aztec UFO Symposium in April.

505/334-9829, 9 A.M.–5 P.M. Mon.–Sat., 10 A.M.–4 P.M. in winter, $3 pp). Old buildings, including a sheriff's office and the city's first jail, stand next to a 1920s oil rig, a narrow-gauge railroad caboose, and collections of historic artifacts, fossils, and minerals. A shoot-out that erupted over a Christmas party is reenacted at high noon on weekdays in the summer.

Tours
Aztec Archaeological Consultants (210 S. Main St., 505/401-6596, mmurin@intergate.com) offer half- and full-day tours of Chaco Canyon, Salmon, and Aztec ruins, and local rock-art sites starting at $110.

Events
The folks at the visitors center run by the **Aztec Chamber of Commerce** (110 N. Ash, 505/334-7648 or 888/838-9551, www.aztecchamber.com, aztec@digii.net, 8 A.M.–5 P.M. Mon.–Sat., extended summer hours) can tell you about the **Aztec UFO Symposium** held in April (see the sidebar *Aliens in Aztec*) and the **Aztec Fiesta Days** in June, which include a parade, food, crafts, the election of new Soreheads, and the burning of an effigy of Old Man Gloom. The **Festival of Lights** in December illuminates

Aztec's downtown with traditional New Mexican *farolitos* (candles in sand-filled bags).

Shopping
Frontiers Trophy Buckles (1312 W. Aztec Blvd., 800/382-3393) specializes in custom-made spurs, knives, key chains, and belt buckles crafted by Native American artisans.

Accommodations
All of Aztec's hotels are in the $50–100 range. **Miss Gail's Inn** (300 S. Main St., 505/334-3452 or 888/534-3452, fax 505/334-9664) has four rooms in a 1907 building near the center of town. Downstairs is **Giovanni's Restaurant,** serving fresh Italian fare for lunch Monday–Friday and dinner by advance reservation. Rooms at the **The Step Back Inn** (103 W. Aztec Blvd, 505/334-1200 or 800/334-1255) are furnished with turn-of-the-20th-century antiques. There's also the **Enchantment Lodge** (1800 W. Aztec Blvd., 505/334-6143) with 20 more rooms, and campsites at the **Ruins Road RV Park** (312 Ruins Rd., 505/334-3160) for $20.

Food
The **Aztec Restaurant** (107 E. Aztec Blvd,

505/334-9586) has a varied menu of healthy breakfasts, steaks, and other fare for $6–8, and an old car impaled on a post marks the **HiWay Grill** (410 N. Aztec Blvd, 505/334-6533), with more Mexican, sandwiches, and blue-plate specials for $6–13. **Oliver's** (1901 W. Aztec Blvd, 505/334-7480) is famous for its breakfast burritos, and serves Mexican dishes, pasta, steaks, and seafood for all meals daily. Grab a cup of coffee and a tasty sandwich at the **Atomic Espresso Bistro** (112 N. Main, 505/334-0109) or a book with your latte at **Hardbacks Books & Espresso** (200 S. Main St., 505/334-5545).

NAVAJO LAKE STATE PARK

Created by the construction of Navajo Dam in 1962, Navajo Lake (505/632-2278, www.navajolake.com) is now a state park. The 35-mile long lake straddles the Colorado border and is very popular, particularly on warm weekends. Visitors come to boat, fish, swim, water-ski, even scuba dive, and they usually start at the visitors center near the dam on Highway 511. The San Juan River, flowing west from the lake toward Aztec and Farmington, is famous for its record trout fishing—get more information on permits and choice spots from **Sandstone Anglers** (505/334-9789 or 888/339-9789, www.sandstoneanglers.com) in Aztec. There are a total of 145 campsites ($10–18) available at three campsites: Sims Mesa and Pine among the piñons and junipers along the lake itself, and Cottonwood, downstream along the river. About half have RV hookups. Primitive camping is permitted along the lakeshore. Keep an eye out for bald eagles November through March.

BLOOMFIELD

Founded in 1877, Bloomfield's story is similar to Farmington's: a farming and agricultural economy supplanted by coal, natural gas, and petroleum discovered in the 1940s and 1950s. To historians, though, Bloomfield is best known as the home of the Stockton Gang, a notorious gang of rustlers who terrorized the town during the late 19th century. The gang was led by Port Stockton, who arrived in Bloomfield fresh off the Lincoln County War down south (where Billy the Kid cut his teeth as an outlaw), supposedly with 15 notches already on his gun barrel. Stockton served briefly as Bloomfield's sheriff before hopping the fence and leading a gang in robbing stagecoaches, seizing widows' ranches, and stealing enough cattle to open their own butcher shop in Durango. All the gang members were eventually killed by locals in a brief flurry of violence called the Stockton War.

Salmon Ruins and Heritage Park

You're better off staying in Aztec or Farmington, but don't miss the Salmon Ruins and Heritage Park (6131 Hwy. 64, 505/632-2103, www .salmonruins.com, 8 A.M.–5 P.M. Mon.–Fri., 9 A.M.–5 P.M. Sat. and Sun. May–Oct., from noon Sun. Nov.–Apr., $3 pp), a Chaco-era ruin built in the shape of a C. This choice spot, overlooking the fertile banks of the San Juan River just west of Bloomfield, was originally inhabited by the Chacoans, who stayed for less than half a century. It stood empty for 50 more years before more settlers arrived from Mesa Verde in the late 1100s and added to the construction. By the late 1200s the buildings stood empty again. One reason for the second abandonment may have been a fire that broke out around 1263. From the evidence, it's thought that a handful of adults and 35 children were standing on the roof of a kiva, perhaps to escape the flames, when it collapsed, killing them all and sealing up a virtual time capsule. The blaze burned hot enough to fuse the kiva sand into glass.

Some 250 rooms made up the two-story complex, which measures 430 by 150 feet. The 13-foot-high tower kiva is unusual, with six-foot-thick walls and six log-and-masonry buttresses similar to those found in European cathedrals. You can walk around the ruins themselves or take a trail down to the **Heritage Park,** where eight reconstructed dwellings represent the valley's wide variety of inhabitants over the last 10,000 years. There's a Navajo hogan, Jicarilla Apache tepees, a Ute lodge, Basketmaker pit houses, a replica trading post, and even an original homestead built by farmer George Salmon near the turn of the 20th century.

NEW MEXICO & COLORADO

Durango and Vicinity

Easily matching Moab and Flagstaff in setting, history, and outdoor offerings, the city of Durango (pop. 14,000) is, in the words of Will Rogers, "out of the way, and glad of it." Durango clings to its heritage as it welcomes visitors on their way to Mesa Verde or the skiing, biking, and hiking in the San Juan Mountains to the north. The 4,400 students attending Fort Lewis College help keep it a young, active place—a kind of Moab in the Mountains, if you will (though here they'd probably call Moab a "Durango of the Desert"). Enviably situated in the Animas River valley between the mountains and the desert, the city boasts plenty of brewpubs, gear stores, and coffee shops, and the scent of pine and patchouli waft through the air. A plethora of old stone buildings in the historic districts of Third and Main Avenues, and the historic rail line to Silverton, hearken back to Durango's raw early days.

HISTORY

Durango was founded in 1881 by the Denver & Rio Grande Railroad, and in its early years was a rough-knuckled frontier town catering to the cattle and mining industries. The grid of the streets, with residential areas uphill from the business district, was the only thing orderly about it. Prospectors, claim-jumpers, gamblers, cowhands, railroad workers, and the occasional desperado crowded the young town's barrooms and dance halls, and brawls and gunfights were common. (An early streetcar line didn't last even a year, according to one historic source, because "the crews were abusive and insulting to patrons, and the cars invariably pulled away from the railroad station before all incoming passengers could get aboard.")

Having faded after the Silver Crash of 1893, Durango found new life in the tourist traffic to Mesa Verde National Park, the restored Silverton railroad, and the lucrative industries spawned by thrill-seeking recreationists—namely skiing, mountain biking, and river-running, not to mention hiking, camping, and fishing.

SIGHTS

◖ Durango & Silverton Narrow Gauge Railroad

One of Durango's biggest tourist draws, this historic railroad (479 Main Ave., 970/247-2733 or 888/872-4607, www.durangotrain .com) has been chugging through the spectacular mountain scenery for over a century. The experience is authentic down to the 36-inch tracks, restored Victorian coaches, and the smoke-spewing engine. Outstanding scenery is part of the package, including precipitous bridges over gorges filled with raging water. In summer you'll probably see backpackers hopping off midway at the Needleton stop and the trailhead to Chicago Basin, a six-mile climb to a gorgeous alpine basin surrounded by three 14,000-foot peaks. (The train stops to pick them up on the way back.)

The train runs daily to Silverton early May–late October, leaving at 8:15 to 9:45 A.M. (check for a current schedule) for $62 adults, $31 children. The trip takes three hours each way, with a two-hour stopover in Silverton. Winter service to Cascade Canyon, 26 miles up the line, leaves daily late November–early January and early March–early May, and Wednesday–Saturday early January–early March ($45/22). Ask about first-class parlor cars, nature-theme trips, and motor coach/train combinations. Hundreds of thousands of people hop on board every year, so advance reservations are a good idea.

Other Sights

Durango's past, from prehistoric times through the Victorian era and beyond, is preserved in the **Animas Museum** (31st St. and W. 2nd Ave., 970/259-2402, www.animasmuseum .org, 10 A.M.–6 P.M. Mon.–Sat., 10 A.M.–4 P.M. Wed.–Sat. in winter, $2.50 pp). It's in the 1904 Animas City School building, and displays everything from Pueblo pottery to an entire 1900 classroom. The **Children's Museum of Durango** (802 E. 2nd Ave., 970/259-9234,

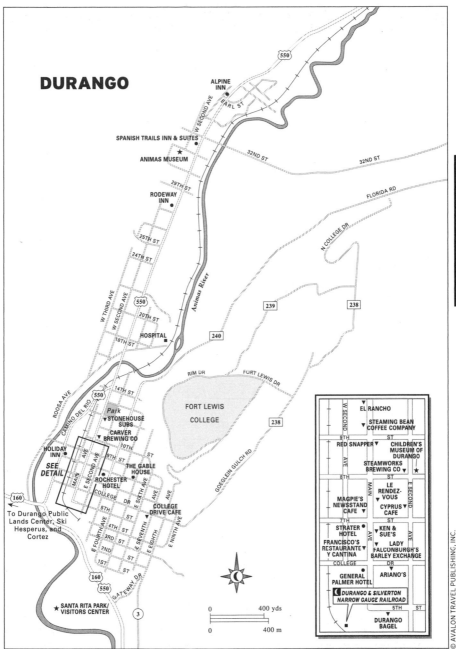

DURANGO

550

ALPINE
INN

EARL ST

SPANISH TRAILS INN & SUITES

★ ANIMAS MUSEUM

32ND ST

32ND ST

FLORIDA RD

29TH ST

RODEWAY
INN

N COLLEGE DR

25TH ST

24TH ST

Animas River

239

238

W THIRD AVE

W SECOND AVE

550

20TH ST

HOSPITAL

240

18TH ST

RIM DR

FORT LEWIS DR

14TH ST

550

ROOSA AVE

CAMINO DEL RIO

Park

STONEHOUSE
SUBS

CARVER
BREWING CO

10TH ST

FORT LEWIS
COLLEGE

238

GOEGLEIN GULCH RD

HOLIDAY
INN

9TH ST

THE GABLE
HOUSE

E SECOND AVE

SEE
DETAIL

MAIN AVE

ROCHESTER
HOTEL

COLLEGE DR

E SIXTH AVE

AVE

AVE

160

COLLEGE
DRIVE CAFE

E NINTH AVE

To Durango Public
Lands Center, Ski
Hesperus, and
Cortez

E FOURTH AVE

E SEVENTH

5TH ST

4TH ST

3RD ST

E EIGHTH

2ND ST

1ST ST

160

550

GATEWAY DR

★ SANTA RITA PARK/
VISITORS CENTER

3

0   400 yds

0   400 m

DETAIL

▼ EL RANCHO

W SECOND

▼ STEAMING BEAN
COFFEE COMPANY

9TH ST

RED SNAPPER ▼

AVE

CHILDREN'S
MUSEUM OF
DURANGO

STEAMWORKS
BREWING CO ▼

★

8TH ST

MAIN

LE
RENDEZ-
VOUS ▼

E SECOND

MAGPIE'S
NEWSSTAND
CAFE ▼

CYPRUS ▼
CAFE

7TH ST

STRATER ●
HOTEL

AVE

KEN &
SUE'S

AVE

FRANCISCO'S
RESTAURANTE ▼
Y CANTINA

▼ LADY
FALCONBURGH'S
BARLEY EXCHANGE

COLLEGE DR

GENERAL ●
PALMER HOTEL

▼ ARIANO'S

☾ DURANGO & SILVERTON
NARROW GAUGE RAILROAD

5TH ST

▼
DURANGO
BAGEL

www.childsmuseum.org, 9:30 A.M.–4:30 P.M. Wed.–Sat., 1–5 P.M. Sun., $5.50 adults, $4 children 3 and up) fills the second floor of the Durango Arts Center with exhibits on robots, take-apart appliances, art projects, and much more. Over $1 million worth of grand pianos and classic cars, including Packards, DeSotos, and Hudsons, are housed in the **Grand Motorcar and Piano Collection** (586 Animas View Dr., 970/247-1250, 9 A.M.–7 P.M. daily, shorter hours in winter, $6 adults, $4 children).

The **Center for Southwest Studies** at Fort Lewis College has a museum (970/247-7456, Mon.–Fri. 1–4 P.M., free) with exhibits on things like ranching and Navajo textiles.

ENTERTAINMENT AND EVENTS

The Strater Hotel's **Diamond Circle Melodrama** (970/247-3400, www.diamondcirclemelodrama.com) has been hailed as one of the best of its kind in the country. Boo the villains and cheer the hero nightly June–August starting at 7:45 P.M. ($20 adults, $15 children).

Advance reservations are a good idea. The musical stage show at the **Bar D Chuckwagon** (970/247-5753 or 888/800-5753, www.bardchuckwagon.com, $17–26 pp) is accompanied by country music and hearty Western cooking. It's nine miles north of Durango at 8080 County Road 250, and happens nightly at 7:30 P.M. Memorial Day–Labor Day.

In town, the **Scoot'n Blues Café and Lounge** (900 Main Ave., 970/259-1400, www.scootnblues.com) is a good bet for live music, and claims Durango's best happy hour 4–6 P.M. Monday–Friday. Grab a pint of Ska Brewery's Pinstripe ale at the century-old **El Rancho Tavern** (975 Main Ave., 970/259-8111). For a schedule of performances at the **Fort Lewis College Community Concert Hall,** contact the box office (970/247-7657, www.durangoconcerts.com).

Durango's Wild West roots live on in its many annual **rodeos,** including the Durango Pro Rodeo Series every Tuesday and Wednesday evening June–August, the Durango Cowgirl Classic over the Fourth of July, and the Family Ranch Rodeo the first week of October.

DURANGO CLIMATE

MONTH	AVG. HIGH	AVG. LOW	MEAN	AVG. PRECIP.
Jan.	39°F	9°F	24°F	1.29 in.
Feb.	45°F	15°F	30°F	1.11 in.
Mar.	53°F	23°F	38°F	1.37 in.
Apr.	62°F	28°F	45°F	0.84 in.
May	72°F	35°F	53°F	0.94 in.
June	83°F	42°F	63°F	0.40 in.
July	87°F	49°F	68°F	1.19 in.
Aug.	85°F	48°F	67°F	1.71 in.
Sept.	77°F	41°F	59°F	1.51 in.
Oct.	65°F	31°F	48°F	1.43 in.
Nov.	50°F	21°F	36°F	1.27 in.
Dec.	41°F	12°F	27°F	1.02 in.

Snowdown (www.snowdown.org) includes a plethora of winter-themed fun in late January. In March, the **Durango Film Festival** (970/259-2291, www.durangofilmfestival. com) brings U.S. and world premieres and juried events. That same month, **Hozhoni Dayz** (http://hozhoni.fortlewis.edu) attracts more than 5,000 people to Native American events on the Fort Lewis College campus.

Early April brings bluegrass picking and plucking to downtown during the **Durango Bluegrass Meltdown** (www.durangomeltdown.com) and over Labor Day weekend the **Iron Horse Bicycle Classic** (www .ironhorsebicycleclassic.com), one of the 10 largest bicycle events in the country, sees cyclists racing the train to Silverton, among other events. Two days of kayak races in June make up the **Animas River Days,** an event attended by many professional paddlers. Contact Four Corner River Sports (970/259-3893, www.riversports.com) for information. **Music in the Mountains** (www.musicin-themountains.com) in July consists of three weeks of classic music performances at the Fort Lewis College campus and the Durango Mountain Resort.

Tractor pulls, auctions, and a livestock show happen in August during the **La Plata County Fair,** the same month the **Main Avenue Juried Arts Festival** comes to the Durango Arts Center. August is also the month of the four-day **Narrow Gauge Railfest,** with visiting locomotives and rail-themed events.

September brings the roar of Harley-Davidson motorcycles **Four Corners Iron Horse Motorcycle Rally** (www.fourcornersrally.com) to nearby Ignacio. Events include scenic tours, bands, and arm-wrestling competitions. In October the **Durango Cowboy Gathering** (www.durangocowboygathering. org) consists of cowboy poetry readings, shooting competitions, and a cowboy parade.

SHOPPING

Many of Durango's art galleries are open late on Friday evenings in season and during gallery walks in early May and late September. **Rain Dance Gallery** (945 Main Ave., 970/375-2708) and **Sorrel Sky** (870 Main

© JULIAN SMITH

Durango-Silverton train

Ave., 970/247-3555) both specialize in Western and Native American art. Stained glass, including works by Tiffany's and local artists, is the focus of **Angels & Lights** (726½ Main Ave., 970/382-9858). The **Toh-Atin Gallery** (145 W. 9th St., 970/247-8277 or 800/525-0384, www.toh-atin.com) has been in business since 1957, and stocks gorgeous and expensive native and Southwest art and crafts, including piles of Navajo rugs. Pick up a handmade chapeau at **O'Farrell Hatmakers** (563 Main Ave., 970/259-5900 or 800/525-0384), with a choice of Panama, palm leaf, beaver-fur, felt, and cowboy models.

Many stores in Durango, such as **Backcountry Experience** (12th and Camino del Rio, 970/247-5830 or 800/648-8519) stock a wide variety of outdoor gear. **Gardenswartz** has two locations: 863 Main Avenue (970/247-2660) and 780 Main Avenue (970/259-6696).

Pine Needle Mountaineering (835 Main Ave., 970/247-8728 or 800/607-0364, www.pine-needle.com) is another good source of gear and info.

RECREATION
Hiking
Durango's choices for hiking are even more extensive, with the steep forested slopes of the La Plata Mountains and the San Juan National Forest practically surrounding the city. Be warned that most trails involve at least some steep slopes. For starters, try a popular trail like the **Animas River Trail,** which runs along the river from Santa Rita Park to 32nd Street, or the easy one-mile climb to **Raider Ridge** overlooking the Fort Lewis College campus, the city, and the La Plata Mountains. (To reach the Raider Ridge trailhead, follow 8th Avenue off College Drive to 3rd Street and go one block east.) The steep, mile-long **Hogsback** trail starts near the Durango Mountain Park east of town; go north on Main Avenue past 22nd Street, turn west (left) on Glenisle and south (left) on Leyden. The trailhead is at the end of the street.

Climb up Haflin Canyon through different ecological zones to reach **Missionary Ridge.** This half-day, 6.5-mile hike takes you through numerous ecological zones from 6,600 to 9,400 feet. Reach the trailhead by heading east on 32nd Street, turning left on County Road 250 at the end, and going five more miles to the sign on the right for Halfin Creek. More good views await from **Animas Mountain** northwest of Durango, which has educational signposts along the way (5 miles round-trip). Start by going north on Main Avenue, left on 32nd Street, and right on 4th Avenue to the trailhead.

Look for peregrine falcons from **Perins Peak,** a difficult five-mile round-trip hike that passes the remains of the Boston Coal Mine and the site of Perins City, an old mining town. Follow directions to the Hogsback trailhead, but start the hike by heading west past the last house on Leyden Street.

DURANGO'S WILD EARLY YEARS

The first mail was carried in by anyone who happened to be coming this way, and was dumped into a cracker box in a store. Water, hauled from springs several miles away, sold at 40¢ a barrel. Court was held in a large room over a general store, and on one occasion when the jury in a murder trail was out, the spectators cleared the floor and had a dance. When the jurors returned, the judge ordered silence while the verdict of guilty was pronounced, after which the dance was resumed, with the judge, lawyers, and jurors, but presumably not the prisoner, participating in great glee.

–The WPA Guide to 1930s Colorado

Mountain Biking

Durango is one of the most fat-tire-happy cities in the county, an infatuation that dates to the 19th-century Durango Wheel Club. In 1990, the city was home to the first-ever Mountain Bike Championships, and in 2001 it hosted one of the World Cup Mountain Biking competitions. Many world-champion riders have or still do live in town. Good rides include the short and long loops at **Log Chutes** (moderately difficult), the tough, steep climb over 11,750-foot **Kennebec Pass** northwest of town (28 miles one-way), and the **Dry Fork Loop** on the edge of town, with six miles of single-track in an 18-mile ride. This is a segment of the 460-mile **Colorado Trail**, which crosses eight mountain ranges, seven national forests, six wilderness areas, and five rivers on its way from Durango to Denver.

Hermosa Creek is another excellent local single-track running 21 miles from Purgatory (see the *Skiing* section) to Hermosa, nine miles north of Durango. Two river crossings are involved, which can get deep in the spring and early summer. For more information on biking in the area, stop by **Durango Cyclery** (143 E. 13th St., 970/247-0747) or **Mountain Bike Specialists** (949 Main Ave., 970/247-4066) who rent bikes starting at $30 per day.

Rafting and Kayaking

The Animas River frothing through downtown Durango is only the beginning; Durango's river offerings extend to the nearby Dolores and Piedras rivers as well. You can get inspired watching kayakers tackle the course set up in the Animas River just off Santa Rita Park, and then sign up with one of the city's many white-water guide services in kiosks along Main Avenue. These include **Flexible Flyers Rafting** (970/247-4628 or 800/346-7741, www.flexibleflyersrafting.com), **Mountain Waters Rafting** (970/259-4191 or 800/585-8243, www.durangorafting.com), and **Mild to Wild Rafting** (970/247-4789 or 800/567-6745, www.mild2wild-rafting.com). Rates start as low as $12 per person ($10 children).

Skiing

Purgatory at Durango Mountain Resort (970/247-9000 or 800/982-6103, www.skipurg.com) is 25 miles north of Durango on Highway 250. This top-flight resort offer 40 miles of trails spread over 1,200 acres and 2,000 vertical feet, with 11 lifts, including a six-person high-speed quad, to get you to the top. The resort receives an average annual snowfall of 260 inches, and backcountry Snow Cat skiing trips take advantage of thousands of acres of untracked terrain. Lift tickets are $55 per day for adults, and a full range of dining, accommodations, equipment rentals, and shopping choices are available at the resort. In summer the slopes are taken over by hikers, mountain bikers, and guests enjoying the alpine slide. Mountain Transport (970/247-9000, ext. 3) runs buses to the resort from Durango November–April for $5 per person round-trip.

At the other end of the spectrum is the family-run hill called **Ski Hesperus** (9848 Hwy. 160, 970/259-3711, www.skihesperus.com), 11 miles west of Durango, with only one lift and a handful of runs. On the bright side, it's cheap (adult passes are $25 per day) and usually much less crowded.

For ski supplies and information in Durango, stop by **The Ski Barn** (3533 Main Ave., 970/247-1923). **Hassle Free Sports** (2615 Main Ave., 970/259-3874 or 800/835-3800, www.hasslefreesports.com) has information on **cross-country skiing** near Durango, including popular trails at Haviland Lake, Molas Pass, and the Purgatory Ski Touring Center.

Fishing

Southwest Colorado has some of the best fishing in the country, from free-flowing rivers to high mountain lakes. Anglers can start with the Animas River in town, and fan out to nearby lakes like Molas, Little Molas, Andrews, Haviland, and Henderson, or rivers like the San Juan, Dolores, and Piedras. The Vallecito, McPhee, and Navajo reservoirs are also good spots for going after trout, salmon, pike, bass, crappie, and bluegill.

Try **Duranglers** (923 Main Ave., 970/385-4081 or 888/347-4346, www.duranglers.com) for guided fly-fishing trips and gear. Their website is a great source of local fishing info.

Other Activities

Trimble Hot Springs, a National Historic Site (6475 County Rd. 203, 970/247-0111, www.trimblehotsprings.com, $11 adults, $7.50 children), is seven miles north of Durango on Highway 550. They offer spa services in addition to hot and cold soaking pools, and are open year-round from 8 or 9 A.M. to 10 or 11 P.M. daily.

For **horseback rides** into the mountains, as well as winter sleigh rides, contact the **Rapp Corral** (970/247-8454, annerapp@frontier.net, www.rappguides.net). Rides start at $28 per person for one hour. The **Durango Soaring Club** (970/247-9037, durangosoaring@frontier.net, www.soardurango.com) offers glider rides over the Animas Valley from mid-May to September, weather permitting, starting at $95 per person for 10–15 minutes of soaring. **Southwest Adventure Guides** (970/259-0370 or 800/642-5389, info@mtnguide.net, www.mtnguide.net) offers rock climbing, backpacking, and mountaineering in summer and ice climbing, mountaineering, and avalanche safety courses in winter.

ACCOMMODATIONS

Many of Durango's hotels offer special winter rates under $50 per night.

$50-100

Durango has lots of inexpensive motels, particularly on Highway 160 toward the outskirts of town. Place in this price range include the **Alpine Inn** (3515 N. Main Ave., 970/247-4042, fax 970/385-4489), and the **Spanish Trails Inn & Suites** (3141 Main Ave., 970/247-4173, www.spanishtrails.com), which has a heated outdoor pool.

$100-150

This price range is mostly the domain of chain hotels, including the **Holiday Inn** (800 Camino del Rio, 970/247-5393), the **Rodeway Inn** (2701 Main Ave., 970/259-2540), and the **Best Western Durango Inn & Suites** (21382 Hwy. 160 W., 970/247-3251, fax 970/385-4835). The **Iron Horse Inn** (5800 N. Main, 970/259-1010 or 800/748-2990, fax 970/385-4791, www.ironhorseinndurango.com) has a fireplace and second-floor loft in every room and an indoor pool and spa.

$150 and Up

Built in 1892, the **Rochester Hotel** (726 E. 2nd Ave., 970/385-1920 or 800/664-1920, fax 970/385-1967, stay@rochesterhotel.com, www.rochesterhotel.com, $150–230) has 14 rooms and suites with high ceilings and "cowboy funky decor," according to *Condé Nast Traveler*. A full breakfast is included with a night's stay. Built the same year, **The Gable House B&B** (805 E. 5th Ave., 970/247-4982, ghbb@frontier.net, www.durangobedandbreakfast.com, $85–195) is a Queen Anne Victorian filled with antique furniture on a quiet street in the heart of town. Breakfast is served on fine china and silver.

Four miles north of town between red cliffs and the Animas River is the **Animas River Guest House** (2725 County Rd. 250, 970/247-7764 or 970/247-3172, fax 970/259-3293, kathydeaderick@msn.com, www.durangoguesthouse.com). The two-bedroom place is fully furnished and is available nightly ($160–200) or weekly ($1,000). A bit farther out is the **Apple Orchard Inn** (7758 County Rd. 203, 970/247-0751 or 800/426-0751, fax 970/385-69776, info@appleorchardinn.com, www.appleorchardinn.com). The only AAA four-diamond B&B in town, it's near Trimble Hot Springs in Hermosa, and has rooms in the main house ($140–160) and separate cottages with covered porches ($170–210). Some rooms feature river-stone fireplaces and views over the old apple orchard.

Main Avenue is home to two outstanding hotels that date back to Durango's 19th-century roots. The ◖ **General Palmer Hotel** (567 Main Ave., 970/247-4747 or 800/523-3358, fax 970/247-1332, gphdurango@yahoo.com, www.generalpalmerhotel.com, $105–170), is the only AAA four-diamond place in town, built in 1898. Brass lamps and hand-crocheted canopies over wooden four-poster beds give you an idea of the Victorian opulence on display here next to the train depot. Grab a bite at the Palace Grill or a tipple at the Quiet Lady Tavern.

A short walk away is the ornate red-and-white facade of the ◖ **Strater Hotel** (699 Main Ave., 970/247-4431 or 800/247-4431, fax 970/259-2208, www.strater.com, $170–245), built in 1887 and run by the third generation of the Barker family. Antiques and hand-printed wallpaper grace the rooms and historical artifacts fill display cases in the lobby. In the Diamond Belle Saloon, waitstaff dress in Victorian finery and a piano player tinkles ragtime beneath an $11,000 chandelier. (Louis L'Amour wrote a few of his Western page-turners here, soaking in the atmosphere.) The Diamond Circle Melodrama (see *Entertainment and Events*) takes place nightly.

Campgrounds

No shortage here: There are more than 900 public and private campsites with 40 miles of Durango. The San Juan National Forest's Columbine Ranger District (970/884-2512) administers campsites ranging from free to $15 per night. Many are northeast of town by the Lemon and Vallecito reservoirs, 20 miles from Durango (head east on Florida Road./County Road 240). The Junction Creek campground is also popular and closer to town; turn right (west) on 25th Street and go eight miles to the campground ($12). Private campgrounds include the **Alpen Rose RV Park** (970/247-5540, camp@alpenroservpark.com, www.alpenroservpark.com, $35–43), five miles north of town on Highway 550; and the **Durango East KOA**

the Strater Hotel, Durango

(970/247-0783, $23–35), seven miles east of town on Highway 160.

FOOD
Coffeeshops and Cafés

The **Steaming Bean Coffee Company** (915 Main Ave., 970/385-7901) is a cozy place with Internet computers and local art on the walls. Another good place for a caffeinated pick-me-up and a newspaper in the morning is **Magpie's Newsstand Cafe** (707 Main Ave., 970/259-1159) with outdoor seating when the weather is nice. **Durango Bagel** (106 E. 5th St., 970/385-7297) is open daily near the train station from 6:30 A.M. and advertises that "Bikers love bagels because they fit easily on your handlebars." The **College Drive Cafe** (666 E. College Dr, 970/247-5322) offers breakfast all day, including half a dozen tasty versions of eggs Benedict, all around $6 (open for all meals Wednesday.–Sunday). More inexpensive fare can be found at **Stonehouse Subs** (140 E. 12th St., 970/247-4882) with sandwiches for $4–8 on bread made from scratch. This locals' favorite makes the best sandwiches in town.

Brewpubs

For local brews of a different sort try the **Carver Brewing Co.** (1022 Main Ave., 970/259-2545, all meals Mon.–Sat., breakfast and lunch Sun.), which has live music and an outdoor beer garden. Their Potato Madness breakfast is a good all-day fuel-up. **Lady Falconburgh's Barley Exchange** (640 N. Main Ave., 970/382-9664) stocks more than 150 microbrews and imported beers downstairs in the Century Mall. Open for lunch and dinner until late. Their Philly cheesesteak is great.

Oven-fired pizza is a specialty (along with the home-brewed beers, of course) of the **Steamworks Brewing Co** (801 E. 2nd Ave., 970/259-9200, lunch and dinner daily). They brew their own sodas, too, and serve food (entrées $7–18) on an outdoor patio. **El Rancho** (975 Main Ave., 970/259-8111) is a tavern that's been around since 1915, when

a 20-year-old Jack Dempsey scored his first knockout on the premises before going on to become World Heavyweight Champion. Some historians now say it happened across the street, but in either case a mural on the wall of the old Central Hotel commemorates the event, which earned the future "Manasa Mauler" $50.

Other Restaurants Downtown

A local favorite for their northern Italian cuisine is **Ariano's** (150 E. College Dr., 970/247-8146, dinner daily). Entrées such as fettuccine with Italian ham and chicken in parchment paper are $10–27. The **Cyprus Cafe** (725 E. 2nd Ave., 970/385-6884) is a charming spot in an old Victorian home that specializes in Mediterranean dishes such as lamb souvlaki and cherry tomato linguine, served daily for lunch ($7–12) and dinner ($12–17). Opened in 1968, **Francisco's Restaurante y Cantina** (619 Main Ave., 970/247-4098) is the oldest restaurant in Durango. Their Mexican fare is available daily for lunch and dinner ($9–16), and includes the best margaritas in town. Pastries, breads, sandwiches, and salads are all on the menu at **Le Rendez-Vous** (750 Main Ave., 970/385-5685), a Swiss bakery and restaurant that offers elegant breakfasts and lunch every day.

Ken and Sue's (636 Main Ave., 970/385-1801) serves New American fare such as pistachio-crusted grouper and southwestern Cobb salad ($10–20) for lunch and dinner daily. Dining is available on the patio near the fountain. **Red Snapper** (144 E. 9th St., 970/259-3417), is a sure bet for good seafood, served daily for dinner in an aquarium-filled dining room, along with steak and other hearty dishes. Their salad bar is Durango's best and biggest.

INFORMATION AND TRANSPORTATION

Durango's main **visitors center** is run by the **Durango Area Tourism Office** (970/247-3500 or 800/525-8855, fax 970/385-7884, info@durango.org, www.durango.org) in the Santa Rita Park at the south end of town.

For destinations out of walking distance, hop aboard the **trolley** that runs up and down Main Avenue ($0.50 pp) every 20 minutes 7 A.M.–10:40 P.M. in summer, or one of the **Durango Lift buses** (970/259-LIFT, 970/259-5438) that go to Fort Lewis College and elsewhere ($1 pp). The **Durango-La Plata County Airport** (www .durangoairport.com) is 14 miles southeast of the city on Highway 172, and is served by United Express (to Denver) and America West Express (to Phoenix), as well as the Avis, Hertz, Dollar, Budget, and National car-rental agencies. Durango's **Greyhound** station (970/247-2756) is at 275 East 8th Avenue.

THE SAN JUAN SKYWAY

A spectacularly scenic loop winds for 236 miles through the San Juan and Uncompahgre national forests north of Durango. This 236-mile national scenic byway passes historic mining towns, prehistoric ruins, and hot springs as it crosses four mountain passes over 10,000 feet. Depending on the season, take your pick from waterfalls, wildflowers, Victorian mansions, alpine forests, icy peaks, and starry skies. Although you can drive the skyway in a day, the views and outdoor offerings merit at least two or three. It's paved the whole way around, but dozens of dirt roads head off into the hills for bicycling, hiking, backpacking, fishing, rafting, and off-roading.

Starting in Durango, the skyway heads north on Highway 550, parallel to the Animas River and the train line past Trimble and Hermosa before heading on its own toward Purgatory Resort. As you climb over Coal Bank Pass (10,640 feet) and Molas Pass (10,910 feet), you'll appreciate how difficult and expensive the "Million Dollar Highway" was to build. (The name is also thought to come from the value of the ore-bearing fill used to build the road.) The town of **Silverton** is a national historic landmark at the other end of the train line from Durango, with Old West gunfights staged in the street during the summer.

Keep going up Highway 550 to Red Mountain Pass (11,008 feet), the highest paved pass in the San Juans, which is surrounded by mining ghost towns and alpine scenery. Following the route of an historic toll road, you'll pass through the rust-colored Red Mountain, a collapsed volcanic cone that gave up $750 million worth of gold, silver, and other minerals to early miners. Keep going through the tunnels and waterfalls of the precipitous Uncompahgre Gorge to reach **Ouray,** another Victorian-era mining town-turned-tourist magnet. Box Canyon Falls and the Ouray Hot Springs are two of the more popular attractions in the area, and Mt. Sneffels (14,150 feet) rises to the west in the center of its own wilderness area. In winter, Ouray becomes a worldwide hot spot for ice climbing, with the Ouray Ice Festival held every January.

Highway 550 continues north to **Ridgway,** home to another great public hot spring (this one is outdoors) and authentic enough to be chosen as the film location for classic Westerns like *How the West Was Won* and *True Grit.* Turn left (west) onto Highway 62 and cross the Dallas Divide (8,970 feet) to reach **Placerville** on the San Miguel River, where you should take Highway 145 southeast. Soon a short side road leads east to the box canyon sheltering the painfully picturesque mining town of **Telluride,** where locals and celebrities rub elbows at music festivals and a world-famous ski resort.

Highway 145 continues south over Lizard Head Pass (10,222 feet), with trails leading into the Lizard Head Wilderness near Mt. Wilson (14,246 feet). Picnic pull-outs and historic markers dot the roadway, as does the Ames Power Plant, producer of the world's first commercial supply of alternating current. The road passes more cliffs and waterfalls to tiny **Rico.** Follow the Dolores River, considered one of the top-50 trout streams in the country, southwest to Dolores, home to the Anasazi Heritage Center and only a short hop from **Cortez.** Highway 160 from Cortez to Mesa Verde National Park and Durango makes up the southern leg of the skyway.

Mesa Verde and Vicinity

◖ MESA VERDE NATIONAL PARK

Between Cortez and the Mancos River looms a series of forested mesas that harbor such a wealth of prehistoric architecture they have been declared both a national park and a World Heritage Site by UNESCO. Amid the steep canyons that slice across this "green table" (from the Spanish) are more than 4,800 known archaeological sites and many more yet undiscovered. About 600 of these are the famous **cliff dwellings,** built when Mesa Verde reached its height between A.D. 1100 and 1300.

Resembling apartment blocks in a city made of stone, these extraordinary structures are built from the same rock as the huge ledges that soar above them. Natural forces and looters have taken their toll—only a few cliff dwellings have been excavated and reinforced enough to admit visitors—but a stroll down these dusty lanes is enough to make 700 years seem like nothing, and the echo of residents' voices and the smoke of their campfires more than just a distant memory.

The Setting

The park covers a series of mesas and canyons that form the northern drainage of the Mancos River, which flows through the Ute Reservation to the south. The fingerlike mesas are formed by three sandstone formations, or layers, that together make up the Mesa Verde Group. Most of the large alcoves are found in Ute, Navaho, Soda, and Morfield canyons, hollowed out of Cliff House Sandstone, the uppermost formation. This sedimentary layer was formed beneath an inland sea between 70 and 100 million years ago. Fine-grained sands deposited in shallow water formed layers of sandstone and shale. When the softer Mancos Shale beneath it crumbles, the harder sandstone splits away in blocks or, occasionally, huge arches, some of which eventually weather into alcoves reaching back deep into the mesa. This often happens near springs, which help

hasten the weathering of the soft sandstone. Percolating rainwater gets redirected horizontally above the less-permeable layer of shale, creating larger alcoves and convenient springs for their inhabitants.

This area is a better place to live than you might think. Sure, the water supply is limited, and no streams run year-round. Most canyons only see flowing water during the summer monsoons or spring runoff. The growing season is long, though—up to 171 days without frost per year, and up this high (7,000 feet) the summer heat isn't so bad, which makes it easier to grow crops. In summer, only the front buildings in the alcoves are hit by the sun's vertical rays, leaving the rest back in the cool shadows. In winter, however, the low sun reaches far back into the alcoves, warming the stone walls as well as the alcoves. It's not unusual for it to be 10–20°F warmer up here than in Montezuma Valley to the north, even though the mesa is 600 feet higher. Over the millennia, dust deposited by winds from the southwest covered the mesa tops with a layer of deep red soil. Combine that with the dependable summer rains in July and August, and Mesa Verde becomes a relatively comfortable, fertile place.

The highest portions of Mesa Verde are covered with large Douglas firs, ponderosa pines, and aspen. Utah juniper and piñon pine are the most common trees, and provided wood for building, tools, and fires, as well as tasty, nutritious nuts. Brush species such as mountain mahogany, Gambrel oak, and serviceberry are concentrated toward the northern end of the park, and big sagebrush, cacti, and flowers occur in the sandy canyon bottoms. More than 200 species of birds live here, from sociable groups of wild turkeys to hummingbirds. Mule deer and coyotes are common, but bears and mountain lions are rarely seen.

History

Mesa Verde has been occupied for about 1,300 years. Nomadic tribes first arrived here at the

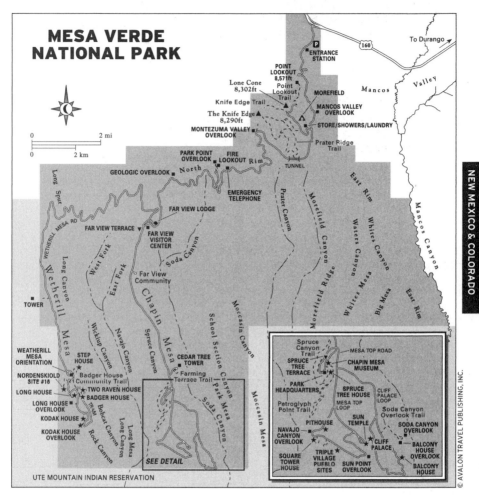

fringe of the Rocky Mountains thousands of years ago, but semipermanent dwellings weren't built until around A.D. 500. People dug pit houses in canyon alcoves and on top of the mesas, covering them with flat or raised roofs of logs and soil. They wove outstanding baskets from plant fibers, and started to make pottery and use the bow and arrow. By A.D. 1000, these houses were being built primarily aboveground on the mesa tops. Roofed dwellings gradually became grouped together to form small villages, called pueblos (Spanish for "village") by archaeologists. Construction methods changed from mud-covered poles to layer masonry, and the builders left open courts amid the rooms. Pit houses deepened until they became the mostly underground ceremonial chambers called kivas.

Mesa Verde culture reached its climax during the Classic Pueblo Period (A.D. 1100–1300), when the inhabitants moved down into the canyons and built most of the grand

FIRE ON THE MOUNTAIN

Wildfires are a natural part of southwestern ecosystems, so when fighting fires becomes part of the management strategy for places like Mesa Verde, it's no surprise that things can quickly get out of balance. Four-fifths of the park has been burned since a policy of total fire suppression was put into effect in 1908, with an average of eight fires racing across the high mesas every year since 1920. Since 1975, the numbers have climbed to 20–25 burns every year, including four major fires between 1996 and 2002 that burned over half the park.

In July 2000, an unusually hot, dry month, a lightning strike outside the park sparked a blaze that eventually scorched 23,607 acres on the eastern side of Mesa Verde. Three-hundred-foot flames were too hot for flame retardants to work, and the path of destruction eventually covered an area eight miles long and four miles wide. It took 1,106 firefighters nine days to put out the Bircher Fire, and much of the area is still scarred.

Unnaturally large wildfires, caused by a combination of hot, dry weather and the buildup of fuels, are expensive by any calculation. The Bircher Fire cost $5.5 million to fight and closed the park for two weeks, spelling lost revenue to the park and local businesses. Big fires can also alter the local ecology: While oak and berry shrubland can regenerate quickly, burned-over piñon and juniper forests can be outcompeted by nonnative grasses, and evergreen woodlands can take centuries to fully regrow. On the bright side, the Bircher Fire burned only a few park buildings, and scorched areas can reveal previously hidden archaeological treasures. After a 1996 fire, one-quarter the size of the Bircher Fire, 372 new sites were discovered.

constructions visible today. Large alcoves facing south or southwest were preferred for the sunlight they captured in the winter. If the floor of an alcove was uneven, builders brought in dirt to even out the surface. Kivas were dug for religious rituals and possibly social events, used by both men and women, and rocks too big to move were incorporated into the construction. It obviously took a large population working in harmony to erect buildings like this—Cliff Place alone had more than 150 rooms and was home to about 100 people. Exquisite pottery was a hallmark of this period, with black geometric designs on a gray or white background. Shell jewelry, bone scrapers, and stone tools have all been unearthed in garbage piles or burial sites.

Farming provided most of the food, mostly from the classic trio of corn, beans, and squash, including the violet-striped bean and a variety of corn resistant to drought. The lack of constantly flowing streams meant the Mesa Verdeans had to depend on what little rain fell, but this was enough. Archaeologists experimented with growing corn in the park from 1918 to 1973 using dryland farming techniques like those of the Hopi, and the crop failed in only three of those years. Storage rooms were incorporated into the buildings to hold excess crops over winter.

Drought arrived around A.D. 1276 and lasted for over a decade. By this point the masonry had begun to decline in quality. The soil may have become less fertile, overtaxed by the demands of a rising population. Residents began to leave as the local springs dried up, moving south into northern Arizona and New Mexico. It's thought that their descendants make up parts of the Hopi and Rio Grande Pueblo tribes. Shortly after A.D. 1300 Mesa Verde was mostly deserted.

The ruins stood empty for centuries. White settlers explored them in the 19th century, after the first official report of the enigmatic sites by Professor J. S. Newberry in an 1859 geological report. In 1874, surveyor W. H. Jackson became the first Anglo to enter a cliff dwelling, when he crawled inside Two-Story Cliff House in Ute Mountain Tribal Park. In December 1888, local rancher Richard Wetherill and his brother-in-law Charles Mason rode out onto Sun Point to look for lost cattle. Through the blowing snow they spotted Cliff Palace. They tied together trees to scramble down into the ruin, and within a day they had discovered Spruce Tree House and Square Tower House as well. Richard returned with three of his brothers to explore the canyons and dig for artifacts. In less than a year and a half they discovered more than 180 cliff dwellings.

Mesa Verde was declared the first (and is still the only) cultural national park in the country in 1906, and it became a World Cultural Heritage Site in 1978.

Entering Mesa Verde

The entrance to the park is off of Highway 160, 10 minutes from Cortez and 45 minutes from Durango. After passing through the entrance station ($10 per vehicle), the park road winds its way up the face of the mesa before reaching the **Moorefield Ranger Station** and the adjacent **Moorefield Campground** after four miles. The ranger station is open late May–August, and the campground (open mid-April–mid-October) is one of the nicest in the national park system. Four hundred sites ($19–25) are first-come, first-served. There's a grocery store, gas station, showers, and laundry facilities in Moorefield Village.

Three **trails** leave from the campground, none of which require permits. The 2.3-mile Point Lookout Trail climbs switchbacks up from a point north of the amphitheater, offering excellent views, and the Knife Edge Trail (1.5 miles) heads to an overlook of Montezuma Valley, which is especially pretty at sunset. The 7.8-mile Prater Ridge Trail was scorched by the Bircher Fire (see the sidebar *Fire on the Mountain*), but it has been reopened.

From the campground the road continues to wind and climb, passing a viewing point at Park Point before reaching the **Far View Visitor Center** (970/529-5036, 8 A.M.–5 P.M. daily Apr.–Oct.), 15 miles from the entrance. The center has exhibits on Native American

crafts and sits next to the **Far View Lodge** (970/529-4421, fax 970/529-4411, Apr.–Oct.), where rooms with great views and private porches are $110–127. The lodge includes the Metate Room restaurant (open daily for breakfast and dinner), the Far View Terrace cafeteria, and a gift shop. Get tickets at the visitors center for tours of Cliff Palace, Balcony House, and Long House ($3 pp).

Here the road splits: head left (south) to reach the Far View Sites complex and Chapin Mesa. Go right (west) to reach Weatherill Mesa, which is open Memorial Day–Labor Day.

Recreation Opportunities

Hiking trails at Mesa Verde take you from mesa-top sites down into the canyons to see the remarkable cliff dwelling up close. Hiking is limited to designated trails only, since the ruins and other cultural resources are so fragile. A park ranger must be present whenever you enter a cliff dwelling, and no backcountry camping is permitted. A number of short trails start near the museum. Keep in mind that most of the park is over 7,000 feet high, and trails can be steep and the weather hot and dry.

One way to have the place almost to yourself (aside from touring Wetherill Mesa on a weekday) is to explore the park in winter on **cross-country skis.** This offers a taste of what it was like when the Weatherills discovered it over a century ago, with walls looming in dark alcoves amid the whiteness. Mesa Verde gets 80–100 inches of snow in an average winter, and all roads beyond the Far View Visitor Center are unplowed and open to skiers. (Stay on roads only, though.) Contact one of the outdoor stores in Durango for ski rentals.

Even if you don't go farther than a few steps from your car, the six-mile **Mesa Top Loop Road** passes a dozen spots of interest with easy access, including pit houses and overlooks.

Chapin Mesa

The road onto Chapin Mesa leads south from the Far View Visitor Center. After passing turnoffs to small sites at the **Far View Sites Complex** and **Cedar Tree Tower,** you'll reach a turnoff 20 miles from the park entrance to **Park Headquarters** (970/529-4465, www .nps.gov/meve) and the **Chapin Mesa Museum** (970/529-4631, 8 A.M.–5 P.M. daily, to 6:30 P.M. Apr.–Oct.). The entire history of Mesa Verde is on display here, with an orientation video shown every half hour. There's also a snack bar and a gift shop.

From here an easy three-mile loop trail to **Petroglyph Point** leads to a petroglyph panel and views over Navajo and Spruce canyons. It starts out low, climbs to the rim, and returns to the museum. A more popular half-mile trail descends into Spruce Tree Canyon to **Spruce Tree House.** The third-largest and the best-preserved cliff dwelling in the park, Spruce Tree House had eight kivas and 130 rooms, and was thought to have 60–90 residents. This is the easiest cliff dwelling to enter. You can tour it yourself for free from spring to fall (rangers are on duty), and take a ranger-guided tour three times a day in the winter. Both trails are gated—only open during visitor hours—and rangers ask that you register before starting out.

The road splits into two loops beyond the park headquarters and museum, leading to three other large cliff dwellings. The Cliff Palace Loop Road, the eastern loop, leads to two cliff dwellings you'll have to have a ticket to tour. To reach **Balcony House** visitors have to climb ladders and stone steps and crawl through a tunnel, so it's not for the faint of heart or the easily winded. The other is the huge **Cliff Palace,** the jewel of Mesa Verde, with 150 rooms and 23 kivas sheltered in an exceptionally large alcove. It's estimated that up to 100 people lived here at its peak. (This tour involves climbing four small ladders.)

Square Tower House is visible from the Chapin Mesa's western loop, and it's easy to see where it gets it name. The 1.5-mile **Soda Canyon Overlook Trail** starts at a parking area on the loop road past the Balcony House parking area, and goes to the canyon edge for views of Balcony House and other sites.

Wetherill Mesa

You'll find less traffic on this side of the park, which is good for at least half a day of exploring. You can reach all the sites here by foot trails or (I kid you not) a tram. Twelve miles from the Far View Visitor Center is a parking area where you can hike to **Step House,** open for self-guided tours via a steep trail. Rangers on duty will explain the evidence of two separate occupations at the site around A.D. 600 and 1200. Otherwise, stop by the snack bar or just load onto the tram, which takes you to the head of the trail to **Long House,** as well as **Bader House, Kodak House,** and the poetically named **Nordenskiold Site #16.** Long House is the second-largest cliff dwelling at Mesa Verde, and the moderately strenuous tour includes a steep staircase and covers almost a mile. This one can only be visited on a ranger-led tour.

Practicalities

Mesa Verde is open daily, year-round, with limited services in winter. You can book hotel and campground reservations, as well as guided tours of the ruins ($39 adults, $28 children), through **Aramark** (970/564-4300 or 800/449-2288, fax 970/564-4311, mesa-verde@aramark.com, www.visitmesaverde.com).

UTE MOUNTAIN RESERVATION

Colorado's southwest corner cradles this 595,787-acre reservation (303/565-3751, www.utemountainute.com) leading up to the Utah and New Mexico lines (and a bit over each). The main town is **Towaoc** (toe-WAY-ock), 11 miles south of Cortez, which was named for the Ute word meaning "all right." This is where most of the reservation's 1,300 residents live, and where you'll find the **Ute Mountain Casino and RV Park** (970/565-8800 or 800/258-8007, www.ute-mountaincasino.com). Take your pick from bingo, keno, poker, and blackjack tables and a variety of slot and video-poker machines. Kuchu's Restaurant serves Southwest-style food (open daily for all meals), and the Sleeping Ute RV Park & Campground (970/565-6544 or 800/889-5072) charges $17 and up per night. Accommodations in the 90-room hotel (888/565-8837) are $70–90. The casino is open 8 A.M.–3 A.M. daily, with free shuttles to and from Cortez (970/565-8800, ext.133). Dances are held in the Indian Village outside, including the **Bear Dance** in late May or early June. At **Ute Mountain Indian Pottery** (800/896-8548), tribal artists paint traditional designs on pottery that is poured into ceramic molds before being turned and cleaned. Each artist signs his or her work before it is glazed and fired.

The area south of Mesa Verde was set aside in 1971 as the **Ute Mountain Tribal Park** (970/565-3751, ext. 330, or 800/847-5485, utepark@fone.net, www.utemountainute.com/tribalpark.htm), centered around **Sleeping Ute Mountain** (9,977 feet), a laccolithic peak that really does look like a slumbering giant with his head pointing north, complete with headdress, folded arms, and volcanic plugs for toes (see the sidebar *The Legend of Sleeping Ute Mountain*). The visitors center (970/749-1452) is 22 miles south of Cortez. With a landscape similar to the national park, the tribal park is also full of Ancestral Puebloan sites and petroglyphs, but they have been left in their natural, unreconstructed state.

The only way to see them is on a native-guided tour, which leave from the visitors center daily at 9 A.M. The half-day tour to Mancos Canyon ($20 pp) is easier, while the full-day tour to Lion Canyon ($40 pp) involves less time spent driving, proportionally. On this one you'll climb five ladders to visit four cliff dwellings including the "Eagle's Nest," which invites comparisons to Mesa Verde's most impressive ruins. Bring lunch and water and your own vehicle; if you don't have your own transportation it costs another $8 per person. Ask about special tours to even more remote sections of the park. Make reservations ahead of time by calling 800/847-5485. The park also offers overnight camping at primitive sites along the Mancos River ($12) as well as cabins ($10).

THE LEGEND OF SLEEPING UTE MOUNTAIN

The mountain was once a great warrior god, they say, whose violent battle against the Evil Ones threw up the mountains and valleys all around. Wounded, he lay down to rest, and his blood formed the Mancos River and its tributaries. When his blanket of trees is light green it means spring has arrived; it turns darker in summer, red and yellow in fall, and white in winter.

SOUTHERN UTE RESERVATION

South of Durango is the smaller (307,000 acres) Ute Reservation (970/563-0100, www.southern-ute.nsn.us). Most of the 7,880 residents live in the town of Ignacio on Highway 172, where tribal crafts and historic artifacts, including powwow outfits and amazing beadwork, are on display at the **Southern Ute Indian Cultural Center** (970/563-9583 www.southernutemuseum.org, 10 A.M.–6 P.M. Mon.–Fri., 10 A.M.–3 P.M. Sat. and Sun., 10 A.M.–5:30 P.M. Tues.–Fri. in winter). Nearby, the **Sky Ute Lodge & Casino** (970/563-3000 or 888/842-4180, www.skyutecasino.com) is the state's only 24-hour house of gambling, with a lineup similar to its cousin in Towaoc. Hotel rooms are $70–85 in season, with the Pino Nuche Restaurant open daily for all meals and free shuttle service to Durango, Farmington, and Pagosa Springs.

CORTEZ AND VICINITY

The closest city to Mesa Verde National Park and the Four Corners Monument is surrounded by mountains and sage flats, with huge mesas rising to the south. Sleepy Cortez (pop. 7,300), occupies land rich in native history, ranging from the Anasazi to the Navajo, who called this spot *Tsaya-toh* ("rock water") for a nearby spring used to water sheep. Irrigation workers trying to bring water from the Dolores River valley to the north were some of Cortez's first white inhabitants, setting up shop in 1886. Sheep and cattle pastured west of town were traded here at the turn of the 20th century, when many of the stone buildings that still line Main Street were built. The 1930s Works Progress Administration (WPA) guide to Colorado described the town's importance as a Native American trading center, painting a livelier picture than you'll probably find today: "Cortez is interesting on Saturday nights, when its main street is filled with ranchers, farmers, and Indians; the latter are usually dressed in brilliant velveteens and calicoes, and aglitter with silver and turquoise jewelry."

Sights

Occupying the ornate 1909 E. R. Lamb & Co. Mercantile Building, the **Cortez Cultural Center** (25 N. Market St., 970/565-1151, www.cortezculturalcenter.org, 10 A.M.–10 P.M. Mon.–Sat., to 5 P.M. Sept.–May) lives up to its name with a museum on the area's rich indigenous heritage, as well as a gallery of local artists and a gift shop. Native dances are held here on some evenings Memorial Day–Labor Day, and there's a local farmers market Sat-

urday mornings June–October. Other native cultural programs at the center include demonstrations of Navajo sandpainting, flute playing, storytelling, and talks on the famous WWII code talkers (see the sidebar *Navajo Code Talkers* in the *Background* chapter).

A bit out of town is the **Crow Canyon Archaeological Center** (970/565-8975 or 800/422-8975, www.crowcanyon.org, 9 A.M.–4:30 P.M. Mon.–Fri.), a nonprofit organization focusing on the long-term archaeological investigation of the earliest inhabitants of the Four Corners. The dusty buses parked at the entrance tell you this place isn't really for casual visits; most people come to participate in the center's long list of research and educational programs or to use the extensive research library. If you've ever wanted to try your hand at the nonlethal half of Indiana Jones's job, this is the place. You might even see something you uncover in a museum someday, since every artifact recovered is professionally curated. They organize trips across the Southwest and as far away as Greece, but also offer day programs in summer for a taste of Mesa Verde archaeology (Wednesday and Thursday June–Aug., $50 adults, $25 children). To get there, go half a mile north of

a junkyard near Cortez

© JULIAN SMITH

town on Highway 491, then take a left on Road L and two more lefts, following the signs for the center. Along the way you'll pass Indian Camp Ranch, "America's first archaeological subdivision," with more than 200 Anasazi sites in situ (not including the fake ruins at the gate).

Events
Late May brings the **Indian Arts and Western Culture Festival,** which spreads to Dolores, Mancos, Towaoc, and Mesa Verde National Park with close to a week of music, arts, crafts, and dancing. Highlights include the traditional Ute Mountain Ute Bear Dance and an Old Time Fiddlers' Contest in Mancos. The **Montezuma County Fair** arrives at Cortez in late July or early August.

Shopping
A large selection of high-quality native crafts fills the **Notah Dineh Trading Company and Museum** (345 W. Main St., 970/565-9607 or 800/444-2024, www.notahdineh.com), including pawned items and weaving supplies. Don't miss the museum downstairs, with its display cases full of old guns, scalps (really!), and beautiful weavings. The centerpiece is the largest Two Gray Hills rug known (12 by 18 feet), woven by Rachel Curly from 1957 to 1960, a year before the original Notah Dineh opened in the center of town. **Mesa Verde Pottery** (27601 Hwy. 160 E., 970/565-4492 or 800/441-9908, also has a large selection, and the **Clay Mesa Gallery** (29 E. Main St., 970/565-1902, www.claymesa .com) displays colorful pottery wall plates by local artists Rick St. John and Lesli Diane.

Accommodations
El Capri Motel (2110 S. Broadway, 970/565-3764 or 877/511-9859) offers very tidy lodgings for under $50. In the $50–100 category, choose from the **Tomahawk Lodge** (728 S. Broadway, 970/565-8521, fax 970/564-9793), the **Anasazi Motor Inn** (640 S. Broadway, 970/565-3773 or 800/972-6232, fax 970/565-1027, www.anasazimotorinn.com), or the **Budget Host Inn** (2040 E. Main St., 970/565-3738, fax 970/565-7623).

Ten miles west of town, in McElmo Canyon at the foot of Sleeping Ute Mountain, is a singular B&B called ☾ **Kelly Place** (970/565-3125 or 800/745-4885, kelly@kellyplace.com, www.kellyplace.com, $75–145). Guests can opt for guided excursions among more than two dozen archaeological sites on the 100-acre property. The lodge itself is an adobe building graced with roses, orchard, and a courtyard, with seven guest rooms, three private cabins with kitchenettes and private patios, and a two-bedroom apartment. Owners Rodney and Kristie Carriker have been in business for over two decades and love what they do.

The ☾ **Grizzly Roadhouse B&B** (3450 Hwy. 160 S., 970/565-7738 or 800/330-7286, info@grizzlyroadhouse.com, www.grizzlyroadhouse.com, $80–160) is more refined than its name might suggest. With two rooms in the main house or a two-bedroom private guest cottage decorated in Victorian style, this getaway is set on 30 acres about 10 miles south of Cortez. Hot-stone massages and blue-corn pancakes are both on the menu.

On the eastern edge of town is the **Cortez-Mesa Verde KOA Kampground** (27432 E. Hwy. 160, 970/565-9301). Tent sites start at $21 and full hookup sites at $26, with tepees going for $30 and cabins for $40. A heated pool and whirlpool are just a few of the amenities.

Food
Quotations about drinking and fools line the walls at the ☾ **Main Street Brewery** (21 E. Main St., 970/564-9112, dinner daily), including my favorite: "Avoid heart attacks—drink beer." They brew their own tasty Mesa Cerveza beers and serve steaks, pizzas, pasta, and burgers for $6–12. An Old-West theme pervades the **Homesteaders Restaurant** (45 E. Main St., 970/565-6253, lunch and dinner Mon.–Sat.), with old-fashioned favorites like liver-and-onions and chicken-fried steaks for $9–20. **Nero's Italian Restaurant** (303 W. Main St., 970/565-7366, dinner daily) puts a Southwest twist on Italian standbys, with entrées for $7–21.

For a step back to the era of beehive hairdos

and lawn flamingos, stop by the **Silver Bean** (410½ W. Main St., 970/946-4404), a drive-through coffee shop in a gleaming 1969 Air-stream International trailer. There are also a few seats inside, where they serve coffee drinks, Italian sodas, smoothies, and a few sandwiches and burritos from early morning to mid-after-noon Monday–Saturday.

Information and Transportation

Stop by the **Colorado Welcome Center** (928 E. Main St. at Mildred, 970/565-3414 or 800/253-1616, 8 A.M.–5 P.M. daily) by City Park, for information on local activities and events. You can also try **Mesa Verde Country Visitor Information** (800/253-1616, www.mesaverdecountry.com).

Great Lakes Airlines (800/554-5111, www.greatlakesav.com) connects the Cortez Municipal Airport (970/565-7458), southwest of town on Highway 160, with Denver. There are **Enterprise** (970/565-6824) and **Budget** (970/564-9012) car-rental offices at the airport.

NEAR CORTEZ
◖ Anasazi Heritage Center

Up in the foothills of the San Juan Moun-tains near Dolores, this excellent museum (970/882-5600, www.co.blm.gov/ahc/index .htm, 9 A.M.–5 P.M. daily Mar.–Oct., to 4 P.M. otherwise, $3 pp) covers all the native cultures of the region, particularly the Anasazi. From the parking lot, a half-mile paved interpretive trail leads uphill to the Escalante Ruins, the size of a modest modern house, with 360-de-gree views of the surrounding countryside. The smaller Dominguez Pueblo ruins are outside the museum itself: imagine four or five fami-lies crammed in these three rooms. More than three million artifacts and records are housed in the museum's research collection, along with hands-on exhibits, computer programs, and a replica of an ancient pit house. This is also the information center for the Canyons of the Ancients National Monument. To get there, turn off Highway 491 onto Highway 184 eight miles north of Cortez, or take Highway 145 north from the east end of town.

Canyons of the Ancients National Monument

The Heritage Center is also the starting point for trips to this monument (www.co.blm.gov/ canm/index.html), covering a ragged 164,000-

Take a break at the Silver Bean in Cortez.

acre chunk of BLM-managed land west of Cortez to the Utah border. Set aside in 2000, the monument protects one of the highest-known densities of archaeological sites in the United States-more than 20,000 all told—belonging to the Ansazi, Ute, and Navajo cultures. That works out to more than 100 per square mile in some cases. The largest and more easily accessible site is Lowry Pueblo, with 40 rooms, eight kivas, and a great kiva, which is along County Road CC nine miles west of Pleasant View, itself on Highway 491 about 20 miles north of Cortez. The huge Sand Canyon Pueblo, with 420 rooms, 90 kivas, and 14 towers, was estimated to hold more than 700 people at its peak. Stop by the Anasazi Heritage Center near Dolores for maps of accessible sites and information.

There's not as much to see here as you might think—most of it is being reburied to protect it after cataloguing—but the road there is a nice mountain bike ride, at least. Take Highway 491 south of Cortez a few miles to County Road G (McElmo Canyon Road), then go west 12 miles to the trailhead. From here, four miles of slickrock and dirt track lead past several cliff dwellings (the last mile is too rough to ride).

◖ Four Corners Monument

The only point in the United States where four states meet is a strange little spot in a blasted landscape, 30 miles from anywhere. The small park surrounding the monument (7 A.M.–8 P.M. daily Mar.–Aug., 8 A.M.–5 P.M. daily otherwise, $3 pp) is run by the Navajo Nation. All there is, really, is a granite-and-brass monument with a small platform from which to take a picture—a hand and foot in each state is popular—surrounded by a ring of vendor stands selling T-shirts, crafts, and food. Picnic tables and restrooms are also available. Cortez, Farmington, and Bluff are all about the same distance away.

Hovenweep National Monument

This remote, little-visited monument straddling the Utah-Colorado border preserves five Ancestral Puebloan villages spread across 20 miles. Astonishingly well-constructed towers balance on the rims of canyons and even on boulders, centuries after their original inhabitants mysteriously vanished.

Most of the structures here were built between A.D. 1200 and 1300 by groups closely associated with those at Mesa Verde (perhaps jealous country cousins?) and abandoned soon after. In addition to the square and circular towers, there are many D-shaped homes and kivas marked by such careful masonry that many structures have survived more or less intact for over 700 years. The classic Hovenweep ruin is a multistory pueblo at the head of a canyon with a perennial spring, and often includes water-control features such as dams to trap and redirect the precious summer rains into gardens. It's unsure what purpose the towers served. They may have been defensive fortifications, homes, storage structures, celestial observatories, or some combination of the above. The worn "Hovenweep" is a Paiute/Ute term that means "Deserted Valley," fittingly adopted by photographer William Henry Jackson in the late 19th century.

Start your tour at the **visitors center** (970/562-4282, www.nps.gov/hove, 8 A.M.– 5 P.M. daily, extended hours in summer, $7 per vehicle), where there is a campground for tents and small RVs ($10). The nearby **Square Tower Group** is the only set of structures accessible by paved road, and the largest collection of ruins in the monument. Close to 30 kivas and the striking three-story Square Tower itself are at the head of Little Ruin Canyon. As many as 500 people may have lived here. A moderately rough trail leads along the canyon rim.

Hovenweep's four outlying groups are accessed by dirt roads that aren't regularly maintained and may be impassible to low-clearance vehicles (and to anything in bad weather). The **Holly Group** includes the multistory Tilted Tower and Boulder House, another tower perched on a large boulder at the head of Keeley Canyon. The top floor of the latter fell when the boulder shifted centuries ago. Access the **Horseshoe Group** via the Canyon Rim Trail (one mile round-trip) to the Tower Point

© JULIAN SMITH

The Four Corners Monument is the only place in the United States where you can stand in four states at once.

Ruin and the four-unit Horseshoe House. Thanks to a perennial spring in Hackberry Canyon, as many as 350 inhabitants may have lived in the **Hackberry Group** a short hike east. Many kivas characterize the **Cutthroat Castle Group,** and a circular tower built on three boulders highlights the **Cajon Group** (ca-HONE).

In 2005 work began on **Goodman Point,** an archaeological site that encompasses seven Ancestral Puebloan communities on the state line. Set aside 17 years before Mesa Verde be- came a park, Goodman Point was ungrazed and is therefore incredibly well preserved. Contact the Crow Canyon Archaeological Center in Cortez for details.

Hovenweep is open year-round, and passes are good for a week. You can get there by taking County Road G (McElmo Canyon Road) west from Highway 491 at Pleasant View, north of Cortez, or via Highway 262, which leaves Highway 191 between Blanding and Bluff. (County Road G is dirt and may be impassible when wet.)

SOUTHEAST UTAH

Mention Southeast Utah to most people who have even heard of the place, and the words typically conjure images of RVs touring Arches National Park, mountain bikes on the Slickrock Trail, and maybe, if you're lucky, the raging white water in the canyons of the Colorado and Green rivers. True, this is the recreation epicenter of southern Utah's canyon country, centered on Moab and full of enough opportunities to hike, bike, raft, and drive through amazing scenery to fill the week or two most visitors can spare.

But there's much more to Southeast Utah than what's pictured on glossy brochures and slick websites. Snowcapped mountains tumbling into thousand-foot river canyons, hot-air balloons soaring over desert towers, and viewing points to make you weak in the knees are just a few of the other options in this land of extremes. The 12,000-foot peaks of the La Sal and Abajo mountains tower over two national parks, a national monument, and plenty of other countryside that could qualify as either. Backcountry trails lead to Anasazi ruins, natural bridges, and quiet towns perfectly spaced for the occasionally meal and hot shower.

About 35,000 people live in Grand County, San Juan County, and the southern half of Emery County, which together spread over 13,500 square miles. Residents are independent, conservative, and hardy, often descended from settlers, homesteaders, and ranchers who arrived when this area was almost completely isolated from the rest of the country—here that means well into the 20th century. Even though it's the poster child of Four Corners recreation,

HIGHLIGHTS

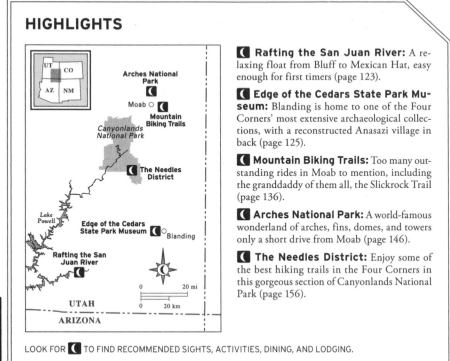

◖ **Rafting the San Juan River:** A relaxing float from Bluff to Mexican Hat, easy enough for first timers (page 123).

◖ **Edge of the Cedars State Park Museum:** Blanding is home to one of the Four Corners' most extensive archaeological collections, with a reconstructed Anasazi village in back (page 125).

◖ **Mountain Biking Trails:** Too many outstanding rides in Moab to mention, including the granddaddy of them all, the Slickrock Trail (page 136).

◖ **Arches National Park:** A world-famous wonderland of arches, fins, domes, and towers only a short drive from Moab (page 146).

◖ **The Needles District:** Enjoy some of the best hiking trails in the Four Corners in this gorgeous section of Canyonlands National Park (page 156).

LOOK FOR ◖ TO FIND RECOMMENDED SIGHTS, ACTIVITIES, DINING, AND LODGING.

Southeast Utah's remoteness and unforgiving landscape still keep much of it off the tourist radar.

PLANNING YOUR TIME

Southeast Utah is worth at least a week of travel time, especially given the long distances between towns and parks. Moab is the obvious hub, and merits a few days itself with its hiking and **mountain biking trails** and shopping and dining options. You can (and definitely should) see the highlights of **Arches National Park** in a day, and spend another at **Canyonlands National Park,** driving to see the views from the Island in the Sky or going on a hike in the Needles district.

If you have more time, take two or three days exploring south of Moab, stopping to see one of the Four Corners' most extensive archae-ological collections at the **Edge of the Cedars State Park Museum** in Blanding. Cedar Mesa is full of Anasazi ruins and rock art, as well as the impressive spans at Natural Bridges National Monument. For more outdoor fun, consider **rafting the San Juan River** from Bluff to Mexican Hat, an easy-enough expedition for first timers. The Green River from the city of Green River to Moab is another moderate overnight float trip.

Highway 191 is the transportation backbone of the region, with side branches at Monticello (Highway 491 east to Cortez, Colorado) and Blanding (Highway 95 northwest to Hanksville). At Mexican Hat, most travelers continue southwest on Highway 163 to Monument Valley on the Arizona border, but Highway 191 continues south across the Navajo Reservation from Bluff.

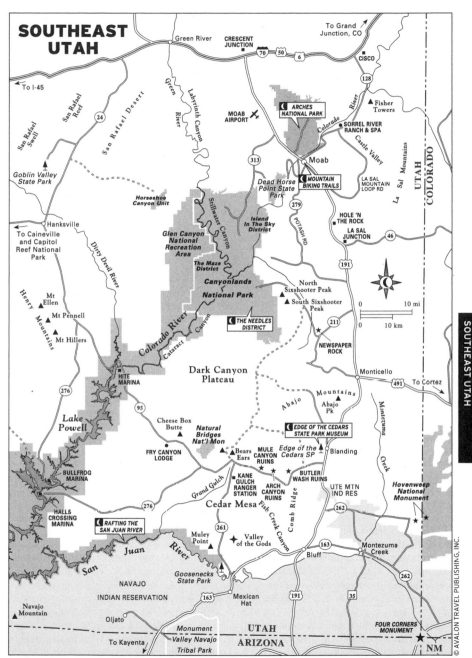

SOUTHEAST UTAH

© AVALON TRAVEL PUBLISHING, INC.

Mexican Hat to Moab

MEXICAN HAT

This tiny town on the San Juan River consists of little more than a few gas stations and hotels, even though it once swelled to as many as 1,000 people during various mining booms in the 20th century. As usual, however, the surrounding geology takes up the slack, from the distinctive rock formation that gives the town its name, standing to the south, to the vibrant patterns in the hillsides above and the black cockscomb of Alhambra Rock across the river.

Recreation

Explore the impressive landscapes around Mexican Hat on horseback with **Slim and Kody's Trail Rides** (435/683-2336), who also offer cookouts and camping for $125 per person for a full day ($75 half day).

Accommodations and Food

Nestled in the gorge of the San Juan River by the Highway 163 bridge, the **San Juan Inn** (435/683-2220 or 800/447-2022, fax 435/683-2210, www.sanjuaninn.net, $70 d Apr.–Oct., $50 Nov.–Mar.) has 37 rooms, including two with kitchens, as well as a small but respectable trading post. Their Olde Bridge Bar & Grill is decorated with Western antiques and has a pool table, a coffee bar, and Internet computers. Sandwiches, Navajo tacos, and burgers are $5, and steaks are $7 and up. They're open daily for dinner year-round, lunch in season, and breakfast only in winter.

Across the street from the Texaco Station, the **Mexican Hat Lodge** (435/683-2222, fax 435/683-2203, $65 d) offers 10 rooms with queen beds and an outdoor restaurant where you can enjoy a steak cooked by a cowboy on a swinging grill over a cedar-wood fire (platters are $9–27). Once the Top O Hat Bar, this place was bought in 1979 by Bobby and Vonnie Mueller, part of a traveling band who fell in love with the area and decided to stay. **Valle's RV Park** (435/683-2226, fax 435/683-2216)

has a dozen sites for $14 including all hookups. They also operate a vehicle shuttle service and storage for river trips, and serve pizzas, buffalo wings, and other quick bites in their convenience store starting at $5.

GOOSENECKS STATE PARK

Just north of Mexican Hat is the turnoff to the west for Highway 261, which climbs the Moki Dugway onto Cedar Mesa. A short side road leads to a small park (435/678-2238) overlooking a tortuous series of curves carved by the San Juan River a thousand feet into the desert. The Goosenecks are a textbook example of "entrenched meanders," which begin when a waterway winds across a relatively flat surface. As the landscape is lifted upwards the river cuts deeper and deeper, eventually becoming trapped in the meandering curves it cut long ago. Here the San Juan winds so tightly that it crams five river miles of curves into one mile of landscape. Facilities include four free primitive campsites, restrooms, and a picnic area.

VALLEY OF THE GODS

At the foot of the precipitous climb up Cedar Mesa, another side road heads east into this Monument Valley in miniature. Hundreds of rock formations jut skyward in the mesa's shadow. The 17-mile dirt road is good enough for cars, but impassable when wet, and eventually reconnects to Highway 163 northeast of Mexican Hat. Along the way you'll pass the **(Valley of the Gods Bed & Breakfast** (970/749-1164, www.valleyofthegods.cjb.net, $120–130), with three rooms in a snug stone 1930s ranch house, more lodging in a two-story converted root cellar next door, and the best porch for hundreds of miles.

BLUFF

Founded in 1880 on the banks of the San Juan River by the exhausted Hole-in-the-Rock expedition, this anomalously liberal enclave is on its way to becoming a sleepier alternative to Moab.

Bluff's tiny size (pop. 400) and dramatic setting gives it one of the highest per-capita populations of archaeologists, naturalists, and artists in the United States. Restored pioneer homes made from buff-colored sandstone stand along dusty streets lined with huge cottonwoods, and crazy formations with names like Locomotive Rock loom above. The **pioneer cemetery** on a hill overlooking the town pays tribute to Bluff's determined settlers. It's next to an ongoing archaeological excavation thought to be a Great House outlier of Chaco Canyon, built by the Anasazi.

Events

The **Bluff Balloon Festival** held the third weekend in January brings dozens of hot-air balloons to the red rock country. They lift off from the Valley of the Gods near Mexican Hat, adding splashes of color to an already-vivid palette. The **Utah Navajo Fair** in late August or early September includes tradition song and dance, crafts, food, and more rodeo action. Writers, artists, and musicians gather in mid-October for the **Bluff Arts Fair.**

Shopping

At the foot of the Navajo Twins, an distinctive pair of stone formations on the edge of town, sits the **Twin Rocks Trading Post** (913 E. Navajo Dr., 435/672-2341 or 800/526-3448, www.twinrocks.com), with one of the best selections of native arts in Southeast Utah. The wide stone building with two cigar-store Indians out front holds plenty of high-quality merchandise, including baskets, knives with inlaid handles, rugs, jewelry, and carvings. A short hop away on Highway 191 is the timeworn **Cow Canyon Trading Post** (435/672-2208), fairly reeking of history from the antique cars out front to the low ceilings and exposed brickwork inside. Built with stones from an old Mormon house in the 1880s, it operated as a trading post in the mid-20th century. They try to be open daily 9 A.M.–5 P.M., and their eclectic collection of souvenirs, art, and books includes lots of pottery and brightly painted wooden representations of Navajo sandpaintings.

Recreation

The highly recommended **Far Out Expeditions** (7th and Mulberry, 435/672-2294, www.faroutexpeditions.com, tours@faroutexpeditions.com, $65 d) offer hikes, backpack trips, and vehicle supported–trips to view rock art and ruins throughout the area, including Monument Valley. Half-day tours with Vaughn and Marcia Hadenfeldt start at $85 per person, and customized day tours are $150 per person (two-person minimum). They also offer vehicle shuttles, cookouts, and a guesthouse in a historic home with a kitchen, living room, and two porches.

Wild River Expeditions (101 Main St., 435/672-2200 or 800/422-7654, fax 435/672-2365, www.riversandruins.com) have been running nearby rivers since 1957. Their trips down the San Juan and the Colorado from one to eight days for $125–1,500 per person. **Buckhorn Llama** (970/667-7411, www.llamapack.com, buckhorn@llamapack.com) organizes llama pack trips into the backcountry of southeast Utah and Colorado's San Juan Mountains. Guided trips are $200–300 per person per day, but if you'd rather do it on your own, they also rent the temperamental camelids to carry your packs for $40–50, including a mandatory getting-to-know-your-llama session. Explore the area on a more familiar animal with **Cottonwood Creek Cowboy Tours** (435/672-2321, rinawhipple@yahoo.com, www.luckyw.com), who have trips ranging from two-hour rides ($60 pp) to overnight trips to Mexican Hat and the Valley of the Gods ($300 pp per day). At the right time of year they can take you to the wild-horse roundup on the Navajo Nation, where untamed range horses are gathered up and branded.

◖ Rafting the San Juan River

A popular, three-day raft trip down the San Juan River starts three miles west of Bluff on Highway 191 at the Sand Island Recreation Area. Primitive camping is available here for $6, and there's an impressive panel of pictographs on a rock wall, including geometric shapes, humanoid figures with three-tiered headdresses, and one half-ram, half-Kokopelli figure brandishing a flute.

The modestly challenging float to Mexican Hat passes through Class III rapids and the famous Goosenecks of the San Juan with lots of rock art and ruins en route. Another five or so days will bring you to Clay Hills Crossing just above Lake Powell, the only viable takeout below Mexican Hat (there's a 30-foot waterfall just downstream). You'll need a Bureau of Land Management (BLM) permit to launch, and mandatory campsites are assigned downstream of Mexican Hat. Contact the Monticello BLM office (435/587-1500) for more details, and pick up a copy of the booklet "Running the San Juan River from San Island to Clay Hills Crossing" from the Canyonlands Natural History Association.

Accommodations

For a motel room around $50, try the **Kokopelli Inn** (435/672-2322 or 800/541-8854, fax 435/672-2385, office@kokoinn.com, www.kokoinn.com) on Main Street (Highway 191) as it passes through town. The **Recapture Lodge** (250 Main St., 435/672-2281, fax 435/672-2284, recapturelodge@hubwest.com, www.bluffutah.org/recapturelodge, $50–60) is a comfy place with a pool, hot tub, and nightly slide shows on the area.

Navajo rugs and art decorate the **(Calf Canyon B&B** (700 E. at Black Locust, 435/672-2470 or 888/922-2470, hosts@calfcanyon.com, www.calfcanyon.com, $80–100), which has three rooms and a shady patio. Breakfast is also included with a room at the **(Decker House Inn** (189 N. 3rd St. E., 435/672-2304 or 888/637-2582, www.deckerhouseinn.com, deckerhouse@frontiernet.net, $50–100). An 1898 pioneer home in Bluff's historic district, the Decker House has five rooms with one to three bedrooms each, kitchenettes, and plenty of space to relax outside. Local artwork adorns the inside.

You can't miss the relatively new **Desert Rose Inn & Cabins** (701 W. Main St., 435/672-2303 or 888/475-7673, fax 435/672-2217, information@desertroseinn.com, www.de-sertroseinn.com, $64–86), a three-story log building on the western edge of town. The 30-room place also has six executive cabins for rent ($84–94). In addition to the Sand Island Recreation Area along the river, you can also camp at the **Cadillac Ranch RV Park** (435/672-2262, $18) or the **Cottonwood RV Park** (435/672-2287, $10–18), both on Highway 191.

Food

Cowboy-style grilled steaks and catfish ($16–20) are served outdoors at the **Cottonwood Steakhouse** (Main St. and 4th W., 435/672-2282, from 6 P.M. daily Apr.–Nov.) You can eat out on the porch of the **Twin Rocks Cafe** (913 E. Navajo Twins Dr., 435/672-2341, all meals daily) next to the trading post of the same name. On the menu are pit BBQ and mesquite-smoked chicken ($7–8) as well as vegetarian fare and microbrewed beers.

At one end of Bluff's historic loop on the east end of town, the **(Cow Canyon Trading Post and Restaurant** (435/672-2208) serves up gourmet Southwest fare with fresh local produce so popular that reservations are often necessary. The dining room is in a glassed-in porch out back of the trading post, looking over green fields on the banks of the San Juan River. You can browse the wares while waiting for your entrée ($8–12), served for dinner April–November.

BLANDING

The largest town in Utah's largest county (San Juan) still only counts about 3,200 residents. Set on White Mesa at the southern edge of rolling plains of sagebrush, Blanding has three museums and one end of Highway 95, the "Trail of the Ancients," appropriate given its location in the middle of the ancient territory of the Anasazi. It's also a strongly conservative town where alcohol is forbidden.

Archaeological excavations show that the Anasazi occupied this area between A.D. 600 and 1200. Later, the Navajo named the location after the abundant sagebrush that rolls into piñon and juniper at the base of Blue Mountain. First known as Grayson, the set-

No, it's not abandoned; in fact, reservations are often required at Cow Canyon Trading Post.

tlement was renamed under somewhat unusual circumstances. In 1914, a wealthy Easterner named Thomas Bicknell offered a thousand-book library to any town in Utah that would take his name. In the ensuing scramble, Grayson came in neck and neck with Thurber, near what is now Capitol Reef National Park. Thurber became Bicknell, Grayson adopted his wife's maiden name of Blanding, and the towns split the books.

In 1923, an abortive uprising by a forlorn group of Utes on the edge of town brought Blanding briefly into the national spotlight as the site of the "Posey War," billed-debatably—as the last Native American uprising in the United States.

(Edge of the Cedars State Park Museum

Displays on the Anasazi, Navajo, and Utes fill this outstanding museum (660 W. 400 N., 435/678-2238, www.stateparks.utah.gov/park_pages/edge.htm, 8 A.M.–7 P.M. daily, 9 A.M.–5 P.M. in winter, $2 pp), which serves as the regional archaeological repository for all

of Southeast Utah. The extensive collection includes hundreds of everyday objects from sandals to pottery. Many of the artifacts, including much of the extensive pottery collection, were found by locals in pot-hunting excursions in nearby canyons. Don't miss the vibrant parrot-feather decoration on the second floor. A partly excavated Anasazi pueblo stands out back.

Dinosaur Museum

Delve even further into the past at the Dinosaur Museum (754 S. 200 W., 435/678-3454, www.dinosaur-museum.org, 9 A.M.–5 P.M. Mon.–Sat. Apr.–Oct., 8 A.M.–8 P.M. June–Aug., $2 pp), a cavernous building filled with the bones, eggs, tracks and even fossilized skin of creatures like the Allosaurus, Utah's official state fossil. The museum also houses dinosaur sculptures, exhibits on the latest research, a 360-pound meteorite, and a great collection of posters from old Hollywood dinosaur movies like *The Beast of Hollow Mountain* and *The Valley of Gwangi.*

Shopping

The **Purple Sage Trading Post** (790 S. Main

St., 435/678-3620 or 877/853-6149, www.purplesagetradingpost.com) stocks a wide range of native crafts including Navajo sandpantings, rugs, pottery, jewelry, and kachinas. You can browse the collection at their website.

Accommodations

All of Blanding's lodgings have rooms for less than $100. The **Rogers House Bed & Breakfast Inn** (412 S. Main St., 435/678-3932 or 800/355-3932, fax 435/678-3276, hosts@rogershouse.com, www.rogershouse.com, $70–90), dates to 1915, with a large front porch and antique furniture.

Chain motels include the **Best Western Gateway Inn** (88 E. Center St., 435/678-2278, fax 435/678-2240) and the **Comfort Inn** (711 S. Main St., 435/678-3271 or 800/622-3250, fax 435/678-3219). Slightly less expensive are the **Four Corners Inn** (131 E. Center St., 435/678-3257, fax 435/678-3186, www.fourcornersinn.com) and the **Prospector Motor Lodge** (591 S. Main St., 435/678-3231).

Food

Choices reflect the town's name—this isn't a stop for gourmands. "Home-style family dining" is the name of the game at the **Old Tymer Restaurant** (733 S. Main St., 435/678-2122, all meals daily), serving mostly Mexican and steaks next to the Comfort Inn. There's also the **Homestead Steak House** (121 E. Center St., 435/678-3456), serving up Navajo tacos, pizza, BBQ ribs, fried ice cream, and homemade pies.

Information

The Blanding Chamber of Commerce runs a **visitors center** (435/678-3662, info@blandingutah.org, www.blandingutah.org, 8 A.M.–8 P.M. Mon.–Sat. in season) on Highway 191 at the north end of town.

HIGHWAY 95: TRAIL OF THE ANCIENTS

Heading west from Highway 191 just south of Blanding, Highway 95 crosses some of the more scenic backcountry in southern Utah. Built in 1946 but unpaved until 1976, the "Bicentennial Highway" came with its share of controversy over opening up beautiful but remote Cedar Mesa to the general, non-four-wheel-drive public. (This road was one target of the environmental saboteurs in Edward Abbey's *The Monkey Wrench Gang*.) The area is particularly rich in archaeology, and is one of the easiest routes in the Four Corners to access dozens of canyons filled with ruins and rock art. Mileposts are measured west to east from I-15.

Between mileposts 111 and 112 is a trailhead for a short, moderate hike over dirt and slickrock to **Butler Wash,** where a well-preserved pueblo with four kivas (one of which is, unusually, square) is visible from an overlook. Look for a hand-and-foot trail chipped into the rock to the left of the alcove. West of that is the unmistakable barrier of **Comb Ridge,** a monocline that slashes 80 miles from north to south in an 800-foot jagged wall like the ramparts of an enormous castle. The road crosses the ridge via a gash dynamited through the sheer stone face, to the horror of environmentalists. There's an overlook between mileposts 108 and 109.

A few miles farther, between mileposts 107 and 108, is the turnoff for **Arch Canyon,** where day hikers can find an Anasazi ruin just past the canyon mouth. The entire canyon is good for two or three days' worth of exploration, with plenty of ruins, arches, and side canyons. Another six miles west on Highway 95 brings you to **Mule Canyon,** where a 12-room dwelling, a kiva, and a two-story circular tower have been excavated and stabilized by the BLM. These structures are all linked by tunnels and were occupied during the Pueblo I–Pueblo III periods. Two miles southeast down the canyon are the **Cave Towers,** with half a dozen towers and several cliff dwellings.

Hiking on Cedar Mesa

Connecting Highway 95 with Highway 191, this road heads out across Cedar Mesa proper, providing access to some of the region's most popular overnight hiking loops, before literally dropping of the edge. Five miles south of Highway 95 is the **Kane Gulch Ranger Station,** starting point for the 23-mile loop hike into **Grand Gulch.** Anasazi aficionados know this loop as one of the easiest and prettiest ways to access a treasure trove of ruins and rock art (although all these canyons off Highway 261 can boast some). The usual 2–3-day hike connects Kane Gulch with Bullet Canyon, and has become so popular that the BLM has instituted a mandatory permit system ($2 pp for day hikers, $8 pp overnight) for trips March–October. The same permit regulations apply to all overnight canyon hikes on Cedar Mesa off Highway 261. Contact the BLM's Monticello Field Office (435/587-1500, www.blm.gov/utah/monticello) for details.

Another loop connects **Owl** and **Fish Creek canyons** to the east of Highway 261. This sees less traffic than Grand Gulch, and is most often done clockwise, starting down Owl Creek Canyon first. The 15-mile hike takes 2–3 days. **Slickhorn Canyon,** 11 miles down Highway 261 from the ranger station, is an-other popular hike, descending 500 feet in 12 miles to the San Juan River to the west. The upper section of **Johns Canyon,** whose trailhead is seven miles north of the Moki Dugway, makes a good day hike with some moderate scrambling involved.

About 23 miles south of Highway 95, Highway 261 gives up the ghost and plunges off the sheer edge of Cedar Mesa in an astounding display of road-building determination known as the **Moki Dugway.** A series of white-knuckled, guardrail-deficient gravel curves descend 1,100 feet in three miles to the Valley of the Gods and the town of Mexican Hat. At the top of the dugway, take a detour down a good dirt road five miles to the west to **Muley Point Overlook,** a stunning view off the edge of the plateau as far as the Goosenecks of the San Juan and Monument Valley. Camping up here for sunset and sunrise is an unforgettable experience.

Natural Bridges National Monument

Back on Highway 95, near the distinctive

Anasazi ruins in Johns Canyon on Cedar Mesa

double peaks know as the **Bears Ears,** are three huge sandstone bridges spanning White Canyon. The monument (435/692-1234, www.nps.gov/nabr, 8 A.M.–5 P.M. daily, $3 pp, $6 per vehicle) also protects many prehistoric cliff dwellings and storage rooms built by the Anasazi. Sipapu, Kachina, and Owachomo bridges were formed when the river changed course and cut across tight bends, eventually tunneling through the fins of rock.

Originally called "President," "Senator," and "Congressman" by prospector Cass Hite in the 1880s, the bridges were briefly renamed "Augusta," "Caroline," and "Edwin" before being re-renamed with native terms. The area was set aside by President Theodore Roosevelt in 1908, four years after *National Geographic* magazine sponsored an expedition here, making it the oldest National Park Service (NPS) unit in the state. The solar array that powers the Park Service facilities—the largest in the world when it was built in 1980—produces up to 50 kilowatts.

You can see each bridge from the overlook drive, and short, steep trails (connected by an 8.5-mile loop) lead to the base of each bridge. The 13-site campground is $10 per night. (A passport to the Southeast Utah Group costs $25 and gives access to Natural Bridges, Arches National Park, Canyonlands National Park, and Hovenweep National Monument for a year).

Dark Canyon Primitive Area

This large, rugged canyon system is one of the wildest and least-explored in the state, even though it's just south of Canyonlands National Park. It takes a multiday trip to do it justice, but if you have the time and determination, you'll be rewarded with thousand-foot-deep gorges spilling from the western slope of the Abajo Mountains all the way to the Colorado River. The lower canyon is hikeable year-round, and water is available throughout (though only intermittently in the upper reaches).

The most direct access is via an unpaved road that heads north from the entrance road to Natural Bridges National Monument

through the 8,500-foot pass between the Bears Ears. Park at the corral shortly thereafter. From here you can descend either Woodenshoe or Peavine canyons, which spill west from Elk Ridge at 8,200 feet in the Manti-La Sal National Forest. Ponderosa pine and Douglas fir grace the wide canyons, which are both contained within a 46,000-acre wilderness area. As you descend you enter BLM land and the canyons become progressively narrower and deeper. The entire canyon is about 30 miles long, and takes three to four days to descend to the uppermost reaches of Lake Powell upstream from Hite. For more information, contact the Forest Service (435/587-2041) or BLM (435/587-1500, www.blm.gov/utah/monticello) offices in Monticello.

West of Natural Bridges

From Natural Bridges National Monument, Highway 95 follows White Canyon west to Lake Powell. The dark-red Organ Rock Shale layer on top of the lighter Cedar Mesa Sandstone contrasts wonderfully with the vibrant green of pine trees. At milepost 75 is **Cheese Box Butte,** which looks like, well, a cheese box. A cairned trail at the end of a short dirt track leads down into White Canyon, which you can cross to ascend **Cheese Box Canyon** and its narrows just a few miles up.

Just west of Cheese Box Butte is the **Fry Canyon Lodge** (435/259-5224, lodge@frycanyon.com, www.frycanyon.com) which bills itself as the "Utah's Most Remote Desert Lodge" but was closed for renovations in 2005. It's hard to imagine a more isolated hotel than this place, established in 1955 as a mining supply center. It served as a post office and school before being transformed into a cozy getaway, and is still the only building on Highway 95 between Blanding and Hanksville.

The next major stop along Highway 95 is **Hite Marina** (435/684-2457) on the upper reaches of Lake Powell near two bridges over what were once the Colorado and Dirty Devil rivers. Before Glen Canyon Dam was built, this was the best natural crossing upriver of Lees Ferry. Prospector Cass Hite dubbed it "Dandy

Crossing" in the 1880s about the time he discovered gold nearby and opened the only post office in Glen Canyon. Here in the northernmost Glen Canyon National Recreation Area the scenery becomes an eye-popping spectacle of red, orange, and white mesas, buttes, and spires sandwiched between the waters of the lake and the gray ramparts of the Henry Mountains. A ranger station, grocery store, boat rentals, a launching ramp, and a primitive campground ($6 per vehicle per night) are available. (As of 2005, low water levels made launching boats here inadvisable.) West of the rivers is a viewing point over the biblical landscape.

About 15 miles west of Hite is the **Hog Springs picnic area** amid red-walled canyons where you should keep an eye out for petroglyphs and pictographs. It's only a few more miles to the junction of Highway 276 at the base of the Henry Mountains, which leads south to Bullfrog Marina and Halls Crossing on Lake Powell. Highway 95 heads north across the Burr Desert to join Highway 24 at Hanksville.

Henry Mountains

The last mountain range to be named in the lower 48 states, the Henrys thrust 2,000 feet from the canyon country. Mount Ellen (11,615 feet) is the highest of three peaks over 10,000 feet, and the northernmost summit in the relatively small range. John Wesley Powell named the range in 1871 after Joseph Henry, his friend at the helm of the Smithsonian Institution, and assigned geologist Grove Karl Gilbert to study their geology. Out of this came Gilbert's classic "Report on the Geology of the Henry Mountains" (1877), which identified the range as laccolithic and made the peaks familiar to geologists worldwide. Near the turn of the 20th century outlaws hid among the mountain among ranches grazing cows, sheep, and goats. Overgrazing still scars the hillsides, which are now home to a herd of about 200 buffalo. One of the few free-roaming herds in the country, these are descended from 18 released in 1941. The Utah Department of Wildlife Resources

manages the herd and organizes a yearly hunt. Rusting equipment and abandoned mine shafts are all that remain of the uranium boom of the 1950s.

The views from the mountains, needless to say, are inspiring, from the tilted layers of the Waterpocket Fold and the Pink Cliffs to the canyons surrounding Lake Powell and the La Sal Mountains. The Bull Creek Pass Backcountry Byway is one way to access viewing points like Burr Point and Angel's Point over the Dirty Devil River. A four-mile trail leads from Bull Creek Pass to the summit of Mt. Ellen. The BLM maintains three campgrounds: Starr Springs, McMillan Springs, and Lonesome Beaver, which is near the Dandelion Flat picnic area. For more information, contact the BLM's Henry Mountains Field Station in Hanksville (435/542-3461).

MONTICELLO

Moab's quiet cousin sits at the foot of the Abajo Mountains, also called the Blue Mountains. Monticello (pop. 2,000), the San Juan County seat, was founded in 1888 near springs known to travelers for centuries. Although it took the name of Thomas Jefferson's Virginia country retreat, here it's pronounced "Mon-ti-SELL-o." It's the closest town to the entrance to the Needles district of Canyonlands National Park, and well placed at the foot of the Abajo Mountains for those in search of activities uphill.

Events

In March the **Blue Mountain Canyonlands Triathlon** comes to town, and July brings the **Blue Mountain Bike Chase** and **Pioneer Days** with parades, games, and food. In August the **San Juan County Fair & Rodeo** arrives in a cloud of dust with various livestock-centered events, dances, and agricultural exhibits.

Recreation

Monticello's nonprofit **Four Corners School of Outdoor Education** (800/525-4456, fcs@fourcornersschool.org, www.fourcornersschool.org) has been running "ed-ventures" (www.sw-adventures.org) throughout the

SOUTHEAST UTAH

Southwest since 1984. Rafting, hiking, and backpacking trips to Lake Powell, Chaco Canyon, the Grand Canyon, and Yellowstone all have a strong conservation bent. The list also includes family tours, llama treks, women-only trips, and explorations of native culture, rock art, and geology. Prices and itineraries vary, but the guides are always top-notch.

Accommodations

The nicest place to stay in town is the **Grist Mill Inn** (64 S. 300 E., 435/587-2597 or 800/645-3762, fax 435/587-2497, reservations@thegristmillinn.com, www.thegristmillinn.com). The B&B occupies the 1933 Monticello Flour Mill, which was used until the mid-1960s. Rooms ($55–75) are full of antiques, and there's a library and a fireplace in the sitting room. A full country breakfast is included in the price. Chain motels include the **Best Western Wayside Inn** (173 E. Central St., 435/587-2261, fax 435/587-2920, $55–75) and a **Days Inn** (549 N. Main St., 435/587-2458, fax 435/587-2191, $60–95), both of which have heated pools. The **Triangle H Motel** (164 E. Hwy. 491, 435/587-2274, fax 435/587-2175) has rooms for under $50.

Campsites at the **Bar-TN RV Park** (348 S. Main St., 435/587-1005 or 866/587-1005, www.bar-tn.com, info@bar-tn.com) run $18 for full hookups and $12 for tents, and they also have cabins for $30 with cable TV. If they're full try the **Mountain View RV Park** (632 N. Main St., 435/587-2974, $12–18). Three **Forest Service campgrounds** can be found in the Abajo Mountains near Monticello: Dalton Springs and Buckboard are both west of town, and Devils Canyon is south off of Highway 191. These sites are open from spring to fall for $4–8 per site per night; call the local Forest Service ranger district (435/587-2041) for more information, or reserve them by calling 877/444-6770.

Food

The "cowboy gourmet" cooking at the **MD Ranch Cookhouse** (380 S. Main St., 435/587-3299) starts with a Buffalo Breakfast of chicken-fried buffalo steak and eggs, and goes from there. Lunch sandwiches are around $5 and dinner entrées are $8 and up. The Western theme continues into the gift stop, art gallery, and antique museum, and live music on weekend evenings. It's open daily in season for lunch and dinner. Inexpensive subs and salads can be found at **Wagon Wheel Pizza** (164 S. Main St., 435/587-2766), and the **Lamplight Restaurant** (655 E. Central, 435/587-2170) serves family-style meals including prime rib and seafood for lunch and dinner daily. (Prices are comparable to the MD Ranch Cookhouse.)

Information and Transportation

The **San Juan County Multi-Agency Visitor Center** (117 S. Main St., 435/587-3235 or 800/574-4386, info@southeastutah.com, www.southeastutah.com, 8 A.M.–5 P.M. Mon.–Fri., 10 A.M.–5 P.M. Sat. and Sun. Apr.–Oct., 9 A.M.–5 P.M. Mon.–Fri. otherwise) is in the San Juan County Administrative Building.

Bighorn Express (801/746-2417 or 888/655-7433, www.bighornexpress.com) runs a shuttle bus to and from Salt Lake City via Price, Green River, and Moab. The trip takes 5.5 hours and costs $60 per person each way from Salt Lake City to Monticello. It runs daily in season; Wednesday, Friday, and Sunday only in January and February.

ABAJO MOUNTAINS

The Abajo Mountains were named with the Spanish word for "below" when early Spanish explorers gazed down on them from the higher La Sals to the north. Peaking at 11,362-foot Abajo Peak, this small laccolithic range was formed by an underground magma bulge like the La Sals and Navajo Mountain. Aspens, firs, pines trees, and alpine lakes are the perfect respite from the desert's summer heat. (Look for the shape of a horse's head formed by the trees towards the north end of the range when seen from Monticello.) A 22-mile paved road connects Monticello with Highway 211 to the Needles, crossing the northeast flank of the range.

Moab and Vicinity

After wandering for 40 years in the wilderness, the Israelites rested in the biblical kingdom of Moab before finally entering the Promised Land. The similarities to the modern seat of Grand County are uncanny: set in a narrow, verdant valley where the Colorado River slices between thousand-foot walls of rock, Moab is surrounded by enough stunning scenery that the Mormons' choice of a name ("beautiful land" in Hebrew) makes perfect sense. The undisputed tourist epicenter of canyon country has gone through more transformations than many cities 10 times its size, and exerts a force on southern Utah and the consciousness of the country—at least the outdoor-loving part—far out of proportion to its population of just under 5,000.

Moab is a diverse community for southern Utah, with Spandex-clad mountain bikers and overall-ed cowboys rubbing elbows with European tourists and frat boys from Boulder. Although still mostly Mormon, Moab has a steadily growing liberal spirit that keeps alive the spirit of Edward Abbey, who penned the classic *Desert Solitaire* after a few seasons as a ranger in Arches in the 1960s. You can stop by Dave's Corner Market on the way to your morning loop on the Slickrock Trail and grab a coffee brewed by mayor Dave Sakrison. Dozens of films have been shot in the immediate environs, from the classic (*Wagon Master* and *Cheyenne Autumn*) to the not-so-classic (*Warlock,* anyone?).

HISTORY

Spanish Valley was formed when a thick layer of underground salt dissolved, causing the valley floor to sink. Native groups from the Anasazi and Fremont to the Sabuagana Utes lived here for the relatively mild climate, riverside soils, and shallow ford of the Colorado River. A Spanish expedition led by Juan Maria Antonio de Rivera arrived in 1765 from New Mexico, and things picked up in 1830 when the blazers of the Spanish Trail between Santa Fe and Los Angeles first took advantage of the easy river crossing.

Mormon settlers came to stay in 1878 after a previous group of missionaries had been run off by native tribes. The biblical name of Moab was adopted two years later. The town site, on the south bank of the river near the foot of the La Sal Mountains, saw its first ferry begin operating in 1885. A modest economy at the turn of the 20th century was based on ranching, farming, and the growing of fruit such as grapes, apples, and peaches. The first bridge spanned the river in 1912, but traffic was sparse.

The Cold War ushered in the town's first economic boom. The sudden demand for uranium brought hundreds of prospectors to comb the hills with jeeps and Geiger counters. Charlie Steen's 1952 discovery of the multi-million-dollar La Vida mine, in the Lisbon Valley southeast of town, proved that there actually were fortunes to be made. Moab's population more than tripled from 1950 to 1960, and almost overnight a sleepy farming community became known as "The Uranium Capital of the World."

A smaller oil boom lasted into the 1960s, but Moab would have to wait another few decades for its next revolution. It was already obvious that Moab was rich in the natural beauty department: Arches National Monument had been set aside in 1929 (and made a park in 1971), Canyonlands National Park had been declared in 1964, and river-running was a tourism staple by the early 1970s. In the 1980s, word started to get out that the slickrock landscape, so beloved by local motorcyclists and jeep drivers, was perfectly suited to a brand-new sport called mountain biking. Knobby tires stuck to the smooth sandstone like glue, and the endless hills, dips, bowls, and mountain trails were soon recognized as some of the best and most challenging off-road biking terrain in the world.

Thus Moab was reborn once again as one of the prime tourist destinations in the Southwest,

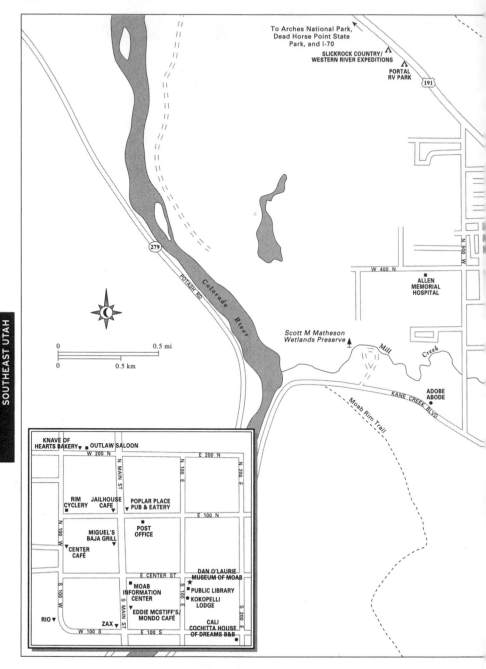

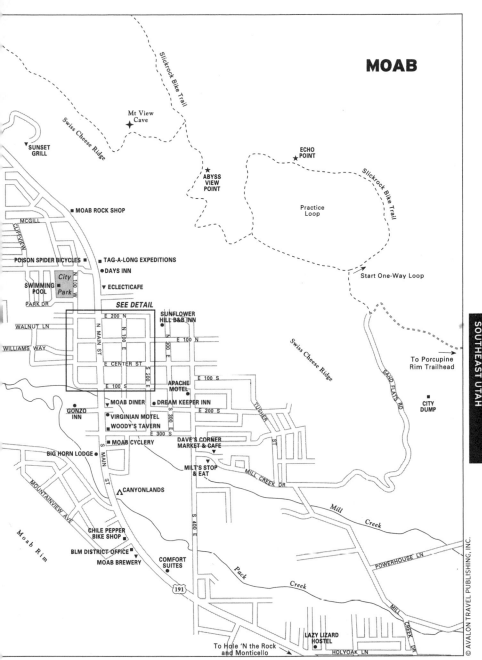

MOAB

Slickrock Bike Trail

Mt View Cave

Swiss Cheese Ridge

▼ SUNSET GRILL

ECHO POINT ★

★ ABYSS VIEW POINT

Slickrock Bike Trail

Practice Loop

■ MOAB ROCK SHOP

MCGILL

CLIFFVIEW

■ POISON SPIDER BICYCLES ■   ■ TAG-A-LONG EXPEDITIONS
● DAYS INN

City Park
SWIMMING POOL ■
N 100 W
▼ ECLECTICAFE

PARK DR

Start One-Way Loop

SEE DETAIL

E 200 N
WALNUT LN
N MAIN ST   N 100 E   E 100 N
WILLIAMS WAY
E CENTER ST
300 E
S 200 E
E 100 S

SUNFLOWER HILL B&B INN ●

Swiss Cheese Ridge

SAND FLATS RD

To Porcupine Rim Trailhead →

APACHE MOTEL
E 100 S   E 200 S

GONZO INN ●   ■ MOAB DINER ● DREAM KEEPER INN
● VIRGINIAN MOTEL
■ WOODY'S TAVERN
S 300 E
TUSHER   ST

■ CITY DUMP

E 300 S
DAVE'S CORNER MARKET & CAFE
■ MOAB CYCLERY

● BIG HORN LODGE ●
S MAIN ST
▼ MILT'S STOP & EAT
MILL CREEK DR

Mill   Creek

∧ CANYONLANDS

MOUNTAINVIEW AVE
S 400 E

Moab Rim

CHILE PEPPER BIKE SHOP ■
BLM DISTRICT OFFICE ■
MOAB BREWERY ▼
COMFORT SUITES ●

POWERHOUSE LN

191

Pack   Creek

To Hole 'N the Rock and Monticello

LAZY LIZARD HOSTEL ●
HOLYOAK LN

MILL CREEK DR

set smack in the middle of an outdoor adventurer's nirvana. Thousands of visitors throng the streets on weekends in the spring and fall, particularly during festivals celebrating mountain biking or four-wheel-drive vehicles. Drawn by famous parks and adrenaline sports, visitors arrive from around the world and just next door; they say you can tell spring has arrived when all the license plates in town turn Colorado green. T-shirt and trinket shops along the town's short Main Street are packed from spring through fall and Main Street is clogged with mountain bikers and 4WD vehicles jacked over head height. In the heat of summer many visitors head up into the La Sals, which tower over town to the east, or onto the Colorado River.

SIGHTS

For a break from the desert, visit the **Scott M. Matheson Wetlands Preserve** (435/259-4629, daily sunrise–sunset, free) which protects 875 acres of marsh between Moab and the Colorado River. Birding is especially good here from spring to fall; more than 180 species have been seen. It's administered by the local office of The Nature Conservancy. Free guided nature walks leave from the main entrance at 8 A.M. on Saturday mornings March–October. The preserve is 0.75 mile down Kane Creek Boulevard from the McDonalds on Main Street.

Another way to escape the heat is **Butch Cassidy's King World Water Park** (435/259-2837, 11:30 A.M.–7 P.M. Tues.–Sat. May–Aug., $11.50 adults, $9.50 children; 1–6 P.M. Sun. and Mon., $10/8), whose entrance is north on Highway 191 almost to the Colorado River bridge. It fills a secluded box canyon, supposedly used by Butch Cassidy's Wild Bunch to hide rustled cattle, with five waterslides, three pools, and a host of other facilities. Also on the premises is a 40-ton boulder carved with strange pictures by an eccentric European immigrant in the early 1930s.

Moab's history gets a good workout at the **Dan O'Laurie Museum of Moab** (118 E. Center St., 435/259-7985, 10 A.M.–6 P.M. Mon.–Fri., noon–6 P.M. Sat. and Sun.). Exhibits on geology, paleontology, and the

MOAB CLIMATE

MONTH	AVG. HIGH	AVG. LOW	MEAN	AVG. PRECIP.
Jan.	43°F	20°F	32°F	0.67 in.
Feb.	53°F	26°F	39°F	0.50 in.
Mar.	64°F	35°F	50°F	0.90 in.
Apr.	73°F	42°F	58°F	0.99 in.
May	84°F	50°F	67°F	0.81 in.
June	95°F	58°F	76°F	0.37 in.
July	101°F	64°F	82°F	0.91 in.
Aug.	98°F	63°F	81°F	0.83 in.
Sept.	89°F	53°F	71°F	0.75 in.
Oct.	75°F	41°F	58°F	1.26 in.
Nov.	57°F	30°F	43°F	0.77 in.
Dec.	46°F	21°F	34°F	0.63 in.

town's human history include dinosaur bones and a 1907 Moab kitchen. It's across from the courthouse.

ENTERTAINMENT AND EVENTS

As a tourist epicenter, Moab has more nightlife than any three other towns in southern Utah combined—which still isn't saying all that much. Zax, Eddie McStiff's, the Moab Brewery (see the *Food* section) are the usual starting points, followed by the **Rio** (2 S. 100 W., 435/259-6666) or **Woody's Tavern** (221 S. Main St., 435/259-9323). The **Outlaw Saloon** (44 W. 200 N., 435/259-2654), set in what looks like an airplane hangar, has pool tables, cheap beer, and a rather startling painting behind the bar.

In late March, runners in the **Canyonlands Half Marathon** thank their guardian angels the desert heat hasn't ramped up to full intensity yet. The **Easter Jeep Safari** in April crams the streets and nearby four-wheel-drive trails with gleaming off-road trucks and their boisterous drivers. April also sees an influx of classic roadsters for the **April Action Car Show,** and the **Green River–Moab Friendship Cruise** on Memorial Day weekend brings a flotilla drifting downstream from the city of Green River. June is the month to catch the **Canyonlands PCRA Rodeo** at the fairgrounds.

The **Grand County Fair** arrives at the fairgrounds in August, and the **Moab Music Festival** brings the strains of chamber music to the area in early September. In October the **Canyonlands Fat Tire Festival** welcomes as many out-of-state bikers as the Jeep Safari does jeepers.

SHOPPING

You'll find two of the best collections of books on all things Southwest *in* the Southwest at **Back of Beyond Books** (83 N. Main St., 435/259-5154) and the **Arches Book Company** (78 N. Main St., 435/259-0782). The **Tom Till Gallery** (61 N. Main St., 435/259-9808 or 888/479-9808), showcases the panoramic work of a local photographer, and the **Hogan Trading Co.** (10 S. Main St., 435/259-8118), sells Native American art, sculpture, jewelry, baskets, kachinas, and pottery. (Main Street is full of souvenir shops specializing in T-shirts, shot glasses, and sunscreen.) Even if you're not a geology buff, you should still drop by the **Moab Rock Shop** (600 N. Main St., 435/259-7312), which stocks amazing fossils, dinosaur bones, meteorites, mining relics, and minerals.

Bike Shops

For obvious reasons, Moab has no shortage of these either. You can buy or rent bikes, browse gear, join a guided riding tour, and have your bike repaired at the **Chile Pepper Bike Shop** (702 S. Main St., 435/259-4688 or 888/677-4688) and **Poison Spider Bicycles** (497 N. Main St., 435/259-7882 or 800/635-1792), which also has showers and a free repair stand out back. The **Rim Cyclery** (94 W. 100 N., 435/259-5333 or 888/304-8219, www.rimcyclery.com) does all of the above and also sells camping gear.

Outdoor Gear

Gearheads (471 S. Main St., 435/259-4327) is crammed with camping and general outdoor gear, including maps, guidebooks, tents, clothes, and hydration systems. Get your climbing gear at **Pagan Mountaineering** (59 S. Main St., 435/259-1117, www.paganmountaineering.com), which has more cams than you've probably even seen in one place before. For topo maps and guidebooks, head to one of the local bookstores (above) or **Times Independent Maps** (29 E. Center St., 435/259-5529).

RECREATION

You're well advised to get a local guidebook, or at least a map, before venturing out into the countryside around Moab. Don't underestimate this landscape—the trails can be highly difficult in spots—and *always* bring enough food and water in case things don't go according to plan in the backcountry. The Latitude 40 maps ("Moab East" and "Moab West") and the Trails Illustrated/National Geographic

("Moab North" and "Moab South") are the best maps, available all around town. (Guidebooks are listed in the *Suggested Reading* section in the *Resources* chapter.)

C Mountain Biking Trails

Moab has enough mountain bike trails to fill a series of guidebooks, so these are just a sample of the best. The granddaddy of all mountain bike routes, the **Slickrock Trail** actually began as a motorcycle path. Mountain bikers have since taken over, with more than 100,000 riders per year attempting the 12-mile loop up, down, and around the petrified sand dunes northeast of town. This is a difficult trail, with sand traps, sheer drop-offs, few rest spots, and nothing but bare rock if you fall. It's also some of the most fun you can have on two wheels—the pedaling equivalent of a roller coaster, with great views to boot. If this is your first time, try the two-mile practice loop first. (**Bartlett Wash** northwest of town is another good slickrock area, albeit smaller, that sees much less traffic.)

To reach the trailhead, take 100 South Street toward the mountains from Main Street, then follow the signs to Tusher Street and Sand Flat Road, where you'll have to pay a fee ($5 per car or $2 per bike) to enter the **Sand Flats Recreation Area** (435/259-2444). Keep going 6.4 miles past the Slickrock parking lot to reach the trailhead for the **Porcupine Rim** trail, an exhausting but exhilarating ride that climbs 1,000 feet up into the La Sal Mountains before peaking at a stunning view of Castle Valley from the southern rim. From here it's almost 3,000 feet downhill to Highway 128 and back to town. A shuttle to the trailhead is a good idea for the 15-mile ride.

Another relentless climb awaits at the **Moab Rim,** but thankfully this one is shorter: almost 1,000 vertical feet in less than a mile. (One biking guidebook says this "may well be the toughest mile in the world.") The top of the climb, 1.6 miles from the trailhead along Kane Creek Boulevard, is reward enough, but you can also continue another six technical miles to Hidden Valley and a downhill bike portage

to rejoin Highway 191 south of Moab. Across the canyon is the **Poison Spider Mesa** trail, overlooking the Colorado above Highway 279. A more moderate ride, this one starts near the dinosaur track and climbs 1,000 feet to the top of the mesa. Drink in the view, all the way to Arches National Park, before deciding if you're up for the Portal Trail, where you are highly advised to dismount and walk your bike down a narrow trail (with a sheer drop to one side) to avoid a potentially deadly fall. Via the Portal Trail this is a 12.7-mile one-way ride, rejoining Highway 279 closer to Moab. Otherwise you can turn around to make it a 12-mile round-trip ride.

On BLM land near the Island in the Sky are two good easy-to-moderate rides that should take about half a day each. The **Gemini Bridges** are a pair of arches at the edge of a mesa you can walk out onto. The trail leaves Highway 313 on its way out to the Island in the Sky, then coasts steadily downhill for 13.7 miles, passing the bridges and one small uphill en route, to Highway 191 just south of the Highway 313 turnoff. You'll need a car shuttle to do the one-way ride. (A bike path has been opened along the north side of Highway 191, which will take you just north of the Colorado River bridge past the Arches entrance to the lower trailhead.)

Another easy trail takes you close to **Monitor and Merrimac buttes** in roughly the same area. Turn off Highway 191 to the left (west) just north of milepost 141, cross the train tracks and park after another half a mile. The 13.2-mile loop tail (take the right fork initially) leads you past the buttes as well as Determination Towers and the Mill Canyon Dinosaur Trail (also accessed off Highway 279). Farther up Highway 191 from Moab (17.3 miles) is a trailhead on the right (east) to the **Klondike Bluffs,** a steady climb 800 feet up slickrock and dirt to an amazing view over the northern part of Arches National Park. This is a medium-difficulty trail that's 14.4 miles round-trip.

The **Sovereign Trail** is a 20-mile single-track north of town that was developed by a group of local motorcyclists who support responsible riding and sharing trails (see www.ridewithrespect.com). Most bikers ride it as a moderate-difficulty out-and-back trail starting from the parking area a few miles out the Willow Springs Road (turn off Highway 191 to the right just past the Highway 313 turnoff).

When the summer heat sets in, bikers head up into the La Sals, where longer trails such as **Moonlight Meadows** (a 10-mile loop) offer great single-track and lung-busting climbs. The **Burro Pass** trail, an 8–19-mile loop, passes two mountain lakes and viewing points of Arches and Canyonlands national parks. Another good ride is the **Three Lake Trail,** a 14-mile figure eight of faint single-track past Oowah, Clark, and Warner lakes.

Mountain Biking Overnight Trips

Several longer trails await riders who are willing to spend a night or more outdoors—and carry everything they need during the day. While more of an undertaking, these really let you get far out into the backcountry, far from the day-pedal crowds. You'll need a set of racks and panniers or a bike trailer to carry your gear. The **White Rim Trail** around Canyonlands' Island in the Sky is a 3–4 day ride, and one of the most incredible mountain bike trips in the country (see *Canyonlands National Park* for more information). **Kokopelli's Trail** is a 142-mile odyssey from the Colorado mountains to the Moab slickrock. It starts just over the border near Loma, Colorado, 15 miles west of Grand Junction, and roughly follows the Colorado River southwest before climbing into the foothills of the La Sals and descending to Moab. Most people take six days to do the entire ride, which covers everything from fire roads to single-track, but it's possible to resupply, start, or stop at several points along the way. Various maps and guides to this epic journey are available. (You can access parts of this trail from some of the day trails north of town.)

Recommended companies for bike tours in Moab include the bike shops listed above, as well as **Rim Mountain Bike Tours** (1233 S.

Hwy. 191, 435/259-5223 or 800/626-7335, info@rimtours.com, www.rimtours.com); **Nichols Expeditions** out of the Chile Pepper bike shop (497 N. Main St., 800/648-8488, info@nicholsexpeditions.com, www.nicholsexpeditions.com); and **Western Spirit Cycling** (478 Mill Creek Dr., 435/259-8732 or 800/845-2453, biking@westernspirit.com, www.westernspirit.com). Prices start around $80 per person for half-day trips including bike rental, and a few, such as Nichols Expeditions, have a long roster of adventure trips around the world.

Hiking

Though most people around here hit the backcountry on two wheels (or four), dozens of hiking trails snake through the desert and hills around Moab. From Potash Road (Highway 279), it's possible to hike two steep miles up to the **Portal Overlook** from the Jaycee Park Recreation Site and, six miles farther down the road, up to **Corona Arch** (1.5 miles one-way). Across the Colorado River on Kane Creek Boulevard, another steep trail leads up to the **Moab Rim** and into the area known as **Behind the Rocks,** a maze of sandstone fins similar to the Fiery Furnace in Arches National Park. Farther down Kane Creek Boulevard, the jeep road up **Pritchett Canyon** leads past (and sometimes through) small pools to a natural bridge, and a trail up **Hunters Canyon** passes Hunter Arch high on the right-hand side above cottonwood trees and pools. (The trailheads for these hikes are 2.6, 3.1, and 7.5 miles from Highway 191/ Main Street, respectively.)

From Highway 128 upstream along the Colorado River, look for the turnoff for **Negro Bill Canyon** on the right after three miles. This slickrock gorge leads to Morning Glory Natural Bridge, the sixth longest in the country at 243 feet, in a side canyon to the right, two miles up. You can keep hiking up the main canyon past the bridge for a few more miles. This was the site of a skirmish in the so-called "Sagebrush Rebellion" in 1979, when anti-government locals used a county bulldozer to break through a dirt barrier—twice—that was

HIKING TIPS

Since most of the Four Corners is accessible only by foot, the possibilities for hiking are almost endless. From paved national park paths to terrifying scrambles along canyon ledges, it's all here. Perhaps more than any other place in the Lower 48, the Four Corners offers something that's become increasingly rare: the opportunity to disappear, really and truly, into the backcountry. You can take a short ramble from your car to a canyon overlook, or descend into that canyon and its tributaries for weeks without seeing another person. Remote ruins, petroglyphs, slot canyons, and hidden springs are only a few of the goodies waiting in the backcountry. For those tired of the desert, there are mountain ranges with peerless views and snow cover from fall to spring. Many trails are developed and even accessible to disabled visitors, while countless more are rough, steep, and un-maintained. Many in this latter category are marked by small piles of rocks called cairns; feel free to add your own pebble, but make sure you really are on the trail – false cairns can be dangerous.

The canyon country is a spectacular terrain, but not one to be taken lightly. Heed the advice on heat and water in the *Health and Safety* section in the *Essentials* chapter, and always carry an emergency survival pack. Be prepared for extreme weather conditions, especially at high altitudes. During the rainy or "monsoon" season (roughly July-September), monumental cloudbursts are an almost daily occurrence. Summer temperatures often climb over 100°F, and subzero winter cold is common.

Since you'll be carrying so much weight in water (one gallon weighs eight pounds), it's smart to minimize the weight of the rest of your gear as much as possible. Many companies are starting to make ultralight camping gear, tested and perfected on long routes like the Appalachian Trail. One outfit specializes in it: **GoLite** (888/5GO-LITE, 888/546-5483, info@golite.com, www.golite.com). Throw one of their Feather-Lite sleeping bags and a Lair tarp shelter inside a Breeze hiking pack, and you have a basic setup that weighs less than five pounds. Inspired and advised by ultralight hiking guru (and inventor of climbing cams) Ray Jardine, they also make clothing.

As you stay safe, protect the environment as well by following the guidelines of the **Leave No Trace** program (800/332-4100, www.lnt.org). These include careful planning (let someone responsible know where you're going and when you plan to return); traveling and camping on durable surfaces (stay off the crypto!); disposing of waste properly (no burning toilet paper); leaving things as you find them (disturbing archaeological sites on federal land is a felony); minimizing the impact of campfires (better yet, just use a stove); leaving wildlife alone; and being considerate of your fellow campers.

put up by the BLM to protect the canyon while it was being considered as a wilderness area.

Climbing and Canyoneering

Although the Wingate Sandstone layer is the only one really worth climbing around here, there are still plenty of options for climbers within a quick trip of Moab. **Wall Street** along Potash Road is frighteningly close to traffic but is a good place to experience desert climbing for the first time. **Castle Valley** up Highway 128 is a broad, flat valley punctuated by towers the size of office buildings with names like the Nuns, the Priest, and the Rectory. Castleton Tower itself is the home of the one of the country's classic multipitch tower climbs, leading to a flat peak the size of a studio apartment—an incredible spot. There are a few routes in Arches and Canyonlands National Park, including Washer Woman Arch off the Island in the Sky and Owl Rock in Arches, but be warned that climbing regulations are more restrictive in the parks than outside (no chalk and no new bolts, for starters). **Indian Creek** on the way to the Needles district of Canyonlands is another world famous climbing area (see *Canyonlands National Park* for more information).

Canyoneering is an exciting, relatively new sport that involves minor rock climbing and rappelling to access canyons that would otherwise be too difficult or dangerous to enter. This is not for the uninitiated or faint of heart, but if you know what you're doing—or are with someone who does—it can provide a feeling of adventure and discovery like few other pursuits.

Stock up on climbing gear at Pagan Mountaineering (see the *Outdoor Gear* section), and book climbing trips and instruction through **Moab Cliffs & Canyons** (63 E. Center St., 435/259-3317 or 877/641-5271, info@cliffsandcanyons.com, www.cliffsandcanyons.com) or **Moab Desert Adventures** (801 Oak St., 435/260-2404 or 877/ROKMOAB, 877/765-6622, emma@moabdesertadventures.com, www.moabdesertadventures.com). Prices start at around $100 for a half-day trip for two people. **Desert Highlights** (50 E. Center St., 435/259-4433 or 800/747-1342, info@deserthighlights.com, www.deserthighlights.com), specializes in canyoneering from $80 per person per day.

Rafting

Moab's location near the confluence of the two biggest rivers in the Four Corners means that outdoor enthusiasts aren't limited to just dry land. Trips range from easy afternoon floats to serious, multiday white water. Permits are necessary whether you're floating through Canyonlands National Park or BLM land outside it.

Between Grand Junction, Colorado, and Moab, the Colorado River provides a great introduction to desert rafting. Rapids ranging from Class II to Class IV have names like Sock-It-To-Me, Last Chance, and Room-of-Doom. In all it's 131 river miles from the border to Moab. **Westwater Canyon,** from the Westwater Ranger Station (4.5 miles from the border)

CANYONEERING

This relatively new pursuit involves descending or ascending narrow canyons that often require rock climbing skills to enter, negotiate, and exit. This is one of the more exciting ways to explore the canyon country, but it's also one of the most potentially hazardous. First there's the risk of falling and hurting or trapping yourself in some of the most remote country around. Add to this the danger of **flash floods** in monsoon season as well as hypothermia, since you'll have to wade and even swim to get through some narrow canyons. Flash floods can arrive with little or no warning, even if the sky is blue overhead, and can fill a canyon with water, mud, trees, and boulders much quicker than you can escape it. For a reminder of the forces involved, look for tree trunks lodged many yards overhead in narrow canyons by seasonal floods. They're often preceded by an earthy smell and sound like a train rushing down the canyon. Smaller ones can be fun to watch from a safe vantage point, but large ones are deadly.

Take wading shoes, synthetic clothing (damp cotton is a killer), waterproof bags for your things, and a walking stick or pole for balance and to check for deep holes hidden under muddy water. Only tackle the really wet canyons in hot weather. If necessary, bring ropes and/or nylon webbing and climbing harnesses, and know how to use them or go with someone who does. Claustrophobes should find something else to do – some slot canyons are so narrow you'll have to remove your backpack and shimmy through sideways. Many excellent guidebooks list canyon hikes in detail; see *Suggested Reading* in the *Resources* chapter for a listing. For more information, contact the **American Canyoneering Association** (435/590-8889, www.canyoneering.net), which offers courses, or check out www.canyoneeringusa.com. The website http://climb-utah.com has good information on hiking and canyoneering in southern Utah.

to the landing at Cisco, does require permits, which are available from the BLM office in Moab (82 E. Dogwood Ave., 435/259-2100). Permittees are chosen by lottery. This trip takes one to two days. From Dewey Bridge to the boat ramp below the Potash Plant along Highway 279 is 46 miles, and takes two to three days. You don't need a permit for this stretch, but check with the BLM for camping rules.

The Potash ramp is the last takeout before Hite Marina on Lake Powell, 118 miles downriver. After two days of leisurely floating through deep canyons, the Colorado River joins with the Green and explodes into **Cataract Canyon,** where 26 rapids have names like Hell-to-Pay and the Big Drops. This stretch provides some of the best whitewater thrills in the country in May and June, its spring surge unfettered by any dam. The still waters of Lake Powell mark the end of the trip. Boating permits ($20–30) are required to cross through Canyonlands National Park.

Moab is full of experienced rafting companies, which run trips from May to September. Prices start at $50 for a half day on The Daily (a short and easy whitewater run) to around $800 per person on a five-day Cataract Canyon adventure. Westwater Canyon will run you about $350 per person for two days or $500 for three.

One of the oldest companies in town is **Tex's Riverways** (435/259-5101, info@texsriverways.com, www.texsriverways.com), which has been operating since 1958 on the Green and Colorado rivers. They run a jet boat down to the confluence and back on a regular basis that can pick you up if you're doing your own trip. **Tag-a-Long** (452 N. Main St., 800/453-3292, tagalong@tagalong.com, www.tagalong.com) has been in business since 1964, and can help you organize self-guided trips. **Sheri Griffith Expeditions** (2231 S. Hwy. 191, 435/259-8229 or 800/332-2439, info@griffithexp.com, www.griffithexp.com) organizes women-only raft trips among many others, while **Adrift Adventures** (378 N. Main St., 435/259-8594 or 800/874-4483, info@adrift.net, www.adrift.net) does horseback and four-wheel-drive excursions as well as raft trips.

MultiSport and Other Tours

Many of the above companies can combine hiking, biking, climbing, and rafting into a customized itinerary. Otherwise, stop by the **Moab Adventure Center** (225 S. Main St., 435/259-7019 or 888/622-4097, www.moabadventurecenter.com), who will happily set up, say, a Hummer safari in the morning and a bike ride in the afternoon. They also arrange tours in Tomcars, which are tough little two-person 4WD vehicles, like Mad Max go-karts.

Hundreds of miles of dirt roads crisscross the rough country of southeastern Utah, and Moab is at the center of it all. Blazed by ranchers and uranium prospectors, many are still popular with four-wheel-drive enthusiasts, who flock to town for the **Easter Jeep Safari** (see the *Entertainment and Events* section). **Tag-a-Long Expeditions** (see the *Rafting* section) has driving tours into Canyonlands National Park, including jet-boat/jeep combination day trips.

The **Camelot Lodge** (435/260-1783, camelot@camelotlodge.com, www.camelotlodge.com) is near Hurrah Pass south of town, and offers half- and full-day trips on camelback for $105–140 per person, in addition to accommodations at their five-room lodge ($125 pp). For horseback trail rides through the canyons, contact **Cowboy Adventures** (435/259-7410, cowboyadventures@hotmail.com). Prices are $60 per person for half-day and $95 per person for full-day rides. Based at the airport, **Skydive Moab** (435/259-JUMP, 435/259-5867, or 800/UGO-JUMP, 800/846-5867, www.skydivemoab.com, info@skydivemoab.com) offers tandem jumps for $210–230 per person.

ACCOMMODATIONS
In Town

Bear in mind that in this tourist town, hotel prices can fall by as much as half out of season (November–February) Aside from camping, Moab's cheapest lodging is at the **Lazy Lizard International Hostel** (1213 S. Hwy. 191, 435/259-6057, reservations@lazylizardhostel.com, www.lazylizardhostel.com). It's chock-full of character, with a full kitchen, laundry, hot tub, and showers ($2 for non-guests). Dorm rooms are $9 per person, and they also have private rooms ($24 d) and log cabins ($29–31 d). Campsites are available for $6 per person with full use of the facilities.

While he was in town filming *Rio Bravo*, John Wayne stayed at the **Apache Motel** (166 S. 400 E., 435/259-5727, fax 435/259-5728). Today their rooms go for $85 in season, as do the rooms at the **Big Horn Lodge** (550 S. Main St., 435/259-6171 or 800/325-6171, fax 435/259-6144, www.moabbighorn.com). The **Virginian Motel** (70 E. 200 S., 435/259-5951, fax 435/259-5468, $75) is slightly less expensive, and for the same price you can have use of the hot tub and shaded backyard of the **Kokopelli Lodge** (72 S. 100 E., 435/259-7615 or 888/530-3134, kokopeli@lasal.net, www.kokopellilodge.com), which offers eight rooms a block from Main Street.

It's easy to see how the **Adobe Abode** (778 W. Kane Creek Blvd., tel./fax 435/259-7716, adobeabode@lasal.net, www.adobeabodemoab.com) got its name. The distinctive building boasts tile floors, a hot tub, and rooms for $100–110, and is set next to the wetland preserve. The attitude of many Moab visitors is summed up in the name of the **Gonzo Inn** (100 W. 200 S., 435/259-2515 or 800/791-4044, fax 435/259-6992, www.gonzoinn.com, gonzoinn@gonzoinn.com), a more-luxurious place with a morning espresso bar and an outdoor pool. Rooms are $135, and the well-appointed suites range $275–300.

A late-1800s Victorian home houses the **Cali Cochitta House of Dreams B&B** (110 S. 200 E., 435/259-4961 or 888/429-8112, fax 435/259-4964, calicochitta@lasal.net, www.moabdreaminn.com). Three rooms and a suite ($105–130) share a wide front porch. Jim and Kathy Kempa have done a good job of making the **Dream Keeper Inn** (191 S. 200 E., 435/259-5998 or 888/230-3247, info@dreamkeeperinn.com, www.dreamkeeperinn.com) a relaxing place. It's tastefully decorated with a pool, hot tub, and rose garden. Rooms are $115–125, and they also offer two cottages at $145 double. Moab's only AAA four-diamond lodging in town is the **◖ Sunflower Hill B&B Inn** (185 N. 300 E., 435/259-2974 or 800/MOAB-SUN, 800/662-2786, fax 435/259-3065, innkeeper@sunflowerhill.com, www.sunflowerhill.com, $135–205). Twelve rooms in two buildings have antique beds (some have private balconies), and wooded pathways lead to an outdoor hot tub.

Outside of Town

Actor Robert Duval and author Edward Abbey are just two of the notables to grace the **Pack Creek Ranch** (435/259-5505, fax 435/259-8879, pcr@packcreekranch.com, www.packcreekranch.com) with their presence. Although it dates to the 19th century, this place is still a working ranch, said to have been named after an incident when a pair of prospectors ditched their gear by a nearby stream to escape Native Americans. The 300-acre ranch has a wide variety of lodging options, including rooms in the ranch house, bunk houses, and fully renovated cabins with full kitchens and rock fireplaces—but emphatically *no* phones or TVs. There's also a sauna and hot tub. In-season rates range from $95 for a two-person cabin to $175 for a four-person one and $225 for a six-person farmhouse. The ranch is in the foothills of the La Sals southeast of Moab, six miles from the southern end of the La Sal Mountain Loop Road on Highway 191.

Seventeen miles north of Moab along Highway 128 is the **◖ Sorrel River Ranch** (435/259-4642 or 877/359-2715, stay@sorrelriver.com, www.sorrelriver.com), probably the area's most luxurious lodging. The contrast between rugged setting and deluxe accommodations is so drastic it's almost surreal. The Colorado flows only yards from the porches and balconies of the rooms ($220–250) and suites ($270–400), while the red towers of Castle Valley and the snowcapped La Sals rise to the east. The 160-acre resort, on the site of a century-old ranch, has a full-service spa, an outdoor pool, an excellent restaurant, and a full slate of activities including horseback riding, rafting, and mountain biking.

Camping

All of these commercial campgrounds are

CAMPING

One of the best things about traveling in the United States – which we Americans often take for granted – is the enormous swatches of public land that belong to all of us. In this respect the Colorado Plateau is a prime example. Much of the land you see out here is owned by the state or federal government, and there's nothing like the freedom of driving for hours, pulling your car off onto a dirt road up in a national forest or across a Bureau of Land Management (BLM)-managed mesa, and finding your own private spot to set up camp just as the sun sets.

Any land managed by the U.S. Forest Service (USFS) and the BLM is open to **dispersed (at-large) camping,** aside from areas specially designated as closed to camping, and places that have already been developed with campsites (in these, stay in the campsites only). Dispersed camping ranges from hike-in backcountry sites to clearings alongside roads where you can park a car, camper, or trailer. Fires are often prohibited, particularly with the recent drought, and land ownership can be a confusing patchwork of public and private holdings, so check with the local office of the USFS or the BLM for details. There is often a maximum stay of two or three weeks, although this is seldom enforced. **Developed campgrounds** usually include bathrooms, picnic tables, and fire rings, and can sometimes be reserved ahead of time. State and national parks are subject to more regulations; here you often have to stay in developed campsites (often first-come, first-served), or at least secure a permit for backcountry camping, and you'll probably have to stay in designated zones or campsites once you're out there. Fees are $5-15 per campsite.

On private land you are limited to **private campgrounds,** which are still plentiful. These offer tent and RV spaces, including electricity, water, and sewer hookups, and often have showers, laundry services, and other activities and services. More-elaborate places, typified by **KOA Kampgrounds** (406/248-7444, fax 406/248-7414, www.koa.com) come complete with pools, game rooms, hot tubs, saunas, and volleyball courts. Occasionally they'll have small **cabins** with air-conditioning and heat for about the price of a budget motel room. Features such as bicycle rental, miniature golf, and summer children's programs cost extra. You can reserve their campsites online. Many campgrounds close for winter, and reservations and/or deposits may be necessary in popular areas like the Grand Canyon or during peak seasons. Private campsites cost around $20-30.

There are also private cabins on the Native American reservations. Otherwise, you must secure permission from the tribes for backcountry camping. On the Navajo Reservation, contact the **Navajo Parks and Recreation Department** office in Window Rock (928/871-6647, fax 928/871-6637, info@navajonationparks.org, www.navajonationparks.org, 8 A.M.-5 P.M.), or the **Cameron Visitor Center** at the junction of Highways 89 and 64 in Cameron, Arizona (928/679-2303, fax 928/679-2330, 8 A.M.-5 P.M.).

You can reserve campsites in national forests and at Arches and Bryce Canyon national parks online at www.reserve-usa.com. Reserve sites at the Grand Canyon and Zion national parks at http://reservations.nps.gov.

open year-round. Sites at the **Canyonlands Campground** (555 S. Main St., tel./fax 435/259-6848 or 800/522-6848, info@canyonlandsrv.com, www.canyonlandsrv.com) are $18 for tents, $25–27 for RVs, and $35 for cabins. The **Portal RV Park** (1261 N. Hwy. 191, 435/259-6108 or 800/574-2028, camp@portalrvpark.com, www.portalrvpark.com) is

north of town on Highway 191, with similarly priced sites and cabins. A heated pool and hot tubs are a few of the many amenities of the **Slickrock Campground** (1301½ N. Hwy. 191, 435/259-7660 or 800/448-8873, info@slickrockcampground.com, www.slickrockcampground.com). Tents are $18, RV sites are $23–25, and cabins with a/c are $32.

In addition to the campground at **Arches National Park, Canyonlands National Park,** and **Dead Horse Point State Park,** many primitive campsites are available on BLM land near Moab. All are open year-round; contact the Moab BLM office (435/259-2100) for more details. There are nine campgrounds up Highway 128 along the Colorado River, from Goose Island (1.4 miles) to Dewey Bridge (28.7 miles), ranging $5–10 per site per night. Four more can be found down Kane Creek Road, from Kings Bottom (2.8 miles) to Echo (8 miles), all of which are $5. The Sand Flats Recreation Area near the Slickrock Trail has 150 sites ($10). Finally, there are two Forest Service campgrounds up the La Sal Mountain Loop Road, Pack Creek and Warner Lake, both $8. Call the local ranger district (435/259-7155) for more information.

FOOD
Along Main Street

Maybe it's all the physical exertion that goes on around here, but Moab has more than its fair share of places to gas up and refuel your internal engines. The **◖ Jailhouse Cafe** (101 N. Main St., 435/259-3900, daily 7 A.M.–noon) occupies a turn-of-the-20th-century courthouse with two-foot adobe walls, serving up ginger pancakes and Southwest eggs Benedict for breakfast ($8). The outdoor porch at the **Eklecticafe** (352 N. Main St., 435/259-6896) is a great place to enjoy some banana nut pancakes when it's sunny out, which it almost always is. Breakfast is served daily, and lunches, like Indonesian satay and curry wraps ($6–8) are served Monday–Saturday.

The java is always fresh and flowing at the **Mondo Cafe** (59 S. Main St., 435/259-5551, 6:30 A.M.–9:30 P.M. daily), which serves coffee drinks and baked goods in McStiff's Plaza. Try their green eggs (breakfast is $4–6) and panini sandwiches ($6.50). They have wireless Internet and a used-book store attached to boot. Breakfast is served anytime at the throwback **Moab Diner** (189 S. Main St., 435/259-4006, all meals daily), starting at $4, and they serve inexpensive lunches and dinners as well.

The **Poplar Place Pub and Eatery** (Main St. and 100 N., 435/259-6018, lunch and dinner daily) specializes in custom pizzas ($13 and up), and offers Guinness on draft as well as a dozen microbrews. On that note, the **Moab Brewery** (686 S. Main St., 435/259-6333, lunch and dinner daily) has pool tables and separate restaurant and bar areas, where they serve steaks, seafood, pasta, and vegetarian dishes starting around $8. Their brews include Dead Horse Ale and Raven Stout. **Eddie McStiff's** (57 S. Main St., 435/259-2337, lunch and dinner daily), has a similar menu but better food, on average. Their brick-oven pizza and pasta dishes are especially good. Burgers start at $5 and everything else is $7 and up.

Miguel's Baja Grill (51 N. Main St., 435/259-6546, dinner daily) serves the best Mexican food in town, and **Zax** (Main St. and 100 S., 435/259-6555, daily lunch and dinner) offers and all-you-can-eat pizza, soup, and salad bar for $11 per person, as well as an outside patio with misters that are more than welcome on hot afternoons.

Elsewhere in Town

One of southern Utah's best restaurants is the **◖ Center Cafe** (60 N. 100 W., 435/259-4295, dinner daily), with a Zagat's award of excellence and a secluded courtyard to its credit. Their "classical and globally inspired" menu lists dishes such as Grilled venison rack and beef bourguignonne for lunch ($6–22) and dinner ($6–32), with homemade ice cream to top it off. It's open daily for all meals.

Homemade breads, pastries, and desserts are the specialty of the **Knave of Hearts Bakery** (84 W. 200 N., 435/259-4116, breakfast and lunch Tues.–Sun.), and **Milt's Stop & Eat** (356 S. 400 E., 435/259-7424, all meals daily) is an authentic 1954 diner with omelets, burgers, and sandwiches for under $5.

Uranium millionaire Charlie Steen built his dream home on a hillside overlooking Moab. Today it goes by the name of the **Sunset Grill** (900 N. Hwy. 191, 435/259-7146, dinner Mon.–Sat.) serving steaks and seafood delivered fresh daily (entrées $13–23) with a wonderful view thrown in for free. Families favor the Wild West show and cowboy supper cookout at the **Bar-M Chuckwagon** (435/259-2276 or 800/214-2085, www.barmchuckwagon.com), served "trail style" on metal plates. It all starts at 7 P.M. daily, faux gunfight and all, seven miles north of town on Highway 191 ($23 adults, $11.50 children).

TRANSPORTATION AND SERVICES
Shuttle Services
If you're not up for tacking a 10-mile pedal onto each end of your exhausting mountain bike ride, ring up one of Moab's many shuttle services, which can drop you off and/or pick you up at either end. They're also handy for raft trips and getting to and from the airport. Prices start at $25 per vehicle for trailhead runs. Options include **Atomic Transfer** (438 N. Castle Valley Dr., 435/259-6475, atomic@moab-canyonlands.com), **Acme Bike Shuttle** (702 S. Main St., 435/260-2534, kymears@yahoo.com), **Coyote Shuttle** (435/259-8656, www.coyoteshuttle.com), and, perhaps inevitably, **Roadrunner Shuttle** (435/259-9402, www.roadrunnershuttle.com).

Bighorn Express (801/746-2417 or 888/655-7433, www.bighornexpress.com) runs a shuttle bus to Salt Lake City ($56 one-way, 4.5 hours) and Monticello ($30, one hour) daily in season; Wednesday, Friday, and Sunday only in January and February.

Airlines
Salmon Air (435/259-0566 or 800/448-3413, www.salmonair.com) flies daily from the airport north of town to Salt Lake City for $104–126 one-way ($178–208 round-trip).

Car Rental
You can rent cars in Moab from **Thrifty** (711 S. Main St., 435/259-7317) at the Moab Valley Inn. **Farabee Jeep Rentals** (401 N. Main St., 435/259-7494, www.moabjeeprentals.com) rents the vehicles for $145–175 per day, as does **Slickrock Jeep Rentals** (900 S. Hwy. 191, 435/259-5678).

Information
While each federal land-management agency has an office in town, they've turned over everything tourist-related to the **Moab Information Center** (Main St. and Center St.,

ODDNESS NEAR MOAB

One of the better offbeat destinations in the Southwest is the **Hole 'N the Rock** (11037 S. Hwy. 191, 435/686-2250, 9 A.M.-6 P.M. daily, to 5 P.M. Labor Day-Memorial Day, $4 pp), a 14-room home that was chipped, blasted, and sculpted out of a sandstone cliff 15 miles south of Moab. It took Albert Chistensen 20 years to blast out his 5,000-square-foot residence, which includes a 65-foot chimney, a creepy taxidermy collection, and a portrait of F.D.R. cut into the outside wall. Albert is buried outside next to his wife Gladys, near the ostrich pen and a concrete sculpture garden. Don't ask – just go. Admission includes a guided tour.

America's Most Scenic Dump, along the road up to the Slickrock Trail, offers unparal-

leled views of snowcapped mountains, redrock arches, and soaring eagles. Rumor has it that Juneau, Alaska, may have an even prettier setting for its garbage, but Moabites still claim their landfill is the most picturesque. At the apocalyptic ghost town of **Cisco,** near where Highway 128 meets I-70, more than 100,000 sheep once grazed in the shadows of the Book Cliffs before being shipped out by train. Founded in 1883, Cisco was abandoned (more or less – a few holdouts remain) when the interstate was built far enough away that passing traffic just kept passing. It's a strange place to visit, especially when overcast skies make the abandoned buildings, including the one-room Cisco post office, even spookier.

435/259-8825 or 800/635-6622, info@discovermoab.com, www.discovermoab.com, 8 A.M.–8 P.M. daily). "The Mic" is the place to go for just about any question you might have; if they don't have the answer, they know who does. They also sell maps and books. The websites www.canyonlands-utah.com and www.southeastutah.com are also both good resources on the area, with links to attractions, activities, tour operators, accommodations, and other online travel resources.

NEAR MOAB
Highway 279 (Potash Road)

This beautiful drive snakes along the bank of the Colorado River after leaving Highway 191 north of the bridge. It's paved for 16 miles as it runs within touching distance of the canyon's north wall. Look for a **rock art** panel five miles from the turnoff from Highway 191, near a popular rock climbing spot called Wall Street (be careful of parked vehicles and climbers). More petroglyphs and set of **dinosaur tracks** are signposted at 6.2 miles, and at 13.6 miles is **Jug Handle Arch** on the right-hand side. The pavement ends at the large evaporation ponds of the **Moab Salt Plant,** also known as the

Potash Plant. From here the dirt road continues to the White Rim Road and the Schaefer Trail inside Canyonlands National Park.

Highway 128

Another scenic byway heads northeast along the Colorado River from the south side of the Highway 191 bridge, and is paved all the way to I-70. It's a longer route than Highway 279 and an even prettier drive. At the turnoff is a picnic area and, just upriver, a natural spring gushing from the canyon wall where you can fill water bottles for hikes up **Negro Bill Canyon.** The turnoff for **Castle Valley** is on the right at 15.5 miles, where huge sandstone towers jut towards the sky against the backdrop of the La Sal Mountains. Head up the wide valley, crosshatched by dirt roads and fields, to access the **La Sal Mountain Loop Road.** Back on Highway 128, the weird muddy spires of the **Fisher Towers** rise above **Professor Valley** near milepost 21. These darker towers are much less photogenic than their cousins in Castle Valley, but they have also been climbed, despite the poor quality of the rock.

The road crosses the river at **Dewey Bridge,** where a one-lane suspension bridge of wood

SOUTHEAST UTAH

© JULIAN SMITH

Castleton Tower, in Castle Valley north of Moab, is a favorite for climbing.

and steel built in 1916 was replaced by a concrete span in the 1980s. The old bridge is still there, near a picnic and boat-launching area. The landscape opens up into barren rolling flatland as the road nears I-70. If you have the time, don't miss the turnoff to the ghost town of **Cisco** (see the sidebar *Oddness near Moab*).

La Sal Mountains

The second-highest range in Utah rises above the high desert east of Moab, tantalizing sweltering visitors with visions of snowcapped peaks well into summer. (The name, meaning "salt" in Spanish, is said to come from Spanish missionaries who couldn't believe there was snow in the midst of such a furnace.)

Six peaks above 12,000 feet are capped by Mount Peale (12,721 feet), and mountain lakes sparkle amid fir and aspen forests throughout. Plenty of trails tempt hikers, bikers, and horseback riders in summer and skiers and snowshoers in winter. The 62-mile **La Sal Mountain Scenic Route** climbs the mountains' flanks between Castle Valley and Highway 191 south of Moab. It's a gorgeous drive with picnic areas, viewing points, and unpaved spur roads its entire length, open late spring–early fall.

Over 60 miles of trails cross the mountains. Mountain bikers get a great workout at these elevations; the two most popular rides each entail about 3,700 feet of elevation change. (See the *Mountain Biking Trails* section for trail details.) Many hikers try to summit **Mt. Tukuhnikivatz,** a five-mile endeavor up and back that starts at 10,000 feet and climbs another 2,400.

◖ ARCHES NATIONAL PARK

The Four Corners' most famous park is, in the minds of many, synonymous with the Southwest itself. The image of Delicate Arch—only one of more than 2,000 found within the park—has been emblazoned on everything from license plates to shot glasses. Although arches occur around the world, there are more here than anywhere else, along with spires, fins, pinnacles, and balanced boulders, and more of these geological oddities are almost

surely waiting to be discovered even inside the park itself.

To say the least, Arches is a popular park. Besides mountain biking, it's the other reason more visitors come to Moab. Its wonders are for the most part easily accessible (i.e. close to a paved road) and the park is just the right size to "do" in a day, making it popular with families and RV drivers. Expect crowds and a full campground in spring and summer, especially around popular weekends like the Jeep Safari and Fat Tire Festival.

The Setting

Like most of the Moab region, Arches sits on top of an ancient underground salt bed left over from the sea that once covered the Colorado Plateau. Over time layers of rock laid down on top of the salt were thrust upward and cracked as the salt shifted and flowed. Water and ice gradually ate away at the exposed cracks to form free-standing fins, many of which are still visible throughout the area (think of them as "proto-arches"). These in turn were carved by erosion until the relatively soft sandstone was worn away.

Sometimes the interplay of weight and balance was just right so that an **arch** was created. The physics of arch formation are complex, but in a nutshell, it takes the least energy for a chunk of rock to drop away in a curve, rather than a straight line. Horizontal **pothole arches** can also be cut through by the chemical reaction of rainwater collecting in natural depressions.

Today the park's sandstone spans range in size from three feet—the minimum size for something to be considered an arch—to 306 feet, in the case of Landscape Arch. Most of them are formed from salmon-colored Entrada Sandstone, with a few made from tan Navajo Sandstone.

Visitors Center

The Arches National Park visitors center (435/719-2299, www.nps.gov/arch) is five miles north of Moab on Highway 191. Entrance is $5 per person or $10 per vehicle and

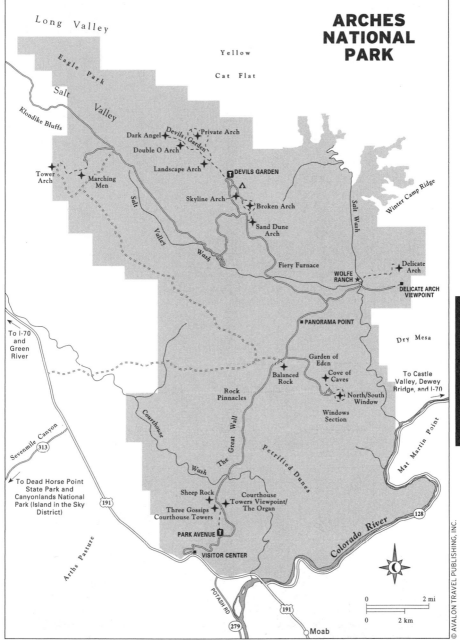

ARCHES NATIONAL PARK

Long Valley

Eagle Park

Salt

Valley

Klondike Bluffs

Yellow

Cat Flat

Dark Angel
Devils Garden
Private Arch
Double O Arch
Landscape Arch
Tower Arch
Marching Men
Salt
Valley
Wash
Skyline Arch
Broken Arch
Sand Dune Arch
Fiery Furnace
DEVILS GARDEN
Salt Wash
Winter Camp Ridge
Delicate Arch
WOLFE RANCH
DELICATE ARCH VIEWPOINT

PANORAMA POINT

Dry Mesa

To I-70 and Green River

Garden of Eden
Balanced Rock
Cove of Caves
North/South Window
Windows Section
Rock Pinnacles

To Castle Valley, Dewey Bridge, and I-70

Courthouse
The Great Wall
Petrified Dunes
Wash
Sheep Rock
Courthouse Towers Viewpoint/ The Organ
Three Gossips
Courthouse Towers
PARK AVENUE
VISITOR CENTER

Mat Martin Point

Sevenmile Canyon
313

To Dead Horse Point State Park and Canyonlands National Park (Island in the Sky District)
191

Arths Pasture

128

Colorado River

POTASH RD
279
191
Moab

0   2 mi
0   2 km

© AVALON TRAVEL PUBLISHING, INC.

SOUTHEAST UTAH

good for a week. (The $25 Southeast Utah Passport gives access to Arches, Canyonlands National Park, Hovenweep National Monument, and Natural Bridges National Monument for a year.) Arches is open daily year-round 8 A.M.–4:30 P.M. (7:30 A.M.–6:30 P.M. Mar.–Oct.). There are books and maps for sale, rangers to question, and exhibits on the park's geology and human history, as well as an orientation film shown every half hour. Ask about guided hikes and campfire-talks programs at the campground.

Scenic Drive and Hikes

From the visitors center, the park's 18-mile scenic drive zigzags up the steep side of the Moab Fault to climb up onto the mesa where most of the park is located. If this is your first taste of the local scenery, be prepared to be impressed. The high-altitude desert is littered with rock towers and formations of every shape imaginable, and the La Sal Mountains stand on the horizon. It's truly an amazing sight, especially in the early morning or late afternoon when the sunlight sets the stone on fire.

The first turnoff is for **Park Avenue** through the **Courthouse Towers** (a set of giant stone formations reminiscent of a row of skyscrapers). A moderate trail descends into a small canyon and leads for a mile through the towers to rejoin the scenic drive, so you can hike it in either direction or arrange for a pickup. At the **Courthouse Towers Viewpoint** at the far end of the trail, look for rock formations with names like the Organ, the Three Gossips, Sheep Rock, and the Tower of Babel.

The scenic drive continues between a set of "petrified" sand dunes to the right (east) and the Great Wall to the west, where you can sometimes spot climbers tackling cracks in the sandstone. A little over nine miles down the road from the entrance is one of the park's most famous formations: **Balanced Rock,** a 3,600-ton boulder that looks like a gentle breeze could knock it over. A short, paved trail leads around the rock. The park's original entrance road, now

Balanced Rock, Arches National Park

called the Willow Flats road, joins the scenic drive from the west here. This is one of the few opportunities for mountain biking in the park; you can ride this road all the way back to Highway 191, eight miles north of the visitors center.

Just past Balanced Rock is a side road to **The Windows,** a pair of huge arches that dwarf hikers. On the way to the Windows section, you'll pass the **Cove of Caves** near a complex of standing rocks called the **Garden of Eden.** An easy trail leads to the North and South Windows and Turret Arch, and a primitive loop trail heads behind them and back to the parking area. A second trail leads to **Double Arch.**

Return to the main road and keep going for another 2.5 miles to reach a second side road. Civil War veteran John Wesley Wolfe built **Wolfe Ranch** near the turn of the 20th century, where he lived with his family for two decades before moving back to Ohio. A nearby petroglyph panel that includes images of men on horseback is thought to be the handiwork of the Ute tribe. From the ranch a three-mile trail leads up across slickrock to the base of **Delicate Arch,** probably the most famous arch in the world. It takes a few hours to make the trip out and back, so bring water. Despite its size, Delicate Arch really does look fragile and unbalanced, as if a touch could send it toppling. (Early settlers had more descriptive names for it, including Cowboy's Chaps and Old Lady's Bloomers.) If you're content with the view from afar, keep driving a mile past the ranch to a parking area where a very short trail leads to a viewing point, with a slightly longer trail climbing closer.

Back on the main road once again, head down into the crazy pastel colors of Salt Valley and back out again to the pullover for the **Fiery Furnace,** a labyrinth of stone fins and canyons that are actually cooler in summer than the surrounding desert. There aren't any marked trails here, so you must obtain a permit or sign up for a ranger-led hike, the best and safest way to explore this fascinating corner of the park. Moderately strenuous three-hour excursions happen twice daily in season and cost $8 per person ($4 children). They're very popular and often fill up a day or two before; make reservations at the visitors center up to a week in advance.

Three more miles brings you to the turnoff for the unpaved **Salt Valley Road** that heads northwest to **Klondike Bluffs,** a striking and little-visited corner of Arches that is also accessible via a moderate mountain bike trail from Highway 191 (see *Mountain Biking Trails* under *Moab*). Out here you'll find **Tower Arch** near the park border, accessed by a 1.7-mile hiking trail that begins from the parking area, nine miles from the scenic drive.

Only another mile of scenic drive remains, ending at the campground and a trailhead for **Devils Garden.** This is one of the park's arch hot spots, with no fewer than seven major arches along a 3.6-mile trail. Pass **Tunnel Arch** and **Pine Tree Arch,** where the trail splits. To the right it quickly becomes primitive (i.e. unmaintained) and loops past **Private Arch** to rejoin the main trail at **Double O Arch.** If you chose to go left you'll pass **Landscape Arch,** the park's largest, an impossibly thin span (only six feet across at one point) that dropped a large piece of rock in 1991. It's an easy two-mile round-trip hike here from the trailhead. The trail becomes more difficult past this point as it leads to the aptly named **Dark Angel** formation.

The **Devils Garden campground** is open year-round, with 52 sites ($15) available on a first-come, first-served basis. It fills quickly in spring and fall, so pre-register your site at the entrance station or visitors center starting at 7:30 A.M. There are tables, grills, toilets, and potable water, but no showers. Most RVs can fit, but there are no hookups. Half the campsites can be reserved ahead of time March–October through the website www.reserveusa.com or by calling the National Recreation Reservation Service (877/444-6777). **Skyline Arch,** a half-mile hike from the campground, doubled in size in November 1940 when a huge chunk fell from underneath.

Canyonlands National Park

If one place encapsulates the heart of the Colorado Plateau, it is Canyonlands, the largest of southern Utah's five national parks. From lightning-swept mesa tops to the roiling depths of the Colorado and Green river gorges, Canyonlands encompasses rock art, prehistoric dwellings, sheer-walled ravines, lush riverside thickets, raging rivers, and abundant desert life. And for all there is to see and do, there are almost as many ways to go about it: scenic drives, easy hikes, placid floats, and sweeping vistas give way to four-wheel-drive tracks, steep trails, frothing white water, and claustrophobic slot canyons the farther you push into the backcountry. Covering 527 square miles and ranging 3,700–7,200 feet, Canyonlands is big enough to offer something for just about everyone. If, by some terrible turns of events, you had to pick only one park to visit on the Colorado Plateau, make it this one.

The Y formed by the confluence of the two rivers neatly divides the park into three sections (four, actually, counting the **River District** itself). The **Island in the Sky District,** north of both rivers and closest to Moab, is a wide-open tableland far above the rivers themselves. Connected to the rest of southern Utah by only a narrow causeway, the Island has many viewing points looking across thousands of square miles of canyon country. Most are easily accessible by a paved scenic drive, along with short trails and the longer White Rim Trail around the mesa's base. Dead Horse Point State Park gives a taste of the Island in miniature.

The **Needles District,** southeast of the Colorado River, takes its name from distinctive red and white spires of Cedar Mesa Sandstone, jumbled like the skyline of an alien city. This is more of a backcountry district, with plenty of excellent trails and four-wheel-drive roads perfect for overnight trips. West of the rivers, the remote **Maze District** is almost a world in itself.

One $10 fee (per vehicle) gives access to all districts of the park for a week. (A passport

to the Southeast Utah Group costs $25 and gives access to Canyonlands, Arches National Park, Hovenweep National Monument, and Natural Bridges National Monument for a year.) Backpacking permits are $15, and 4WD and mountain bike camping permits are $30; both are good for 14 days. Some 4WD roads in the Needles require permits for day use. For more information, contact the park in Moab (435/719-2313, backcountry reservations 435/259-4351, www.nps.gov/cany). All national park visitors centers are open 9 A.M.– 4:30 P.M. daily, with extended hours spring through fall.

The Setting

Canyonlands owes its stunning topography to the usual culprits of layered deposits, dramatic uplift, and gradual erosion. From the Paradox Formation at the bottom of Cataract Canyon to the Navajo Sandstone on top of the Island in the Sky, the park's geologic history spans hundreds of millions of years. Many of its most outstanding features occur in the Cutler Formation, dating to the Permian Period (245–286 million years ago). The unmistakable White Rim around the Island in the Sky, 200 feet thick and flat as a pancake, and the Cedar Mesa Sandstone formations in the Needles and Maze districts are both part of the Cutler Formation.

Above the White Rim, in order, are the brownish, silty Moenkopi Formation, the uranium-rich shale of the Chinle Formation, the soaring vertical cliffs of Wingate Sandstone topped by the harder protective layer of the Kayenta Formation, and the creamy curves of Navajo Sandstone, the youngest layer in the park. Another 140 million years of geology above all this is now gone, swept away by weather and the rivers.

History

For such an inhospitable-looking place, Canyonlands has had many inhabitants over the years. The Fremont people left some of the most spectacular pictographs and petroglyphs in the country in Horseshoe Canyon near the Maze and Salt Canyon in the Needles. Not to be outdone, the Ancestral Puebloans left their own share of rock art and stone dwellings, including dozens of small granaries and more-impressive structures like Tower Ruin in the Needles.

Trapper Denis Julien carved his named along the canyons of the Green and Colorado in the 1830s, and on an 1859 expedition to the Confluence, Captain John N. Macomb wrote while overlooking the Needles, "I cannot conceive of a more worthless and impracticable region than the one we now found ourselves in." Undeterred (or perhaps inspired) by this, Captain John Wesley Powell led two celebrated and nearly fatal expeditions down the Green and the Colorado in 1869 and 1871.

Utes and Navajos lived in the canyons until the late 19th century, when cowboys and their cattle crowded them out. At one point, tens of thousands of cattle were grazed in the region, including many in the lower canyons and up on the Island. Remains of cowboy camps are preserved in the Needles District, and Butch Cassidy and his Wild Bunch hid from the law in Robber's Roost Canyon near the Maze. In 1964, despite considerable opposition from within the state, Canyonlands National Park was signed into existence by President Lyndon Johnson.

ISLAND IN THE SKY DISTRICT

The park's lofty district is the closest to Moab and thus sees the most visitors. The Island is a plateau that soars 2,000 feet above the river canyons in two giant steps: one from the plateau top, at over 6,000 feet, down to the White Rim, and another from the White Rim to the rivers themselves.

To reach the Island, take Highway 191 north from Moab and turn left (west) on Highway 313, 6.5 miles north of the Colorado River bridge. This road winds southwest up onto the plateau. Just over 14 miles from the turnoff, a side road leads to Dead Horse Point State Park, which offers similar panoramic views as the Island but in a more compact package.

SOUTHEAST UTAH

© JULIAN SMITH

Canyonlands National Park

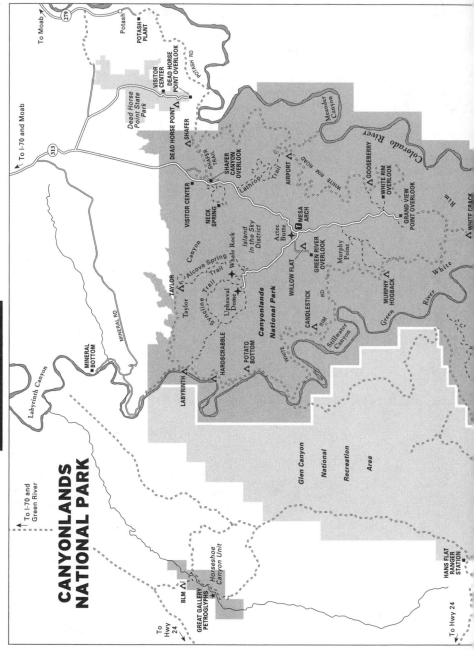

CANYONLANDS NATIONAL PARK

To Moab
279
Potash
POTASH PLANT
POTASH RD
VISITOR CENTER
DEAD HORSE POINT OVERLOOK
To I-70 and Moab
Dead Horse Point State Park
DEAD HORSE POINT
313
SHAFER
SHAFER TRAIL
SHAFER CANYON OVERLOOK
Meander Canyon
Colorado River
Lathrop Trail
AIRPORT
WHITE RIM ROAD
GOOSEBERRY
WHITE RIM OVERLOOK
GRAND VIEW POINT OVERLOOK
White Rim
WHITE CRACK
VISITOR CENTER
NECK SPRING
Island in the Sky District
Aztec Butte
MESA ARCH
GREEN RIVER OVERLOOK
Murphy Point
TAYLOR
Taylor Canyon
Alcove Spring Trail
Whale Rock
Syncline Trail
Upheaval Dome
WILLOW FLAT
Canyonlands National Park
CANDLESTICK
RIM RD
MURPHY HOGBACK
White
Green River
WHITE
Stillwater Canyon
HARDSCRABBLE
POTATO BOTTOM
MINERAL BOTTOM
MINERAL RD
LABYRINTH
Labyrinth Canyon

To I-70 and Green River

Glen Canyon
National Recreation Area

To Hwy 24
BLM
GREAT GALLERY PETROGLYPHS
Horseshoe Canyon Unit

HANS FLAT RANGER STATION

To Hwy 24

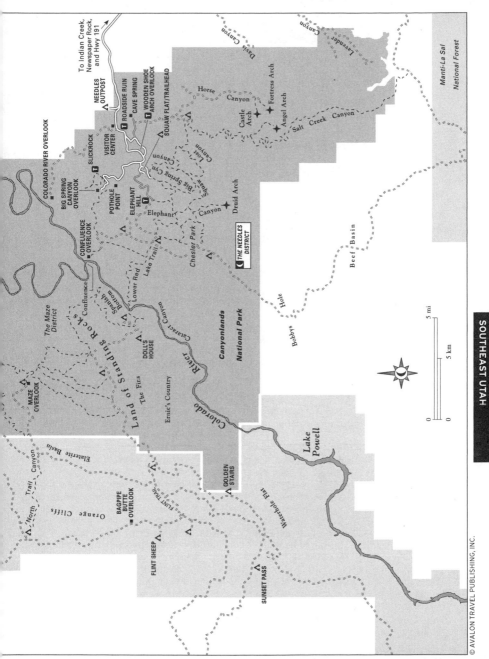

To Indian Creek,
Newspaper Rock,
and Hwy 191

NEEDLES OUTPOST
ROADSIDE RUIN
CAVE SPRING
WOODEN SHOE ARCH OVERLOOK
SQUAW FLAT/TRAILHEAD
VISITOR CENTER
SLICKROCK
COLORADO RIVER OVERLOOK
BIG SPRING CANYON OVERLOOK
POTHOLE POINT
ELEPHANT HILL
CONFLUENCE OVERLOOK

Horse   Canyon
Davis Canyon
Lavender   Canyon
Castle Arch
Fortress Arch
Angel Arch
Salt   Creek   Canyon
Manti-La Sal National Forest

Elephant   Canyon
Druid Arch
Lost   Canyon
Squaw   Canyon
Big Spring Cyn.
THE NEEDLES DISTRICT

Chesler Park
Lake Trail
Lower Red
Spanish Bottom
Confluence

The Maze District
Land of Standing Rocks
DOLL'S HOUSE
Cataract Canyon
Colorado River
Canyonlands National Park

Beef   Basin
Bobbys   Hole

The Fins
Ernie's Country
MAZE OVERLOOK

Elaterite Basin
North   Trail   Canyon
Orange   Cliffs
BAGPIPE BUTTE OVERLOOK
FLINT TRAIL
FLINT SHEEP

SUNSET PASS
GOLDEN STAIRS
Waterhole Flat
Lake Powell

SOUTHEAST UTAH

5 mi
5 km
0
0

© AVALON TRAVEL PUBLISHING, INC.

JOHN WESLEY POWELL

We are now ready to start on our way down the Great Unknown.
– John Wesley Powell, starting down the unmapped Green and Colorado rivers

Opening up the last unknown region of the continental United States was just one item on John Wesley Powell's long résumé. The one-armed Civil War veteran also laid the groundwork for some of the fundamental principles of geology, and raised a firm but ultimately futile voice for the wise development of the American West and the principled treatment of its natural resources and native tribes.

Powell was born on March 24, 1834, in western New York, the son of a Methodist preacher. He picked up his interest in natural history while being tutored by George Crookham, a farmer and amateur naturalist, who encouraged him to go out and get his hands dirty collecting specimens of plants, rocks, and animals. Powell defied his father's wishes to follow him into the clergy, instead working as a teacher and attending college at Wheaton and Oberlin. He collected geologic samples along the rivers of the Midwest, but when the Civil War erupted in 1861, he dropped his studies and enlisted in the Union Army.

In April 1862, one month after he had married his cousin Emma Dean, Powell was struck by a rifle ball in the right forearm during the battle of Shiloh. Hasty surgery saved his life but not his arm, which was amputated above the elbow. Nonetheless, he returned to service, was promoted to major, and took part in the siege of Vicksburg, where he collected fossils in the trenches. Discharged in 1865, Powell taught geology and curated museums at colleges in Illinois.

Two years later, Powell began a series of scientific expeditions into the little-known country of the West. With the help of the Smithsonian, He led a group of students and his wife into the Rocky Mountains in the Colorado Territory to collect museum specimens. In 1868 he returned with a similar group and climbed 14,255-foot Long's Peak. Gazing down on the headwaters of the Grand River, as the Colorado was then called, Powell decided that he would descend the river in small boats, despite stories of earlier explorers who had never emerged from the canyon country into which the rushing waters descended.

The country the Colorado River passed through was probably the least-known land remaining in the lower 48 states. Powell did some research, talked with mountain men and Native Americans, and studied the few documents the existed on the region. The first expedition set off from Green River Station in the Wyoming Territory on May 24, 1869. Funding came from private sources and the Illinois State Natural History Society. A crew of nine, including his brother Walter, packed into four small boats of Powell's design. They had no idea what lay ahead. "What falls there are," wrote Powell, "we know not; what rocks beset the channel, we know not; what walls rise over the river, we know not." His headstrong nature, his insatiable curiosity, and his ability to inspire others were about to be put to the supreme test.

The thousand-mile journey took only three months, as opposed to the six to nine they had planned for. Raging rapids tossed the wooden dories like corks, equipment sank as the boats overturned repeatedly, and muddy water worked its way into precious stores of food. One crew member had enough and left after a month. After weeks in the dark depths of the Grand Canyon, three others left to find an overland route home. They were killed soon after they emerged from the canyon, and different theories blame this on local Native Americans or Mormon settlers. Two days later, the remaining five emerged at the mouth of the Virgin River, Arizona, to the astonishment of the nation and local Native American tribes, all of whom had thought the plan was certain suicide.

Frustrated by how little scientific data he

had been able to collect while trying to keep his party alive, Powell lost no time in readying a second expedition. He secured $10,000 from Congress, planned supply caches along the route, and improved the design of his boats. On May 22, 1871, the second expedition set out from Green River Station in three boats, with Powell perched in a chair tied to the deck of the lead vessel. The roster included surveyor and professor Amon Thompson, Powell's brother-in-law, and photographer E. O. Beaman. During the initial easy miles, Powell spent much of the time on land, studying the local tribes and traveling back east to find more funding. He also became a father on September 8, naming his only child Mary Dean.

In the spring of 1872 the expedition discovered the last unknown river in the country while trying to get supplies to the riverbank. They named it the Escalante, after a Catholic priest who done some Southwest exploring himself centuries before, and continued to Lees Ferry, where the river, fed with heavy snowmelt and spring rains, raged through Marble Canyon. The ride got so rough that Powell ended the journey at Kanab Canyon in the Grand Canyon. Although abbreviated, the second expedition was a scientific success. Thompson had finished his topographic maps of the Grand Canyon and the surrounding region, and hundreds of photographs recorded the group's progress and captured the canyon's majesty for eager Eastern audiences. The Smithsonian published Powell's *Exploration of the Colorado River of the West and Its Tributaries* (revised as *Canyons of Colorado* in 1895), which is still required reading for anyone who runs the rapids or dreams of it.

As a result of his courageous leadership, Powell had become a national figure. Despite his exploits, he always maintained that he was a scientist first and foremost, not an adventurer, and he was eager to get back to his true calling. In 1873, Powell was appointed special commissioner to the Native Americans in Utah and eastern Nevada, where he worked to improve native tribes' education and economic situation. His *Introduction to the Study of Indian Languages* was published in 1877, cementing his reputation as an anthropologist. Powell's true landmark work, however, was his prescient *Report on the Lands of the Arid Region of the United States* (1878).

In this weighty tome, produced for Congress, Powell addressed the problem of settling the arid West. He knew firsthand how unsuited the region was for unplanned settlement, huge populations, and Eastern-style agriculture. With wisdom and remarkable foresight, he advised classifying the land according to its physical characteristics — chiefly rainfall — as well as its economic potential. Counties should be demarked by watershed boundaries, he said, not arbitrary political lines. The Homestead Act's 160-acre plots were far too small to graze animals, he added, recommending a farm of at least 2,560 acres for adequate pasturage. Most of his advice was ignored in the country's rush to achieve its Manifest Destiny, but today it is recognized today as a watershed document and a milestone of conservation literature.

In 1879, Powell founded the Smithsonian Institution's Bureau of Ethnology and became its first director. Here he continued his work on the languages of the tribes of the Intermountain West, which he had studied in person on his various journeys. (At one point he had even been adopted into a Hopi clan.) A year later, Powell became director of the newly organized U.S. Geological Survey, where he continued with his mapping and helped plan irrigation projects for settlers pouring toward the California coast. He held the post until 1892. Powell died September 23, 1902 in Haven, Maine, and was buried in the officer's section of Arlington National Cemetery.

SOUTHEAST UTAH

The name supposedly came from a herd of horses left to graze at the end of the mesa, which became confused about the way down and died of thirst within sight of the river far below. There's a **visitors center** (435/259-2614, 8 A.M.–6 P.M., to 5 P.M. in winter). You can reserve sites at the campground ($14) by calling 800/322-3770. Entrance is $7 per vehicle. Ask rangers to point you toward "Thelma and Louise Point," where the movie heroines (actually, stunt dummies) drove off into what was supposed to be the Grand Canyon. The climbing sequence at the beginning of *Mission: Impossible II* was also filmed here.

Back on Highway 313, another six miles brings you to the Canyonlands park boundary and the district **visitors center** (435/259-4712). Exhibits and an orientation video give introductory information on this section of the park, and books and maps are for sale. It's a good idea to get a weather report, even in summer—lightning is a real danger out in the open this high up. The road continues another six miles across the top of the plateau and forks near the **Willow Flat Campground,** with 12 sites (but no water) open all year ($5). In spring and fall all the sites fill early, and for good reason: The views from here, particularly at sunset, are dazzling. Head right (northwest) five miles to the road's end at **Whale Rock** and the edge of **Upheaval Dome,** a two-mile-wide crater whose origins geologists have been debating for decades. Most think it is a collapsed salt dome, but some still hold that it is an eroded astrobleme (meteorite crater).

In the opposite direction at the fork, a six-mile drive brings you to the true edge of things: **Grandview Point,** one of the great panoramas of the American West. Over 10,000 square miles of canyon country are on magnificent display, including the La Sal and Abajo Mountains, the Needles, Thousand Lake and Boulder mountains, Ekker and Elaterite buttes in the Maze, and the Orange Cliffs. It's a vista to lose yourself in, but be careful near the edge: it's a long way down.

The Island has fewer **hiking trails** than the park's other districts. Short trails (under two miles round-trip) lead to the very tip of the mesa at Grandview Point, to an overlook over Upheaval Dome, up on top of the stone domes of Whale Rock and Aztec Butte, and to Mesa Arch, perched right on the edge of the precipice. (Sunrise through Mesa Arch is worth rising early.) Longer trails lead down off the mesa to the White Rim and even the rivers. If you tackle one of these, remember that you'll have to climb back up whatever you descend, and there is very little water along the way. These include the Syncline Loop around Upheaval Dome, Lathrop Canyon, Taylor Canyon, and Murphy Loop. You can stop at Murphy Point for the night, but the rest of the overnight routes all involve at least a thousand-foot descent and involve steep switchbacks that are often very rough.

It's hard to miss the **White Rim,** a broad geologic layer midway between the Island and the rivers. A dirt track snakes across this mostly level plain, giving the adventurous the opportunity to enter the scenery so many others just look upon. The **White Rim Trail** is a 100-mile route gaining fame as one of the best multiday mountain bike rides in the United States. It's also popular with four-wheel-drive drivers and motorcyclists. There are eight campgrounds along the way, and you must reserve sites ahead of time for this popular excursion. If you go counterclockwise, as most people do, you'll head down the gradually descending Mineral Bottom Road, and at the other end ascend the merciless switchbacks of the Schafer Trail, visible near the visitors center. The entire trail can be driven in a day, but mountain bikers typically take 3–4 days depending on whether they're self-supported or have a support vehicle. (Some superhuman local bikers can ride it in a day.) Many companies in Moab organize trips.

◖ THE NEEDLES DISTRICT

Multicolored Church Rock marks the turnoff to the Needles from Highway 191, 40 miles south of Moab and 14 miles north of Monticello. From here, Highway 211 snakes west across the flats before dropping steeply into the valley cut by Indian Creek. This marks the beginning of one of Utah's prettiest drives, a winding route around the feet of looming mesas. Ten miles in is **Newspaper Rock,** where ancient passersby carved everything from bear tracks to mounted warriors into the dark desert varnish up to 4,000 years ago. There's a BLM campsite under the cottonwoods by the water, and more petroglyphs in nearby canyons. The soaring red cliffs of Wingate Sandstone along Indian Creek boast the best **crack climbing** in the world, with legendary routes like Supercrack (rated 5.10) slicing upwards for hundreds of flawless feet. Keep your eyes out for climbers on the blank-looking walls, and if you're climbing, bring plenty of medium-sized cams and tape up your hands—these are tough, sustained routes.

A few miles farther at the mouth of Cottonwood Creek sits the **Dugout Ranch,** a private spread established in 1885. After it was bought up by the S&S Cattle Company in 1919, it became part of the largest cattle operation in Utah, with more than 10,000 cows grazing on 1.8 million acres. The Redd family bought the spread in 1967 and in the late 1990s handed it over to The Nature Conservancy to manage on the condition that it continue as a working, conservation-minded ranch. From here you can see the unmistakable North and South Six-Shooter Peaks that mark the entrance to the Needles. From the right (north) comes the dirt road through Lockhart Basin, where there's another BLM campsite about a mile down. Just past the park boundary is a turnoff to the **Needles Outpost** (435/979-4007, cno@sanjuan.net, www.canyonlands-needlesoutpost.com), with a privately owned camp store, café, gas station, and campground ($15 per night) that's open more or less regularly from spring to fall.

Thirty-five miles from Highway 191 is the Needles **visitors center** (435/259-4711). Get your hiking and 4WD permits here, and get your bearings at the scale model of the entire park. The pavement continues to **Squaw Flat Campground** with 26 sites ($10). This one also fills quickly in spring and fall. The road continues 3.5 miles to the Big Spring Canyon Overlook.

Most visitors come to the Needles for the

SOUTHEAST UTAH

© JULIAN SMITH

Newspaper Rock

EVERETT RUESS:
LOST WANDERER OF CANYON COUNTRY

Poet, artist, nomad, naturalist: These terms and more applied to Everett Ruess, who saw more of the Southwest in his teens than most do in a lifetime, and eventually vanished into the very canyons that captured his vivid imagination. Born in Los Angeles in 1914, Everett grew up in a heady household. His mother was a noted art patron and his father a graduate of the Harvard Divinity School. After graduating from Hollywood High School, the slim, baby-faced boy set out for the Southwest. He bought a burro from a Navajo and led the animal throughout northern Arizona and southern Utah, exploring for months on end the remote reaches of the Grand Canyon, Zion, the Painted Desert, the canyons of the Escalante, Monument Valley, and Canyon de Chelly.

Flush with artistic zeal and the idealism of youth, Everett captured the wonders he saw in fervent journal entries and lyrical letters to his family and friends. "The wind is in my hair," he wrote, "there's a fire in my heels, and I shall always be a rover." In the days before the parks and monuments, few places were out of bounds. His mother cringed to read of him climbing cliffs to remote ruins and trudging alone across the desert for weeks. "There is a splendid freedom in solitude," Everett responded, "and after all, it is for solitude that I go to the mountains and deserts, not for companionship. In solitude I can bare my soul to the mountains unabashed ... and nothing stands between me and the Wild."

Everett quickly won over those he met along the way with his enthusiasm and openness. The Hopi granted him the rare honor of participating in their Antelope Dance, and Ruess taught himself enough Navajo to sing with a medicine man at a sick girl's bedside. He supported himself by selling paintings and woodblock prints of the landscapes he traveled through, and spent the winters in California, where artists like Edward Weston, Dorothea Lange, Maynard Dixon, and Ansel Adams recognized his potential and encouraged him to continue.

His writings grew more impassioned with every season. "I have loved the red rocks, the twisted trees, the red sand blowing in the wind, the slow sunny clouds crossing the sky, the shafts of moonlight on my bed at night. I have seemed to be at one with the world. ... I have really lived." His journeys became a spiritual quest, and Everett began taking greater and greater risks. "I have been flirting pretty

---

easily accessible backcountry, and they are seldom disappointed. Four short self-guided **hiking trails** leave the paved main road for Ancestral Puebloan ruins and an old cowboy camp in a smoke-blackened cave. Over 60 miles of longer trails snake over the slickrock and down into canyon bottoms, easily connected into challenging day hikes or overnight trips. The trail to **Chessler Park** is one of the most popular, leading to an open grassy area surrounded by slickrock. It can easily be extended to include the **Joint Trail** through narrow, deep cracks in the rock. For more hikes of about 10 miles, try the Big Spring to Squaw Canyon Loop, Squaw Canyon to Lost Canyon, Elephant Canyon to Druid Arch, the Peekaboo trail, and (my favorite) the loop that starts and ends at Squaw Flat, head-

ing up Big Spring and back past campsites EC2 and EC1. Lower Red Lake Canyon leads down to the Colorado River just across from Spanish Bottom and the Doll's House in the Maze. You'll have to reserve a spot at one of more than a dozen backcountry campsites. (Four vehicle campsites are set aside for drivers.)

Mountain bikers are limited to roads, but you can still ride nine miles to the **Confluence Overlook** trailhead, where after a half-mile walk you'll be able to see that the Green River is actually brown and the Colorado flows green. **Elephant Hill,** a short but ridiculously difficult climb in the heart of the district, is also popular with 4WD enthusiasts, who descend on the park in droves during Easter Jeep Week. (The back side, even worse than the front, includes heavily with death, the old clown," he wrote, describing premonitions of vanishing into the wild. "I shall go on some last wilderness trip to a place I have known and loved. I shall not return. When I go I leave no trace."

In November 1934, Everett rode into the town of Escalante, where he stocked up on provisions and talked with townsfolk in the dusty streets. Intending to spend the winter in Arizona, he then set off down the Hole-in-the-Rock Road as an early blizzard moved in across the Kaiparowits Plateau. A week later he camped with a pair of sheepherders, and may have bumped into a party of cattlemen soon after. If so, they were the last to ever see Everett alive. In February, his two burros were found in Davis Gulch near what was thought to be his last campsite. Everett had vanished.

Search parties organized by his parents and friends from his travels combed the canyons of the Escalante to no avail. An expert tracker, a half-Navajo, half-Ute named Dougeye, led one party across the Colorado into Davis Canyon, where he wandered stymied for days. Everett had entered the canyon, he agreed, but there was no sign that he had ever left. As reports came in of supposed sightings from Moab to Florida, theories flew around the canyon coun-try: Everett had orchestrated his own disappearance; he had been killed in a flood or fell from a cliff; he had been killed by Indians and his scalp used in squaw dances. He appeared in the visions of Navajo medicine men and his signature inscription "NEMO" – meaning "no one" in Latin, and probably a reference to the ill-fated submarine captain in Jules Verne's *Twenty Thousands Leagues Under the Sea* – kept turning up in caves and canyon walls. (Many are still visible today.)

As time passed, Everett's disappearance became a canyon country legend. In the early 1960s, archaeologists found his canteen and a box of razor blades from the Owl Drug Company of Los Angeles. The most widely accepted theory is that he was killed for his gear, and his body hidden in one of the countless nooks in the country he loved so much. His older brother Waldo eventually oversaw the installation of a plaque high on the wall of Davis Canyon, bearing a quote from Everett's journals:

Oh but the desert is glorious now, with marching clouds in the blue sky and cool winds blowing. The smell of the sage is sweet in my nostrils, and the luring trail leads onwards.

SOUTHEAST UTAH

a section with such tight corners that vehicles have to shift into reverse and back down part of the way.) Elephant Hill leads to a loop road through the **grabens,** an area of straight-sided, flat-bottomed valleys like city streets.

Salt Creek Canyon, once one of the most popular drives in the park, was closed to vehicles after research showed that its delicate riparian ecosystem—growing around the most extensive perennial water source in the entire park—could be damaged by 4WD traffic. It's here that the Needle's rich archaeology reaches its apex. Ancient granaries and rock art fill the upper canyon, including the famous red-white-and-blue "All-American Man" pictograph. (The blue is actually charcoal.) The entire canyon takes 2–4 days to hike. Vehicles can still drive up **Horse Canyon** to the east, which leads to Tower Ruin and a pothole (horizontal) arch called Paul Bunyan's Potty, as well as **Davis** and **Lavender canyons** off of Highway 211. Lavender and Horse Canyons require a $5 permit for day use.

THE MAZE DISTRICT

Accessed by river or off Highway 24, the Maze is by far the least-visited and least-accessible part of the park. The Maze, which includes the separate **Horseshoe Canyon** section of Highway 24 between Green River and Hanksville, offers plenty of opportunity for isolation and adventure. With its rough roads, faint trails, and rare water sources, it also demands a higher degree of backcountry experience than most parts of the Colorado Plateau. Even if you're driving in, as many visitors do, you *must* go prepared, and always let someone know where you're going and when you should be back.

Three days is considered a minimum to visit the Maze, and you can easily spend a week here. The only services of any kind are at the **Hans Flat Ranger Station** (8 A.M.–4:30 P.M. daily), which is 46 miles from Highway 24 along a two-wheel-drive dirt road. (Turn off to the east just south of Goblin Valley State Park, 24 miles from the interstate.) All you'll find here is information—no water, food, gas, or entrance fees. Beyond this you'll need a high-clearance four-wheel-drive to negotiate the tracks in the park. It's possible to drive all the way to The Doll House, a distinctive rock formation overlooking Spanish Bottom along the Colorado River, but expect this to take hours if not days. Make sure to bring extra gas, water, at least one full-sized spare tire, chains, a shovel, and a high-lift jack; towing bills out here run in the thousands of dollars. There are 17 primitive vehicle campsites.

Hiking trails in the Maze are very rugged and not always well marked. Look for rock cairns, and be prepared to raise and lower your packs with ropes at some points. Often the main concern is getting from one source of water to the next. Popular destinations include the Land of Standing Rocks and the network of canyons that make up the Maze proper—South Fork, Shot Canyon, and others—where you'll find the famous Harvest Scene pictograph panel. Permits are required for overnight trips.

Horseshoe Canyon

A small, separate section of the Maze protects one of the most remarkable collections of rock art in the Four Corners. Turn off Highway 24 to the east between Goblin Valley State Park and Hanksville; from here it's 30 miles of graded dirt road to the parking area. (You can camp here at the canyon rim.) A 6.5-mile (round-trip) trail leads down 750 feet into Horseshoe Canyon along an old 4WD route. It's a beautiful, relatively lush canyon filled with cottonwoods. After three miles you'll suddenly catch a glimpse of the **Great Gallery,** an extensive lineup of figures up to eight feet tall presided over by the haunting, hollow-eyed "Holy Ghost." This "Barrier Canyon" style of rock art is believed to have been painted between 2000 B.C. and A.D. 500. Other pictographs and petroglyphs are scattered along the trail.

Land of Standing Rocks in the Maze District of Canyonlands National Park

© JULIAN SMITH

SOUTHEAST UTAH

Highway 24: Green River to Torrey

Leaving I-40 west of the town of Green River (not to be confused with Green River, Wyoming, which is also on the waterway of the same name), Highway 24 heads bravely south across the San Rafael Desert. To the west rises the San Rafael Swell, a stone bulge carved by narrow canyons and protected by the serrated barricade of the San Rafael Reef. Goblin Valley State Park and Horseshoe Canyon, a detached portion of the Maze District of Canyonlands National Park, offer two versions of the fantastic on either side of the roadway, but past Hanksville the scenery really starts to get strange. A sickly expanse of badlands make up the western San Rafael Desert, a gorgeous but forbidding wilderness of purples, grays, mustards, and tans. This landscape is so extraterrestrial that the Mars Society, a group dedicated to reaching the Red Planet, has set up a research station near Hanksville. It's dominated by Factory Butte, a massive wedge of dark Mancos Shale topped with tougher Mesa Verde Sandstone near Caineville. The topography gets older as you continue west along the Fremont River, through the huge monocline of the Waterpocket Fold, the backbone of Capitol Reef National Park.

GREEN RIVER

An easy river crossing is a rarity in canyon country, so this valley south of the Book Cliffs, between Gray and Labyrinth canyons, has been known since prehistoric times. During the Mexican occupation, the Spanish Trail forded the river just upstream on its way from Santa Fe to Los Angeles. Americans began to arrive from the east in the late 1870s, and in 1883 the Denver & Rio Grande Western Railway first dropped off mining supplies and carried away livestock. This ended when the railroad moved to Helper, Utah, and began a pattern of booms and busts that continued through eras of oil exploration, fruit growing, and the establishment of the Utah Launch Complex of the White Sands Missile Base in 1963. Test rockets were fired from along the river to land in White Sands Missile Range in New Mexico until 1979.

Today the town survives on farming, ranching, and above all the traffic off I-70, whose 105-mile run west to Salina is the longest stretch of interstate without services in the country. Green River (pop. 1,000) has been an obvious supply and staging point for river travel since Powell and his men floated through town. Hot summers, little winter frost, and just the right elevation (4,000 feet) give Green River the ideal climate for growing melons, and the town's justifiably famous cantaloupe and watermelons are sold from roadside stands in summer and celebrated during a fall festival.

Sights

The **John Wesley Powell River History Museum** (885 E. Main St., 435/564-3427, www.jwprhm.com, 8 A.M.–8 P.M. daily Apr.–Oct., to 5 P.M. otherwise, $2 pp) celebrates the career of the man whose descents of the Green River put much of this part of the country on the map. Exhibits on the geology and human history of the Green and Colorado rivers includes the fascinating River Runner's Hall of Fame and models of the various boats that have made (or attempted) the difficult descents. It all leads to a mock-up of the man himself in a chair on the bow of the *Emma Dean*.

Towering cottonwoods shade green lawns on the east bank of the river at the **Green River State Park** (450 S. Green River Blvd., 435/564-3633, $5 pp). It's a popular put-in place for trips down Labyrinth and Stillwater canyons, and has 42 RV or tent campsites ($14), hot showers, and a nine-hole golf course.

Events

If you're in the area the third weekend in September, keep your eye out for the 25-foot watermelon that's rolled out to help celebrate **Melon Days,** accompanied by music, games, a parade, canoe races and, of course, lots and lots of melons.

Recreation

River-running is the main diversion in Green River, and trips are run in both directions: through Desolation and Gray canyons to the north, and Labyrinth and Stillwater canyons to the south. **Moki-Mac River Expeditions** (800/284-7280, mokimac@mokimac.com, www.mokimac.com) run river trips on both the Green and the Colorado rivers, including the Grand Canyon. Their voyages last 3–14 days, and include one-day excursions through Westwater Canyon on the Colorado ($150 adults, $135 children) and Gray Canyon ($60/$50). If you want to do Labyrinth and Stillwater canyons on your own, they'll rent you canoes for $17 per day and retrieve up to four people from Mineral Canyon for $250.

Holiday Expeditions (435/564-3273 or 800/624-6323, holiday@bikeraft.com, www.bikeraft.com) are located behind the Comfort Inn, and offer white-water rafting and mountain bikes trips.

Accommodations

Two of Green River's least-expensive lodgings are known by their classic neon signs: the reclining woman at the **Robber's Roost** (225 W. Main St., 435/564-3452, fax 435/564-8809) and the flower and arrow of the **Sleepy Hollow Motel** (94 E. Main St., 435/564-8189), which welcomes "Hip Cats and Kittens." Both are under $50 per night.

The **Best Western River Terrace** (880 E. Main St., 435/564-3401, fax 435/564-3403, $90–130) has rooms with views of the river as well as the **Tamarisk Restaurant,** serving all meals, downstairs near the pool. Close by is a **Comfort Inn** (1065 E. Main St., 435/564-3300, fax 435/564-3299, $65–75).

Beautiful antique furniture fills the **Bankurz Hatt Bed & Breakfast** (214 Farrer St., 435/564-3382, www.bankurzhatt.com), built in the late 1890s by the town's first banker, with wood shipped from St. Louis. Owners Ben and Lana Coomer are full of information on things to do in the area. Rates are in the $100–150 range.

Next to the state park, the **Shady Acres RV Park** (360 E. Main St., 435/564-8290 or 800/537-8674, www.shadyacresrv.com) has 101 sites as well as a Blimpie restaurant and a gas station. Tent sites are $20, RV sites run $24–29, and cabins with a/c are $42. Green River also hosts the **United Campground** (910 E. Main St., 435/564-8195) with sites for $16–22.

Food

Ray's Tavern (25 S. Broadway, 435/564-3511) is a classic roadhouse with excellent burgers and other meaty delights, which are even better paired with a microbrew and a few rounds of pool or pinball. They have a covered outdoor patio and occasional live music on weekends. Mexican and American dishes start at $6 at **Ben's Cafe** (115 W. Main, 435/564-3352, daily for all meals) whose diner atmosphere comes from countertop jukeboxes and orange vinyl upholstery.

Information and Transportation

The **Green River City Travel Center** (885 E. Main St., 435/564-3526, www.greenriver-utah.com) is in the same building as the John Wesley Powell River History Museum.

To arrange vehicle pickup from Mineral Bottom or elsewhere along the river, contact one of the tour companies listed above or **Green River Shuttle Service** (435/564-8292). **Bighorn Express** (801/746-2417 or 888/655-7433, www.bighornexpress.com) runs a shuttle bus to and from Salt Lake City via Price and continuing to Moab and Monticello (daily in season; Wed., Fri. and Sun. only in Jan. and Feb.). Green River's **Greyhound** stop (435/564-3421) is at the West Winds Truck Stop at 525 East Main Street.

CRYSTAL GEYSER

An unsuccessful petroleum test well drilled in the 1930s concentrated bubbling, mineral-rich waters into a cold-water gusher that shoots up to 100 feet in the air two to four times per day. It's on the east bank of the river, 4.5 river miles south of the state park, and is surrounded by maroon deposits of travertine. To drive there, turn south onto Frontage Road off Main Street near milepost 4, and head south for three miles until you pass under a railroad overpass. Turn right and go six miles west to the river, on a road that quickly turns to dirt and passes under I-70.

FLOATING LABYRINTH AND STILLWATER CANYONS

If you've cut your teeth on daylong river trips and want to try something a little longer, but still on your own, this float just might be the perfect step up. It's a calm, winding journey downstream from Green River, with plenty of side canyons to explore and historic artifacts to puzzle over. You probably won't have it all to yourself—powerboats zoom past pretty regularly, and it's popular with the canoe-and-kayak crowd—but for a relaxing, pretty trip that doesn't take all that much planning or expertise, these canyons are hard to beat.

The trip can be done year-round, but try to avoid Memorial Day Weekend, when the Annual Friendship Cruise fills the wide canyon with boaters. You'll need a free permit available from the BLM, and you must be completely self-contained, with toilets and a keen eye for collecting all your own garbage.

Labyrinth Canyon begins south of Green River and winds for 68 miles to Mineral Bottom just north of Canyonlands National Park. Along the way you'll pass an old cabin at Doc Bishop Bottom, the privately owned Ruby Ranch, and the names of early river-runners chiseled into the stone at Register Rock and the Post Office at the Bow Knot. The trip takes three to four days, leaving time to explore side canyons. You can arrange a vehicle pickup a Mineral Bottom through rafting or shuttle companies in Green River or Moab. The rafting companies can also arrange guided trips down this section of the Green. For more information, contact the BLM office in Price, Utah (435/636-3622, www.blm.gov/utah/price/labyrinth.htm).

Stillwater Canyon continues another 53 miles from Mineral Bottom to the confluence of the Green and Colorado rivers. You'll need an NPS permit for this section, since it crosses Canyonlands National Park, and you'll also have to arrange a pickup from one of the jet boats that descend to the confluence daily in season.

SAN RAFAEL SWELL

This kidney-shaped anticline covers 900 square miles on either side of I-70, stretching for 80 miles from north to south. Its southeastern edge along Highway 24 is marked by the **San Rafael Reef,** a jagged line of thousand-foot hills like the teeth of some gigantic monster. Two perennial streams cut through this imposing wall, revealing 250-million-year-old Coconino Sandstone—one of the area's oldest exposed rocks layers—on their way east toward the Green River.

Pictographs found here, similar to those in Horseshoe Canyon, have been estimated to be at least 2,000 years old. In 1853, the head of a railroad survey team charting a route for the transcontinental railroad wrote:

As we approached the [Green] river yesterday, the ridges on either side of its banks to the west appeared broken into a thousand forms – columns, shafts, temples, buildings, and ruined cities could be seen, or imagined, from the high points along our route.

A member of Powell's second expedition down the Green River wrote in his journal that local Native Americans called the formations of the Reed "Sau-auger-towip," or the "Stone House Lands," and conductors on the Denver & Rio Grande Western Railroad pointed out the "silent city" to passengers. Butch Cassidy is only one of dozens of outlaws who have sought refuge among the tortuous canyons after various misdeeds.

Dozens of canyons and hundreds of side canyons lace through the reef as well, making it a canyoneer's playground. Flood debris hangs 50 feet high between the walls of slot canyons. Others are filled with water for most of the year, meaning that if you're truly prepared, you'll find yourself hiking across the desert carrying a wetsuit and an inner tube.

You probably won't be alone in the swell. With the construction of I-70, the once-remote area was made suddenly more accessible, and off-road vehicle (ORV) use continues to be a contentious issue. A population of bighorn sheep has been established by the Utah Department of Wildlife Resources (at last count it was some 70 strong), and hundreds of pronghorn antelope live in the desert to the east and occasionally venture into the swell itself.

Originally the San Rafael Swell was considered for national park status, but mineral development interests kept that from happening. There has been a growing push to have 600,000 acres of it declared a national monument, a proposal even Utah's Republican politicians have endorsed. This would be an especially welcome move to opponents of ORVs, whose tire marks scar hillsides on both sides of the highway.

Exploring the Southern San Rafael Swell

Always take a topographical map; it's possible to get lost even among the slot canyons, which empty out into a confusing landscape beyond the reef. By far the most detailed guide to exploring the swell is Steve Allen's *Canyoneering I* (see *Suggested Reading* in the *Resources* chapter).

Aside from I-70, the easiest way into the southern Reef is the road that leads to Goblin Valley State Park from Highway 24. Instead of turning south toward the park, keep going west. Seven miles from Highway 24 is a parking area on the right for the trail around **Temple Mountain,** a colorful pointed peak north of the road. The seven-mile mining road around its base makes a good ramble or mountain bike ride. Keep an eye out for open mine shafts.

Just past the Temple Mountain turnoff, head left (southwest) to reach a series of short but spectacular slot canyons cutting through the reef. First is **Wild Horse Canyon,** an easy walk past a number of pictographs, which eventu-

ally intersects with the Temple Mountain road. Keep going down the road past the turnoff for Goblin Valley to reach **Chute** and **Crack canyons,** which are slightly more narrow and difficult, with some scrambling required. This is a longer hike, but can still be done in a day. The hike starts by heading up Chute Canyon, 6.5 miles from the Temple Mountain road.

Just over five miles past the Goblin Valley turnoff is the parking area for **Little Wild Horse Canyon,** the reef's most popular hike, which joins with **Bell Canyon** into a relatively easy loop hike that can be done in a day. It's narrow and beautiful, and will get a smile out of even veteran slot canyoneers. Just under a mile farther (6.5 miles past Goblin Valley) is a wash coming from the north. Head up here about 20 minutes to reach the mouths of **Ding** and **Dang canyons,** a challenging (and less-traveled) pair of slots. Look for pointy Ding Dang Dome at the top of the Ding Canyon, which is your signal to head left (west) and return via Dang Canyon.

This is just a taste of what the San Rafael Swell has to offer. Some of the other choices are serious undertakings, and every year some people underestimate them and have to be rescued. West of the reef, via the road past Temple Mountain, is **Muddy Creek,** with a sinuous, deep section of narrows called simply **The Chute.** One of the best canyon hikes in the Southwest, this involves going down a deep sinuous chasm beneath logs jammed high overhead by raging spring floodwaters. The hike from Hondoo Arch to the Hidden Splendor Mine can be done, with a two-car shuttle, in a long day. Aside from spring, the water shouldn't be more than knee deep.

North of I-70, a section of the San Rafael River known as the **Black Box** has 400-foot-high walls that are sometimes only 10 feet apart. The problem is that it's full of water, and thus requires a wetsuit and inner tubes to avoid hypothermia and drowning. Also north of the interstate (turn off just west of mile marker 145) is a dirt road to **Black Dragon Wash,** where an amazing panel of Barrier Canyon–style pictographs is half a mile up.

GOBLIN VALLEY STATE PARK

About 20 miles north of Hanksville on Highway 24 is a signed turnoff to the west that leads, after another 12 miles and one more left turn, to one of the odder sights in this landscape of visual extremes. Imagine an amphitheater of house-high chocolate mushrooms left out in the sun, and you'll have a general idea of the crazily eroded sandstone formations that fill this small but detour-worthy park.

You can admire the stubby formations from a picnic area overlook or hike down among them—best of all, you're even allowed to climb them. (Movie buffs might recognize this place from a scene in the comedy *Galaxy Quest;* during filming, some friends of mine unwittingly stumbled on a fake spaceship among the formations and were, let's just say, briefly but intensely confused.)

Entrance to the park (435/564-3633) is $5 per vehicle, and there's a 21-site campground ($14) with showers. You can reserve sites ahead of time through the website www .reserveamerica.com.

HANKSVILLE

Established in 1882 on the bank of the Fremont River, Hanksville was named for one of its original settlers, Ebenezer Hanks. The only remnant of a string of Mormon communities along the river decimated by floods near the turn of the 20th century, Hanksville has always been a remote town. Mail was once carried by horse from Green River three times a week, with riders making the 110-mile round-trip in two days. Electricity only arrived in 1960. Today Hanksville, with a population of about 400, survives on mining, farming, ranching, and, increasingly, the tourist traffic to Lake Powell and parks to the west.

At the intersection of Highways 24 and 95 is the **Hollow Mountain Gas & Grocery** (435/542-3298), a filling station that has been hollowed out of a sandstone hillside. Next door, **Blondie's Eatery & Gift** (435/542-3255) has a restaurant/deli serving all meals, including ice cream, vegetarian burgers, and platters starting at $6. There's a nice view from the picnic tables on the front patio.

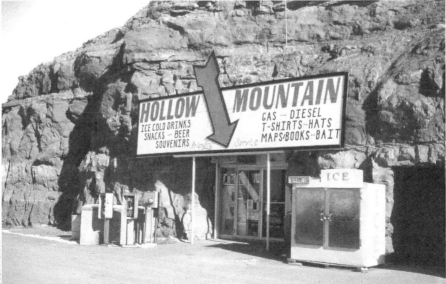

Hollow Mountain Gas & Grocery in Hanksville is actually carved into the side of a cliff.

SOUTHEAST UTAH

© JULIAN SMITH

Also near the intersection is the **Redrock Restaurant and Campground** (226 E. 100 N., 435/542-3235, all meals Apr.–Oct.), probably the best eatery in town, with sandwiches from $3 and chicken, steak, and seafood entrées from $7. They offer campsites in back for tents ($12) and RVs ($18).

Lodging options in town include **Fern's Place** (99 E. 100 N., 435/542-3251), the **Whispering Sands Motel** (140 S. Hwy. 95, 435/542-3238, $60–70), and the **Best Value Inn** (322 E. 100 N., 435/542-3471). You can't miss the **Desert Inn Motel** (197 E. 100 N., 435/542-3241)—just look for the scrap-metal dinosaur skeletons out front, especially the one with the hood and trunk lid of a Volkswagen Beetle for a skull. None of these places charges over $50 per night.

SOUTH-CENTRAL UTAH

South-Central Utah is big, beautiful, remote, and nearly empty. Garfield and Wayne counties combined are larger than five entire U.S. states, but have fewer than 7,000 residents between them. That's more than a square mile for every inhabitant, and not just any square mile, either. On your winding way across the state's emptiest quarter, you'll cross through some of the country's wildest topography.

Southern Utah is defined by geographical features on a monumental scale. The outlandish cliffs of the Waterpocket Fold in Capitol Reef National Park are evidence of an almost incomprehensibly large uplift. Passing over the cool evergreen slopes of Boulder Mountain and the Aquarius Plateau, you'll be riding yet another geologic bulge, this one not yet eroded away. From here the tortuous canyons of the Escalante

River drain southeast to Lake Powell, and the vast sweep of the Grand Staircase–Escalante National Monument, littered with the leftovers of long-gone cultures, spreads south and west. The vividly named steps of the Grand Staircase march from north to south in the monument's western reaches. Along the way, isolated towns such as Boulder and Escalante are just beginning to see an influx of visitors and new residents drawn by the landscape and seclusion.

For all intents and purposes, the city of Page, Arizona, and the Paria Plateau to the west can be considered part of South-Central Utah, and so they are included in this chapter. Built to house workers on the Glen Canyon Dam, the tidy little tourist town of Page sits at the southern end of Lake Powell, the region's water-sport mecca, and offers plenty of budget accommodations

© JULIAN SMITH

HIGHLIGHTS

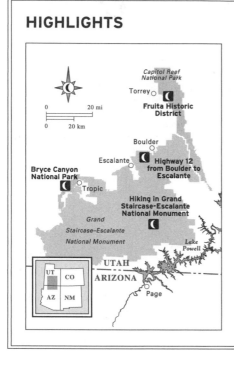

◖ **Fruita Historic District:** Pick your own apples and cherries among pioneer cabins in the middle of the red-rock desert in Capitol Reef National Park (page 169).

◖ **Highway 12 from Boulder to Escalante:** Panoramas of the Escalante canyons on either side of the Hogback, barely wide enough for two lanes of pavement (page 180).

◖ **Hiking in Grand Staircase-Escalante National Monument:** The town of Escalante offers easy access to the innumerable canyon hikes—including claustrophobic slots—along the Hole-in-the-Rock Road (page 188).

◖ **Bryce Canyon National Park:** Multihued rock hoodoos were "A hell of a place to lose a cow," in the words of an early settler (page 191).

LOOK FOR ◖ TO FIND RECOMMENDED SIGHTS, ACTIVITIES, DINING, AND LODGING.

and options for outdoor fun. Canyon hikers flock to the Paria Plateau, where the multiday hike down Paria Canyon, including the legendary Buckskin Gulch narrows, is one of the best in the Four Corners.

Each of these features would be worth a trip in itself, but luckily you can get a tantalizing but substantial taste of them all in a few days' drive along the meandering byways of Highways 24 and 12, which connect I-70 with Highway 89 near Bryce Canyon National Park. Page is connected to Kanab, Utah, and Flagstaff, Arizona, by Highway 89, whose spur 89A crosses south of the Paria Plateau and offers access to the North Rim of the Grand Canyon. The paved road is only the beginning, however. Most of this area is backcountry—*way* backcountry—and can be explored only by four-wheel-drive, horse, mountain bike, or sweat and boot leather.

PLANNING YOUR TIME

"Outback" implies lots of big, beautiful distances to cover, so ideally you'd have a week to explore South-Central Utah—five days minimum. Tiny Page is the only city of any size out here, so it's better to thinking terms of moving rather than touring out of a home base. Starting in the east, Capitol Reef National Park merits a few days of exploring. Start at the **Fruita Historic District,** a historic haven that contrasts the overwhelming scenery along the Waterpocket Fold with lush orchards. Keep going along Highway 12 from Torrey, whose stretch from **Boulder to Escalante** is among the most scenic drives in the country. The towns of Boulder and Escalante are jumping-off points for **hiking in Grand Staircase-Escalante.** At the western end of Highway 12 you'll find yourself among the stone spires of **Bryce Canyon National Park**—another completely unique sight in this land of visual extremes.

Capitol Reef National Park and Vicinity

Word is starting to get out about Utah's least-known national park, but Capitol Reef still gets only a fraction as many visitors as its more famous neighbors. The long, narrow park—the second largest in the state—follows the Waterpocket Fold, a gigantic north–south wrinkle in the earth's crust that stretches for more than 100 miles. Highway 24 bisects the northern end of the park along the Fremont River, but those who venture south past the startling green oasis of the historic Fruita settlement will find a world of dreamlike rock formations, narrow slot canyons, and silent battlements of stone. And the best part, at least for the moment, is that you still stand a very good chance of having it, or at least a sizable chunk of it, all to yourself.

The Setting

Geology is the language of the reef. In all, almost 10,000 feet of sedimentary layers are on display here, ranging from the Permian period (270 million years ago) to the late Cretaceous (80 million years ago). The park's main feature, the **Waterpocket Fold,** is a classic monocline (a single-step fold) and is all that remains of a huge bulge in the planet's surface thrust skyward 65 million years ago. After the fold was formed, it eroded away until only jagged ranks of stone remained along what was once its base.

Since the Waterpocket Fold tilted up to the west, the rock layers are in order of age, with younger layers to the east and older (once deeper) layers to the west. It's easy to recognize the domes of light-colored Navajo Sandstone, like Capitol Dome and the Golden Throne. Cathedral Valley's formations in the north end of the park are of darker Entrada Sandstone.

The term "Waterpocket" refers to natural sandstone basins that collect rainwater, and "Capitol" came about because the huge round white domes of sandstone concentrated in the Navajo Sandstone reminded early settlers of the Capitol building in Washington, DC. The other half of the park's name has its roots in the high-seas experiences of early prospectors, so that anything that blocked travel—such as a huge ridge of rock—they called a "reef."

(FRUITA HISTORIC DISTRICT

The first stop after turning off Highway 24 is the Capitol Reef **visitors center** (435/425-3791, www.nps.gov/care, 8 A.M.–4:30 P.M. daily with extended summer hours). Various exhibits explain the park's geology, history, and archaeology, and books and maps are for sale. Pick up free backcountry camping permits here, and check on the weather before setting off down any of the park's dirt roads. (In addition to the park's visitors center, another good source of info is the **Capitol Reef Country Travel Council** (435/425-3365 or 800/858-7951, info@capitolreef.org, www.capitolreef.org).

Keep going south into the **historic district** (where Mormon settlers planted orchards on

© JULIAN SMITH

Capitol Reef National Park

SOUTH-

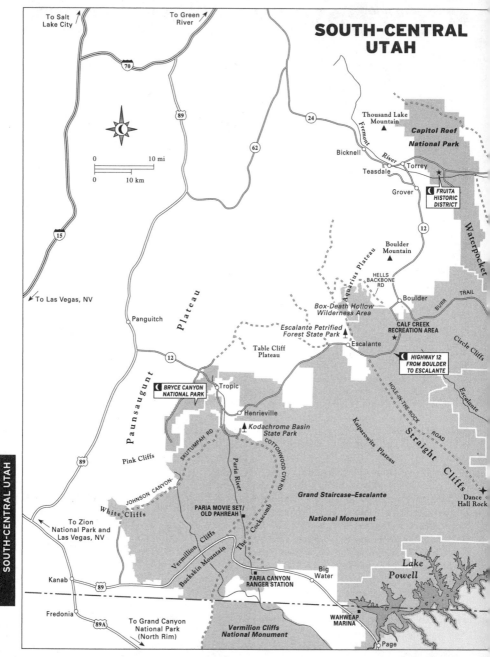

SOUTH-CENTRAL UTAH

To Salt Lake City

To Green River

To Las Vegas, NV

0   10 mi
0   10 km

Thousand Lake Mountain

Capitol Reef National Park

Bicknell

Fremont River

Torrey

Teasdale

Grover

FRUITA HISTORIC DISTRICT

Boulder Mountain

Aquarius Plateau

HELLS BACKBONE RD

Waterpocket

Boulder

BURR TRAIL

Box-Death Hollow Wilderness Area

CALF CREEK RECREATION AREA

Panguitch

Plateau

Escalante Petrified Forest State Park

Escalante

Circle Cliffs

Table Cliff Plateau

HIGHWAY 12 FROM BOULDER TO ESCALANTE

BRYCE CANYON NATIONAL PARK

Tropic

Paunsaugunt

Henrieville

Kodachrome Basin State Park

HOLE-IN-THE-ROCK

Escalante

ROAD

Straight Cliffs

Pink Cliffs

SKUTUMPAH RD

Paria River

COTTONWOOD CVN RD

Kalparowits Plateau

Grand Staircase–Escalante

Dance Hall Rock

JOHNSON CANYON

White Cliffs

PARIA MOVIE SET/ OLD PAHREAH

Cockscomb

National Monument

To Zion National Park and Las Vegas, NV

Vermillion Cliffs

Buckskin Mountain

The

Big Water

Lake Powell

Kanab

PARIA CANYON RANGER STATION

Fredonia

To Grand Canyon National Park (North Rim)

WAHWEAP MARINA

Vermilion Cliffs National Monument

Page

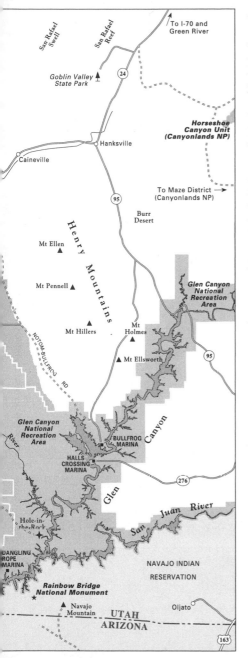

the green banks of the Fremont River in the 1880s. Originally called Junction, as it stood at the intersection of the Fremont River and Sulphur Creek, the settlement quickly became known as the "Eden of Wayne County" about around the time when Butch Cassidy and his Wild Bunch are said to have hidden out in the nearby canyons. The settlement changed its name to Fruita in 1902 after the apple, cherry, peach, apricot, mulberry, and pear trees started bearing fruit.

In the early 1900s the population hovered around 10 families, who raised sorghum, alfalfa, and vegetables. Fruit still provided most of the income, though, and only rough tracks connected Fruita with the rest of the world. A mainly barter economy helped the tiny community weather the Great Depression, and the first tractor didn't arrive until World War II. Visitors began to arrive with the declaration of Capitol Reef National Monument in 1937, and the National Park Service eventually purchased most of the land peacefully by the late 1960s. The last resident moved away in 1969.

Today you can see the historic **school** on Highway 24, the **Gifford farmhouse and barn,** the **Holt Farmstead,** and the famous Fruita **orchards.** The Park Service maintains about 2,700 trees with year-round irrigation and care, and in season each fruit crop is available to visitors on a pick-your-own basis for a small fee. Fruits are ready for harvest anywhere between late June (cherries) and early October (apples)—contact the visitors center for a schedule. Follow the **Fremont River Trail** through the orchards to an overlook 800 feet above the valley. It's easy for its first half mile but starts to climb steeply after that, and is just over a mile long.

Another, steeper trail leaves the road to the east just before the campground, and climbs up to **Cohab Canyon,** named after the Mormon polygamists who sought refuge from the law in this classic "hanging" canyon that's hard to see from below. The 1.5-mile trail climbs steeply at first, and has short side spurs leading to various overlooks.

There's a pleasantly shady picnic area among

SOUTH-CENTRAL UTAH

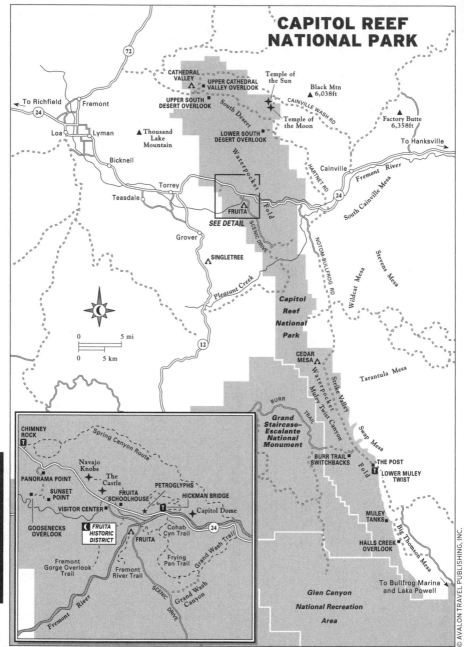

CAPITOL REEF NATIONAL PARK

To Richfield

72

Fremont

Loa

Lyman

Bicknell

Torrey

Teasdale

Grover

CATHEDRAL VALLEY

UPPER CATHEDRAL VALLEY OVERLOOK

UPPER SOUTH DESERT OVERLOOK

▲ Thousand Lake Mountain

LOWER SOUTH DESERT OVERLOOK

South Desert

Temple of the Sun

Black Mtn
▲ 6,038ft

CAINVILLE WASH RD

Temple of the Moon

▲ Factory Butte 6,358ft

To Hanksville

Waterpocket Fold

Cainville

Fremont River

HARTNET RD

24

South Cainville Mesa

FRUITA

SEE DETAIL

SCENIC DRIVE

SINGLETREE

Pleasant Creek

Capitol Reef National Park

Stevens Mesa

Wildcat Mesa

0   5 mi

0   5 km

12

NOTOM-BULLFROG RD

CEDAR MESA

Tarantula Mesa

Waterpocket Fold

Strike Valley

Muley Twist Canyon

BURR TRAIL

Grand Staircase–Escalante National Monument

Swap Mesa

BURR TRAIL SWITCHBACKS

THE POST
LOWER MULEY TWIST

MULEY TANKS

Big Thomson Mesa

HALLS CREEK OVERLOOK

To Bullfrog Marina and Lake Powell

Glen Canyon National Recreation Area

Detail Inset

CHIMNEY ROCK

Spring Canyon Route

Navajo Knobs

The Castle

PANORAMA POINT

SUNSET POINT

VISITOR CENTER

PETROGLYPHS

FRUITA SCHOOLHOUSE

HICKMAN BRIDGE

Capitol Dome

GOOSENECKS OVERLOOK

FRUITA HISTORIC DISTRICT

FRUITA

Cohab Cyn Trail

24

Fremont Gorge Overlook Trail

Fremont River Trail

Frying Pan Trail

Grand Wash Trail

SCENIC DRIVE

Grand Wash Canyon

Fremont River

the cottonwood and willows by the river, and interpreters at the Gifford farmhouse explain and demonstrate various aspects of pioneer life. The **Fruita Campground** just down the road has 71 sites for $10, open year-round. The park is free up to this point, but to continue down the scenic drive you'll have to pay a $5 **entrance fee** per car.

SCENIC DRIVE

The Reef's main thoroughfare, relatively speaking, starts at the visitors center and heads south for 12.5 paved miles. Past Fruita, the first major point of interest is the short dirt spur into **Grand Wash,** which is good enough for two-wheel-drive vehicles in dry weather. Butch Cassidy was said to have a hideout in this narrow, sheer-sided canyon. True or not, there's an arch named after him today, and the trail to **Cassidy Arch** (1.75 miles) climbs steeply to a spot above it.

Keep driving south past the **Egyptian Temple** and the **Golden Throne,** two of the park's more unusual landmarks. The Egyptian Temple looks like a vertical accordion of dark Moenkopi Sandstone topped by the harder Shinarump Layer, and the Golden Throne is an unmistakable dome of gleaming Navajo Sandstone. A tough two-mile trail climbs to the top of the cliffs to a view over the Golden Throne and the surrounding landscape.

A short distance farther down the road another dirt spur heads east into **Capitol Gorge,** which is just as deep and narrow as Grand Wash. This used to be the only way vehicles could cross the Waterpocket Fold before Highway 24 was built, and is probably the closest thing you will ever come to driving through a slot canyon, weather permitting. Look for Fremont petroglyphs and the "Pioneer Register," where passing settlers carved their names on the canyon wall near the turn of the 20th century.

Beyond Capitol Gorge the pavement ends and the scenic drive crosses Pleasant Creek and becomes the **South Draw Road,** a rougher track that curves around to the southwest to join Highway 12 near the Pleasant Creek and Oak Creek campgrounds up on Boulder Mountain.

CATHEDRAL VALLEY

North of Highway 24 is some of the reef's most unusual landscapes—and by now you should know that's saying a lot. It's a four-wheel-drive-only adventure past stone formations jutting abruptly from a nearly level plain, formed by a layer of Curtis Sandstone capping softer Entrada Sandstone. Check with the visitors center for current weather conditions before setting out on this or any other dirt roads in the park.

Most visitors see Cathedral Valley from a 60-mile loop that starts at the **Fremont River Ford** 12 miles east of the visitors center on Highway 24. (It's a good idea to start here to make sure you can make the crossing, which can be flooded after thunderstorms or during spring runoff.) Please close the gate behind you and don't park or camp on private property along the road.

The loop follows the **Hartnet Road** past sweeping views over the stark South Desert. Turn off onto the **Caineville Wash Road** at **Hartnet Junction,** 28 miles from the ford,

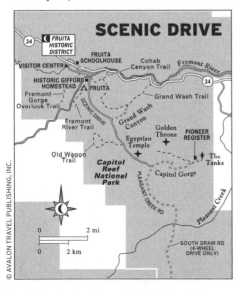

SOUTH-CENTRAL UTAH

BUTCH CASSIDY AND THE WILD BUNCH

One of the West's most famous outlaws, Butch Cassidy is remembered as much for his wit, charm, and outright benevolence as for his utter disregard for the law. He was born Robert LeRoy Parker on April 13, 1866, to Mormon parents in Beaver, Utah. Raised on a ranch near Circleville, he fell under the wing of an old rustler named Mike Cassidy before leaving home to seek his fortune by any means necessary. Two years as a cowboy was followed by a stint as a butcher in Rock Springs, Wyoming. By adding his mentor's last name to his profession, Parker came up with the nickname that he would ride to worldwide fame: Butch Cassidy.

In Telluride, Colorado, Cassidy joined forces with another Utahan, Matt Warner, and in 1899 they staged their first major bank robbery in the mountain mining town. Butch served two years in a Wyoming jail for cattle rustling before finding his true calling as the leader of the "Wild Bunch," a loosely knit gang that kept the peacekeepers of the intermountain West on their toes for the better part of a decade. Several famous outlaws belonged to the Wild Bunch at one time or another, including Ben Kilpatrick (the "Tall Texan"), Harvey Logan (aka "Kid Curry"), and Butch's best friend Elzy

Lay. When Lay was captured and jailed in 1899, Butch teamed up with Harry Longabaugh, a gunslinger from Pennsylvania better known as the Sundance Kid.

Led by Butch and Sundance, the Wild Bunch embarked on one of the most successful crime sprees in the history of the West. They robbed banks and trains and rustled horses and cattle throughout Colorado, Utah, Wyoming, and the surrounding territories. The gang had a number of hideouts to retreat to when the heat was on, each with its own corrals for rustled livestock. There were inaccessible canyons like the grassy Hole in the Wall in northern Wyoming, and the remote Robber's Roost in South-Central Utah, south of the San Rafael Swell. Brown's Hole (now called Brown's Park), a valley along the Green River where Utah, Colorado, and Wyoming come together, was another favorite lair.

Most of the Wild Bunch eventually found themselves in jail or pine boxes by the turn of the 20th century, but Butch and Sundance kept going. Cassidy's gentlemanly charm no doubt helped, earning him the reputation of a fearless outlaw who never killed anyone and was polite to the ladies. Stories have him help-

---

which is near the primitive **Cathedral Valley** campsite (six sites) at 7,000 feet on the base of **Thousand Lake Mountain.** Notice the changes in the landscape as the road's elevation rises. Heading east on the Caineville Wash Road, the loop passes innumerable volcanic dikes and plugs in **Cathedral Valley** proper, of which the sharp spires of the **Temple of the Moon** and the **Temple of the Sun** are the two most striking examples. Eventually the road rejoins Highway 24 just west of Caineville.

HIGHWAY 24 THROUGH THE PARK

East of the **Fruita schoolhouse,** built in 1896 and used until 1941, are a set of beautifully made **pictographs** chipped into the canyon wall a stone's throw above the river made by

the Fremont people. (The culture was actually named after sites found along the river in 1929.) You can't approach the stone carvings, but the view through binoculars or the telescopes provided is still impressive. Deer like to congregate in the grass below and in the orchards across the road. Keep going east past **Hickman Bridge** and **Capitol Dome**—short, steep trails lead up to both—to reach the pioneer-era **Behunin Cabin** and eventually leave the park for the Caineville badlands.

West of the visitors center, Highway 24 passes **The Castle,** formed of angular Wingate Sandstone, and a turnoff to **Panorama Point** and a very short dirt track leading to the **Goosenecks Overlook** over Sulphur Creek. The bulbous **Twin Rocks** are the last formation of note before you leave the park to the west.

ing those in need, including a lost priest whom he helped back home, and ejecting a member from his gang who had stolen a horse from a young boy. He split up his crimes with interludes as a legitimate rancher, but the straight-and-narrow lifestyle never seemed to stick.

As the West filled with settlers and police, the once-easy life of an outlaw became more of an effort. The Pinkerton Agency, hired by the railroads, pursued the pair relentlessly. Butch sought an amnesty first from the governor of Utah, then from the Union Pacific Railroad, but neither worked. Along with Sundance and his girlfriend, Etta Place, Cassidy fled to New York City, where on February 20, 1902, he departed on a steamer for Buenos Aires, Argentina. The trio took aliases and bought a ranch in Patagonia, where for four years they tried to make a go at an honest living. When Etta returned to the United States In 1907, though, Butch and Sundance reverted to their old ways, robbing trains, banks, and rich mine stations in several countries.

The events surrounding the supposed death of Butch Cassidy and the Sundance Kid are still debated. On November 4, 1908, the pair found themselves at the Concordia Tin Mines near San Vicente, Bolivia. What happened there remains a mystery. According to an official document signed by the mayor, a pair of gringos who had robbed a mine payroll holed up in a local house, where they exchanged gunfire with a number of soldiers. When the troops approached the house the next morning, they found both men dead inside, one apparently from a self-inflicted gunshot. The men were quickly buried.

But were they Butch and Sundance? Many say they were actually another pair of outlaws, and that it would be just like Butch to spread the word that it had been him and his partner instead. According to this version, the pair returned to the United States and lived out the rest of their lives in peaceful anonymity. Some have sworn they spotted or even met with Butch in the 1920s and 1930s, including his sister Lula and Matt Warner's daughter Joyce. The myth got a boost with the 1969 hit movie starring Paul Newman and Robert Redford, although that had them meet their end at the hands of half the Bolivian army. It seems that no one knows for sure but Butch himself, and he probably would have wanted it that way.

NOTOM-BULLFROG ROAD

A little more than nine miles east of the visitors center on Highway 24 is a turnoff to the south for another popular Capitol Reef back road. The 65-mile route is paved only on either end, and runs down the east side of the Waterpocket Fold. About 17 miles south of Highway 24 it passes the primitive **Cedar Mesa Campground** (five sites) and then enters Strike Valley to intersect the Burr Trail from Boulder after 29 miles.

Past the Burr Trail switchbacks is the entrance to **Lower Muley Twist,** a popular narrows hike through a canyon so sinuous they say it could tie a mule in knots. If you hike the canyon south of the road, you can exit east to Halls Creek after four miles and climb a cutoff trail back to the road at a parking area

on the Notom-Bullfrog Road called The Post. This six-mile hike can be done in a day. Otherwise, keep heading south down the canyon, which becomes more interesting after it joins Halls Creek. Keep an eye out for pour-offs, pools, huge undercuts, and a cowboy camp, and imagine being a Mormon pioneer hauling wagons and cattle through here in the 1880s.

The Notom-Bullfrog Road leaves the park soon just south of The Post, and become paved once again as it nears Bullfrog Marina and Glen Canyon National Recreation Area. A side (dirt) loop off the paved southern end leads across Big Thompson Mesa to the **Halls Creek Overlook** and the trailhead to another outstanding narrows hike: the **Halls Creek Narrows.** The narrows themselves, three miles long and 328 feet

SOUTH-CENTRAL UTAH

deep, are 10 miles south of the overlook, so getting there and back is an overnight trip or a long day hike, but deep shade and a trickling perennial stream help make it worth the effort. An old wagon trail to Halls Crossing on the Colorado River once ran down this canyon, and is still visible in many stretches.

Another trail leads west from the overlook to **Brimhall Bridge,** a moderately challenging route that's five miles round-trip. Head upcanyon for three miles to **Hamburger Rocks,** dark hoodoos of stone that look like burgers on a white stone grill.

TORREY

Capitol Reef's gateway town stretches for a half mile or so along Highway 24 near its intersection with Highway 12, west of the park. Large cottonwoods and a canal follow the road, along with a growing handful of hotels, restaurants, and other businesses.

Everything tourist-related in Torrey closes down from late fall through spring. These listings are ordered from west to east along Highway 24 (called Main Street in town).

Shopping

For a dose of caffeine and/or literature, look for the conical roof of **Robber's Roost Books & Beverages** (185 W. Main St., 435/425-3265). It's a great place to lounge and sip, with couches and a wood-burning stove inside and a glassed-in porch out back. They have a small but well-chosen assortment of titles, and many works by local authors. **The Torrey Gallery** (80 E. Main St., 435/425-3909, www.torreygallery.com) offers paintings, photography, and sculpture by Utah artists, as well as antique and contemporary Navajo rugs.

Recreation

Anglers who swoon at the potential of a place called Thousand Lake Mountain should head for the **Alpine Anglers Flyshop and Boulder Mountain Adventures** (310 W. Main St., 435/425-3660 or 888/484-3331, www.fly-fishing-utah.net). Southern Utah's only full-service fly shop and fishing gu service offers trips into the mountains the nearby Fremont River starting at $ per person per day and lasting up to a v in length. Fly-fishing horse pack trips sta $715 per person for two days.

Wild Hare Expeditions (116 W. Main St., 435/425-3999 or 888/304-4273, thehare@ color-country.net, http://members.color-country.net/~thehare) organizes half-, full-, and multiday trips all over the area. Choose from hiking, biking, backpacking, and four-wheel-drive ventures, with gear for rent and well-trained guides available. They can also shuttle you to a trailhead and/or pick you up after a hike. Their "Hare Lair" headquarters is a combination gift shop and gear store, stocking maps and guidebooks.

Hondoo Rivers and Trails (90 E. Main St., 435/425-3519 or 800/332-2696, hondoo@color-country.net, www.hondoo.com) do multiday trail rides to Capitol Reef, the Escalante canyons, the San Rafael Swell, and other destinations in the vicinity, as well as guided day hikes (from $90 pp), backcountry jeep tours, and women-only trips.

For more on Torrey stop by www.torrey-utah.com.

Accommodations and Food

Starting from the west end of town on Highway 24 (a.k.a. Main Street), the **Thousand Lake RV Park** (1050 W. Main St., 435/425-3500 or 800/355-8995, www.thousandlakes-rvpark.com) has tent and RV sites ($14–20) as well as camping cabin ($30–55) open late March–October. They also boast a heated pool, grocery store, showers, and Western cookouts five nights a week, and they're a Wi-Fi hot spot to boot. They rent four-wheel-drive Geo Trackers for $90 per day. The **Café Diablo** (599 W. Main St., 435/425-3070, www.cafediablo.net, dinner daily Apr.–Oct.) may not look all that fancy from the outside, but their nouveaux southwestern dishes, like pecan chicken and pumpkin-seed trout ($170–25), are outstanding. Try the rattlesnake cakes appetizer ($8). They have an outdoor patio that's lovely once it starts to cool off at night.

Another hidden gem of the southern Utah dining scene (there are more than you'd think!) is the restaurant at the ◖ **Capitol Reef Inn & Cafe** (360 W. Main, 435/425-3271, cri@capitolreefinn.com, www.capitolreefinn.com, all meals Apr.–Oct.). Fresh local produce goes into their healthy creations spanning the spectrum from 10-vegetable salads to lemon hickory chicken dinners. Dinner entrées are $9–19, and lunch sandwiches run $6–8. Southwest-style rooms with handmade furniture are $52, complete with satellite movies and a shared hot tub. Elm trees, a waterfall, and a desert garden decorate the grounds, and the owners have built an Anasazi-style kiva next door.

Austin's Chuckwagon Lodge (12 W. Main St., 435/425-3335 or 800/863-3288, info@AustinsChuckwagonMotel.com, www.austinschuckwagonmotel.com) offers rooms for $45–65 and two-bedroom log cabins, with full kitchens and enough room for six people, for $110. Outdoors is a large heated pool with a whirlpool, and the general store on the premises has a full selection of groceries and a bakery. Atop a mesa above the Highways 12 and 24 intersection is the **Wonderland Inn** (435/425-3775 or 877/854-0184, dianewonderland@yahoo.com, www.capitolreefwonderland.com, $60). This sprawling complex boasts 50 rooms, a heated pool, a whirlpool tub, and a sauna, as well as a 39-space RV park and a restaurant serving all meals (entrées $9–14). A more intimate experience awaits at the ◖ **Sky Ridge B&B** (tel./fax 435/425-3222, tel. 800/448-6990, info@skyridgeinn.com, www.skyridgeinn.com, $120–190), a AAA four-diamond property that's also above the Highways 12/24 intersection. Six rooms with names like Juniper and Tumbleweed are eclectically decorated and include a full, tasty breakfast. The views up here are great.

Two miles east of Torrey towards the park are two chain hotels: a **Best Western Capitol Reef Resort** (2600 E. Hwy. 24, 435/425-3761, fax 435/425-3300, $80–140) and a **Comfort Inn** (2424 E. Hwy. 24, 435/425-3866, fax 435/425-2150, $40–110). Continue east another mile to find the **Rim Rock Inn** (2523 E. Hwy. 24, 435/425-3398, fax 435/425-3378, $50–65), set on a cliff in the middle of a 120-acre ranch. Ten large windows overlook the Waterpocket Fold and Boulder Mountain, and two stone fireplaces keep things snug in colder weather. Their restaurant serves southwestern fare for dinner March–November (entrées $12–22).

Three miles south of town on Highway 12 are the **Cowboy Homestead Cabins** (2100 S. Hwy. 12, tel./fax 435/425-3414 or 888/854-5871, info@cowboyhomesteadcabins.com), set on an original pioneer family's homestead that still covers 150 acres. Their cabins ($60–65) all have covered decks facing Boulder Mountain, as well as TVs and VCRs.

Highway 12 Scenic Byway

The most spectacular drive in a land of superlatives, this road takes the cake by a wide margin. It's one of the most beautiful routes in the country, the kind that can make you swerve in awe—a definite problem when it's the 500-foot drop off the shoulder that's making you gasp. Take turns at the wheel, or stop often if you're alone and admire the view. This is a drive not to be missed.

Starting at Torrey, Highway 12 climbs to almost 10,000 feet at the top of the Aquarius Plateau before dropping down to skewer two of the most remote towns in the lower 48, Boulder and Escalante. Meandering across the slickrock expanses of the northern edge of the Grand Staircase–Escalante National Monument, the road passes livestock grazing in green fields near Henrieville, continues west for the neon spires of Bryce Canyon National Park, and climbs the Paunsaugunt Plateau to Highway 89 just south of Panguitch.

You could drive it in an afternoon or spend a lifetime exploring the canyons visible from just one of the overlooks. Well worth at least a few days' meandering, Highway 12 showcases the amazing diversity of what was one of the last blank spots on the map of the United States. For more information try the website www.scenicbyway12.com.

WEST ON HIGHWAY 12

On its way up over the flank of **Boulder Mountain,** Highway 12 cuts across the eastern edge of the Aquarius Plateau and the Dixie National Forest, the largest in Utah. Peaking at 11,322 feet, Boulder Mountain is the highest timbered plateau in North America, and is home to hundreds of small lakes above 10,000 feet elevation. (The mountains around here seem to be deliberately misnamed: most of the lakes are on Boulder Mountain, and most of the boulders are on Thousand Lake Mountain.) As the road climbs, piñon pine and juniper gradually give way to aspen, fir, and spruce. Pullouts lead to stupendous over-

looks wide enough to encompass entire Eastern states. Paving on this stretch of Highway 12 was not completed until 1985.

About 25 miles east of Boulder is the **Singletree Campground,** followed five miles later by the **Oak Creek Campground.** A spur road after another mile leads to **Pleasant Creek Campground** near the **Wildcat Ranger Station,** open in summer only. Highway 12 tops out at 9,400 feet at Roundtop Flat before dropping down to Boulder, 39 miles from Torrey.

BOULDER

A cattle ranching community settled in 1889, Boulder is little more than a wide spot on Highway 12. The tiny community is so isolated by the canyons of the Escalante River and its tributaries that it was the last community to receive its mail by mule in the country. It did so until 1935, when the river was finally bridged, making Boulder one of the last towns in the United States to gain automobile access.

Ranches spread to the south and west and Boulder mountain rises to the north. Around the town tower huge, glowing domes of Navajo Sandstone cracked into patterns like the skins of huge creatures. Boulder itself is a pretty, green oasis that's seen land values rise significantly since the declaration of the Grand Staircase–Escalante National Monument.

Sights

Part of one of the largest Anasazi villages west of the Colorado River has been excavated and partially reconstructed on the grounds of the **Anasazi State Park Museum** (435/335-7308, 8 A.M.–6 P.M. daily, $2 pp or $6 per car). There's an indoor museum with thousands of artifacts inside the museum building, and out back is the Coombs Site, believed to have been occupied by up to 200 people A.D. 1160–1235.

Recreation

The **Boulder Mountain Ranch** (435/335-7480,

fax 435/335-7352, bmr@boulderutah.com, www.boulderutah.com/bmr/) has lodge rooms ($55–60) and cabins ($66–83), but specializes in guided horseback rides. Pick from a half-day trip ($65 pp), an all-day "No Pansy" ride ($118), or a six-day "Long in the Saddle" adventure for experienced riders ($1,070). The turn-off for this working cattle ranch is 3.5 miles up the Hell's Backbone Road. Campers can find a spot at the **Deer Creek Campground** 6.7 miles down the Burr Trail (see *Near Boulder*) for $5 per night.

Red Rock 'n Llama Tours (435/335-7533 or 877/955-2627, rllama@color-country.net, www.redrocknllamas.com) has 4–5-day guided hikes to Glen Canyon, Rainbow Bridge, and the Escalante and Colorado rivers starting at $750 per person. Llamas carry most of the gear, and are easier on the scenery than horses or mules. Other guide services operating out of Boulder include **Escalante Canyon Outfitters** (888/326-4453, ecohike@color-country.net, www.ecohike.com), with 10 different trips starting at $820 per person for four days, and **Earth Tours** (435/691-1241, info@earth-tours.com, www.earth-tours.com), which starts with half-day and full-day guided hiking trips for $50 and $75 per person, respectively, and goes from there.

Local fishing guide Steve Stoner runs **Boulder Mountain Fly Fishing** (435/335-7306, stevestoner@direcway.com, www.bouldermountainflyfishing.com) and offers trips in search of the cutthroat and brook trout that fill the many lakes up on Boulder Mountain. He provides all the equipment. And if you happen to see a bedraggled group limp into town and head straight for the burgers at Pole's Place, they're probably with the **Boulder Outdoor Survival School** (303/444-9779, info@boss-inc.com, www.boss-inc.com), which is actually based in Boulder, Colorado. Their desert survival courses are only a few of the many educational trips they offer.

Accommodations and Food

Just down the road from the state park is the **Boulder Mountain Lodge** (435/335-7460 or 800/556-3446, fax 435/335-7461, info@boulder-utah.com, www.boulder-utah.com, $70–85), one of the Four Corner's most enticing getaways. The luxury eco-lodge combines Western coziness with first-class comfort. Tapestries and local artists' works decorate the tasteful interior, and the whole timbered thing is set around an 11-acre private waterfowl sanctuary complete with pond and marsh. (Birders can spot ibises from the outdoor hot tub.) There's also a library and a sandstone fireplace for lounging. The inspired food at the lodge's **Hell's Backbone Grill** (435/335-7464, www.hellsbackbonegrill.com, breakfast and dinner Mar.–Oct.) is good enough to inspire some to make the drive here just for dinner. The best cooking in this part of Utah combines local meats and organically grown veggies into Southwest delicacies like chipotle meat loaf and pecan skillet trout. (The Grill is also the only place in the city you can buy wine and microbrewed beer, after a fight against the town government that went all the way to the Utah Supreme Court.) Entrées are $14–27, and they'll make you a picnic lunch to go for $6–8 if you order the night before.

Across from the state park, **Poles Place** (435/355-7422 or 800/730-7422, www.boulder-utah.com/polesplace, $55–65) is a motel with 12 guest rooms and a café with good burgers and shakes at their walk-up window. The **Circle Cliffs Motel** (225 N. Hwy. 12, 435/335-7333, circle@boulderutah.com, $40–60) is located downtown and has three rooms available year-round. One is an apartment with a full kitchenette.

Information

More details about the area's attractions and businesses can be found at the website of the **Boulder Business Alliance** (info@boulder-utah.com, www.boulderutah.com).

BURR TRAIL

This old cattle trail winds east from Boulder, crosses the Circle Cliffs and the southern end of Capitol Reef National Park, and joins the Notom-Bullfrog Road to reach Bullfrog

Marina on Lake Powell after 66 miles. The route was blazed by rancher John Atlantic Burr in the late 1800s to move cattle between winter and summer ranges and to market. In 1882, a pioneer wrote of it in her journal:

*It is the most God-forsaken and wild look-
ing country that was ever traveled.....It is
mostly uphill and sandy knee and then
sheets of solid rock for the poor animals
to pull over and slide down. I never saw
the poor horses pull and paw as they
done today.*

After the trail was improved by the Atomic Energy Commission to help uranium prospectors access the backcountry, controversy erupted in the 1970s over whether it should be paved its entire length. Garfield County officials held that paving would boost the local economy and improve transportation, while conservationists argued that off-road vehicle (ORV) damage would increase. Things reached a bitter peak in the 1980s, when directors of the Southern Utah Wilderness Association were hanged in effigy in Escalante, and four county bulldozers were sabotaged near the switchbacks.

The Burr Trail is paved for a few dozen miles on either end, but dirt otherwise, and through the Waterpocket Fold and the park, the going can get rough in inclement weather. Steep winding switchbacks in Capitol Reef make RVs a bad idea. There are no services the entire length, so carry all the water and gasoline you think you'll need, plus some extra. Intermittent posts along the road serve as reference markers for some of the more major turnoffs. Find more information on the Internet at www.nps.gov/glca/burrtr.htm.

Dozens of side roads and trails branch off from the main route. After passing the Deer Creek Campground at mile 6.5, you'll cross The Gulch at 10.7 miles, a popular trailhead from which you can reach the Escalante River in about two days. The Burr Trail then follows Long Canyon, a colorful gorge reminiscent of Zion Canyon, for about seven miles. Twenty-five miles from Boulder is the intersection with

the west end of the Wolverine Road, a 28-mile loop through remote, rugged terrain that rejoins the Burr Trail 11 miles west near Long Canyon. The Wolverine Road is a rougher route that passes an area of petrified logs on Bureau of Land Management (BLM) land (collecting any is illegal).

Once inside Capitol Reef National Park, the Burr Trail turns to dirt and is recommended for four-wheel-drive vehicles only. Soon you'll cross Muley Twist Canyon. From Muley Twist, the Burr Trail climbs a daunting series of switchbacks—climbing 800 feet in half a mile—and intersects with the Notom-Bullfrog Road. The view to the east is outstanding. From here the Notom-Bullfrog Road leaves the park and parallels the Waterpocket Fold north and south. Head south to join UT-276 after 66 miles from Boulder, and Bullfrog is only a short distance ahead.

❰ HIGHWAY 12 FROM BOULDER TO ESCALANTE

The most scenic stretch of Highway 12 runs for less than 30 miles between Boulder and Escalante. Finished by the Civilian Conservation Corps in 1940, the "Million-Dollar Highway to Boulder" allowed the first year-round car access to the towns cut off from the rest of the world by the Escalante canyons. It wasn't fully paved until 1971.

Drive it and you'll agree the nickname refers to the views as much as the cost: Blond and rosy slickrock undulate toward the horizon, with green lines of cottonwoods following invisible watercourses down in the brown canyon bottoms and the Henry Mountains, Navajo Mountain, and the Straight Cliffs standing above it all. Try to do this drive in the morning or late afternoon to fully appreciate the three-dimensionality of the landscape. Few roads interact with their scenery as spectacularly as this one, and it's worth doing it right.

Heading west from Boulder, the **Hells Backbone Road** soon joins the highway from the right. Highway 12 crosses a winding section called the **Hogback,** a rocky spine just wide enough for the two-lane road, a narrow shoulder, and a few small pullouts. It then descends the Haymaker Bench to Calf Creek. Just over 11 miles west of Boulder is the popular **Calf Creek Canyon Recreation Area,** run by the BLM, with 13 campsites for $8 per night (day use is $2 per car). From here a trail heads up Calf Canyon for just under three miles to the beautiful **Lower Calf Creek Falls,** plunging 126 feet into a sandy pool. River otters were reintroduced into the Escalante River in 2005 and are occasionally seen in Calf Creek, so keep your eyes open! Also look for ruins and pictographs along the way as you pass beaver-dammed pools lined with reeds. The trail is a moderate walk and offers an easy taste of the Escalante canyons, so it can get relatively crowded on weekends. Fewer people take the one-mile trail to the 90-foot **Upper Calf Creek Falls,** starting at a dirt road between mileposts 81 and 82 on Highway 12, just uphill toward Boulder.

Continuing toward Escalante, you'll cross the Escalante River at another popular trailhead for hikes down the canyon. Next comes Boynton Overlook, offering a glimpse of the Escalante River and Calf Creek. (Get out your binoculars and look for a pictograph panel of handprints on the opposite canyon wall, just above the mouth of Calf Creek.) Head of the Rocks four miles later offers more great views, and beyond that bare rock is replaced by farmland as you pass the turnoff for the **Hole-in-the-Rock Road.** Escalante is 27 miles from Boulder.

ESCALANTE

For some reason the Mormon pioneers who founded this town in 1875 decided to name it after the Spanish priest Francisco Silvestre Vélez de Escalante, who didn't come within 150 miles of the place during his 1776 wanderings. Drawn to the area's mild climate, 6,000 feet high between the Kaiparowits and Aquarius plateaus, the settlers nicknamed their new home "Potato Valley" for a local variety of wild tuber and set about exploring the grazing potential of the nearby canyons and benches. Families drew numbers from a hat to decide who got which 1.25-acre lot, logs houses went up, and the new town was off and running. When the Centennial rolled around in July 1876, no one had an American flag yet, so a striped Navajo blanket was proudly hoisted instead. Piped drinking water arrived in 1937.

Today tiny Escalante (pop. 900) still has an economy based on farming and livestock, but change began to roll across the horizon like a stampede with the declaration of the huge national monument next door. As the main gateway to the wonders of the Grand Staircase and the Escalante canyons, the town is also at the center of controversy, since government restrictions on grazing could deeply affect local ranchers. Among the pioneer homes and barns you'll see signs demanding the government give locals their backyard back, and for every "Wild Utah" bumper sticker you'll see one proclaiming "Wilderness: Land of No Use." The local old guard is slowly coming round, grudgingly admitting the monument's economic potential, as real estate prices seem to rise with every SUV that rolls into town. Some business close in winter, so check ahead if you're visiting November–March.

Sights

If you need a break from the unending swells of slickrock, the **Escalante Petrified Forest State Park** (435/826-4466, 7 A.M.–10 P.M. daily, $5 pp) offers a 130-acre reservoir for fishing and swimming, as well as two short self-guided trails past rainbow-colored chunks of petrified wood and fossilized dinosaur bones. The park is 1.5 miles west of Escalante on UT-12, and has a 22-site campground for $14 per night.

Entertainment and Events

The **Escalante Festival and Craft Fair** comes to town in late May, followed by the **Pioneer Days Celebration** in late July. In early October, the legacy of Everett Ruess (see the sidebar *Everett Ruess: Lost Wanderer of Canyon Country* in the *Southeast Utah* chapter) is celebrated with art and music during the **Everett Ruess Festival** (www.everettruessdays.org).

Shopping

An espresso bar isn't the rarity it once was in southern Utah, but the "Esca-Latte" sign at **Escalante Outfitters** (310 W. Main St., 435/826-4266, www.escalanteoutfitters.com) is still a welcome sight to road-tripping caffeine hounds. Along with a small wine shop and pizza parlor, this all-inclusive place stocks gear, guidebooks, and microbrews, and has log cabins next door for $45. They can also arrange lodgings at the Vagabond Inn B&B in town for $130 double. (Campsites are $14, and RV hookups are $30.)

Right across the street, **Utah Canyons** (325 W. Main St., 435/826-4967 or 877/777-7988, www.utahcanyons.com) offers maps, gear, guidebooks, a small BBQ restaurant, and a wealth of friendly advice about the surrounding countryside.

Pick up the "Escalante Arts & Crafts Guide" pamphlet anywhere in town for information on local artists and their galleries. **Brigitte and David Delthony** (1540 W. Hwy. 12, 435/826-4631, www.sculpturedfurnitureartandceramics.com) have a gallery half a mile west of town on UT-12. Brigitte creates pit-fired pottery and ceramics inspired by the area's prehistoric cultures, and offers workshops occasionally. David sculpts beautiful, organically inspired wooden furniture.

Recreation

Day hikes and trailhead shuttle service are only two of the services Utah Canyons offers under the guise of **Escalante Outback Adventures** (www.escalante-utah.com, tours@utahcanyons.com). Guided tours to slot canyons and waterfalls run $30–150 per person for two people.

If you'd like to explore the Escalante canyons but would rather have someone (or something) else carry your pack, sign up with **Escape Goats** (435/826-4652, smillers@scinternet.net, www.utahpackgoats.com), which offer goat-supported day and evening hikes for $40–65 per person.

Rick Green's **Excursions of Escalante** (800/839-7567, rickgreen435@msn.com,

www.excursionsescalante.com,) advertises archaeology, fishing, mountain biking, backpacking, and photography trips. He operates out of the Trail Head Cafe & Grill at 125 East Main Street. For more camping supplies and hardware, try the Griffin Grocery (see the *Food* section).

Accommodations

Escalante has a number of modest motels with room for under $50, including the **Circle D Motel** (475 W. Main St., 435/826-4297, fax 435/826-4402, circledmotel@color-country.net, www.utahcanyons.com/circled.htm) and the **Padre Motel** (20 E. Main St., 435/826-4276, www.padremotel.com). The 50 rooms at the **Prospector Inn** (380 W. Main St., 435/826-4653, fax 435/826-4285, prospectorinn@color-country.net, www.prospectorinn.com) start at $50. A night at **Escalante's Grand Staircase B&B/Inn** (280 W. Main St., 435/826-4890, escalbnb@color-country.net, www.escalantebnb.com) starts at $95, and they have two-night packages that including guided hikes in a slot canyon for $360 per person. Four comfortable suites in the Coach House include a full breakfast, while the three rooms in the Carriage House don't (but they do come with a complimentary cell phone). The **Rainbow Country Bed & Breakfast Inn** (300 S. 586 East, 435/826-4567 or 800/252-8824, fax 435/826-4557, rainbow@color-country.net, www.color-country.net/~rainbow, $50–84) has a great view from the large sundeck. Four guest rooms include a hearty breakfast and access to the pool table and outdoor hot tub.

The **Serenidad Retreat** (2610 E. Hwy. 12, 435/826-4720 or 888/826-4577, hpriska@escalanteretreat.com, www.escalanteretreat.com) takes its name from the Spanish word for (you guessed it) "serenity," and has the secluded location and views to back it up. Three bedrooms, two baths, and a complete kitchen are available year-round ($95 for the whole place). There's a wood-burning stove and a large redwood deck, and pets are welcome. They also have an art gallery on the premises. The owners of **Escalante's Wild West Retreat** (300 S. 200 East, 866/292-3043, yahoo@wildwestretreat.com, www.wildwestretreat.com) took a 1930s barn and restored it into a luxury-rustic getaway with a full kitchen, hot tub, covered porches, and a stargazing upper deck. Rates start at $100 double, and horses and mules are boarded free. Another private building for rent in the same price range is the **Southwestern Retreat** (435/826-4967, retreat@utahcanyons.com, www.southwesternretreat.com, $100 d). It sleeps seven people in three bedrooms and comes complete with kitchen, laundry, deck, and entertainment center.

On the southwest edge of town, **《 La Luz Desert Retreat** (435/826-4967, stay@laluz.net, www.laluz.net, $120 d) is a wedge-shaped vacation home built in the Usonian architectural style of Frank Lloyd Wright. It sleeps up to six people and has wonderful views through many windows. The owners also have another similar place (La Luz II) in town for rent for the same rates.

The **Broken Bow RV Camp** (495 W. Main St., 435/826-4959 or 888/241-8785, $18) has 48 full-hookup sites, cabins, hot showers, and a laundry room. Escalante Outfitters (see the *Shopping* section) also has cabins and campsites. You can pitch a tent at the Escalante Petrified Forest State Park (see *Sights*), the Calf Creek Canyon Recreation Area (see *Highway 12 from Boulder to Escalante*), and up in the Dixie National Forest, along the Hell's Backbone Road (see *Highway 12 Scenic Byway*).

Food

All restaurants in Escalante (there aren't many) are open daily for all meals. The Prospector Inn's **Ponderosa Restaurant** (45 N. 400 West, 435/826-4775, all meals daily) is probably the nicest of the bunch, serving American and European dishes. Burgers at the **Golden Loop Cafe** (39 W. Main St., 435/826-4433) start at $3, and they also have sandwiches, tacos, and steaks topping out at $10. There's a similar menu at the **Cowboy Blues Restaurant** (530 W. Main St., 435/826-4577) and the **Trail Head Cafe & Grill** (125 E. Main St.,

7 A.M.–8 P.M. Wed.–Mon. Apr.–Nov.) serves up baked goods, soups, sandwiches, smoothies, and espresso drinks on their outdoor patio.

Both Utah Canyons and Escalante Outfitters (see the *Shopping* section) have small eateries on premises. For outfitting yourself, stop by the mom-and-pop **Griffin Grocery** (30 W. Main St., 435/826-4226) for groceries, ice, and a deli.

Information

The U.S. National Park Service, National Forest Service, and Bureau of Land Management have set aside their differences long enough to establish the **Escalante Interagency Visitor Center** (435/826-5499, 8 A.M.–5 P.M. daily) on the western edge of town. Direct any other questions to the **Escalante Chamber of Commerce** (escalante@escalante-cc.com, www.escalante-cc.com).

NEAR ESCALANTE

The name enough would be reason to recommend it, but the **Hells Backbone Road** goes one better: this 40-mile loop takes you up into the 25,000-acre **Box-Death Hollow Wilderness Area** north of Escalante. The four-wheel-drive track follows sheer ridge tops and crosses gorges lined with orange-gray walls of Navajo Sandstone. Along the way it passes **Posey Lake Campground** at 8,700 feet (22 sites, $8 per night) and the **Blue Spruce Campground** at 7,800 feet (6 sites, $7). The eastern end of the road meets Highway 12 at mile 60.2 east of Escalante (head east and north past the cemetery and the old garbage dump).

This end of the road is the terminus of a number of popular **hikes** in the canyons that flow into the upper reaches of the Escalante River. Pine Creek, which parallels the Hells Backbone Road initially, offers a stretch of narrow, tree-lined streambed called the **Pine Creek Box.** Most people drive up the road about eight miles, descend to the streambed, and follow it back to Escalante in a day. **Death Hollow** itself, east of Pine Creek, is much more of an undertaking. You'll need up to five days to do the entire canyon from the trailhead, which is 22.5 miles up the Hells Backbone Road, back down to Escalante. Along the way you'll thread about three miles of high-quality narrows and encounter pools that may require some swimming to cross. This is a serious hike, but one of the best in southern Utah. It should not be your first canyoneering trip, and climbing experience and gear wouldn't hurt either. Both of these hikes are easier with a two-car shuttle.

One way out of Death Hollow is via the **Boulder Mail Trail,** which until 1935 was the only way the U.S. Postal Service could reach the remote town. This 16-mile route cuts across the Pine Creek, Death Hollow, and Sand Creek canyons and the exposed slickrock in between. You can do it in a day, but take two to fully enjoy it. You'll need some cross-country route-finding ability, but look for sporadic rock cairns and old telegraph wire. Its eastern end intersects Highway 12 near where the Hells Backbone Road rejoins it, near milepost 84.

Grand Staircase-Escalante

At 1.9 million acres—almost 3,000 square miles—the latest addition to Utah's protected lands dwarfs the surrounding national parks. Grand Staircase–Escalante National Monument is almost as big as Delaware and Rhode Island put together, yet few people outside the Four Corners could place it on a map, and even fewer have been lucky enough to venture inside. Word is starting to get out, however, and thousands of visitors are already arriving each year to explore this little-known wonderland of cliffs, canyons, rivers, and desert plateaus. Whatever your interest—archaeology, geology, history, biology, paleontology, desert scenery, or just escaping into the wild—the monument is more than big enough to accommodate.

The monument can be roughly divided into three regions from west to east:

Grand Staircase

The southwest corner of the monument is the kind of landscape that makes geologists drool. First described by geologist Clarence Dutton in his classic *Report of the Geology of the High Plateaus of Utah* (1880), it consists of a series of huge geological steps rising 3,500 feet from the North Rim of the Grand Canyon to the top of the Paunsaugunt Plateau at Bryce Canyon National Park, 150 miles to the north. More than 250 million years of uplift and erosion are on stark display in five major terraces named for their gaudy colors: the Chocolate Cliffs, the

Vermilion Cliffs, the White Cliffs, the Gray Cliffs, and the Pink Cliffs. Five distinct life zones, from Sonoran desert to coniferous forests, shelter a wide variety of plant and animal life, including bald eagles, peregrine falcons, and California condors.

Kaiparowits Plateau

The monument's middle section is the most rugged, one of the largest remaining blank spots on a road map of the Four Corners. Some have likened this region of canyons and mesas to an "American Outback," and if it's solitude you're after—and you can handle yourself in the desert—this is the place to go. Desert bighorn sheep and mountain lions roam among rare plants and remnants of the Fremont and Anasazi cultures. Kaiparowits means "Big Mountain's Little Brother" in the Paiute language, referring to the point near its north end the region was named after. It has recently begun to be recognized as a world-class hot spot for late-Cretaceous paleontology, and many prehistoric human sites have been recorded.

Escalante Canyons

Dinosaur tracks and historic pioneer routes converge near the spiderweb canyons of the Escalante River, the last major river to be discovered by Anglo explorers in the contiguous United States. The runoff from the southern edge of the Aquarius Plateau has created a thousand-mile labyrinth of converging canyons that eventually drain into the upper reaches of Lake Powell. Many of the monument's 200 or so bird species congregate here along the leafy drainages, including some from the neotropics. This is the easiest part of the monument to access (relatively speaking, of course) and thus sees the most visitors. It was named after Spanish priest Francisco Silvestre Vélez de Escalante by the Powell survey team in 1872, although the padre hadn't ever seen the river himself.

HISTORY
Early Inhabitants

It goes to show how remote this region is that humans didn't settle more or less permanently here until about A.D. 500, during the late Basketmaker II period. Both the Fremont and Kayenta Anasazi took advantage of the wide climatic range and lived in the area around the same time. While the Anasazi farmed in the Escalante canyons and up on the Kaiparowits Plateau, the Fremont tended to hunt and gather below the plateau and near the Escalante Valley. Both groups grew corn, beans, and squash, and built brush-roofed pit houses or took advantage of natural rock shelters. The largest Kayenta Anasazi settlements were scattered across the Kaiparowits Plateau near the present town of Boulder, while the Fremont lived in Calf Creek Canyon, Harris Wash, and near the town of Escalante.

Today it's hard to find a corner of the monument without some evidence of early human use, whether it's a prehistoric ruin, a line of carefully chipped Moqui steps up a rock wall, or a rock art panel with characteristic trapezoidal bodies, animals figures, and abstract designs. Once these groups left or were absorbed into other cultures that arrived around A.D. 1300, the canyons were quiet. Later, groups that would become today's Paiute, Ute, and Navajo tribes arrived; the Navajo hunted deer and sheep and began herding livestock into the eastern reaches of what would be declared the monument.

European Settlement

The first record of Anglo settlers in the region dates to 1866, when Captain James Andrus led a group of cavalry to the headwaters of the Escalante River. Five years later, Jacob Hamblin of Kanab, on his way to the Colorado River to resupply the second Powell Expedition, mistook the Escalante for the Dirty Devil River and thus became the first European to travel the length of the canyon. The unforgiving topography was never demonstrated more clearly than during the 1879–80 Hole-in-the-Rock Expedition (see the sidebar *The Hole-in-the-Rock Expedition*). To this day, the canyons of the Escalante remain a major barrier to east–west vehicle travel, and the river is only bridged at its upper end.

Recent News

Although the Department of the Interior had proposed the creation of a national monument as early as 1936, it took another 60 years for reality to catch up. In September 1996, President Bill Clinton used the authority given to him through the Antiquities Act and created the

rock formations in Grand Staircase-Escalante National Monument

© JULIAN SMITH

SOUTH-CENTRAL UTAH

Grand Staircase–Escalante National Monument, and the sparks immediately started to fly. Utah politicians, no big fans of Washington "meddling" to begin with, were enraged they weren't consulted in the transfer of such a huge chunk of their state to federal jurisdiction. The fact that the declaration was made from the rim of the Grand Canyon, in *Arizona,* just added fuel to the fire.

Tensions have sprouted between local ranchers, miners, and farmers, who feel that their land and way of life is being legislated out of existence, and newly arrived environmentalists and government employees scrambling to protect the huge area. Many of the latter camp see tourism and tourist dollars as inevitable (and point out that many of the former have quietly stuck their fingers in the tourism pot already). Land values and visitation are already rising.

The monument's proclamation was vague enough on what is and isn't allowed within the boundaries to ensure years of land-use controversies. In 1991, the Dutch mining company Andalex applied for a state permit to mine the estimated 62 billion tons of coal under the surface of the Kaiparowits Plateau, the largest deposit of its kind in the United States. Although the proclamation didn't specifically prohibit the development of existing mining leases, the roads, traffic, and construction that mining would bring conflict enough with the monument's stated purpose of preserving the "unspoiled natural area" that the company eventually withdrew the proposal. They've since begun negotiating land exchanges with the federal government for the leases. Legal and political battles are still being fought over the future of grazing within the monument.

VISITING THE MONUMENT
Access and Roads

Most access roads are from the north branches off Highway 12 between Bryce Canyon National Park and Boulder. A few of these run all the way through the monument to Highway 89, on the southwest side between Kanab, Utah, and Page, Arizona. Both highways are paved, but the rest of the monument's graded

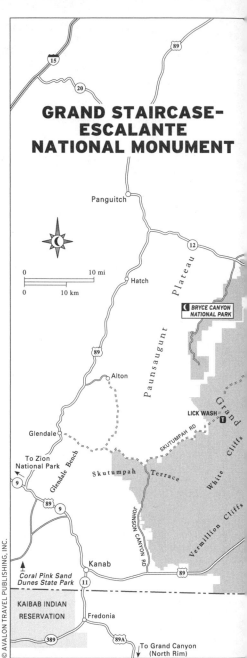

GRAND STAIRCASE-ESCALANTE NATIONAL MONUMENT

Panguitch

0   10 mi
0   10 km

Hatch

Plateau

BRYCE CANYON NATIONAL PARK

Paunsaugunt

Alton

Grand

LICK WASH

Cliffs

Glendale

SKUTUMPAH RD

To Zion National Park

Glendale Bench

Skutumpah   Terrace

White

JOHNSON CANYON RD

Vermillion Cliffs

Kanab

Coral Pink Sand Dunes State Park

KAIBAB INDIAN RESERVATION

Fredonia

To Grand Canyon (North Rim)

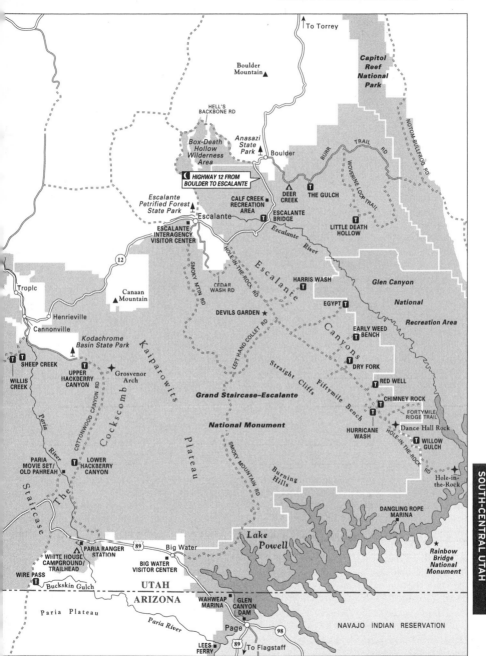

To Torrey

Capitol
Reef
National
Park

Boulder
Mountain

HELL'S
BACKBONE RD

Box-Death
Hollow
Wilderness
Area

Anasazi
State
Park   Boulder

**HIGHWAY 12 FROM
BOULDER TO ESCALANTE**

BURR   TRAIL   RD

NOTOM-BULLFROG RD

WOLVERINE LOOP TRAIL

Escalante
Petrified Forest
State Park

CALF CREEK
RECREATION
AREA

DEER
CREEK   THE GULCH

Escalante   ESCALANTE
BRIDGE

LITTLE DEATH
HOLLOW

ESCALANTE
INTERAGENCY
VISITOR CENTER

Escalante   River

12

Tropic   Canaan
Mountain

SMOKY MTN RD

HOLE-IN-THE-ROCK RD

CEDAR
WASH RD

Escalante

HARRIS WASH

EGYPT

Glen Canyon

National

Recreation Area

DEVILS GARDEN

Canyons

EARLY WEED
BENCH

Henrieville

Cannonville

Kodachrome
Basin State Park

LEFT HAND COLLET RD

DRY FORK

Straight   Cliffs

Fiftymile   Bench

RED WELL

SHEEP CREEK

Kaiparowits

UPPER
HACKBERRY
CANYON   Grosvenor
Arch

WILLIS
CREEK

COTTONWOOD CANYON RD

Cockscomb

Grand Staircase-Escalante

National Monument

CHIMNEY ROCK

FORTYMILE
RIDGE TRAIL

HURRICANE
WASH   Dance Hall Rock

HOLE-IN-THE-ROCK RD

WILLOW
GULCH

Paria   River

Plateau

SMOKY MOUNTAIN RD

Burning
Hills

Hole-in-
the-Rock

PARIA
MOVIE SET/
OLD PAHREAH   LOWER
HACKBERRY
CANYON

DANGLING ROPE
MARINA

Staircase   The

Lake
Powell

Rainbow
Bridge
National
Monument

PARIA RANGER
STATION   89   Big Water

WHITE HOUSE
CAMPGROUND/
TRAILHEAD

BIG WATER
VISITOR CENTER

WIRE PASS

Buckskin Gulch   **UTAH**

ARIZONA

WAHWEAP
MARINA   GLEN
CANYON
DAM

Paria   Plateau

Paria River   Page   98

NAVAJO   INDIAN   RESERVATION

LEES
FERRY   89   To Flagstaff

and/or gravel roads can quickly become impassable when wet. Even when dry, they're often rough enough to loosen the bolts on most two-wheel-drive vehicles.

The **Johnson Canyon/Skutumpah Road** connects Kodachrome Basin State Park with Highway 89 about 10 miles east of Kanab. The 46-mile graded dirt road offers glimpses of the Grand Staircase and access to trailheads at Sheep Creek, Willis Creek, and Lick Wash. It's paved for its southernmost half. The **Cottonwood Canyon Road** runs for 46 miles along the Cockscomb (aka the East Kaibab Monocline), a huge north–south fold in the earth that divides the Grand Staircase from the Kaiparowits Plateau. Along this road, which heads southeast from Kodachrome Basin, are trailheads for Upper and Lower Hackberry Canyon and Grosvenor Arch, 17 miles south of Highway 12. From Escalante, the **Smoky Mountain Road** winds for 78 rough miles across the Kaiparowits Plateau, providing the best access to the remote area. It eventually hits Highway 89 at Big Water.

Perhaps the most popular way to access the eastern half of the monument is via the **Hole-in-the-Rock Road,** blazed by a courageous band of Mormon pioneers on their way to the Colorado River (see the sidebar *The Hole-in-the-Rock Expedition*). This official scenic byway runs for 57 miles parallel to the Straight Cliffs, from Highway 12 just east of Escalante to the Hole-in-the-Rock itself, overlooking Lake Powell. In good weather, passenger cars can usually negotiate most of the graded dirt road, except for the last six or so miles that require a high-clearance four-wheel-drive. At 10.4 miles from Highway 12, a side road leaves to the east for Harris Wash and a large primitive campsite near a corral. Devil's Garden is on the right at 12.1 miles, a small but beautiful area of rock hoodoos. There's a picnic area but no overnight camping allowed.

More turnoffs from the Hole-in-the-Rock Road lead to side tracks and trailheads. (All of the following are to the east.) At 16.5 miles is the turnoff to the Egypt area, followed by ones for Early Weed Bench (23.6 miles), Dry Fork

(25.9 miles), and Fortymile Ridge (36.1 miles). Half a mile past Fortymile Ridge is a natural red-rock amphitheater known as Dance Hall Rock, where the original pioneer group held dances. At 50 miles from Highway 12 are the access points to Llewelyn, Cottonwood, and David canyons. Finally, after 56 miles, are great views of Lake Powell from the Hole-in-the-Rock overlook, the true end of the road. A steep ravine trail leads downward a third of a mile to the rocky lakeshore, but the remnants of the pioneer track itself have been drowned by Lake Powell.

For details on the **Burr Trail** in the northern tip of the monument, see *Boulder*.

(Hiking in Grand Staircase–Escalante National Monument

Entire books have been written about hiking in the monument, so this listing is just a taste. It also means that hikers and bikers should acquire a more detailed guidebook and maps before heading out, and ideally stop by the Escalante Interagency Visitor Center for more recent route information.

Most of the more popular trails are concentrated along the Escalante River drainage, which is accessed via the Hole-in-the-Rock Road. Trails descend side canyons to the Escalante canyon itself, and either ascend via the same route or else form a loop using the Escalante River or an overland trail as a connector. These include pastoral **Harris Wash,** a relatively easy 2–3-day hike that starts 10.5 miles down the road from Highway 12. The **Egypt 3** slot, down the next turnoff from the Hold in the Rock Road, is legendarily long and tight, not for beginners or anyone freaked out by tight spaces. Return overland to the east of the north–south slot. Also from the Egypt trailhead, the triangular route down **Fence Canyon,** then down the Escalante River (some wading required) and back up. **Twentyfive Mile Canyon** is an excellent, moderate canyon trip that can be done in two or three days. Don't miss the Golden Cathedral at the end of pretty little Neon Canyon.

Spooky, Peek-a-Boo, and **Brimstone** are

THE HOLE-IN-THE-ROCK EXPEDITION

It was 1879, and Mormon Church President John Taylor had called on a group of believers to colonize Montezuma Creek in Southeast Utah to secure a remote corner of the rapidly expanding Mormon empire and "breed goodwill among the Indians." And so they went – 236 people, many recent arrivals to the Western desert, in 82 wagons surrounded by hundreds of horses and cattle, on one of the most arduous journeys in the history of the American West.

From the start they knew the trip would not be easy. Leader Silas Smith had chosen to cut straight across the barren Escalante Desert to save 250 miles over alternate routes to the north and south. Cattle could find hardly any forage in the wasteland, and resourceful Mormon wives, lacking wood, had to burn weeds and sagebrush to cook the food.

In December, with snow blocking any hope of retreat through the mountains behind, the ragged party reached the edge of Glen Canyon, took one look over the 1,800-foot drop, and immediately sent Smith and two boys back to Salt Lake for blasting powder, mining equipment, and food. When they returned, the pioneers sat down to figure out how to get everything down to the river in one piece.

Plagued by bitter cold and dwindling food, 60 men set about building a road where, as author Wallace Stegner writes, "God certainly never intended a road to be." While one team hung from the cliff edge in barrels, chiseling blasting holes to widen and level an existing crack, another group essentially began tacking a road onto the sheer rock face below it. First they blasted a small ledge just wide enough for the uphill wagon wheels, then drove two-foot cottonwood stakes into a row of holes gouged every 18 inches into the sandstone. Rocks, dirt, and vegetation were piled on top of the stakes, and gradually a makeshift road began to take shape. At an average angle of 50 degrees, the dizzying route was named Uncle Ben's Dugout for its designer, engineer Benjamin Perkins. Far below, a third party was busy building a fer-ryboat to cross the river. On weekends everyone returned to camp to nurse their bruises, and still found enough energy to fill the icy nights with fiddle music and singing.

On January 25, after six weeks of backbreaking labor, the Hole-in-the-Rock Road was finished. Perkins went first, his horses rearing and shying away from the drop-off. (Other accounts say he had to use horses blinded by pinkeye.) The settlers tried everything they could think of to slow the wagons – holding ropes and chains wrapped around the wheels, tying large juniper trees to the frames, rigging a pulley system from the top. Each wagon smoothed the passage more, making it harder and harder to hold the vehicles back. The women and children walked.

By February 10, everyone was down with all their possessions. Amazingly, no lives had been lost, human or otherwise, but many had been injured and all were exhausted. In passing they had worn the road down to almost nothing, so once again there would be no going back. It took a week to get across the river and up the equally steep wall on the other side. There they met a Ute who, on hearing their story, called them liars and rode away insulted.

After that, things got even worse. Scouts almost died of thirst and starvation trying to find the route ahead, which they only stumbled on by following a herd of mountain sheep. One hundred fifty more miles took almost four months – an average of two miles a day – as they pulled, pushed, and dragged the wagons over slickrock and through sandy wash bottoms. By the time they reached the banks of the San Juan River, everyone had had enough. The six-week trip has taken six months, and nobody had the strength or will to push on another mile. Instead, they settled the town of Bluff, which faltered over the years but always managed to pull through, perhaps drawing strength from the echoes of its founders.

three small gulches off the Dry Fork of Coyote Gulch, accessed from the Early Weed Bench Road or the Dry Fork Coyote Trailhead, 26 miles down the Hole-in-the-Rock Road. Along with Egypt, these are three of the best slots in the Four Corners, and all three can be done in a day.

Coyote Gulch is probably the most popular canyon in the Escalante drainage. Tree-lined and wet, it can hiked down to the Escalante River in a day, but leave two or three to explore all the side canyons and get back to the trail-head. At 50 miles from Highway 12—almost all the way to the Hole-in-the-Rock itself—are the access points to **Llewelyn** and **Cottonwood canyons,** two difficult slots that lead southeast to Lake Powell. These require three to five days and some climbing experience. **Davis Gulch** heads north from the same trailhead, and is too narrow for large packs. This is a very long and strenuous day hike, or a good two-day venture. Keep an eye open near the end of the slot for a memorial plaque to Everett Ruess (see the sidebar *Everett Ruess: Lost Wanderer of Canyon Country* in the *Southeast Utah* chapter), high on the wall to the right.

Near Highway 12 between Escalante and Boulder are the **Lower Calf Creek Falls** trail and the **Boulder Mail Trail,** and **Death Hollow,** described under *Near Escalante.* From the Highway 12 bridge over the Escalante River, an easy two-mile trail leads upstream to **Escalante Natural Bridge** on the south side of the canyon. Many people hike down this section of the river from the town of Escalante to the bridge, taking three to four days to cover the 16 miles. Be prepared for some scrambling and plenty of wading and bush-whacking. **Phipps Wash,** about 1.5 miles downstream from the bridge, has a natural bridge in a west-side drainage and an arch in an east-side drainage

In the western part of the monument you can find **Bull Valley Gorge** and **Willis Creek** off the Skutumpah Road about 10 miles south of Cannonville. You can explore the good nar-rows in the upper parts of both in a day, or connect them via Sheep Creek for a good over-

night hike. (In 1954, three people were killed when their pickup ran off the road at the bridge over Bull Valley Gorge—the truck is still vis-ible, wedged into the slot.) Farther down the Skutumpah Road toward Kanab is **Lick Wash,** an easy day hike southeast toward No Mans Mesa.

About 13 miles down the Cottonwood Canyon Road from Cannonville is **Round Valley Draw,** a tributary of upper Hackberry Canyon. Explore the upper slots in a day, or else continue down narrow **Hackberry Canyon** on a multiday adventure. It eventually rejoins the Cottonwood Canyon Road after 22 miles. You can explore the side canyons Booker, Stone Donkey, and Pollock (which contains an arch), and look for the old Watson Cabin near the bottom. Keep going down the road from Round Valley Draw to reach the turnoff to the east for **Grosvenor Arch**—actually a cluster of cream and gold double arches—and adjoining picnic area, It's another three miles south to **Cottonwood Creek,** a short slot can-yon that runs parallel to the road on the west side for half a mile.

Ten miles west of the Paria Canyon Ranger Station on Highway 89 is a sandstone obelisk marking the turnoff for a post-post-modern blend of fantasy and reality in the shadows of one of the most colorful hillsides in the hemi-sphere. Six miles down the graded dirt road is the **Paria Movie Set,** where parts of *The Out-law Josie Wales* and episodes of *Gunsmoke* were filmed—well, kind of. The original weathered buildings had become so rickety that they were torn down and replaced with replicas, so the faux town is really a copy of a copy. The eroded hillsides above are a geological kaleidoscope, particularly at sunset. Keep going down the road to the river for a dose of the real thing: the foundations of the actual **Pahreah Town Site,** abandoned in the 1930s after nearby gold mines played out and the river kept flooding. The town's graveyard is on the near side of the river, which can often be easily waded, while the town itself is across the water. Hike upriver to **Starlight Arch,** a scenic trip that can be done in a day.

Mountain Biking

With all this backcountry available, mountain bikers may groan to learn that they must stay on roads inside the monument. This still leaves hundreds of miles of remote riding, though. Any of the access roads described above are fair game, although some—particularly the Hole-in-the-Rock Road—see a good bit of dust-raising vehicle traffic. Try to aim for lesser-used routes like the **Cedar Wash Loop,** a 20-mile back road connecting Escalante to the Hole-in-the-Rock Road, or the **Wolverine Loop Road** off the Burr Trail. Roads to trailheads, some of which get pretty rough, are also recommended, like the **Egypt** road (10 miles one-way) or the one up to **Fiftymile Bench** (27 miles round-trip), which leaves the Hole-in-the-Rock Road at the Willow Tank slide just past the Hurricane Wash trail head parking area and rejoins it just south of Sooner Wash.

Nipple Creek Wash and **Tibbet Canyon** near Big Water on Highway 89 are good, steep rides, as is the **Smokey Hollow Loop** off the Smoky Mountain Road. **Sand Gulch** is an alternate way to get to the Paria Movie Set, leaving Highway 89 from a corral one mile west of the obelisk. It's 12 mostly level miles round-trip.

Camping

There are only two developed campgrounds in the monument: Calf Creek (see *Boulder to Escalante*) and Deer Creek (see *Boulder*). Beyond that, and the campgrounds in nearby parks, you're on your own—which is exactly how most visitors to the Escalante like it. Free backcountry permits are required for overnight trips, and minimum-impact camping techniques are crucial to keeping this delicate area as pristine as possible.

Information and Permits

The **Escalante Interagency Visitors Center** (755 W. Main St., 435/826-5499, 7:30 A.M.–5:30 P.M. daily in summer) in Escalante is the main source of information for the monument. The Cannonville Contact Station (10 Center St., 435/679-8981, 8 A.M.–4:30 P.M. in summer), in Cannonville near Bryce Canyon Na-

tional Park, focuses on Mormon history. A third visitors center is in Big Water (100 Upper Revolution Way, 435/675-3200) on Highway 89 along the southern edge of the monument, and focuses on paleontology. There's a fourth visitors center in Kanab (75 E. Hwy. 89, 435/644-4680, 7:30 A.M.–5:30 P.M. daily in summer) on the west edge of the monument, and an information desk at Anasazi State Park in Boulder (435/335-7382). For more information contact the BLM's Utah office (801/539-4001, http://utah.blm.gov).

Backcountry visitors currently need free **backcountry permits** to spend the night in the monument. These are available at any of the stations listed above, and in register boxes at major trailheads. They're as much to find you if something goes wrong as anything, so it's a good idea to fill one out.

NEAR THE MONUMENT
◖ Bryce Canyon National Park

The Paiute told of the "Legend People" who lived in a beautiful city, but misbehaved and were turned to stone as punishment. They remain standing to this day, filling the gigantic amphitheater of Bryce Canyon National Park with peculiar limestone hoodoos in every imaginable shade of white, yellow, pink, and brown. This section of the Pink Cliffs (remember your Grand Staircase geology?) has eroded out of the eastern edge of the Paunsaugunt Plateau, so it lights up best at sunrise. The park was named for Mormon pioneer Ebenezer Bryce, who lived here in the late 19th century. Leaving for Arizona after only a few years, all he had to say of the stunning amphitheater was that it was "a hell of a place to lose a cow."

At the main **visitors center** (435/834-5322, www.nps.gov/brca, 8 A.M.–8 P.M. daily in season), pay your entrance fees ($20 per car) and get backcountry permits ($5). A 17-mile scenic drive follows the rim, and hikers can choose from 61 miles of trails ranging from 9,100 feet elevation at the rim to 6,500 feet down in the fantasyland of rock. To ease congestion, a free shuttle service has been instituted that runs from the entrance to Pryce Point (every 10–15

SOUTH-CENTRAL UTAH

minutes, 9 A.M.–5 P.M. June–early Sept.). There are two first-come, first-served campgrounds ($10), one of which is open year-round. Reserve campsites by calling 877/444-6777 or online at www.reserveusa.com.

In addition to hiking, cross-country skiing along the rim is popular in winter, when the park is practically deserted. Canyon Trail Rides (435/679-8665, www.canyonrides.com) offers guided **horseback rides** for $40 (two hours) to $55 (half day) per person.

While you're here you can stay at the rustic but comfortable **(** **Bryce Canyon Lodge** (888/297-2757, fax 303/297-3175, www.brycecanyonlodge.com, $110–140, Apr.–Oct.), built near the rim by the Union Pacific Railroad Company in the 1920s, or at the **Best Western Ruby's Inn** (435/834-5341, www.rubysinn.com, $105–150), a monstrous resort-style spread just north of the park boundary. Cheaper accommodations and more

food choices can be found in the nearby towns of Tropic and Panguitch.

Kodachrome Basin State Park

It's hard to believe, but according to geologists, the area south of Cannonville on Highway 12 once had hot springs and geysers like those in Yellowstone National Park. Over time they stopped spurting and filled in with sediment, which outlasted the surrounding terrain and left large vertical pipes of hardened sand. In 1949, photographers from *National Geographic* used a new type of film to shoot the colorful arches and 67 chimneys in the area, some of which are 170 feet high.

Since then, the area has been set aside as **Kodachrome Basin State Park** (435/679-8562) which offers a 27-unit year-round campground ($14), short hiking trails, and horseback and stagecoach rides. The day-use fee is $5.

Lake Powell and Glen Canyon

Coming upon Lake Powell unprepared is like stumbling on a mirage. Wavering between red rock and blue sky, the lake's turquoise waters seem outrageously out of place, yet at the same time are undeniably inviting in the heart of the desert. Regardless of your feelings, Lake Powell is an impressive piece of engineering. It's one of the largest man-made lakes in the country, stretching for 186 miles from Glen Canyon Dam up what used to be the Colorado and San Juan rivers to its upper end at Hite Marina.

In between is nearly 2,000 miles of convoluted shoreline—more than the entire West Coast—that is perforated by 96 major canyons. When it's full the reservoir can hold enough water to cover 27 million acres a foot deep. Around the lake's northern shore, the Glen Canyon National Recreation Area protects the upper reaches of canyons that once took weeks to reach by horseback. Countless

secluded beaches dot the shoreline, and fish now swim where eagles soared.

In the process, opponents of the dam will point out, one of the most beautiful canyons in the Southwest was drowned, along with countless sites of historical and archaeological value. (See the sidebar *Glen Canyon Dammed.*) Rainbow Bridge, at one time a week on horseback from anywhere, now stands at the very edge of the water. As of 2005, an ongoing drought had reduced Lake Powell to its lowest level since it first filled completely in 1980—less than 50 percent of capacity. Ten-story white cliffs are now exposed around much of the shoreline, while boaters are able to reach places not seen since before the lake was filled.

SIGHTS AND RECREATION
Rainbow Bridge
National Monument
The largest natural bridge in the world (275

RAINBOW BRIDGE, THE OLD-FASHIONED WAY

If you're up for a bit of a trek, you can reach Rainbow Bridge the only way it was possible before the filling of Lake Powell – by land. The Rainbow Trail circles Navajo Mountain, and begins off Highway 98 between Page and Kayenta. Between mileposts 349 and 350, turn north onto the partly paved Navajo Mountain Road. Drive 32 miles and turn left at the fork to reach the ruins of the old Rainbow Lodge. (If you arrive at the Navajo Mountain Mission, you turned right.)

From here the South Rainbow Trail (marked by red mileposts) leads west across First and Horse canyons, then down into Cliff Canyon, where you'll find first water at a campsite after eight miles. Take a side canyon to the right another mile down, then climb out and over Redbud Pass (blasted out by John Wetherell's party in 1922) to Redbud Creek, which you'll follow down to the bridge at the water's edge, about 13 miles from the trailhead. The remains of the old Echo Camp tourist camp are under an overhang nearby. Remember, don't camp under the bridge or approach it too closely, as it is still holy to the Navajo.

You can return the same way, or take the North Rainbow Trail back to complete the circle. This leaves the bridge to the east up Bridge Canyon, and crosses Oak, Masja, Blad Rock, and Cha canyons and the tablelands between them. From Cha Canyon a dirt road takes you back around to the Navajo Mountain Mission. A vehicle or mountain bike shuttle will save you another 10 miles of walking back to the Rainbow Lodge. The whole loop should take 3-5 days, and there is little water away from the lake (which you should take care to purify carefully).

You can also climb Navajo Mountain from the mission; take a rough road west that eventually turns into a track as it reaches the summit at 10,388 feet. Since the route crosses the Navajo Reservation, you'll have to get a permit in advance from the Parks and Recreation Department office in Window Rock (928/871-6647, info@navajonationparks.org), the Cameron visitors center (928/679-2303), the LeChee Chapter House in Page (928/698-2808), or the Monument Valley visitors center (435/727-3353).

feet across), once one of the most remote spots in the Lower 48, now stands at the very edge of Lake Powell. If you don't have access to a boat, the only other way to see the multihued sandstone span, 50 miles from Wahweap, is the hike from the end of the Navajo Mountain Road west of Kayenta, Arizona (see the sidebar *Rainbow Bridge, the Old-Fashioned Way*).

Long known to local tribes, the bridge symbolizes rainfall and fertility to the Navajo. It was formally "discovered" by white men in August 1909, when two Paiutes guided two expeditions that joined forces and surveyed the scene.

Rainbow Bridge sits on a 160-acre national monument (www.nps.gov/rabr) surrounded by the Navajo Indian Reservation. Soaring 290 feet above Bridge Creek, the salmon-pink bridge is only 32 feet across at its narrowest

point. It's an extraordinary sight that inspired Zane Grey to write a novel about it, and Theodore Roosevelt woke several times during a 1913 visit to gaze on it by moonlight.

Boating

The incongruous sight of an SUV towing a boat across the San Rafael Desert starts to make sense at any one of Lake Powell's marinas, where houseboats, fishing boats, kayaks, and personal watercraft vie for space. A houseboat is one of the most popular ways to explore the lake, with many visitors renting one for a week or more and finding and holding up in their own private side canyon.

Boat rentals are available at Wahweap and Bullfrog marinas from Lake Powell Resorts & Marinas (928/645-1111 or 800/528-6154, lake-powell@aramark.com, www.lakepowell.com).

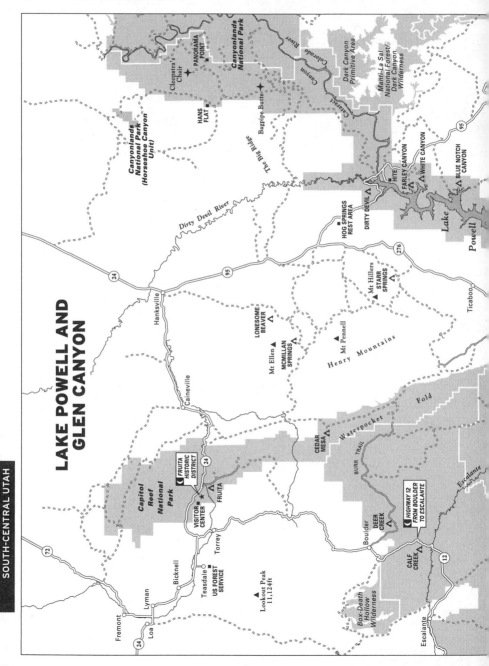

LAKE POWELL AND GLEN CANYON

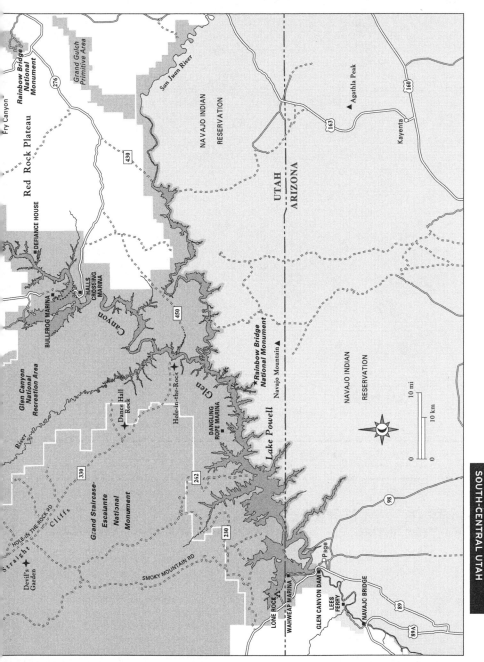

Four classes of houseboats range 44–75 feet and start at $1,371 for three days in summer. Powerboats, fishing boats, kayaks, and personal watercraft are also available. Boaters must be aware of all state boating regulations, as well as those imposed by the National Park Service, which requires a $16 boating permit, good for a week.

Kayaking

A quieter way to reach the lakeside backcountry is by paddling a kayak. From September to May the weather is at its mildest and the powerboaters are fewer. The possibilities are almost limitless; you can take an afternoon to explore the crannies of Wahweap Bay, one of the biggest in the lake, or take a day or two to ascend long, narrow Navajo Canyon east of Page. Crosby Canyon and Antelope Canyon are also popular and within a day of Wahweap, while the lower Escalante and San Juan rivers are good for multiday trips.

Fishing

The Colorado River's native catfish, suckers, and squawfish have been largely supplanted by introduced species such as bluegill sunfish, black crappie, walleye, and bass (striped, largemouth, and smallmouth). Hook and line is the only permitted fishing technique, and if you're over 14 years old a license is required. (Trout require their own additional license.) The lake's now-endangered native fish, including the Colorado squawfish, humpback, and bonytail chub, and the razorback sucker, are off-limits.

FACILITIES AND SERVICES
Wahweap Marina

Just about anything you could do on, under, or near the surface of Lake Powell is available at the main marina just west of Glen Canyon Dam on Lakeshore Drive. Wahweap, which means "bitter water" in the Ute language, is the largest freshwater marina west of the Mississippi. Hundreds of boats bob at anchor in front of the (Lake Powell Resort (928/645-2433). Many of the hotel's 350 units ($100–160) have

patios or balconies overlooking Wahweap Basin, while the excellent **Rainbow Room** restaurant provides fine dining with a panoramic view of the water. They serve all meals daily, with buffets for breakfast and lunch in the Navajo Room and a café for snacks.

Marina services are offered by ARAMARK's **Lake Powell Resorts & Marinas** (928/645-2433 or 800/528-6154, www.lakepowell.com). Boat rentals and tours are offered at the front desk, ranging from a short cruise to Antelope Canyon to all-day tours to Rainbow Bridge. You can also enjoy breakfast or a sunset dinner aboard the *Canyon King* paddle wheeler. Advance reservations are recommended; call or visit their website for the latest prices.

The **Wahweap Campground** is open all year, with sites ($15) open on a first-come, first-served basis. The **Wahweap RV Park** is also open year-round, with full hookup sites for $30 in summer. Primitive camping at **Lone Rock,** six miles northwest on Highway 89, costs $6 per vehicle, and free camping is also permitted anywhere along the lake shore beyond the developed areas.

Dangling Rope Marina

This outpost, 40 miles east of Wahweap, is accessible only by boat, and is the closest to Rainbow Bridge National Monument. There's a ranger station, restrooms, a boat fueling station (the only one between Wahweap and Bullfrog), and limited marina facilities.

Halls Crossing Marina

The south side of a popular river crossing, Halls Crossing (435/684-7000) is named for Charles Hall, one of the founders of Escalante and the builder of a ferry he operated here from 1881 to 1884. Highway 276 connects Halls Crossing with Highway 95 at Natural Bridges National Monument, 48 miles to the east. Ninety-five miles upriver from Wahweap, Halls Crossing has a ranger station, campground ($18), RV park ($30), and a marina. A camp store is also available. The ferry **John Atlantic Burr** (www.nps.gov/glca/ferry.htm) crosses between Halls Crossing and Bullfrog 4–11 times a day mid-April–late October (every two hours mid-May–mid-Sept.). Rates are $4 per person on foot, $6 on a bicycle, and $16–60 for vehicles, depending on length.

Bullfrog Marina

Glen Canyon's second-largest marina is opposite Halls Crossing. Here you'll find a ranger station/visitors center (435/684-7400, 8 A.M.–5 P.M. Apr.–Oct.) along with a marina, a campground ($18), and an RV park ($30). The luxury Defiance House Lodge (435/684-3000, $83–128) has a restaurant that serves all meals. Primitive camping is also available nearby for $6 per vehicle (call 435/684-3000 for information on the developed campsites). You can rent boats and arrange tours here as well. Highway 276 heads north to meet Highway 95, 20 miles west of Hite.

Hite Marina

As of 2005, Lake Powell's northernmost marina was closed as falling lake levels left it high and dry. Hite (435/684-2457) still has a ranger station and an undeveloped campground ($6). It's off Highway 95, 57 miles west of Natural Bridges National Monument, near a pair of bridges over the flooded mouths of the Dirty Devil and Colorado river canyons.

INFORMATION AND TRANSPORTATION
Fees, Regulations, and Safety

The National Park Service charges $10 per vehicle for entrance to the Glen Canyon National Recreation Area (928/608-6404 or 928/608-6200, www.nps.gov/glca), good for a week. Annual boat and vehicle passes are $20.

Life jackets are highly recommended out on the water, and there's no boating after dark. Cliff diving into the lake is prohibited.

Getting There and Around

Lake Powell and the Glen Canyon National Recreation Area are accessible by two-wheel-drive vehicles at Lees Ferry off Highway 89A, at Wahweap Marina near Page, and at Bullfrog and Halls Crossing, both on Highway 276 west of Natural Bridges National Monument. Four-wheel-drive vehicles can use the Hole-in-the-Rock Road from Highway 12 at Escalante, the Burr Trail from Boulder, or a dirt road that leaves Highway 89A at Big Water and heads up onto the Kaiparowits Plateau.

Page, Arizona, and the Paria Plateau

PAGE

This tidy little town (pop. 9,000) was built from scratch in 1957 for workers on the Glen Canyon Dam, at the time one of the largest construction projects in the world. Since then it's become the tourist center of northernmost Arizona. With a good museum and plenty of outdoor activities within easy range, Page is a good base for visiting the Paria Plateau, Glen Canyon and Lake Powell, the northern Navajo Nation, and the southern Grand Staircase–Escalante National Monument. Every other vehicle seems to be towing some kind of watercraft, which together with marinas and swimwear shops give Page an odd beach-town-in-the-

desert feel. It's sandwiched between the dam and the Navajo Generating Station—two of the most important revenue-generators (and worst environmental insults, according to some) in the Four Corners.

About two-thirds of Page's workforce is Navajo, and most of the town's economy comes from tourism and the generating station, whose three towers jut from desert plain to the east. Built in 1974, this coal-fired station can produce up to 2,250 megawatts of power for cities such as Tucson, Las Vegas, and Los Angeles. This takes 1,000 tons of coal per hour, though, brought in by electric train from the controversial mines at Black Mesa, 70 miles south on the Hopi

Reservation. Scrubbers were installed on each of the three generating units by 1999, and now remove about 90 percent of the sulfur dioxide from the gases emitted by the chimneys. With these in place, it has become one of the cleanest coal-fired power plants in the United States.

For information on Wahweap Marina on Lake Powell, seven miles northwest of Page on Highway 89, see *Lake Powell and Glen Canyon* earlier in this chapter.

Sights

The **John Wesley Powell Memorial Museum** (6 N. Lake Powell Blvd., 928/645-9496 or 888/597-6873, visitorinfo@powellmuseum.org, www.powellmuseum.org, 9 A.M.–5 P.M. Mon.–Fri. Feb.–Dec., $3) houses an excellent collection covering early cultures, river-runners, and natural history. Displays on Powell's life and explorations include an interesting set of photos from his expeditions, paired with pictures taken a century later to

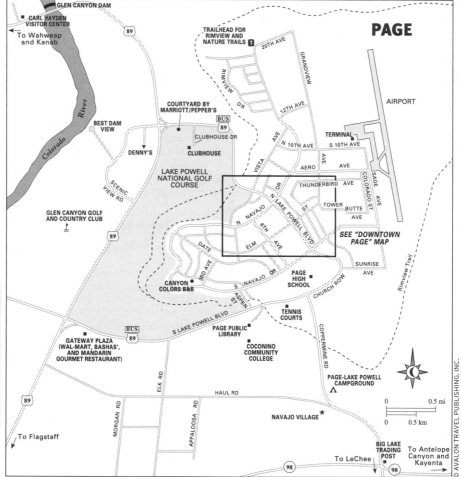

show the environmental changes. Kids can grind corn amid the exhibits on native cultures and early explorers, and nearby are displays by local artists and a pictorial history of the dam and Lake Powell. The museum is also the local **information center,** and you can make reservations for tours of the lake and Antelope Canyon here as well.

Get a taste of Navajo culture through programs held at **Navajo Village** (928/660-0304, 9 A.M.–3 P.M. daily Apr.–Oct., $10 adults, $5 children 6–13), a living museum where you can take a guided tour of a traditional Navajo home during the day. Otherwise, opt for the full four-hour evening program, which includes demonstrations of weaving and silversmithing; a traditional dinner; and singing, dancing, and stories around the campfire ($50 adults, $35 children). Shorter evening programs are also available; get tickets at the Powell Museum or the Chamber of Commerce visitors center. It's a little hard to find, off Haul Road near the intersection with Coppermine Road.

Shopping

Blair's Dinnebito Trading Post (626 N. Navajo Dr., 928/645-3008 or 800/644-3008, www.blairstradingpost.com), in the Dam Plaza shopping center, evolved from a remote trading post deep in the Navajo Reservation. Along with a large selection of rugs, kachinas, pottery, baskets, and paintings, they also stock raw wool, saddle leather, and pawned jewelry. Ask to see the private collection upstairs, collected over half a century by patriarch Elijah Blair, who helped create the black-background Dinnebito style of Navajo weaving. The old cash registers, guns, historical photos, jewelry, and rugs are not for sale, but worth a peek nonetheless.

Hiking

In Page's best-known hike, you can't even see the sun for a good part of it. Discovered in 1931, **Antelope Canyon** is probably this most famous slot canyon in the world, thanks to countless photographs of shafts of light penetrating its sensual sandstone curves. (Also, per-

haps, because of a flash flood in 1997 that left 11 European tourists dead and spit out their Navajo guide, alive, after tearing his clothes off.) The canyon is 120 feet deep and only a few yards wide in spots, but easy going on a flat sandy bottom most of the way. The rosily lighted grottoes and hairpin corners are a photographer's dream—bring a tripod and cable release, and try to shoot near noon.

Many companies in Page offer tours—the only way to see the canyon, as it's now a Navajo tribal park. **Overland Canyon Tours** (695 N. Navajo, 928/608-4072, overland@overlandcanyon.com, www.overlandcanyon.com) takes visitors to Antelope Canyon as well as the less-visited (and just as impressive) **Canyon X,** to which they have exclusive access. Waterholes Canyon is another guided slot option. **Roger Ekis' Antelope Canyon Tours** (22 S. Lake Powell Blvd., 928/645-9102 or 866/645-9102, carolene_ekis@hotmail.com, www.antelopecanyon.com) offers tours starting at $20 per person ($10 children 6–13) for a 90-minute visit to the upper canyon. Longer custom

© JULIAN SMITH

SOUTH-CENTRAL UTAH

Canyon X, near Page

photography tours are also possible with both outfits.

Antelope Canyon is a mile east on Highway 98 from the Big Lake Trading Post. Like any slot, Antelope is prone to flash flooding from storms upstream, even if the sky is blue overhead. If your Navajo guide says get out, listen to him—something 11 European tourists didn't do in 1997. Their bodies took months to dig out of the mud and debris. Call the park at 928/698-2808 for more information.

The **Rim Trail** is an eight-mile bike- and footpath around the edge of Manson Mesa, with great views of the lake and desert. One access point is via the nature trail at the north end of town near the Lake View School at North Navajo Drive and 20th Avenue. Another short trail (1.5 miles round-trip) leads to an overlook above the impressive **Horseshoe Bend** of the Colorado, from a parking area just south of milepost 545 on Highway 89 south. Watch your footing here—there aren't any guardrails—and try to come at sunset, when flocks of birds swarm after insects above the abyss.

The trail to **Wiregrass Canyon,** a steep wash down to Lake Powell, begins off Highway 89 between mileposts 7 and 8 toward Big Water. Turn right and go about five miles down a dirt road to a parking area. The hike follows the unmarked wash about three miles to the lake, and involves some scrambling around pouroffs. Keep an eye out for arches, balanced rocks, and a natural bridge.

Other Recreation

In addition to the ARAMARK tours of Lake Powell (see *Lake Powell and Glen Canyon*), you can explore the waters in a kayak with **Kayak Powell** (888/854-7862, seldomseenkyle@hawaiicity.com, www.kayakpowell.com). Kyle Walker offers half-day ($85 pp) and full-day ($125 pp) paddling trips, as well as overnighters ($200 pp per day) and rentals for $25–45 per day. He also runs hiking and four-wheel-drive tours, and offers shuttle service for people hiking the Paria River's Buckskin Gulch. The **Twin Finn Dive Center** (811 Vista Ave., 928/645-3114, www.twin-

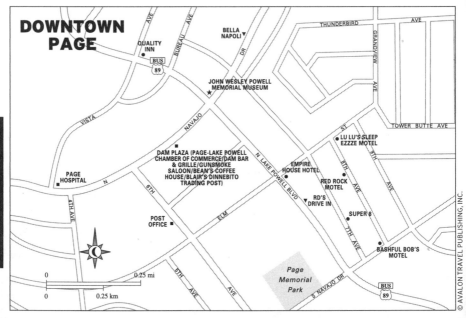

SOUTH-CENTRAL UTAH

finn.com) is the only dive shop in own, and they also rents kayaks year-round starting at $35/day.

Rent a personal watercraft, boat, or kayak at **Bill & Toni's Marine** (803 Vista Ave., 928/645-5990) and sign up for raft trips through the Grand Canyon with **Wilderness River Adventures** (928/645-3296 or 800/992-8022, www.riveradventures.com). Choose from either the whole shebang or just the placid stretch through Marble Canyon to Lees Ferry. Pick up a game of pool or bowling at **The Bowl** (24 N. Lake Powell Blvd., 928/645-2682) which also has a bistro and a bar.

Accommodations

Since Page is such a busy tourist hub, it's a good idea to call ahead for reservations, particularly in summer. The summer rates listed here drop dramatically in winter. Plenty of inexpensive accommodations line 8th Avenue, Page's "Street of Little Motels," which originally housed supervisors during the construction of the dam. Clean, comfortable double rooms for under $50 can be found at **Lu Lu's Sleep Ezzze Motel** (105 8th Ave., 928/608-0273), **Bashful Bob's Motel** (750 S. Navajo Dr., 928/645-3919), and the **Red Rock Motel** (114 8th Ave., 928/645-0062).

Chain hotels galore are sprinkled throughout the rest of the town; in the $50–100 category are a **Super 8** (75 S. 7th Ave., 928/645-2858, fax 928/645-2890) and a **Quality Inn** (287 N. Lake Powell Blvd., 928/645-8851, fax 928/645-2523). A pool and patio await at the **Canyon Colors B&B** (225 S. Navajo Dr., 928/645-5979 or 800/536-2530, fax 928/645-5979, canyoncolors@webtv.net, www.canyoncolors.com, $85–95), run by a friendly Belgian couple.

On a hillside overlooking the dam and the lake is the ◖ **Courtyard by Marriott** (600 Clubhouse Dr., 928/645-5000, fax 928/645-5004, $100–130) with a golf course, heated outdoor pool, and **Pepper's** restaurant, voted one of Arizona's 100 best in 1995. The **Page-Lake Powell Campground** (849 S. Coppermine Rd, 928/645-374, http://campground.page-lake-powell.com) is southeast of downtown. Full

PAGE CLIMATE

MONTH	AVG. HIGH	AVG. LOW	MEAN	AVG. PRECIP.
Jan.	43°F	26°F	35°F	0.61 in.
Feb.	50°F	30°F	41°F	0.48 in.
Mar.	59°F	37°F	48°F	0.65 in.
Apr.	69°F	44°F	56°F	0.50 in.
May	78°F	53°F	66°F	0.40 in.
June	90°F	62°F	76°F	0.14 in.
July	95°F	68°F	82°F	0.58 in.
Aug.	92°F	66°F	79°F	0.69 in.
Sept.	84°F	58°F	71°F	0.66 in.
Oct.	70°F	47°F	58°F	0.99 in.
Nov.	54°F	35°F	44°F	0.56 in.
Dec.	44°F	27°F	35°F	0.48 in.

SOUTH-CENTRAL UTAH

hookup sites are $26, and tent sites are $17. (Showers are $4.) More campsites are available west of the dam at Wahweap Marina.

Food

🄲 **Peppers** (928/645-1347, all meals daily) at the Courtyard by Marriott, is probably the best restaurant in town, serving Southwest fare (dinner runs $15–20) and a good lunch buffet. On the other end of the price range, the **Empire House Hotel** (107 S. Lake Powell Blvd., 928/645-2406) has a $2 all-you-can-eat pancake special for the thrifty or impecunious. **RD's Drive In,** (143 Lake Powell Blvd., 928/645-2791) was the first in town when Glen Canyon Dam was only a dream on paper. It's a local hangout for burgers and ice cream, especially for high schoolers around lunchtime. Hardly anything is over $4.

Bella Napoli (810 N. Navajo Dr., 928/645-2706, lunch Mon.–Fri., dinner Mon.–Sat.) does a good Italian dinner, with pasta, fish, and seafood entrées around $10. In the Dam Plaza shopping center is the **Dam Bar & Grille** (644 N. Navajo Dr., 928/645-2161, lunch and dinner Mon.–Sat.), serving BBQ ribs and steaks ($15–20). It includes the Gunsmoke Saloon, a sports bar with live music (mostly country) Wednesday–Saturday evenings. Next door, **Bean's Coffee House** (928/645-6858, 6 A.M.–5 P.M. Mon.–Fri., 7 A.M.–5 P.M. Sat., 8 A.M.–noon Sun.) offers breakfast and lunch ($3–5) on weekdays, and coffee and Internet access all hours.

Information and Transportation

The **Page/Lake Powell Chamber of Commerce** (928/645-2741 or 888/261-7243, chamber@pagelakepowellchamber.org, www.pagelakepowellchamber.org) operates a visitors center (8 A.M.–8 P.M. Mon.–Sat., 9 A.M.–6 P.M. Sun. in season, 9 A.M.–5 P.M. Mon.–Fri. otherwise) in the Dam Plaza shopping center, next to the Dam Bar and Grill. They stock plenty of information about the area, and offer reservations for local tours.

Find more information on the area, especially its natural and human history,

from the **Glen Canyon Natural History Association** (928/608-6358 or 877/453-6296, www.pagelakepowell.org). They fund research projects, help staff park visitor centers, and sell books and maps by mail order.

Great Lakes Airlines (800/554-5111, www.greatlakesav.com) flies to Denver ($164, once daily), Farmington ($100–120, once daily) and Phoenix ($134, three times daily).

GLEN CANYON DAM

Page's raison d'être plugs Marble Canyon a few miles west of town with nearly five million cubic yards of concrete, poured around the clock for three years. It was built between 1960 and 1963, stands 710 feet high, and holds back 27,000,000 acre-feet of water when the reservoir is full. Free tours of the dam's cave-cool innards are given at the National Park Service's **Carl Hayden Visitor Center** (928/608-6404, 8 A.M.–6 P.M. daily Memorial Day–Labor Day, to 5 P.M. otherwise) on the west side of the Highway 89 bridge. Depending on the national security alert level, these occur four

Glen Canyon Dam

times daily with a maximum of 20 people per tour, and take you from the gigantic turbines and transformers to an incongruous patch of green grass at the base.

The **best dam view** in Page can be found behind the Denny's off Highway 89. Go down Scenic View Drive to the sign for the overlook. To take in the entire sweep of this end of the lake, head west about a mile past the dam visitors center, then climb the steep but short hill to your right (north). The sight is startling, bizarre, and undeniably beautiful—the blue of the lake, the green oasis of Page, the monolithic dam, and Navajo Mountain, all in one grand panorama.

PARIA PLATEAU

As the Grand Staircase marches down to the Colorado River, this plateau between the Kaibab Mountains and the Vermilion Cliffs forms one of its bottom steps. Outlined by Highways 89 and 89A, the Paria Plateau forms the eastern end of the Arizona Strip, the isolated piece of the state north of the Grand Canyon. It centers on the Big Knoll (6,844 feet) and is sliced neatly in two by the lower reaches of the Paria River, which offers one of the Four Corners' great canyon hikes. If you're going to do just one overnight narrows hike in the Four Corners, make it this one.

The canyon constricts in its upper reaches into some of the longest and tightest slot canyons in the world, before opening up into a majestic gorge with thousand-foot walls that empties into the Colorado at Lees Ferry. To keep a handle on the canyon's growing popularity, 112,500 acres have been set aside as the **Paria Canyon-Vermilion Cliffs Wilderness,** enclosed by the little-known, 293,000-acre **Vermilion Cliffs National Monument.**

Hiking the Canyons

You have a few different options for hikes. The easiest access is off Highway 89, 43 miles east of Kanab and just less than 14 miles west of Big Water. Here, near the Paria River Bridge, is the **Paria Contact Station** (8:30 A.M.–4:15 P.M. daily mid-Mar.–mid-Nov.). You can pick up

permits, ask advice, and buy maps and guidebooks, including the BLM's "Hiker's Guide to Paria Canyon." Just down the gravel road is the **White House Campground,** where primitive sites are $10. The **Paria River Trailhead** is two miles farther down the road. A trail meanders along the riverbanks, which are wide for four miles before closing in sharply and rising to about 200 feet. The play of light and shadow and the gurgle of water make the seven miles to the Buckskin Gulch confluence an enchanting hike that can be done in one long day.

Keep going west on Highway 89 five miles past the contact station until the road curves sharply north at the Cockscomb, an unmistakable monocline. A reasonably good dirt road heads south here parallel to the gigantic ridge; follow it south to the **Buckskin Trailhead** (4.5 miles) or the **Wire Pass Trailhead** (8.5 miles). (The road continues all the way to Highway 89A near Jacob Lake.) There is good at-large camping nearby—just don't sleep in your car at the trailhead, as it's prohibited. Wire Pass offers the quickest access to the narrows—less than two miles—which are on most desert rats' lists of the best slot canyons in the Southwest. Deep, dark, and drop-dead gorgeous, Buckskin Gulch gives even slot veterans goose bumps. At points the canyon walls are barely shoulder width apart. From Wire Pass it's 14 miles downstream to the confluence with Paria Canyon (it's 16 miles from the Buckskin trailhead). The Buckskin–Wire Pass loop is good for a day hike, but you can make it to White House in a long day. To descend all the way down to Lee's Ferry (38 miles) takes 4–5 days.

About three miles farther south is the access point to **Coyote Buttes,** another popular spot nicknamed "The Wave." By now you've probably seen the amazing photos of red-and-white rock layers swirling like ice cream frozen in an ocean wave. Day-use permits are required as well.

Permits and Information

Since this is such a popular hiking area, the BLM has instituted a permit system. You can get these at the contact station or secure them

GLEN CANYON DAMMED

When Interior Secretary Bruce Babbit brought a sledgehammer down on McPherrin Dam near Chico, California, in 1998, the symbolic blow – ostensibly for the good of spawning salmon – struck more than the dam itself. In recent years cracks have appeared in an entire ideology begun over a century ago when settlers first began using dams and irrigation to feed crops and cities in the deserts of the American West. Nowhere is the controversy more heated than over the 710-foot face of Glen Canyon Dam.

Water has always been the limiting factor in the settlement of the West, and it's a problem whose solutions are, at best, temporary. Dam supporters include ranchers, farmers, developers, and anyone else who benefits from water where it doesn't occur naturally (i.e., most of the United States between Colorado and California), along with government agencies like the Bureau of Reclamation and the U.S. Army Corps of engineers that threw dams up by the hundreds in the early and middle 20th century. These groups espouse benefits like pollution-free power, irrigation, flood control, and smooth waterways to transport goods.

On the other hand are scientists, conservation groups, and fish- and river-lovers citing growing evidence of the catastrophic effects dams have on river ecosystems – fish runs decimated, fertile banks turned barren – as well as practical considerations (surpluses of crops and power) and even aesthetics, like golf courses in Phoenix and the fact that the Colorado River no longer even reaches the Gulf of California, instead trickling to nothing in the sands of Mexico.

Many dam opponents look at Glen Canyon Dam as environmental author Edward Abbey did: as the ultimate symbol of the bulldozing of the West by overeager engineers and shortsighted developers. From the moment the last spillway closed on March 13, 1963, the dam's opponents have mourned the loss of one of the West's most beautiful canyons, pointing out how the river ecosystem is so altered that trout – cold, clear-water fish, mountain fish – now thrive in the once-warm and muddy river; how sediment has filled one-seventh of the lake; and how pollutants have become so concentrated that pregnant women have been warned to stay out of the water. But opponents of the dam are in for a fight from the three million tourists who enjoy the lake every year, as well as from anyone who pulls in part of the $400 million those tourists spend, and from

---

ahead of time from the BLM's **Arizona Strip Field Office** in St. George, Utah (345 E. Riverside Dr., 435/688-3230, azafoweb@blm.gov, www.az.blm.gov/paria/, 7:45 A.M.–5 P.M. Mon.–Fri., 10 A.M.–3 P.M. Sat.). The fee is $5 per person per day, and you can pay this at the trailheads for day use. Permits are also available online. Permits for Coyote Buttes North (the Wave) are limited to 20 people per day, and are claimed within minutes of being put up online at midnight Mountain Standard Time on the first of each month. Coyote Butte South and Paria Canyon are easier to get permits for the same month.

Campfires are prohibited in the canyons, toilet paper must be packed out, and you should pay particular attention to the weather. Precip-

itation is highest July–September, peaking in August, and a cloudburst can fill the narrows much faster than you can get out—notice the logs jammed between the canyon walls high overhead.

Car shuttles can be arranged through Kayak Powell in Page, Arizona, for $50–100 for up to five people.

Paria Canyon Adventure Ranch

This friendly, sprawling operation (928/660-2674, easton@pariacampground.com, www.pariacampground.com) is between mileposts 21 and 22 on Highway 89. They offer a wide range of service: trail rides in the Grand Staircase, volleyball, horseshoes, horseback riding to the Paria River ($45 pp), ATV rentals, those who draw water from the lake or power from the dam.

Abbey advocated the dam's destruction for decades in his novels and essays, but only recently has the idea begun to seem possible. The environmental group Earth First! kicked off its career in 1981 by unfurling a gigantic plastic "crack" down the face of the dam, and in 1996 the Sierra Club, which had let the dam be built unopposed in the first place in a Faustian bargain to keep two more out of Dinosaur National Monument, passed a resolution calling for the draining of Lake Powell. The proposal was heard before a subcommittee of the House Committee on Resources in September 1997.

Five years later, the worst drought in a quarter century gripped the Four Corners. At its peak, three inches of Lake Powell was evaporating every day, until the upper part of the long-drowned Cathedral in the Desert came into view. As water levels dropped 15 percent, the idea of keeping the lake half full suddenly didn't seem as crazy. In a normal year, a full Lake Powell loses 163 billion gallons to evaporation. This is wasted water, according to the lake's original purpose of providing a steady supply to states downriver. Dropping the level by even one-quarter, re-ducing surface area, and eliminating shallows could eliminate up to half the loss to evaporation. And out here, water is money – that's about $100 million saved.

Proponents present it as a win-win situation – more water is available for irrigation and thirsty cities, and at least some of the lake remains – and they are starting to gain the ear of California politicians. Opponents, including local groups like Friends of Lake Powell, see this as the first step to draining the lake completely, and the end to electricity generated by the Glen Canyon Dam and the elimination of the recreation industry that brings in $500 million per year to Page alone.

The battle lines have been drawn, with groups like the Sierra Club, the Glen Canyon Institute, and the Glen Canyon Action Network lobbying for the dam's removal, while the Friends of Lake Powell (and just about everyone employed in Page and South-Central Utah) fight to keep it in place.

Over it all hangs the irony of naming a dam after the canyon it covered, and an artificial lake after the explorer and scientist who spent much of his life campaigning against the unwise use of the West's most precious resource.

and a climbing wall are a few of the options. To spend the night you can choose between the bunkhouse hostel ($12 pp), tent spaces and RV sites ($7.50 pp), or their cabin ($35). They also have a shuttle service for hiking the Paria canyons. Next door is the **Paria Outpost Restaurant** (928/691-1047, dinner Fri. and Sat. in season), with great BBQ, live music, and a big wraparound porch to enjoy the scenery. Food, drinks, maps, and guidebooks are available in the general store.

LEES FERRY AND VICINITY

Highway 89A leaves Highway 89 105 miles north of Flagstaff and 25 miles south of Page, at the north end of the Echo Cliffs. It heads north across what looks like an unbroken plain to-ward the Vermilion Cliffs. Before you know it, though up rise two shining metal arches across the Colorado, flowing deep in a canyon that remains invisible until you reach its edge.

Marble Canyon

Navajo Bridge crosses the river at an area of spectacular scenery and intriguing history. When it was opened in 1929, the original bridge was the highest cantilevered steel arch in the world, soaring 467 feet above the river, and was the only place to cross between Moab and the Hoover Dam. During its construction, the two cantilevered halves were gradually extended across the abyss until they met in the middle. Parts had to be shipped from one side to the other all the way through Needles,

SOUTH-CENTRAL UTAH

California—an 800-mile trip to travel 800 feet across the river. The road was paved in 1937.

The bridge was replaced in 1995 by a stronger, wider twin—it is still one of only seven river crossings in 750 miles—and the original is now open only to pedestrians. It's worth a walk across to gaze down at the Colorado River, colored a Caribbean turquoise from its source at the base of the Glen Canyon Dam. You'll often see rafters heading downstream from Lees Ferry. There is a national park **interpretive center** (9 A.M.–5 P.M. daily Apr.–Oct., 10 A.M.–4 P.M. Sat. and Sun. early Apr. and Nov.) at the western end. The Civilian Conservation Corps built the rustic stone observation structure in the 1930s; now you can listen to Charlton Heston narrate a documentary video in a kiosk outside, next to a memorial plaque to John Doyle Lee, a "man of great faith, sound judgment, and indomitable courage" (more on him soon).

Just up the road is the **Marble Canyon Lodge** (928/355-2225 or 800/726-1789, fax 928/355-2227) built in 1926 in anticipation of the bridge's construction. It was owned and operated by Lorenzo Hubbell's trading company 1937–1950, and the master trader's influence still shows in the excellent crafts shop, with a large selection of books as well. It's a comfortable, rustic place of stone and logs, with wide porches and cottonwoods for shade. Rooms are $75, with cottages for $95 and apartments for $145. They also offer a full-service fly shop (www.mcg-leesferry.com), convenience store, gas station, general store, and post office. The restaurant is decorated with photos of river-runners and serves entrées ($11–22) like pan-fried trout and veggie melts ($7).

Lees Ferry

Descend to the river's edge past house-size rocks balanced on pedestals of compressed earth. Six miles down the paved road, where the Paria River empties into the Colorado, is a small historic district and the major put-in spot for raft trips heading into the Grand Canyon. Before the era of pavement and suspension bridges, Lees Ferry was an impor-

Navajo Bridge crosses Marble Canyon and the Colorado River near Lees Ferry.

© JULIAN SMITH

THE CONDOR SOARS AGAIN

If you see a huge silhouette gliding across the sun near the Vermilion Cliffs, it might be one of six California Condors *(Gymnogyps californianus)* released near here in 1996. The genus *Gymnogpys* once ranged over what is now west Texas, Arizona, and New Mexico. Fossil bones, eggshells, and feathers have been found in the Grand Canyon, dated between 10,000 and 22,000 years ago. By 1982, there were only 22 of the giant birds, whose wingspan can reach 10 feet across, left in the mountains of California, making them the most endangered vertebrates in the world. In a last-ditch effort, all the wild California condors were rounded up and placed in captivity, where it was hoped they could breed themselves back from the brink.

The program has seen some success, but also some setbacks. Of the 35 condors released so far in Arizona, 14 have been killed by predators, power lines, or people. In 2000, five died from lead poisoning, probably from eating a carcass contaminated by buckshot. The recovery plan calls for three self-supporting populations, two in the wild and one in captivity, with at least 150 birds in each. So far, so good, but keep your fingers crossed.

Your best chance of seeing a condor is near the release site at the intersection of Highway 89A and House Rock Valley Road, about 15 miles east of Jacob Lake.

tant passage from Utah to Arizona and New Mexico.

The area was named for John Doyle Lee, who is most well known as the engineer—or

© JULIAN SMITH

rafters getting ready for a Colorado River trip

scapegoat—behind the Mountain Meadows Massacre, one of the darkest chapters in the history of the Mormon pioneers. In 1857, a party of 137 Arkansas emigrants was crossing southern Utah on the way to California. In early September, they were ambushed near Cedar City, Utah, by a group of Paiute and Mormons, angered by U.S. government interference in what they saw as their territory. Led by Lee, the group promised the emigrants safe passage, convinced them to lay down their arms, and then killed everyone except the young children.

Details of the crime were slow in leaking out (and are still being debated today), but Lee was worried enough to seek refuge here in 1871. He built the Lonely Dell Ranch with the help of Emma, his 17th wife out of 19. The Lees saw a good bit of traffic, in part because their home was on the Honeymoon Trail for newly married Mormons traveling by wagon from new settlements in Arizona to have their marriages officially sanctioned in St. George, Utah. Lee was eventually tracked down and arrested in 1875, but the trial resulted in a hung jury. He was arrested again the next year, convicted of first-degree murder, and in 1877 was shot at the site of

SOUTH-CENTRAL UTAH

the massacre, standing in front of his own open grave.

Lonely or not, it's hard to imagine a prettier setting, with green cottonwoods and fruit trees contrasting with red and gold cliffs and surging blue water. The Lees' log cabin, built in the 1870s, stands near an orchard of peach, pear, apricot, and plum trees and a stone building built in 1916 for the Bar Z Ranch. It's maintained by the National Park Service and is open to the public.

From April to October, chances are you will see a raft trip packing up at the boat launch ramp. More than 20,000 people brave the rapids and drink in the scenery (and some of the river) every year. About 100 yards upriver are the remains of a few stone buildings that served as trading post and post office, near the sunken carcass of a steamboat brought here in the early 1900s in an unsuccessful attempt to extract gold from the Chinle Shale. The old ferry crossing, in operation 1873–1928, is another mile upstream, reachable via the old wagon road from the ruins. A campground ($10/night) is on the hillside overlooking the river.

Along the Vermilion Cliffs

Highway 89A continues west through a wild landscape at the foot of the cliffs, with huge tumbled boulders and condors soaring overhead (see the sidebar *The Condor Soars Again*). Nine miles west of Marble Canyon is the **Cliff Dwellers Lodge** (928/355-2261 or 800/962-9755, fax 928/355-2271, info@cliffdwellerslodge.com, www.cliffdwellerslodge.com, $45 d) with a gas station, a restaurant, and a small store. The spread includes **Lees Ferry Anglers** (928/355-2261 or 800/962-9755, anglers@leesferry.com, www.leesferry.com), which has a fly shop, guiding services, and gear rental. A few hundred yards away are the ruins of the original Cliff Dwellers lodge, built by a Ziegfeld Follies dancer and her tubercular husband during the Great Depression.

BACKGROUND

The Land

The Four Corners is part of the larger **Colorado Plateau,** one of the major physiographic provinces of the western United States. Bounded by the Rocky Mountains to the north and east, the Sonoran Desert to the south, and Nevada's Great Basin to the west, the Colorado Plateau consists of 130,000 square miles of southern Utah, northern Arizona, northwestern New Mexico, and southwestern Colorado—most of it relatively flat country sliced by rivers and punctuated by buttes and isolated mountains and small ranges.

GEOLOGY
Geologic History
The combined forces of weather, gravity, and plate tectonics have filled this region with an amazing variety of topography. If you remember nothing else about the complex surface of the Four Corners (and there is a lot), keep these three words in mind: deposition, uplift, and erosion. At its simplest, the Four Corners' stupendous scenery can be summed up in three steps. First, layers of sediment were laid down like Navajo blankets on a bed. Next, these were bent, abused, and generally lifted toward the sky by huge energies below ground. Finally, they were worn away by wind, rain, ice, and above all flowing water, into the mesas and canyons and endless other shapes that fill the region.

© JULIAN SMITH

In all, some 300 million years of geologic history are visible in the Four Corners, a display with few equals in the world. The oldest rocks in the region, at the bottom of the Grand Canyon, date to the middle of the Precambrian Era (4.6 billion–570 million years ago). During the Cambrian, Devonian, Mississippian, and Permian periods, (570–320 million years ago), the region was much closer to the equator, and warm tropical seas left behind layers of early marine fossils. A series of mountain ranges called the Ancestral Rockies rose during the Pennsylvanian Period (320–286 million years ago), including the **Uncompahgre Uplift** in what is now eastern Utah and western Colorado. These were probably as high as today's Rockies, and shed sediments into lower-elevation depressions such as the **Paradox Basin,** southwest of the Uncompahgre Uplift, which filled and emptied of water as deep geologic faults shifted well into the Permian Period (286–245 million years ago).

During the Triassic Period (245–208 million years ago), continental drift carried the land north into warmer climates. Increased rainfall fed lakes, streams, marshes, and early forests, some of which were buried and turned to stone. Ferns and early conifers were also covered in silt, mud, and sand along with primitive amphibians and reptiles. Dinosaur fossils were added to the mix during the Jurassic Period (208–144 million years ago), when the local climate cooled somewhat as the continent moved even farther north. By this time the Uncompahgre Uplift had been mostly worn away, and seas flowing in from the west and north created muddy tidal flats whose petrified ripples turn up near sand dunes also frozen by the forces of time.

More marine fossils are found in layers dating to the Cretaceous Period (104–66 million years ago), when waters spread across North America from Alaska to Mexico. The modern Rocky Mountains rose during this period as well, taking 20–30 million years to reach their current heights. More uplift followed during the Tertiary Period (66–2 million years ago), starting with the formation of the **laccolithic mountains** that rise above the plateau today. The La Sals, the Abajos, the Henry Mountains, and Navajo Mountain are all laccolithic peaks, formed over huge blisters of magma that pushed upward without breaking through to the surface.

Beginning about 15 million years ago, the entire plateau, which until now had existed close sea level, was lifted up about 3,000 feet. Steeper slopes made rivers flow faster, increasing erosion, and rapid downcutting occurred along the course of the Colorado and Green rivers. About 10,000 feet of sedimentary deposits have eroded in the last 10–15 million years, exposing millions of years of older rock layers. About 5.5 million years ago, the San Andres Fault opened the Gulf of California, freeing the Colorado River to flow into the ocean to the southwest.

The forces of erosion continued through the Quaternary period (2 million years ago–present), and the youngest geologic features are constantly being created and destroyed. The forces of weather, gravity, and chance shape arches, spires, natural bridges, and hoodoos, and volcanic necks and dikes are exposed as their softer outer layers wear away. The timescale involved is immense, but if you're lucky you might even see this process at work—although hopefully from a safe distance. Pieces have fallen from arches and towers have collapsed well into the 20th century, and rocks tumble from cliffs on an almost daily basis.

Major Features

Elevations in the Four Corners range from 2,000 feet at the bottom of the Grand Canyon to 12,700 feet in the La Sal Mountains near Moab, but average 3,000–5,000 feet. The tension between lifting up and tearing down shows in the contrast between huge, shallow basins, such as the Paradox Basin and the oil-rich San Juan Basin of northern New Mexico, and smaller uplifted areas with names like Defiance, Monument, Zuni, and the Circle Cliffs.

GEOLOGIC TERMS

anticline: arch-shaped upfold in rock layers

arch: freestanding stone curve formed by erosion

butte: flat-topped hill with sloping sides

concretion: rounded mineral mass found in sedimentary rock

cross-bedding: linear patterns in sandstone created by shifting wind directions (also called cross stratification)

desert varnish: dark rock coating formed by water and microbes

diatreme: solidified neck of an explosive volcano, later exposed by erosion

dike: vertical ridge of exposed igneous rock formed by fissures filling with magma

fault: fracture or break in a rock mass that has moved

graben: straight-walled canyon formed by down-shifted fault blocks (German for "ditch" or "grave")

horst: uplifted block remaining between grabens

joint: fracture or break in a rock mass that has not moved

mesa: flat-topped hill with at least one steeply sloping side

monocline: steplike fold in rock layers

natural bridge: freestanding stone curve formed by flowing water

pothole: shallow, water-collecting depression created by erosion

slickrock: bare sandstone

syncline: trough-shaped downfold in rock layers

talus: rock fragments that accumulate at the bottom of eroding slopes or cliffs

Dark-green forests cover the largest ranges: the **La Sal Mountains** east of Moab, the **Abajo Mountains** west of Monticello, and the **Henry Mountains** east of Capitol Reef National Park. On the Navajo Reservation, **Navajo Mountain** rises south of Lake Powell, and the **Chuska** and **Carrizo mountains** follow the Arizona–New Mexico border. Boulder and Thousand-Lake Mountain form the bulk of the **Aquarius Plateau** in South-Central Utah, near the colorfully named cliffs that make up the **Grand Staircase** to the west. Other dramatic features include stair-step **monoclines** stretching for dozens of miles; the Waterpocket Fold is the largest of these, but the list includes Comb Ridge on Cedar Mesa and The Cockscomb in the southern Escalante. Black Mesa, rich in coal, underlies most of the Hopi Reservation and the central Navajo Reservation.

The list goes on: buttes and mesas, looming cliffs, and volcanic necks and dikes dot the terrain by the hundreds. Long, brown rivers meander for miles before exploding into white water in deep, shaded canyons. The **Colorado River,** creator of the Grand Canyon, is the unquestioned champion, even though it has been flooded by dams and reservoirs for much of its length, and more often than not it trickles to nothing in the desert of northern Mexico instead of reaching the Gulf of California. Born in the Colorado Rockies, it follows a major fault zone running northeast to southwest from Southeast Utah into northern Arizona, and is joined in the heart of Canyonlands National Park by the **Green River,** which flows south from Wyoming. The **San Juan River** runs west across northern New Mexico and Arizona before joining **Lake Powell,** the huge reservoir in southern Utah formed by the Colorado River backing up behind Glen Canyon Dam. The **Little Colorado River** drains the southern Navajo Reservation before it joins the Colorado in the Grand Canyon. Verdant valleys line some sections of riverbank. These are fed by countless smaller streams and washes, many of which flow only a few days out of the year.

Major Rock Layers

Some of the Four Corners' rock layers, like

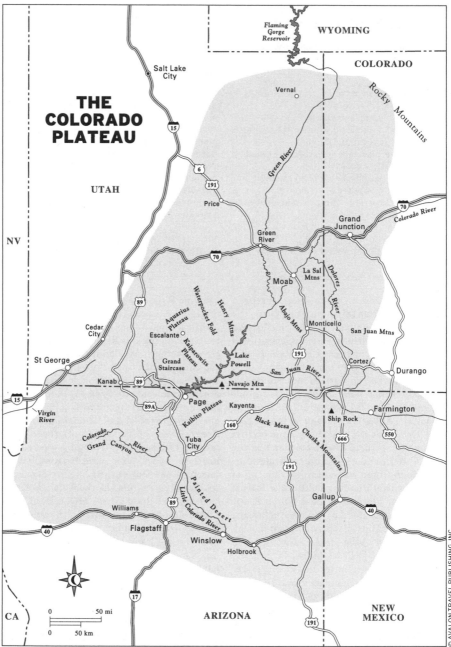

THE
COLORADO
PLATEAU

the distinctive sheer walls of Wingate Sandstone near Moab, are easy to recognize. Others aren't, especially when they change from place to place, like the ubiquitous Navajo Sandstone, deposited as dunes during the Jurassic Period. In Canyonlands and Capitol Reef national parks its distinctive rounded contours are the color of chalk and cream; it starts turning pink in the lower reaches of Zion Canyon; and the walls of Glen Canyon are still salmon-colored somewhere beneath the silty waters of Lake Powell to the south.

A few mnemonic devices can help with the names. Heading up the Colorado River from Lee's Ferry, remember "Many Canyon Walls Know No Capitalist Exploitation," which stands for the layers visible from bottom (oldest) to top: Moenkopi, Chinle, Wingate, Kayenta, Navajo, Carmel, and Entrada. Another saying goes from top to bottom: "Every New Kangaroo Wants Chocolate Milk" (Entrada, Navajo, Kayenta, Wingate, Chinle, Moenkopi). The three most visible layers in Southeast Utah are the red-brown mud/shale of the Kayenta layer, the lighter Navajo Sandstone, and red-brown Entrada Sandstone—if you can recognize these, you're doing pretty well.

CLIMATE

The Colorado Plateau is classified as arid to semiarid, receiving an average of 11.8 inches of rain per year—a little too much to qualify as desert, but close enough. This, along with the fact that the plateau sits an average of 5,000 feet above sea level, means that **extreme temperatures** are the norm. Summer heat over 100°F changes to a winter chill below 0°F—and not only that, but the **daily**

temperature fluctuations can be tremendous. Without much cloud cover or vegetation to get in the way, most of the sunlight tends to reach the ground (up to 90 percent, compared to less than 50 percent in other temperate regions). Ground temperatures skyrocket by day, particularly during the sweltering summer months of June–September. At night, however, the dry air lets the heat escape just as quickly, and temperatures plummet. A drop of 40°F between noon and night is not unusual.

Deserts are characterized as much by **seasonal rainfall** as by low rainfall. When it does come, most **precipitation** falls during **summer monsoons** (the "male rain" of the Navajo) and winter snows. Cloudbursts are usually heralded by black clouds and anvil-shaped thunderheads visible for miles. Occasionally the air is so dry that rain evaporates before it hits the ground, a phenomenon called virga. This happened more often in winter, when low-level air is very dry. Lightning is a danger on high-altitude plateaus; seek shelter if you're caught in the open. These downpours can dump inches of water in just a few minutes, and the topography has a tendency to channel the rain over a wide area into narrow gullies. (The ground is also usually too dry to absorb that much moisture that quickly.) This results in rivers that suddenly rise, dry washes that abruptly flow, or the most extreme example, **flash floods** that can scour a narrow canyon with little or no warning. Moisture that falls as snow is useless to plants until it melts in the spring, when the occasional showers are more gentle (the Navajo's nourishing "female rain") than summer rainstorms.

The Natural World

The Colorado Plateau is blessed with a wide range of biological diversity, inhabiting everything from bare rock to lush riverbanks, sweltering canyon interiors to snowy alpine tundra. Most of the habitat is dry and high, averaging about 4,000 feet above sea level and only 12 inches of rain per year. The result is an arid landscape whose inhabitants are well adapted to life where water is a precious commodity. Numerous microclimates give rise to special mini-ecosystems, including hanging gardens, potholes, and cryptobiotic soil crusts (see the sidebar *Cryptobiotic Soil*). It helps that this region is one of the largest roadless areas (some say *the* largest) in the Lower 48, but human encroachment has already taken a toll.

PLANTS

The arid reaches of the Colorado Plateau favor sparse, scrubby vegetation spread widely across the land. There are more than 2,500 species of vascular plants in the region, and more than 200 are endemic. Species from the Great Basin to the west mix with those from the Rocky Mountains to the east. Forests cover the mountains, with different tree communities occurring at different heights, and the banks of streams and rivers are lined with lush vegetation—some native, some not.

Dealing with Drought

A desert (or near-desert) calls for a special set of adaptations to collect water and hold onto it once you do. Even when it does fall, moisture doesn't stick around for long: heavy rains tend to run off hard, dry soils without much soaking in. Between soil evaporation and plant transpiration (water loss during photosynthesis), collectively termed "evapotranspiration," water loss can approach the ridiculous—regions that receive less than five inches of rain a year may have the potential to lose 120 inches. (In Moab, the potential evapotranspiration is over 80 inches per year.) Plants, which can't move on when things get tough, have to do the best with what is on hand.

Most plants are able to wait for the right time to throw energy into making flowers or seeds. After a summer thundershower, a barren plateau can erupt with color within days as dead-looking plants put out blossoms almost overnight. Grass and flower seeds can lie dormant in the soil for years, waiting until the right amount of precipitation falls. Some plants flower only at night to avoid losing water to the daytime heat. Many perennial plants resist drought by getting rid of a plant's biggest water-wasters: its leaves. Thorns on cacti minimize water loss, and small, hairy or scalelike leaves and waxy coverings on other plants cut down on moisture lost to moving air.

CRYPTOBIOTIC SOIL

The dark, rough covering that grows on undisturbed sandy soil takes its name from the Greek words for "hidden" and "life," and for a long time it was a mystery to biologists. It turns out this crust is a mix of mosses, lichens, algae, and fungi, and is crucial to the ecology of the desert. "Crypto" starts as a dark scattering across the sand, and can take centuries to grow three or four inches, the ground-level equivalent of old-growth forests. Frost buckling cracks the spongy covering and lifts it into tiny waves that solidify and help trap moisture and windblown seeds and spores. In addition to absorbing and holding water, crypto helps keep the soil from eroding, and provides nutrients such as nitrogen that help plants grow. Without it, plant communities would take much longer to develop, or they might not develop at all. Cryptobiotic crust is very fragile, and can take years to recover from a boot print or tire track. Sometime it's impossible to avoid it in the backcountry, but keep this in mind as you do your best to avoid crunching the crypto.

Still other plants take the most direct route by growing only where there is a constant water supply, such as streamside areas or the unique, fragile **hanging gardens** found at springs and seeps, which are full of ferns, monkey-flowers, and other species that are rare elsewhere. Willows and cottonwoods sends roots deep to reach the water table along rivers and sporadic streams. When rain falls, the best idea is to gather as much as possible, as quickly as possible. With this in mind (evolutionarily speaking), the lethal leaves of the narrowleaf yucca channel moisture into the plant's center, and the wide, shallow roots of the prickly pear cactus collects water dropped during brief rain showers.

Trees and Shrubs

The woody plants of the Colorado Plateau are usually small, widely spaced, and tough. Their roots can split rocks, and they can live up to a century. One of the most common shrubs is **Mormon tea,** an odd-looking, broomlike plant that contains pseudoephedrine, a drug used in nasal decongestants. Early settlers boiled this relative of pines and junipers into a bitter but effective medicinal tea. **Blackbrush** is also ubiquitous, and although it's full of thorns, that doesn't keep desert bighorn sheep from eating it. **Four-winged saltbush** can grow in soils too salty for other plants, which give its leaves a distinctively saline taste. (It's still an important food for many creatures.)

Fremont's cottonwood is unmistakable anywhere there is water, with its huge, gnarled trunks and delicate green leaves. It takes its name from the downy, highly flammable cotton produced by female trees, and can grow up to 90 feet tall. Other common plants in riparian areas include **netleaf hackberry,** and the invasive **Russian olive** and **tamarisk,** which can crowd out native vegetation. One of the most interesting partnerships in the Colorado Plateau involves the **narrowleaf yucca,** which looks like a collection of green swords all pointing outward. Unlike its relative the agave, or century plant, which flowers only once before dying, the narrowleaf yucca sends up a towering flower stalk every spring. After mating, female yucca moths gather yucca pollen into a ball and spread it to other yucca plants, so the larvae that hatch from the eggs they lay

© JULIAN SMITH

Junipers are often as beautiful dead as alive.

will have something to eat. In the process, the moths pollinate the plants. Each would be lost without the other: yucca moth larvae feed only on yucca pollen, and the moths are the plant's only pollinators.

Between 4,500 and 5,500 feet, the most common plants are the **Utah juniper** and the **piñon pine.** This plant community covers an estimated 75,000 square miles of the dry, rocky West, making it one of the regions' most common forest types. The juniper, whose scale-colored leaves look like broccoli from a distance, is covered with shaggy bark that indigenous tribes used as kindling and to line baby cradle boards. It's not a true cedar, but a cypress, and it can stop circulation to its twisted outer branches during a drought to keep the rest of the tree alive. The scientific name of the **piñon pine,** *pinus edulis,* hints at its seasonal treasure: The delicious, protein-rich seeds inside its compact cones, produced in huge crops every 3–7 years in such abundance that predators can't possibly eat them all, insures that some survive. Roasted or eaten raw, pine nuts have 5,000 calories per pound, making them an important food source for prehistoric people and animals alike. (Some birds breed late or not at all between pine nut crops.) The smallest member of the pine family smells sweet in a campfire, and its pitch was used to make baskets, mend pottery, and dress wounds.

Other common plants in this zone include the **cliffrose,** with its fragrant yellow blossoms; **mountain mahogany,** which resembles blackbrush (mahogany branches alternate, those of blackbrush sprout opposite each other); and **big sagebrush,** one of the classic plants of the West. Mark Twain called it the "fag-end of vegetable creation," but this fragrant shrub that shelters smaller plants and animals has been eliminated from half of its historic acreage.

Between 6,500 and 8,000 feet, the most common tree is the **ponderosa pine,** with long needles grouped into threes and puzzlelike bark that smells like vanilla. Northern Arizona is home to the largest ponderosa pine forest in the world, with members averaging about 100 feet tall and 3 feet in diameter. Ponderosas are resistant to the fires that periodically clear the undergrowth, leaving pine forests wide open at eye level. The **Gambrel oak, bigtooth maple,** and **Utah serviceberry** are also found in the pine-oak belt.

Higher up the isolated mountain ranges, from 8,00 to 9,500 feet, is the domain of the **Douglas fir** and the **quaking aspen.** The fir has distinctive "mouse tails" (technically called bracts) poking out from between its cone scales, and it's not really a fir, but a separate species altogether. In its first two decades, it can grow two feet per year. The white bark and shimmering green leaves of the aspen are unmistakable, and the plants—which grow in clusters that are actually clones of each other, connected under ground—are often of the first things to grow in land cleared by humans or fire. This zone includes the **white fir** and **berry bushes** such as raspberry, gooseberry, and thimbleberry. The highest plant zone, from 9,500 feet to tree line at 11,500 feet, is home to the **Englemann spruce, blue spruce, subalpine fir, limber pine,** and **lodgepole pine.**

Flowers

Desert flowers are also a hardy bunch, and easy to underestimate—many visitors are amazed to see the plateau's color potential fully realized after a long-awaited downpour. Red blooms of the **Eaton's penstemon, common globe mallow,** and **Indian paintbrush** are easy to spot, as are yellow flowers like the **sunflower, rough mule's ear,** and **newberry's twinpod.** I still have trouble telling the purplish **milkvetch** and **locoweed** apart, so it's good I'm not a cow; the latter contains an alkaloid that can drive grazers crazy or even kill them if they eat too much. The **dwarf lupine** and **showy four-o'clock** have bluish-purple flowers that are more easily distinguishable.

White flowers like the **Apache plume** and the delicate **sego lily** often have a dual purpose: They're pretty and easier for pollinators to see at night. That's why both the **sacred datura** and the **dwarf evening primrose** also have white blossoms, as well as distinctive perfumes—to attract pollinators. The bell-like blooms of the datura, the largest flowers in canyon country, are pollinated by moths the size of small birds, and contain toxic compounds that have been used to induce religious hallucinations. Moths aren't the only pollinators out there; butterflies, bees, wasps, birds, flies, and beetles are also hard at work, doing good with only their own selfish interests in mind.

Cacti

Cacti are desert plants *par excellence*—the Ferraris of drought resistance. Succulent stems and pads store moisture and expand to hold more, while letting very little leak out through their waxy coatings. Spines protect the plant, and stomata open only at night to collect carbon dioxide for photosynthesis, conserving even more moisture. The cacti you're most likely to see include the **prickly pear,** with its flattened, palm-sized pads and yellow or red blooms, which appear for only a few days. The fleshy interior of its red fruit, called *tuna* in Spanish, is eaten by people and animals (just make sure you get all those tiny little spines out—trust me). The **claret cup cactus** produces crimson blooms in April and May on densely packed stems, and are pollinated by hummingbirds.

Invaders

It's hard to believe, but even in this inhospitable land some late-arriving plants have taken root and spread like wildfire. **Tamarisk,** also known as salt cedar, was brought from the Mediterranean in the 19th century, and planted as an ornamental and to control streamside erosion. The water-loving shrub took off at 12 miles per year until it was found in nearly every tributary of the Colorado River. The tough, tenacious plant sounds like something designed by engineers to take over ecosystems. It reproduces prolifically, even in poor, salty soils—a mature tree can produce up to 500,000 seeds a year—and if it's cut down or burned it simply sprouts new shoots. It grows in stands so dense that it crowds out other plants, and sucks up an astonishing amount of water through taproots that can be 50 feet deep. A single tamarisk plant can suck up 300 gallons of water a day, more than twice as much water as any native species. Across the Southwest, where the plant is estimated to cover one million acres, tamarisks absorb as much water in a year as 20 million people. To add insult to injury, tamarisks provide little food or habitat for wildlife and burn very easily.

Fighting an invader like this isn't easy, but some efforts are paying off. Rangers in the Maze district of Canyonlands National Park spray choked waterways with herbicides, and have already cleared some canyons of the intruder and increased cottonwood seedling counts. Tamarisk has even inspired Congressional legislation: the Tamarisk Research and Control Act of 2003. The U.S. Department of Agriculture has begun plans to introduce leaf beetles from Asia to 13 Western states to eat tamarisks (and, in theory, leave others alone). One concern is the effect on the endangered Southwest willow flycatcher, which has been forced to nest in salt cedars as native plants have been pushed out.

Shipments of wheat from Europe in the late 1800s brought the first seeds of **cheatgrass,** which now covers some 100 million acres across the West. Since it germinates in fall and spends the winter storing energy and growing roots (as native plants lie dormant), it gets the jump when spring comes. It's also more efficient at using underground water and colonizing areas disturbed by cultivation, overgrazing, or fire. Animals don't like to eat it, and its seed heads are really annoying when they latch on to your socks. In all, cheatgrass is a formidable competitor, and has replaced native grasslands on a scale seldom seen in botanical history.

ANIMALS

Though the largest living things you see out here, aside from other hikers, are mostly birds and the occasional fleeing cottontail, a wide variety of critters call the Colorado Plateau home. Most wisely avoid the triple threats of heat, drought, and other animals by venturing into the open only at certain times of day or year.

Desert Adaptations

Many animals avoid the stress of daytime temperatures by coming out only at dawn and dusk (crepuscular) or at night (nocturnal). Fields of sagebrush start hopping near sunset as cottontails and jackrabbits emerge from their burrows, bringing their eager predators, the coyotes. Porcupines, mule deer, and many birds also favor the cooler and dimmer in-between times, while many rodents, bobcats, mountain lions, and foxes wait until full darkness.

Those that do come out by day (diurnal) have other strategies for surviving the heat. Some animals alter their activity patterns depending on the temperature—mosquitoes come out at different times of day, or not at all, depending on how hot it is. Reptiles such as lizards and snakes are crepuscular in summer, diurnal in spring and fall, and go into a state of semi-hibernation (torpor) in winter. If the moisture content of their plant food is over 75 percent, pronghorns can survive without drinking any water, as can the nocturnal Ord's kangaroo rat, which can extract all the liquids it needs from the seeds it eats.

Mammals

Desert bighorn sheep, driven close to extinction by livestock diseases and hunting, have been reintroduced into Southeast Utah by the National Park Service (NPS). If you venture into the backcountry, you may spot one of the sure-footed ungulates, often in bands of females and young. During the fall and winter rut, males charge each other with a crash of their large curved horns. Herds of **pronghorns** roam the flats, where they can leap up to eight feet high and run up to 65 miles per hour. **Mule deer** thrive throughout the plateau, now that most of their predators have been eliminated. They migrate to high ground in summer, and males sport large racks of antlers. Their odd, bounding leap is called "stotting."

You can tell **desert cottontails** and **black-tailed jackrabbits** apart by size; jackrabbits are larger and more gangly, with long black-tipped ears useful for getting rid of excess heat. Similarly, a **gray fox** is larger than a **kit fox**—

the latter's large ears and big bushy tail make it one of the cutest desert creatures. Like these others, **coyotes** blend in well with the scenery in their buff and gray pelts. They're as big as medium-sized dogs, and flourish everywhere from the Escalante to backyards in Phoenix. A pack of coyotes yipping at the stars is one of the most hauntingly distinctive noises in the Four Corners.

Ringtails are related to raccoons, and have the striped, bushy tails to prove it. They love the cracks and ledges of canyon country, and their incredible agility, balance, and daring (plus hind feet that can rotate 180 degrees for a better grip) let them climb places nothing else can. A host of chipmunks, squirrels, rats, and mice keeps these larger animals well fed. **Deer mice** are infamous for harboring the horrific hantavirus, which killed a handful of people in the area in 1993. You'll probably see the conglomerated nests (middens) of four species of **woodrats** beneath rock overhangs. These are useful to scientists trying to reconstruct the ancient ecology of the Four Corners, since—like their common name, pack rat, suggests—their nests contain a little bit of just about everything under the sun. The nighttime skies are the domain of close to two dozen types of bats, from the **big brown bat** to the **western pipistrelle,** the smallest bat in the United States.

Beavers and grizzly bears were both once native, but they have been exterminated from the area. On the other hand, the black-footed ferret has been reintroduced, and conservationists hope (and ranchers fear) that it's only a matter of time before reintroduced gray wolves work their way back into the area.

Birds

Those far-off silhouettes soaring on the thermals are hard to distinguish. If it holds its wings in a V and wobbles as it glides, it's a **turkey vulture,** who help keep the desert clean of carrion with their excellent eyesight and sense of smell. A large bird with flat wings and an even flight could be a **golden eagle,** with its six-foot wingspan, or a **red-tailed hawk,** the most common large bird of prey in the country. The red-tail's screeching call has added atmosphere to so many classic Westerns it's become an auditory cliché. Other raptors you might spot include the **sharp-shinned hawk** and **Cooper's hawk,** which look very similar (Cooper's are bigger). **Peregrine falcons,** the poster children of successful wildlife conservation, dive after prey at 180 mph, making them the world's fastest animal.

The **common raven** is one of the smartest animals, let alone birds, in the world. They can learn to speak, count to at least 10, and outperform graduate students in tests of memory. You'll often see these playful, jet-black birds cavorting in midair, doing barrel rolls or playing tag or catch. The black-and-white **black-billed magpies** are also in the crow family, and quite bright as well. Like ravens, they also mate for life and have a wide range of vocalizations. Speaking of bird calls, the liquid descending notes of the seldom-seen **canyon wren** could be the theme song of the Colorado Plateau. The high desert scrub is the domain of the **piñon jay** and the **western scrub jay,** while the **mountain bluebird** sticks out like a sore (but beautiful) thumb.

Other common birds on the Colorado Plateau include **hummingbirds** (black-chinned and broad-tailed), **woodpeckers** (hairy and downy), and various **chickadees, warblers, flycatchers,** and the occasional **spotted towhee** rustling in the underbrush. After dark the **great horned owl** soars silently after rabbits, skunks, and even other birds.

Reptiles and Amphibians

The yellow-and-green **collared lizard** seems enamored with its own beauty, perching prominently on rocks and stumps (males are actually defending their territory). Like other Four Corners lizards, such as the **plateau lizard** and various kinds of **whiptail lizards,** they do push-ups to display their markings and regulate their temperature, and sprint after insects, spiders, and small arthropods. **Gopher** and **racer snakes** kill their prey through constriction, while **garter** snakes sit in wait near potholes for frogs and tadpoles. There probably aren't as many poisonous snakes out here as you think, based on how many movie characters they kill. The **midget-faded rattlesnake** packs a potent wallop for its size, however, while the **prairie rattler** migrates miles in search of deer mice to swallow.

Aside from the months of waiting for the rain to fall, the life of a **Great Basin spadefoot toad** doesn't sound so bad: find water, drink to bursting, eat up to half your weight in a single night, and mate like crazy—then burrow back into the mud and do it again next year. Potholes are often full of their eggs and tadpoles in early summer. **Canyon tree frogs** often sit immobile near water, hoping their excellent camouflage will keep them safe. Like the spadefoot, this frog can survive desiccation and heat that would kill a nondesert amphibian.

Insects and Arachnids

Contrary to popular myth, the stings of **tarantulas** are no more dangerous than those of bees. Tarantulas grow up to six inches across, and their hairy legs and giant fangs are enough to give arachniphobes the screaming fits. Besides a bad rap, they also have to deal with the depredations of the **tarantula hawk.** These wasps paralyze tarantulas and lay their eggs on the living body, which provides food for the hatching larvae. **Scorpions** are incredibly ancient creatures, evolutionarily speaking, and some glow under ultraviolet light; if you have a chance to shine one after dark, you'll be amazed at how many scorpions are out there. Their sting can be fatal to small children.

Female **black widow spiders** are highly poisonous—steer clear of a black spider with a red hourglass on its abdomen. **Velvet ants** are also no fun to play with. They look like colorful, hairy ants, but have a bite toxic enough to earn the nickname "cow-killer." Shiny black **darkling beetles** spray a noxious liquid from the end of their abdomen. These inch-long beetles are very common. They don't fool the grasshopper mouse with their threat posture, rear end raised. It simply sticks the spraying end in the ground and starts eating at the other one.

CONSERVATION ISSUES

Most conservation conflicts in the Four Corners concern public land use, and have reached their most heated peak in southern Utah. Once you strip away the details, most of the debate boils down to the fact that many residents resent outside influences—whether it's the federal government, recent arrivals, or environmental groups based elsewhere—telling them how to manage the vast surrounding federal lands, which locals feel they have more stake in, and experience with, than anyone else. The other groups point out that generations of land leasing and use don't mean it is being used sustainably—and in many cases is being mined, logged, or grazed to death. Old ways of life die hard as the economy shifts, and the most beautiful acres on earth can cause some of the most apoplectic arguments you've ever seen.

Monuments and Wilderness Areas

President Clinton ruffled feathers nationwide when he created 15 national monuments, including in the Four Corners the Canyons of the Ancients, the Vermilion Cliffs, the Grand Canyon–Parashant in northern Arizona, and the gigantic Grand Staircase–Escalante in southern Utah. A lawsuit by a coalition including the Utah Association of Counties, the Colorado-based Mountain States Legal Foundation, and the Blue Ribbon Coalition, an off-road vehicle (ORV) advocacy group, was defeated in 2002, when a federal court ruled that the president acted within his authority under the 1906 Antiquities Act in authorizing the monuments. (Even land use within monuments remains controversial; local ranchers refused to remove their livestock from the Grand Staircase–Escalante for years after the monument was set aside.)

Still up in the air is the fate of millions of acres of desert that environmental groups are hoping to protect under **America's Red Rock Wilderness Act,** first introduced in Congress in 1989. This legislation would designate more than nine million acres of southern Utah—85 percent of which is already within two miles of a road—as off-limits to development and me-

chanical access. The efforts of the Sierra Club and the Southern Utah Wilderness Alliance (SUWA) gained the bill 162 sponsors in the House and 15 in the Senate.

An area can be set aside as wilderness only if it has little or no roads, and here the legal wrangling starts to get esoteric. A one-sentence statute known as **R. S. 2477** is invoked by local landowners and counties to prevent the creation of wilderness areas, even though it was passed in 1866. Originally intended to give Civil War–era prospectors easy access to claims, the provision says simply that "The right of way for the construction of highways across public lands not otherwise reserved for public purposes is hereby granted"—in this case, to the state and country legislatures. It was repealed by the 1976 Federal Lands Policy and Management Act, but a grandfather clause continues to honor valid existing rights.

The result is endless, deadly, serious arguments over what is and isn't a road. Areas being considered for wilderness protection are marbled with thousands of dirt trails, sandy washes, ORV tracks, seismic exploration lines, and cow paths. In Utah alone, about 15,000 road claims are being debated. The more these un-maintained tracks can be declared "roads," the smaller the chance of a given acre being declared wilderness. Passions are high and there is little middle ground. County officials send out bulldozers to improve rights-of-way, and environmental groups sue to stop them.

In 2002 the drama played out on the side of the environmental groups when the National Park Service decided to permanently close Salt Creek Canyon in the Needles district of Canyonlands National Park to vehicles. San Juan County had invoked R. S. 2477 in its claim over the popular route up the creek bed, but the Park Service's own studies found that motor vehicles were harming vegetation and water quality. A federal judge ruled that the county had to show evidence that the road was actually built and led somewhere—more than aerial photos and affidavits from cowboys who rode the route decades before—and the Park Service followed suit. Two years later, the sec-

ond Bush administration delighted ORV enthusiasts by pledging to finalize a rule making
it easier for Western states, counties, and cities
to enforce R. S. 2477 claims.

Off-Road Vehicles

A key issue in the argument over roads is off-
road vehicles (ORVs), including motorcycles
and four-wheel all-terrain vehicles (ATVs).
(The easily tipped three-wheeled ATVs have
been gradually phased out.) With 80,000 reg-
istered ORVs, Utah is second only to California, so it's lucky for them that 94 percent of
Bureau of Land Management (BLM) land in
the state is open to their use. Popular areas like
the San Rafael Swell, however, are still being
fought over by ORV groups, who question the
worth of wilderness that few people ever see,
and their opponents, who cringe at the spiral-
ing tracks, noise, and pollution. They also cite
surveys that suggest most public lands visitors
prefer nonmotorized access, and claim that
ATVs disturb six acres of topsoil for every 20
miles of travel. With only one BLM ranger to
patrol 2.5 million acres in the swell, any ORV
ban may well depend on the honor system regardless.

Mining and Drilling

The high desert plateaus of the Four Corners
hide substantial reserves of uranium, coal, oil,
gas, and other things that take much more
than a pick and shovel to unearth. The BLM
leases its immense holdings to oil and gas companies to search for new deposits, raising the
ire of conservation groups, tribal members, and
some local residents. The dispute has reached
a peak under the second Bush administration,
which has directed the BLM to consider opening more public lands in the Rocky Mountains
and the Southwest to oil and gas drilling, as
part of its push to expand national energy reserves.

In 2001, the Department of the Interior au-
thorized the use of "thumper trucks" around
Canyonlands and Arches national parks near
Moab. These vehicles send seismic waves deep
into the earth to map underground struc-

POTHOLES OF LIFE

The sandstone depressions that pepper
the Four Corners sit bone-dry and lifeless
for much of the year. After a good-sized
rain, though, the eruption of activity that
follows is as astounding as it is rapid. Eggs,
larvae, and small organisms that have survived temperatures from freezing to 140°F
burst into life, which may be compressed
into only a few weeks or even days until the
pothole dries up again. Algae are present
even in the smallest pools, providing a bottom rung to the abbreviated food chain.
In bigger pools, tadpoles and fairy shrimp
larvae squiggle in the muddy depths, back-
swimmer insects dive for the bottom, and
predaceous diving beetles pursue the
newly hatched. Take a closer look the next
time you're gulping down a mouthful, and
try not to disturb potholes any more than
necessary, whether they're full or empty –
these amazing ecosystems are tenacious
but delicate.

tures and leave huge gouges in the desert as
they go. A year later, a federal judge tempo-
rarily blocked this activity in the 25,000-acre
Dome Plateau region east of Arches, accusing
the BLM of failing to accurately predict the effects on the ecosystem. The parks remain safe,
for now, but areas near the Needles such as
Lockhart Basin and Hatch Point were left open
for exploration.

Overgrazing

It may be hard to believe, but much of the
Colorado Plateau was once covered by lush
grasslands. As they migrated through, native
bison and other ungulates not only cropped
the shoots, but also churned up the earth and
fertilized it with their dung. Now they have
been replaced by cows and sheep, which are
kept in much smaller areas year-round. In their
search for water, livestock tear up delicate riparian areas and graze anything green and edible down to the ground. Fast-growing invaders

such as cheatgrass move in, and delicate ecosystems are drastically changed.

This process was already well underway by the turn of the 20th century, when overgrazing had stopped forest regeneration in the highlands and trampled lowland soils to a bare crust. With improved range management techniques, things have improved over the decades, but only to a limited extent. The effect goes deeper, as well—some 85–90 percent of the Colorado River water still goes to farms to grow feed for livestock, including water-hungry plants like alfalfa. Ranching has always been a marginal enterprise in the West, where alkaline soils and low rainfall add up to a losing equation. It's astounding to many visitors that anyone ever thought this area would be a good place to raise livestock, and Western beef makes up only a small fraction of the country's supply. But the cowboy's hold on the national identity is a tight one, and the ranching industry, helped by inexpensive grazing permits for federal land, still has political clout far out of proportion to its size.

History

PREHISTORY
Early Cultures
The history of the Four Corners is largely the history of the Southwest itself, a region that generally includes all of Arizona and New Mexico and parts of Texas, Oklahoma, Colorado, Utah, and Nevada. Some of the oldest records of human occupation in the New World have been found here, dating as far back as 18,000 years ago. As early at 10,000 B.C., small groups of humans lived in the basin of prehistoric Lake Bonneville, an inland sea that covered much of modern-day Utah and left behind the Great Salt Lake. During the **desert archaic** cultural period, starting about 6000 B.C., nomadic hunters and gatherers spread throughout the region in search of game and edible plants, living in caves or temporary brush shelters and leaving little trace of their passing.

Agriculture spread north from Mexico between 2000 and 500 B.C., allowing larger, more permanent settlements to supplement wild forage with a more nutritious diet of squash, corn, and beans. People made crude pottery to cook and store food and water. Farming techniques improved in the first millennium A.D., and the construction of partially underground pit houses became widespread.

The Basketmakers
Between about A.D. 100 and 700, the **Basketmaker** culture concentrated on growing crops and domesticated wild animals such as dogs and turkeys, which provided companionship, meat, bones for tools, and feathers for clothing. They wove yucca fibers into cord and sandals, and wore ornaments of stones and shells traded from the south. Crops were grown in small garden plots, and large game like deer and elk was taken down with spears thrown using a device called the atlatl. Their baskets were true works of art, elaborately decorated and woven tightly enough that, lined with pitch, they could be used for cooking by dropping in red-hot stones. Around A.D. 500, villages grew in size, with many food storage bins and the first **kivas**—round ceremonial chambers built partly underground. These were lined with benches and centered around fire pits and a sipapu, a small hole symbolizing the one through which their ancestors had emerged from the underworld.

Rise of the Anasazi
The Basketmaker culture gradually developed into what is known as the **Anasazi,** an Athapascan (Navajo) word which translates roughly as "ancient enemies" or "enemies of my ancestors." (This term has come under fire lately from the group's Pueblo descendents, who claim it is derogatory and prefer the less-offensive "Ancestral Puebloans"—

you'll hear both, but "Anasazi" is still more widely used.) In the **Developmental period** (A.D. 700–1050), Pueblo culture centered on planned villages that were frequently built on a north–south axis. These often held several hundred people in hundreds of rooms built of stone masonry, as well as pit houses, and were surrounded by tilled fields where cotton may have been grown. Infants were carried in cradle boards whose hard backs flattened their skulls, perhaps on purpose, and pottery grew finer and more elaborately decorated.

Anasazi settlements expanded into the **Classic Pueblo** period (A.D. 1050–1300), which saw the construction of the great cliff houses that still draw thousands of visitors every year. Built in large natural alcoves in canyon walls, these freestanding structures resembled apartment blocks made of stone, with up to four stories designed so that the roof on one would be the porch for the one above. This period also brought what has been called the **Chaco Phenomenon,** referring to the massive constructions in Chaco Canyon of northwest New Mexico. Perhaps influenced by Central American cultures, the Puebloans built a series of great houses at Chaco unlike anything the Southwest had ever seen. Huge timbers were carried from the Chuska and San Mateo mountains to serve as floor and roof beams in structures with up to 1,000 rooms. A radiating network of roads made Chaco the Rome of the ancient Southwest, concentrating the religious, cultural, and political energies of some 30,000 people spread over 40,000 square miles. The Chacoans built many "Great Kivas" up to 16 feet deep and 70 feet in diameter, and developed their pottery skills to new heights.

End of an Era

After a peak around 1300, Chaco and the entire Pueblo culture experienced a startlingly rapid decline that left cliff houses and great houses abandoned. It was as if their inhabitants had simply picked up one day and walked off. This was probably due to a combination of factors, including overpopulation, resource depletion, raids by new tribes arriving from the north, widespread droughts in A.D. 1130–1180 and 1276–1299, and ill-fated changes in religious and political leadership. It may also have been a time of hunger and terror; it's hard to visit some of these inaccessible ruins and not feel a touch of paranoia. Archaeologists have turned up evidence of violence around this time, including some recent, controversial finds that

© JULIAN SMITH

Anasazi mortar, Aztec Ruins National Monument

indicate cannibalism. This is a touchy subject among descendents of the Anasazi, who view the dead as something not to be discussed and cannibalism as the worst sort of insult. Still, stop for a moment at the next cliff house and imagine desperate raiders approaching across withered fields, as you call in the children and try to pull up the ladders in time.

During the **Regressive Pueblo** period (1300–1700), a civilization that once numbered in the hundreds of thousands was scattered to the winds. Anasazi offshoots rose briefly in this tail-end time, including the **Kayenta Anasazi** of northeastern Arizona, who left the ruins in Canyon de Chelly and Navajo National Monument. (Some researchers think the Chacoans simply moved north to Aztec, where very similar ruins remain, and then south to Casas Grandes in northern Mexico for a third try.) The **Mesa Verde Anasazi** of southwest Colorado and Southeast Utah reached their peak as Chaco faded, but suffered the same fate soon after. On the whole, however, the descendents of the Anasazi merged with other groups on the more fertile lands to the south and east, along the Rio Grande and the Hopi mesas.

North of the Anasazi, a group known as the **Fremont** flourished in the western Colorado Plateau and the eastern Great Basin of Nevada from about A.D. 750–1250. Originally thought to be a primitive branch of the Anasazi, the Fremont have been accepted as a distinct culture, although a much less cohesive one. They settled in villages, grew similar crops, and made baskets and pottery like their neighbors, but left fewer artifacts and nothing approaching the grandeur of the cliff palaces. The groups did seem to mingle at least somewhat in South-Central Utah, but like the Anasazi, and probably for many of the same reasons, the Fremont went into decline and vanished by A.D. 1500.

More Recent Tribes

As the Anasazi and the Fremont faded, new cultural groups moved in from the north. These more aggressive, nomadic peoples spoke dialects of the Athapascan languages of western Canada, and would eventually evolve into the **Navajo** and **Apache** tribes. The exact timing of the immigration is unclear, but it was definitely underway by the time the Spanish arrived in the 16th century. These groups would become some of the most feared raiders in the history of the Southwest as the cultures of the old and new worlds clashed. The Apache moved south of the Colorado Plateau, but the Navajo stayed in the area around the Four Corners. They adopted many Pueblo customs, including farming, weaving, livestock herding, a matrilineal society, and the clan system. Their traditional log hogans have been traced to origins in Asia, and they kept up the habit of adopting from other cultures—horses from the Spanish, and the art of silversmithing from the Mexicans.

Like the Pueblo tribes along the Rio Grande in New Mexico, the **Hopi** are considered to be more or less direct descendants of the Anasazi. The origins of the **Ute** tribe are less clear; it is known their ancestors came from the north and west, but when is uncertain.

THE EUROPEANS ARRIVE

Spanish missionaries and explorers were the first Europeans to traverse the American Southwest. They came in search of souls and gold, respectively, and were spurred in their often miserable and deadly travels by the thousands of "heathens" waiting to be converted, and legends of golden cities in the sand. Even more encouraging were the stories of the conquistadores who had already met with success: Hernán Cortés, who in 1521 defeated the entire Aztec empire of central Mexico with only 500 men; and Francisco Pizarro, who helped topple the fabulously wealthy Andean kingdom of the Inca in the 1530s. The legends of El Dorado ("The Golden One") and the Seven Golden Cities of Cibola got a boost from the stories of Alvar Nuñez Cabeza de Vaca who, after being shipwrecked on the Florida coast in 1528, spent eight years wandering across the Southwest with a small group of survivors until eventually reaching the Spanish colonies in Mexico.

Early Explorers

In 1540, **Francisco Vázquez de Coronado** led a party of 300 into Arizona in search of the cities of gold and to claim the region for Spain. Finding no treasure in the Zuñi pueblos, the heavily armed group advanced north, where a side expedition led by García López de Cárdenas became the first Europeans the gaze into the Grand Canyon. Indigenous groups, including the Hopi, kept using the legend of the golden cities to urge the Spaniards onwards ("Cibola? Uh, yeah—it's just a few days that way. Keep going, you can't miss it!"). The party advanced through northern New Mexico and Texas, and made it as far as Kansas before realizing that the only gold in sight was the setting sun reflecting from the walls of the adobe pueblos. Only 100 men made it back to Mexico City, where Coronado died in 1554 after being found guilty of corruption and atrocities against the Indians.

Half a century later, Juan de Oñate established the colony of New Mexico for Spain. Married to a granddaughter of Cortés, Oñate led 400 settlers across the Rio Grande and sent scouting parties in search of treasure in Quivira (central Kansas). He quickly earned a reputation for brutality among the settlers, which served as a warm-up for his response to an uprising among the residents of the pueblo of Acoma, high atop a mesa in what is now western New Mexico. When 11 Spaniards, including one of Oñate's nephews, were killed in 1598, the furious conquistador laid siege to the sheer-walled mesa and burned the pueblo. About 800 Native Americans were killed, and every adult male survivor had one foot cut off. (Feelings are still sore: A modern statue of Oñate erected near Santa Fe has had its foot sawed off repeatedly.) In 1601, Oñate returned from an unsuccessful treasure hunt to find his colony mostly deserted. A further quest to the Colorado River and the Gulf of California were also failures, and he resigned his post in 1607.

SPANISH NEW MEXICO

These early expeditions soured relations between Europeans and native tribes for centuries. The Spanish gradually assumed control over much of the Southwest in the 18th century from their capital city of La Villa Real de la Santa Fe de San Francisco de Asis, today known simply as Santa Fe, founded in 1610. Subsistence agriculture in river valleys, trade with Mexico, and the raising of sheep and horses formed the basis of the economy, despite regular attacks by Apache, Comanche, and Navajo warriors. The effects of missionaries varied: While some served as intermediaries, speaking out for Native Americans' rights in the face of European settlement, others did their best to supplant indigenous cultural traditions with Christianity and suppress all things native.

By the late 17th century, things had reached a head. Continued persecution, punishment, and executions for "witchcraft" and "idolatry" had pushed native tribes to the edge. Abortive revolts in the Zuñi, Hopi, and Rio Grande Pueblos served as prelude to a massive uprising in 1680 known as the **Pueblo Revolt.** Led by a Tewa medicine man named Pope, the insurrection was organized by runners carrying knotted strings encoding the fateful date. On August 10, some 17,000 Puebloans, including 6,000 warriors in battle paint, rose against 3,000 Spanish colonists. The furious tribes burned churches and their holy icons, threw friars from cliffs, and massacred entire communities as the Spanish survivors retreated to Santa Fe. After a six-day siege, a ragged column was allowed to march south down the Rio Grande valley, leaving some 400 dead amid the ruins. It remains one of the most successful uprisings in the history of the Americas.

Even as they retreated, however, the Spanish were already planning their return, and by 1700 they had reconquered much of the Southwest, extending their New World empire from Panama to California and Santa Fe. Albuquerque was founded in 1706, and during the 1700s the Spanish population of New Mexico had increased to as much as 25,000, many times the size of the Texas and California colonies. Priests once again visited tribes to try and convert them to Christianity, but these efforts met with mixed success. They did discover more about the geography of the region, however, particularly during the **Dominguez-Escalante Expedition** led by Fathers Francisco Atanasio Dominguez and Silvestre Velez de Escalante. In 1776, as a new nation was declaring its independence across the continent, 14 men set out to find a northern route between the missions of Santa Fe and Monterey, California.

They made their way through western Colorado, crossing the Green River and going as far north as what is now Cedar City, Utah, before heading west, becoming the first Europeans to venture into Nevada's Great Basin Desert. Bludgeoned by blizzards and starvation, they survived on the kindness of groups of Utes and Paiutes before drawing lots to see if they should press on or turn back. The result—turn back—probably saved their lives. The fathers crossed northern Arizona along the Vermilion Cliffs and the Paria River before fording the Colorado River at Marble Canyon, at a spot still known as the Crossing of the Fathers. In six months and 2,000 miles, they had failed in their goal but added much to European knowledge of the intermountain West.

The colony of New Mexico continued to limp along, far from the resources and attention of Mexico City, the center of Spanish authority in the New World. The opening of the **Old Spanish Trail** in the early 19th century allowed the transport of livestock and slaves from Santa Fe to central Utah and, eventually, Los Angeles. Slave raids were only one of a long list of reasons the Navajo had become the colony's most dangerous enemies. They raided settlements from horseback along with Comanche and Ute warriors. (The Canyon del Muerto in Canyon de Chelly was named after a slave raid that left hundreds of Navajo women and children dead in 1805.)

THE UNITED STATES TAKES OVER

Taking advantage of the Spanish colony's relative weakness, explorers, surveyors, and adventurers pushed west from the young United States. Zebulon Pike, John Frémont, and John Gunnison all led parties exploring the intermountain West. A vast territory had been added to the country's borders by the 1803 Louisiana Purchase, and in 1821 the Republic of Mexico's independence from Spain transferred much of the Southwest to new ownership. Anglo settlers continued to trickle in, including Mormons led by Brigham Young, whose wagons entered the Great Salt Lake valley in 1847. Fleeing religious persecution, the Latter-Day Saints busily set about establishing a highly regulated, self-sufficient colony that stretched from the Sierra Nevada to the Rockies and from Oregon to Arizona. Colonists were organized by skill and leadership and sent out to settle the farthest corners of the territory to strengthen the church's hold on the land. The unforgiving land made settlement a grueling experience, wrote Wallace Stegner in *Mormon Country:*

Its destiny was plain on its face, its contempt of man and his history and his theological immortality, his Millennium, his Heaven on Earth, was monumentally obvious. Its distances were terrifying, its cloudbursts catastrophic, its beauty flamboyant and bizarre and allied with death.

In 1846, Brigadier General Stephen Watts Kearny arrived in Santa Fe to proclaim the beginning of American dominion over the Southwest. The one-sided **Mexican-America War** (1846–1848), sparked by unresolved border issues left by the U.S. annexation of the Republic of Texas in 1845, made good on this promise. It resulted in the **Treaty of Guadalupe Hidalgo,** which transferred the northern half of Mexico—what is today most of California, Nevada, Arizona, New Mexico, and Utah—to American hands. The $10 million **Gadsden Purchase** in 1853 shifted another 30,000 square miles of southern Arizona and New Mexico from Mexico to the United States. The United States now had a Southwest, but by the end of the 19th century, only a relative handful of explorers, trappers, soldiers, miners, and missionaries had ventured onto the Colorado Plateau. The government began to build army posts to protect immigrants and settlers from Native Americans, and the frontier territories were dominated by cabals that made fortunes off the livestock industry and the newly laid railroads, while mostly ignoring the needs of native groups.

Utah, however, was off and running. By 1860, more than 150 communities, with a total of 40,000 inhabitants, had taken root. The desert bloomed with crops grown using ingenious irrigation projects, despite raids by local tribes. The Mormons' autonomy (and their penchant for polygamy) rankled the federal government and, in 1857, President James Buchanan declared Utah in rebellion of the U.S. government and sent 2,500 soldiers to the territory to replace Young as governor. Mormon leaders saw this as more religious persecution, declared martial law, and got ready to defend themselves. Young eventually came to his senses and handed over the title of governor to Alfred Cumming, and the **"Utah War"** ended without bloodshed.

RAILROADS AND STATEHOOD

The latter half of the 19th century brought the American Civil War, which had relatively little effect in the Southwest, and the completion of the **transcontinental railroad.** On May 10, 1869, a symbolic golden spike was driven at Promontory, Utah, and the linking of rail lines to both coasts officially closed the American frontier. This had the immediate impact of bringing in immigrants and allowing the transport of products such as timber, minerals, and livestock across huge distances. Where the rail lines went, so did life. Cities, often named after railroad engineers, sprang up almost overnight along the tracks, bringing jobs and radically altering lives in long-isolated towns and settlements. If a town refused to grant privileges to the railroads, they simply built another town down the line. The Atchison, Topeka, and Santa Fe Railway from St. Louis reached Albuquerque in 1880, northern Arizona in 1883, and Los Angeles in 1885, the same year the Northern Pacific Railway reached Seattle. Another golden-spike moment occurred in Tucson in 1880, when the

© JULIAN SMITH

a Mormon wagon on display at the Nations of the Four Corners Cultural Center in Bluff

Southern Pacific Railroad connected California with New Orleans.

The arrival of the "Iron Horse," along with the advent of barbed wire in the 1870s, signaled the end of the freedom enjoyed by native tribes, who found themselves being crowded from their homelands by European immigrants. They didn't take it lying down, but they never really had a chance—by sheer force of numbers and technology, Americans rolled over the West and its indigenous cultures in a steady, unstoppable tide.

In 1863, the famous frontiersman and Civil War veteran Kit Carson was ordered to end the problem of Navajo raids once and for all. Once considered a good friend by native groups, Carson began a brutal military campaign that ended with a futile last stand by the Navajo in the Canyon de Chelly. Some 8,000 men, women, and children were then marched 300 miles to Bosque Redondo (later called Fort Sumner), on the Pecos River in eastern New Mexico. Many did not survive the infamous **"Long Walk,"** and many of those who made it probably wished they hadn't. The poorly planned site was called a reservation but was more of a gulag. Sicknesses and disease compounded a meager wood supply, and worms destroyed the corn crops. Four years of misery ended when the U.S. government relented and Navajo leader Barboncito negotiated the return of his people to their ancestral lands in Arizona and New Mexico in 1868. In return, the Navajo had to agree never to raise arms against the United States or her citizens and to send their children to American schools. The reservation was later expanded to its current boundaries, and in 1882, 4,000 square miles out of the center of the Navajo Reservation was set aside for the Hopi tribe. (Land disputes between the traditionally distrustful tribes continue to this day.) The Apache were forced onto reservations in the 1880s, despite fierce resistance from bands led by chiefs such as Geronimo, Cochise, and Victorio.

The "Wild" West

The last decades of the 1800s encompassed that mythic intersection of time and place whose images have spread around the world. Sure, it was in the West, and it was wild, but it bore little resemblance to the operatic, fresh-scrubbed version of dime novels and the silver screen. Lawmen like the legendary Pat Garrett and Wyatt Earp were tough as nails but few and far between, and lawlessness most often took the form of cattle rustling and shady land dealings. Alcohol, prostitution, and gambling dulled the growing pains of a frontier that was no longer really a frontier, but in many ways still felt like one. Homesteaders, including many Mormons, eked out a living by farming along streams and rivers. Ranchers grazed thousands of sheep, cows, and horses on the seemingly endless acres of the Colorado Plateau, even though much of it offered substandard forage, and moved their herds from the lowlands to the mountains as the seasons shifted. Much of the rural economy centered on trading posts, which served as combination bank, store, and social club.

Powell's Expeditions

The age of exploration was not over yet. Much of the Four Corners was still terra incognita, the last blank spot on the map of the continental United States. To remedy this, the professor and one-armed Civil War hero **Major John Wesley Powell** led two survey trips down the Colorado River through the Grand Canyon in 1869 and 1871. Braving terrifying rapids in sluggish wooden boats, Powell's expeditions had little idea what they were getting into, particularly the first time through. They still managed to collect specimens, take photographs, and complete a topographic map of the previously unknown Grand Canyon region, and had the honor of naming the last river (the Escalante) and mountain range (the Henrys) to be added to the map of the United States. Powell wrote his classic knuckle-biter *Exploration of the Colorado River of the West and Its Tributaries* about the experience, and went on to direct the U.S. Geological Survey, to plead for justice for native tribes as special commissioner to the Native Americans in Utah and Nevada, and to argue futilely for the wise use of the West's scant water.

Colorado achieved statehood in 1876, followed by Utah in 1896. Mormon settlers had already applied to join the Union numerous times, and were forced to discontinue polygamy and the church's political activities before they were finally admitted.

INTO THE 20TH CENTURY

In 1912, New Mexico and Arizona became the 47th and 48th states, respectively. Both remained very undeveloped—stagecoaches still carried passengers and mules delivered mail to isolated settlements. The region's stark beauty was starting to gain national attention, though, and the first few decades of the 20th century brought an influx of tourists, retirees, and winter residents (still called "snowbirds") and the construction of motor courts and "dude ranches" to house them. Native Americans became U.S. citizens with the passage of the Indian Citizenship Act in 1924—just in time for the Great Depression, which brought drought, rural emigration, and the relief programs of the New Deal. Artists and writers were employed by the Works Progress Administration to sing the praises of this grubby but gorgeous corner of the country in guidebooks and national park posters, and infrastructure in many parks enjoyed the fruits of cheap, eager labor. Many emigrants moved to California in search of work along the new Route 66, the "Mother Road" from Chicago to Los Angeles, which ran through Albuquerque and Flagstaff.

Relations with native tribes in the early days of the reservations remained tense. Things weren't helped by the government's plan of livestock reduction among the Navajo that was implemented in the 1930s, out of concerns over soil erosion and overgrazing. Thousands of sheep, goats, and horses were slaughtered in front of their horrified owners, who considered them to be almost members of the family. Along with the Long Walk, this cemented a legacy of distrust of the federal government that still lingers.

The Hollywood Version

By now the legend of the Old West was firmly entrenched in the national consciousness, mostly as a result of the **Westerns** churned out by Hollywood as an increasing rate. With roots in the radio dramas of the 1930s and 1940s, early Westerns often involved singing by the likes of Dale Autry and Roy Rogers. It was the epic films of director John Ford, however, that defined the genre for decades to come. Larger-than-life characters played by iconic actors like John Wayne were shown in clear-cut struggles against evil, against, as often as not, the sweeping panorama of Monument Valley. Ford and Wayne collaborated on the classics *Stagecoach* (1939), *Rio Grande* (1950), *The Searchers* (1956), and *How the West Was Won* (1962). *Cheyenne Autumn* (1964) was Ford's final tribute to the tribes he had often depicted in a less than positive light. When they weren't the bad guys, native characters were mostly interchangeable and played by dark-skinned Europeans or Navajo, regardless of their supposed tribe. (In some of the films, Navajo actors apparently worked some racy bits into their dialogue, which had reservation audiences snickering when they were first shown.)

The turn of the 20th century also saw the beginnings of the serious Southwest **tourism industry.** Instrumental in opening the region were the restaurants and lodges operated by the **Fred Harvey Company** along the Atchison, Topeka, and Santa Fe Railway. With the help of pioneering architect Mary Colter, Harvey erected landmark buildings in Zion, Bryce, and the North Rim of the Grand Canyon, as well as places like Winslow's La Posada, to cater to the moneyed crowd who came by train for the views, the service, and the "Harvey Girls," a famously smart and pretty bunch of waitresses. Harvey's hotels operated from the 1880s through the 1950s, and showed that the rugged wonders of the Southwest could be enjoyed in comfort.

Fruits of the Land

The pace of change quickened during World

War II, when many rural young men—Anglo, Native American, and Hispanic alike—were drafted into the military or found jobs with the government. During World War II, a handful of Navajo served as code talkers for the Marines in the Pacific, helping ensure a U.S. victory. By the middle of the century, the Colorado Plateau's **resource-based economy** was firmly entrenched, dependent on the extraction and/or processing of natural products such as lumber, minerals, gas, oil, and grass (through grazing). Those activities that required water or power, including agriculture, grazing, and mining, were supported by major public works projects which began with the 1902 Reclamation Act and led to the construction of the Roosevelt Dam (1911), the Hoover Dam (1936), and the Glen Canyon Dam (1966). Much of this region would still be barren desert without the federal government's concerted effort to transform it into a tamed, productive landscape—an important point to remember in light of frequent cries for local autonomy and freedom from federal tyranny. Crops such as cotton, grain, fruit, and alfalfa helped support the rural economies, along with cattle and sheep ranching.

Mining had been important in the Southwest for centuries, particularly in Arizona, whose copper reserves were exposed in massive open-pit excavations. The discovery of natural gas and petroleum in Texas and Oklahoma in the early 1900s was only the beginning. Oil was discovered on the Navajo Reservation in 1922, suspicions about coal beneath Black Mesa were proved true, and major oil and natural-gas fields were discovered in the San Juan Basin of northwestern New Mexico and southwestern Colorado in the 1940s. In the 1950s, the Cold War brought a sharp demand for **uranium,** a key ingredient in the atomic bomb. Prospectors armed with Geiger counters combed the Colorado Plateau in Army-surplus jeeps, opening new roads and occasionally even striking it rich. By 1955, about 800 uranium mines were spread across the plateau, but when the Atomic Energy Commission stopped buying uranium ore in 1970, the market collapsed.

RECENT HISTORY

Rachel Carson's book *Silent Spring,* published in 1962, is usually credited with sparking the modern **environmental movement.** Its account of the effects of pesticides on birds struck a nerve with readers around the world, and provided the motivation for the passage of a number of environmental laws in the United States, including the Wilderness Act (1964); the National Environmental Policy Act (1969), which created the Environmental Protection Agency; and the Clean Air Act (1970). In 1966, three years after the gates of Glen Canyon Dam were closed, the Sierra Club fought the Bureau of Reclamation's plans to dam the Grand Canyon. In response to the Bureau's claim that a dammed river would let tourists get closer to the canyon walls, the Club ran full-page ads in the *New York Times* and the *Washington Post* asking "Should we flood the Sistine Chapel so tourists can get closer to the ceiling?" The bold move cost the group its tax-exempt status, but boosted membership and helped defeat the plan three years later.

Published in 1968, Edward Abbey's *Desert Solitaire* would do for the Southwest deserts what *Silent Spring* did for birds and forests. The pithy account of two seasons as a ranger in Arches, liberally laced with calls to protect the Four Corners' natural wonders from the forces of development and tourism, has become an environmental classic. The first Earth Day was held on April 22, 1970, followed in 1980 by the "Sagebrush Rebellion" near Moab. During a July 4th Earth First! rally, a local county commission responded by sending a flag-flying bulldozer to carve a road into what the BLM had identified as a potential wilderness study area.

Winds of Change

The resource economy is struggling, but even as "sustainability" becomes the new buzzword, old ways die hard. The long-term value of the coal deposits beneath Black Mesa on the Navajo and Hopi lands has been estimated as high as $100 billion, but the effects of draining a billion gallons per year from the underground aquifer to carry coal slurry to power plants is being hotly debated. Recent controversies over land use in the San Juan Basin have pitted oil and gas drillers against an unlikely alliance of environmentalists and sixth-generation ranchers. More than 10,000 head of cattle graze in the basin, and ranchers say that oil drilling—which produced $2.4 billion in 2001—has contaminated water and led to erosion and the death of livestock. Instead of turning local communities into ghost towns by cutting off access to minerals, the creation of new parks and monuments has brought a new economic boom: **tourism.**

Outdoor recreation is becoming the Four Corners' modern gold mine. Mountain bikers, hikers, river runners, and families in vans and RVs have discovered the scenic and cultural wonders of the Colorado Plateau, and support growing numbers of hotels, restaurants, tour companies, and other businesses. Retirees are drawn to the scenery and climate, particularly in Arizona. As populations rise, though, the already meager water supply is stretched even thinner.

To make things worse, starting in the late 1990s, the region has been entering the throes of the worst drought in over a century, and by some estimates, perhaps one of the worst droughts in the past 1,400 years. According to the U.S. Geological Survey, the period 1999–2004 was the driest in 98 years of recorded history of the Colorado River. Reservoirs sat at record lows, farms shriveled, and bone-dry forests ignited at the slightest spark. At times, soil moisture levels were barely registering, and a plague of bark beetles had decimated pine trees weakened by the drought—two million in northern Arizona alone.

As a result, southwestern states fight over shares of diverted water flows, especially from the Colorado River, which has been over-allotted since a miscalculation of the river's average flow was locked into the Colorado River Compact in 1922. Climatologists have begun to suspect that the past century was abnormally wet, meaning that the calculations that did and still do drive the development of the urbanized West were, to put it bluntly, flat-out wrong.

On the bright side, New Mexico passed a law requiring utilities to get 10 percent of their electricity supply from renewable energy sources, such as solar, by the year 2011. The future of this amazing, austere, but still fragile region depends on whether we can find the right balance between leaving it alone, living on its terms, and loving it to death.

Native Cultures

Over a third of all Native Americans live in the Southwest, mostly in Arizona and New Mexico. The tribes you'll encounter in the Four Corners are the Navajo, the Hopi, and the Ute, but other Pueblo tribes, as well as the Apache, have reservations nearby. The United States has always had a schizophrenic relationship with its native cultures, alternately idealizing and scorning them, while leaving mostly unaddressed the national legacy of guilt over their wholesale destruction during the European settlement of the continent. The old ways are fading in the face of modern technological civilization, but some are determined to preserve traditional culture, arts, and ceremonies no matter what. A visit to a reservation can be like a cold bucket of water in the face, replacing hazy romantic notions with harsh reality. With their high unemployment and alcohol abuse, low average income, and rough living conditions, Native American reservations can be disheartening places at first glance. But a visit can also be incredibly enjoyable and enlightening experience, and meeting tribe members in person can offer a glimpse into a fascinating way of life that has endured despite all the odds.

There is evidence that attitudes are improving. The **Native American Graves**

Protection and Repatriation Act (NAG-PRA) of 1990 made it a crime to disturb or dig up funerary objects and human remains on federal or tribal land. If a tribal affiliation can be determined, the tribe must be given the opportunity to claim the remains. Thanks to this law and a philosophical shift in the practice of archaeology, remains and objects in museums are slowly being returned to the care of their parent tribes, and large-scale excavations are shifting out of vogue in place of smaller projects where relics are left in place.

In May 2004, a **"Resolution of Apology to the Native American Peoples"** was introduced in the U.S. Congress, which, among other things, "commends and honors the Native Peoples for the thousands of years that they have stewarded and protected this land" and "apologizes on behalf of the people of the United States to all Native Peoples for the many instances of violence, maltreatment, and neglect inflicted on Native Peoples by citizens of the United States."

NAVAJO
Demography

The Diné, as the Navajo call themselves, are the second-largest tribe in the United States after the Cherokee, with 282,000 members. About 165,000 of these live on the country's largest reservation, which covers 25,000 square miles—about a quarter of the state of Arizona and small slivers of New Mexico and Utah. This traditional territory is called Dinetah, meaning "among the People," or Din'e Bike'yah, "the land between the sacred mountains," referring to the tribe's traditional territorial boundaries: to the north is Sisnaajinii (Blanca Peak) near Alamosa, Colorado, representing dawn; Tsoodzil (Mt. Taylor) rises near Grants, New Mexico and symbolizes the daytime sky; Dook'o'oosliid (the San Francisco Peaks) near Flagstaff signify twilight; and Dibe Nitsaa (Mt. Hesperus) near Durango represents night.

Despite significant natural resources, including massive reserves of coal, natural gas, and oil, the "Rez" is still a very poor place. Ac-cording to the 1990 census, more than half of its residents lived below the poverty line, with unemployment as high as 50 percent and an average income of just over $14,000 per year (vs. the national average of $39,000). Only two-thirds of houses have electricity and half lack running water. One cause of the poverty is a booming population—the tribe grew almost 80 percent from 1980 to 2000.

Gambling on the reservation has been voted down repeatedly, in part because it is seen as a sickness in traditional Navajo teachings, so you won't find any casinos—yet. (In 2005, the 2,800-member To'hajiilee band of Navajo, which have their own reservation in New Mexico, planned to build a casino near Albuquerque.) Tribe members support themselves through industry, farming, and raising livestock such as goats, sheep, and horses. Tourism and the sale of traditional crafts, including weaving, pottery, and silverwork—mostly to *belagaana* (Anglos)—are also important moneymakers.

Organization

The Navajo Nation (this term is also used to refer to the reservation itself) is a sovereign entity within the United States, with its own government and courts. Navajo land is held in trust by the federal government, which under the original treaties assumed responsibility for the tribe members' health and welfare. The Navajo Nation is divided into about 110 political divisions called chapters. Elected leaders address local community problems and select delegates for the Tribal Council, based in Window Rock. The Navajo Police has jurisdiction over the reservation, but they share duties with the state and federal law enforcement agencies as well, including the FBI and the Bureau of Indian Affairs (BIA). The BIA still has some administrative and maintenance duties on the reservation, but these are gradually being turned over to the tribe.

Language

The Navajo speak an Athapascan language similar to that of the Apache, their cultural cousins who arrived with them from the north

NAVAJO CODE TALKERS

During World War II, the obscurity of the Navajo language helped win the battle for the Pacific. The idea came from engineer Philip Johnston, who had grown up on the Navajo Reservation as the son of a Protestant missionary. Johnston knew that only a few dozen people outside the reservation spoke the tribe's language, and figured it would make an excellent code. He set up a demonstration to convince the Marine Corps, and 30 tribe members were soon recruited as "code talkers."

Native American languages, including Choctaw, had been used as codes in World War I, but the pilot program took things a step further. Navajo is an extremely complex language, full of dialect and nuance, and at the time was still unwritten. Johnston had the idea to use ordinary Navajo words for military terms to add an extra layer of encoding. *Cha* ("beaver") meant "minesweeper," *gini* ("chicken hawk") became "dive bomber," and *besh-lo* ("iron fish") meant "submarine." Four hundred eleven words were encoded, and multiple Navajo words were assigned to 12 commonly used letters. For example, *Be-la-sana* ("apple") and *tse-nil* ("axe") both stood for "A." The code talkers, many of whom had never been off the reservation, were drilled repeatedly. There was no room for error—transmissions had to be fast and accurate, and a single mistake could cost lives. Twenty-seven code talkers were sent to Guadalcanal and two stayed behind to train others. (One dropped out of training.)

The brass were skeptical, but the code talkers quickly proved their value. From 1942 to 1945, the Navajo participated in every Marine assault in the Pacific, including Guadalcanal, Peliliu, Tarawa, and Iwo Jima. They transmitted from trenches, foxholes, and jungle redoubts, reporting on battlefield conditions and calling in air support and supplies. The Native Americans were often mistaken for Japanese soldiers by their fellow soldiers, and some were nearly shot. Each was given a bodyguard to keep him safe and to prevent the code, which was not written down on the battlefield, from falling into enemy hands. (This arrangement was the basis for the movie *Windtalkers*.) During the first two days of the battle for Iwo Jima, six code talkers worked around the clock to deliver more than 800 messages without error.

The Japanese, experts at breaking codes, were mystified; they had never heard anything like the sounds that burbled from the radio. Even a Navajo soldier captured at Bataan was bewildered. The code that helped ensure victory in the Pacific was never broken, and the code talkers have only recently been getting the recognition they deserve. There is a good display on the code talkers at the Burger King in Kayenta, Arizona, since owner Richard Mike's father King was one.

NAVAJO CODE WORDS
Officers
commanding general: *bih-keh-he* ("War Chief")
major general: *so-na-kih* ("two star")
brigadier general: *so-a-la-ih* ("one star")
colonel: *atsah-besh-le-gai* ("silver eagle")

Places
Alaska: *beh-hga* ("with winter")
America: *ne-he-mah* ("our mother")
Australia: *cha-yes-desi* ("rolled hat")
Britain: *toh-ta* ("between waters")
Germany: *besh-be-cha-he* ("iron hat")
India: *ah-le-gai* ("white clothes")
Russia: *sila-gol-chi-ih* ("red army")
Spain: *deba-de-nih* ("sheep pain")

Airplanes
torpedo plane: *tas-chizzie* ("swallow")
fighter plane: *da-he-tih-hi* ("hummingbird")
bomber plane: *jay-sho* ("buzzard")

Ships
battleship: *lo-tso* ("whale")
aircraft: *tsidi-moffa-ye-hi* ("bird carrier")
destroyer: *ca-lo* ("shark")
cruiser: *lo-tso-yazzie* ("small whale")

around the 1400s. Navajo is a colorful, descriptive language, full of subtle nuance and puns, and it incorporates words from other languages, such as *beeso* for "money" from the Spanish *peso*. Navajo is also incredibly difficult to learn well, so it was perfect for a WWII code that remained unbroken through the Pacific theater. (It is ironic that before and after World War II, Navajo children were being punished for speaking their own language in government-run boarding schools that were trying to "take the Indian out of the Indian.")

Arts

Experts at borrowing useful skills from other cultures, the Navajo adopted weaving from their Pueblo neighbors and silversmithing from Mexican artisans during the Spanish occupation of the Southwest. Handwoven wool rugs have reached an exquisite level of artistry, although fewer and fewer young women are learning the skills and patience to weave like their grandmothers. Navajo silverwork is equally intricate. Other crafts include baskets, pottery, sandpaintings, and kachina dolls copied from the Hopi.

Traditional Culture

Traditional Navajo beliefs revolve around the idea that the proper state of the universe is one of order, balance, and happiness called *hózhó*, often translated as "beauty." When *hózhó* is present, all is well. When it is lost through violence or the breaking of cultural taboos, things swing out of kilter and evil witches called Skinwalkers roam at night. Particularly stringent rules surround incest and death—a spiritual contagion called *chindi* following the loss of a life can pollute a dwelling if it happens indoors. Disharmony must be put right through rituals called "sings," which have been handed down through generations. Days of chanting, drumming, and ceremonial purification are supervised by a medicine man. Sings include the Blessing Way and the Enemy Way for cleansing after battle, and communal dances with names such as When the Thunder Sleeps are also held.

Often the setting is inside a traditional log hogan, which means "home" in Navajo. These eight-sided, one-room structures have a packed clay floor and a domed roof of mud or sod pierced by a smoke hole. The doorway faces east to greet the rising sun. Hogans are slowly being replaced by modern buildings with tar paper and shingle roofs or plywood walls, but you'll still see traditional hogans out in the countryside.

Navajo mythology includes a rich cast of characters including Turquoise Boy, Talking God, Spider Woman, and Water Monster. Their origin stories recount a progression through three underworlds into this, the Fourth or Glittering World. Of the Navajo Holy People, one of the most important is Changing Woman *(Asdzaan Nadleehe),* considered the tribe's spiritual mother. Impregnated by the sun, she bore twin sons called Monster Slayer *(Naaee' Neezghani)* and Born for Water *(Tobdjishchini).* The Hero Twins went on to slay a series of monsters to make the earth safe for human beings. Several who plead for their lives were spared as a lesson to humanity, including Sleepiness, Hunger, Old Age, and Poverty.

The Navajo live in a matrilineal clan system, in which kinship is extremely important. There are more than 140 clans today, with names like Bitter Water Clan and the Corn People. Traditional greetings include a recitation of one's mother's ("born-to") and father's ("born-for") clans, and marriages must be to someone outside of one's clan. A complex chain of clan relationships can make avoiding this form of "incest" very difficult.

HOPI
Demography

The westernmost group of Pueblo Indians, once called the Moqui, occupy 12 villages on three mesas in the middle of the Navajo Reservation. Most of the approximately 12,000 tribe members live on the 1.6 million-acre Hopi Reservation. It was created in 1882 with little thought given to the traditional boundaries of the Navajo and the Hopi, and subsequent legal rulings have only complicated things. The Hopi Reservation is as poor as its surrounding neighbor; the average annual income is $17,500, unemployment is around 25 percent, and more than half of tribe members live below the poverty line. The Hopi live mostly on tourism, government aid, and farm products such as beans, corn, squash, melons, fruit, and wheat. They also herd cows and sheep. Despite the once-popular T-shirts saying "Don't Worry, Be Hopi," the tribe's traditional culture has had to struggle to survive. Many members have moved away from the mesas and abandoned the complex instructions of *Sootukwnangwu,* the Supreme Creator. Yet the core values remain, and the lofty villages endure.

Organization

The 12 Hopi villages are largely autonomous, but are loosely united under the Hopi Tribal Council. The majority rule incorporated by the 1936 Hopi constitution conflicts with the tribe's traditional ways of making decisions, which rely more on building consensus. Like the Navajo Nation, the Hopi tribal government maintains relationships with the federal government, which acts as a trustee for the tribe, as well as surrounding state and local agencies. Three villages have adopted Western-style governments, and the others have held onto the traditional Hopi form of government to different degrees. (Oraibi is the most traditional and independent.) A chief *(kikmongwi)* oversees each village's social and ceremonial life, while still bowing to community consensus.

Language

The Hopi speak a Uto-Aztecan language, part of a linguistic family that ranges from California to Mexico.

Arts

The most famous Hopi crafts are the figurines that represent the kachina spirits who reside in the San Francisco Mountains near Flagstaff. Tribe members also make beautiful silver jewelry using an overlay technique, as well as pottery, baskets, and paintings.

THE HAPPY HOPI

Louis Tewanima, one of the United States' greatest distance runners, grew up chasing jackrabbits on the Hopi Reservation. It's said that he would run 120 miles to Winslow and back just to see the trains pass. He met the legendary Native American athlete Jim Thorpe at an Indian school in Pennsylvania, where Tewanima once had to run 18 miles to a race after missing the train — he arrived in time and won the two-mile event. He went on to represent the United States at the 1908 and 1912 Olympic Games. At the second he won a silver medal and set an American record that stood for 52 years before it was broken by another Native American. The "Happy Hopi from Shongopovi" returned to his home, were he died at age 92, by falling off Second Mesa in the dark coming home from a ceremony.

Traditional Culture

The Hopi live according to the translation of their correct name, *Hopitu,* which means "peaceful people." Their worldview is based on humility, respect, cooperation, and caring for the earth. This last part is particularly important since, as farmers without a permanent water supply, they have had to learn dry-farming techniques that take extraordinary care and diligence. In this unforgiving land, it is crucial that the tribe follow the ceremonial Hopi Way—not only to ensure their own survival, but the well-being of everyone on earth.

The Hopi have a similar origin story to the Navajo. The Bear Clan, they say, led the Hopi from a *sipapu* (a small opening in the earth) into this, the Fourth World, where they wandered the globe before settling in the *Tuuwanasave,* or "earth center." Here the Hopi follow the laws of *Maa'sau,* the Guardian of the Fourth World, which tell them to live in harmony and balance with their surroundings. Only a careful balance keeps the world from disaster. Help is available in the form of the kachinas *(katsinam),* benevolent spirit beings who live in the San Francisco Mountains and appear to the tribe between the winter solstice and mid-July. Hundreds of kachinas serve as messengers between the Hopi and the spiritual realm, by controlling natural forces such as rain and meting out punishment for infringements of Hopi law. The spirits themselves can be represented in two other ways: by men dressing up for ceremonies, and as dolls *(tihu* or *tithu)* that are used to teach children, and also sold. Some kachinas are frightening figures who concentrate on discipline, while others serve as comic relief, including the Navajo Clown *(Tasavu)* who mocks the neighboring tribe.

Hopi culture is divided into matrilineal clans, with villages providing an extra level of self-identification. A sophisticated religious calendar is followed closely, with spiritual leaders calculating ceremonial dates by the position of the sun. Like other Pueblo tribes, the Hopi use ceremonial underground kivas, which a number of secret societies use for meditation and prayer. Important ceremonies include *Soyal,* the celebration of the winter solstice, and *Niman,* the Home Dance. Once all Hopi ceremonies were open to nonmembers, but so many visitors broke the rules against recording that many dances have been closed, including the famous Snake Dance held in late August. The public portion was only the end of nine days of secret ceremonies in the kivas of the Snake and Antelope clans, and included dancers performing with live snakes in their mouths.

UTE

The smallest tribal group in the Four Corners occupies two reservations in southwest Colorado and just over the border into New Mexico. Colorado's oldest native residents began as a loose confederation of seven nomadic bands spread across Colorado, Arizona, New Mexico, Wyoming, and Utah, which was named after them. Ute means "land of the sun," and although it is known that they originally came

from the north and west, when is still unclear. The Ute adopted horses from the Spanish and became respected hunters and feared raiders, going after buffalo on the eastern plains and settlers' livestock with equal ferocity. Utes speak a Shoshonean language similar to that of the Shoshones, Paiutes, and Comanches.

The Ute mythos centers on animal deities. In spring they would gather for the Bear Dance, which had its origins in a story of a bear who taught the song and dance steps to a young hunter. Spring was a time of reawakening for both man and beast, and after the four-day dance, participants would place plumes they had worn in a cedar tree, symbolically leaving their troubles behind. The Sundance, the most important social and religious ceremony, took place in summer. Participants underwent a four-day fast, called *tagu-wuni,* or "standing thirsty," while dancing inside a special lodge. (Both dances are still held today, but only the Bear Dance is open to the public.)

Two of the bands, the Mouache and the Capote, became the **Southern Ute Tribe,** which now lives on a 818,000-acre reservation that was left a checkerboard of Native American and non–Native American lands due to the homesteading system. The tribe owns just over 300,000 acres, and counts 1,250 members out of the reservation's total population of 7,900. Tribal headquarters are in Ignacio, Colorado, with a smaller group living in White Mesa.

The Weeminuche band is now called the **Ute Mountain Tribe,** which occupies a 600,000-acre reservation bordering Mesa Verde National Park, with the anthropomorphic mountain at its center. A population of about 2,000 lives mostly in Towaoc.

Both Four Corners Ute tribes are run by elected Tribal Councils, and depend on income from agriculture, livestock, construction, forestry, mining, and casinos on both reservations. (The other four Ute bands became the Northern Ute tribe, which lives on the Uintah-Ouray Reservation near Fort Duchesne, Utah.)

ESSENTIALS
Getting There and Around

In a nutshell, the easiest way to explore the Four Corners is to fly to one of the nearest major airports, such as Salt Lake City or Las Vegas, rent a car, and drive wherever you want to go. It is possible to arrive and even get around—somewhat—by bus, train, and local airline, but service is limited to a few cities, and the distances involved and the remoteness of many of the attractions make a private vehicle the only practical way to travel here. A network of highways connect the major cities and points of interest, but this still leaves much of the region inaccessible to drivers without four-wheel-drive, or in many cases, any vehicles at all.

BY AIR

The nearest **international airports** are in Albuquerque (ABQ; 140 miles from Gallup), Phoenix (PHX; 145 miles from Flagstaff), Denver (DEN; 335 miles from Durango), Salt Lake City (SLC; 182 miles from Green River, 235 miles from Moab), and Las Vegas (LAS; 250 miles from Flagstaff, 270 miles from Page). Each of these cities is a major travel gateway served by most major airlines, and all offer a full range of hotels, restaurants, and tourist-related services. There are smaller **local airports** in Moab (CNY), Cortez (CEZ), Grand Junction (GJT), Flagstaff (FLG), and Page (PGA), with limited service to each other and larger

© JULIAN SMITH

STATE FAST FACTS

STATE	TOTAL AREA, SQUARE MILES (RANK)	PERCENT OWNED FEDERAL BY GOVERNMENT (RANK)	NICKNAME
Arizona	113,635 (6th)	44.3% (8th)	Grand Canyon State
Colorado	103,718 (8th)	38.9% (9th)	Centennial State
New Mexico	121,356 (5th)	36.2% (10th)	Land of Enchantment
Utah	82,144 (13th)	67.9% (2nd)	Beehive State

cities; information on these is included in the travel chapters.

BY CAR

The Four Corners is sandwiched between I-40 to the south, running between Albuquerque and California, and I-70 to the north, which runs from Denver to I-15 in the middle of Utah. I-15 runs from Salt Lake City southwest to St. George, Las Vegas, and beyond. Major travel arteries within the area include **Highway 89** and **Highway 89A,** which connect Flagstaff

LARGEST CITIES IN THE FOUR CORNERS

CITY	POPULATION (2000)
Flagstaff, AZ	52,894
Farmington, NM	37,844
Gallup, NM	20,209
Durango, CO	13,922
Winslow, AZ	9,520
Cortez, CO	7,977
Page, AZ	6,809
Aztec, NM	6,378
Holbrook, AZ	4,917
Moab, UT	4,779

to Kanab, close to I-15 at St. George. **Highway 160** connects with Highway 89 north of Flagstaff and runs east to the Four Corners monument itself, Cortez, and Durango.

Highway 491 leads north from Gallup across the Navajo Reservation, joining briefly with Highway 160 and eventually meeting Highway 191 at Monticello. **Highway 191** joins I-70 near Green River, and runs south through Moab and the other towns of Southeast Utah before crossing the state line and the Navajo Reservation. It passes the Canyon de Chelly and joins I-40 at Chambers. Other major routes—and out here that means a two-lane paved road—include **Highway 24** and **Highway 95** across remote South-Central Utah, and the spectacular **Highway 12,** which winds across the northern border of the Grand Staircase–Escalante National Monument.

Car rental agencies can be found in the Four Corners' larger cities, including Moab, Durango, Flagstaff, Gallup, and Farmington. When renting a car, consider how far out into the backcountry you want to go; four-wheel-drive vehicles are available, but these cost more. A good option if you plan on sticking to the pavement is to rent a Recreational Vehicle (RV), which is like piloting your own little mobile hotel. You can find developed campsites with water, electric, and sewer hookups for $20–30 per night, or just park on public land and rough it, relatively speaking. **Cruise America** (800/327-7799, fax 480/464-7321, info@cruiseamerica.com, www.cruiseamerica

CAPITAL	POPULATION (2003 EST.)	POPULATION DENSITY PER SQUARE MILE (RANK, 1990)	PER CAPITA INCOME (2000)
Phoenix	5,580,811	45.2 (37th)	$24,988
Denver	4,550,688	41.5 (38th)	$32,434
Santa Fe	1,874,614	15 (46th)	$21,931
Salt Lake City	2,351,467	27.2 (42nd)	$23,436

.com) has RV rental offices in Phoenix, Albuquerque, Salt Lake City, and Denver.

BY BUS

There's not as much bus service out here as you might expect (or hope). **Greyhound** (800/231-2222, www.greyhound.com) has regular service to cities along the interstates: Green River, Durango, Gallup, Farmington, Holbrook, Winslow, and Flagstaff. Contact them for a schedule and information on special discounts and passes. **Golden State Bus Lines** stops at Ben's Cafe in Green River on the way from Las Vegas to Denver. This line goes all over the Southwest and into northern Mexico; for information, contact them in Las Vegas (607 Maple St., 213/627-2940) or Denver (2301 Champa St., 303/675-0110). The Navajo Reservation is served by the **Navajo Transit System** (928/729-4002), which sends buses along seven routes: Tuba City/Window Rock, Toyei/Window Rock, Kayenta/Fort Defiance, Crownpoint/Fort Defiance, Fort Defiance/Window Rock/Gallup, and Shiprock/Farmington/Window Rock. All are daily except Shiprock/Farmington/Window Rock, which runs a few times a week. None are over $15 one-way.

A few companies offer bus tours of the Southwest very different from the typical Greyhound experience. Both **Adventure Bus** (888/737-5263, info@adventurebus.com, www.adventurebus.com) and **Green Tortoise Adventure Travel** (800/867-8647, tortoise@greentortoise.com, www.greentortoise.com) have buses that double as rolling hostels. These trips usually include a food fund and communal cooking, and concentrate on outdoor activities and national parks.

BY TRAIN

Amtrak (800/872-7245, www.amtrak.com) runs the luxury Southwest Chief line along the path, more or less, of old Route 66. On its way between Chicago to Los Angeles, the Chief stops in Gallup, Winslow, and Flagstaff daily in both directions. This is a more-comfortable but more-expensive and much less flexible way to travel than by bus. Fares vary depending on time of year, and there are a number of discounts available; contact Amtrak for details.

HITCHHIKING

This is still a common form of transport in the Southwest, particularly on the Native American reservations. It can be a good way to meet locals and get around for little or nothing, but it can also be an adventure in patience, not to mention luck and personal safety. I do it from time to time—mostly on the driving end nowadays—and have never had a bad experience, but that's just one person's story. Trust your instincts when deciding whether or not to accept or offer a ride. It's polite to offer some money for gas if you do get picked up. Women traveling alone should not hitchhike. **Ride boards** at universities such as Northern Arizona University in Flagstaff list people looking for rides or riders to specific locations to help share the costs.

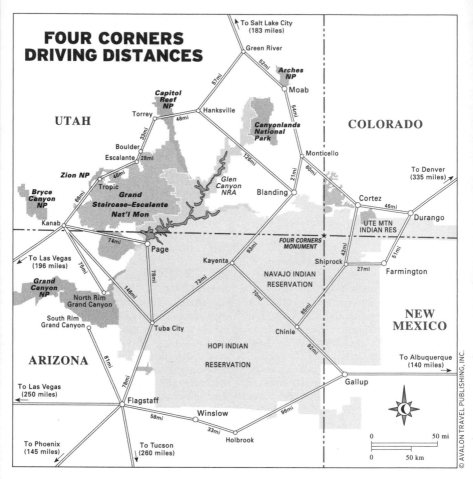

FOUR CORNERS DRIVING DISTANCES

Health and Safety

HEAT, WATER, AND SUN

In the high desert you have two things working against you whenever you step outside: the strong, nearly constant sunlight, and the thin, dry air. It's remarkably easy to get a **sunburn,** so use sunscreen (at least SPF 15) liberally, and always have a hat with you—the bigger the brim, the better. Consider wearing long sleeves and pants, preferably in light colors; they can

actually keep you cooler than shorts and T-shirts (just ask the Beduin). A handkerchief is handy to protect your neck if you burn easily. "Desert-rat" hats with built-in neck flaps are available at outdoor gear stores. Sunburn is the first step on the road to **hyperthermia** (overheating). This progresses through relatively common **heat exhaustion,** with its flulike symptoms such as vomiting and dizziness, to

heat stroke, a very serious condition in which the body's cooling mechanism breaks down. Heat stroke is marked by a significant change in behavior and brain activity, and has an 80 percent mortality rate when untreated. If you suspect any of the above, get out of the sun, remove any restrictive clothing, and drink plenty of fluids, preferably with salts or electrolytes. If you can, splash cool water on the victim or use ice packs (over clothing) to cool them off.

Most visitors to the Four Corners will experience **dehydration** at some point; in this thin, dry, warm air, it's almost a way of life. Pay attention, though, and you'll soon be able to head it off before things get serious. The easiest way to judge how well you are hydrated, not to mince words, is to keep track of the color of your pee. Clear or barely tinted urine is good; dark urine is bad. Get in the habit of paying attention to this and *drink constantly,* even if it's only a few sips of something decaffeinated every so often. Carbohydrate drinks such as Gatorade or Cytomax help restore lost electrolytes. These are available in powered form, along with electrolyte tablets you can add to water in emergencies.

Backpack hydration systems make constant sipping easier. Remember (or know) that you become dehydrated *before* you get thirsty. Even if you aren't thirsty, drink! Just get in the habit. Anyway, it's good for you.

Another thing to keep in mind is that you often won't have sweat to remind you you're losing water—the moisture evaporates straight into the air instead. During hard exercise in the hot sun—hiking or mountain biking, for instance—it's possible to lose up to two quarts of water per hour, and two gallons of water per day. That's why it's crucial to carry at least **one gallon of water per person per day** when doing these kinds of activities from spring through fall. *Always* carry more water than you think you'll need, to have some left over in case things go wrong. Stashing an extra gallon in the car or a quart in the backpack can make all the difference. Consider staying put, or in the shade, during the hottest part of the day, especially in summer. Night hiking by the light of the moon is cool and magical. Take a water bottle with you whenever you venture off the pavement, even if it's only a short hike to a

© JULIAN SMITH

If you're heading to the Tuweep entrance of Grand Canyon National Park, be sure you go prepared.

ruin or overlook. Out here, water is life—don't get caught without it.

OTHER HEALTH ISSUES
Hypothermia
Too far at the other end of the thermometer is also reason to worry. Temperatures drop amazingly fast in the dry desert air—a plunge of 40°F from day to night is not unusual. Heat vanishes into the stratosphere as the sun falls, and if your body temperature drops below 95°F, you're in trouble. Shivering is a sign of mild hypothermia—if this happens, remove any wet clothes, find the warmest spot possible, and get the victim to eat and drink, preferable hot, sugary liquids like Jell-O mix. If weakness, slurred speech, apathy, and poor judgment appear, cover the victim gently with clothing or a sleeping bag and seek medical attention.

Impure Water
Thanks in part to grazing cattle, nearly all natural water sources in the country can be considered contaminated. **Giardia** is the most common bug, causing diarrhea and cramps that can become quite serious. Always filter or chemically treat all water with iodine before drinking it. Rivers like the Colorado, which, like the Mississippi, could be called "too thick to drink, too thin to plow," often carry runoff from fertilized fields and mine tailings rich in heavy metals. I try never to drink directly out of big rivers in the Four Corners. If you must, let the sediment settle before filtering, and considering double-treating the water.

In the Backcountry
Getting lost is a very real possibility in the trackless desert and canyon mazes that make up the Colorado Plateau. Always let someone responsible know where you're going and when you plan to return when you head off on a trip, or else you risk having to do something drastic to survive. Consider the case of hiker Aaron Ralston, who in 2003 went canyoneering alone near Horseshoe Canyon in the Maze district of Canyonlands National Park. When a shifting boulder crushed

and pinned his hand, he was forced to cut if off to escape after five days of exposure.

Keep an eye out for unusual landmarks as you progress, and look back frequently so you can pick out the way home, if necessary. If you think you've lost the trail, backtrack to your last known point—a tree, a junction, or a trail marker. If this doesn't work, *stay put* and try to **signal** for help. Use your signal mirror, wave brightly colored clothing, and blow your whistle. Although it may be tough to just sit and wait, that is better than wandering farther off when a search party is trying to find you. *Always* check the weather forecast before venturing into narrow canyons to avoid **flash floods.**

Plants and Animals
At times it seems like every living thing in the desert either stings, bites, scratches, or impales. Life here is a struggle, and the plants and ani-

---

DESERT SURVIVAL KIT

If you plan on doing any desert hiking or biking, throw these items into a small plastic bag and keep it in the bottom of your pack – it could make all the difference.

Lighter: small, childproof to prevent leaking

Swiss Army knife or pocketknife

Light source: Mini Maglite flashlight or LED headlamp

Compass: to go with your map

Extra food: a few energy bars, gels, or some hard candy

Space blanket: emergency versions roll up very small

First-aid kit: just the essentials

Signal mirror: plastic models available – practice first!

Signal whistle: much better than screaming yourself hoarse

Water purification tablets: iodine drops work as well

Electrolyte tablets: you sweat this off, too

mals have evolved many ways to secure and protect scant resources, and themselves. A fearsome appearance is often deceiving, however—for example, tarantulas aren't dangerous to humans. **Rattlesnakes,** however, are often found sunning themselves on ledges or trails when the ground temperature is over 80°F. They're as afraid of you as you are of them, so if you don't torment them—or grab one unexpectedly—you should have nothing to worry about. The rattle is unmistakable; simply back off and go another way. **Scorpions, centipedes,** and poisonous **spiders** like the black widow are also present. The easiest way to avoid all of these creatures is to avoid putting your hands and feet where you can't see, including ledges, overhangs, and behind logs. Don't leave clothing or sleeping bags lying around on the ground, and if you have, shake it out before putting it on or crawling inside.

The most you'll probably ever see of a **mountain lion** is a flash of movement, if you're lucky, but these large cats are present in the higher mountain ranges. **Coyotes** are ubiquitous, but have never been recorded to attack people (nor have wolves, for that matter). **Black bears** also live in the mountains; store your food in a bag hung from a branch, and don't leave any sitting around a campsite.

Poison ivy grows in wet areas; avoid its waxy leaves which grow in groups of three. **Nettles** can also cause severe itching, and grow in drier, rocky locations. The sharp, stiff leaves of **agaves** and **yuccas** can be dangerous if you stumble into them (one species of yucca is called the Spanish Bayonet). **Cacti** are covered with spines, often including tiny ones you can't even see. Needless to say, avoid these plants, particularly the cholla, whose needles leave a nearly invisible sheath behind that itches madly.

Hantavirus

This nasty virus appeared in the Four Corners in 1993, when a number of people suddenly developed acute breathing problems. About half died with alarming speed. When health authorities investigated, they realized that heavy snowmelt had caused a bumper crop of piñon nuts, which in turn supported an unusually high mouse population. They figured out that the mice droppings carried the airborne virus that causes Hantavirus Pulmonary Syndrome (HPV). The symptoms, which appear one to five weeks after exposure, include fever, fatigue, aching muscles, nausea, and other flu-like symptoms. If untreated, though, HPV is fatal. It is very rare, but to avoid it, minimize your contact with rodents and their droppings, particularly in enclosed spaces like old cabins. Clean up infested areas by wetting the droppings with a bleach solution (wear latex gloves) and mopping them up—don't sweep dry particles into the air. In the backcountry, avoid pack rat middens, and don't encourage the little critters into your campsite by leaving food within easy reach.

Interestingly, the Navajo were not surprised by the 1993 hantavirus outbreak. In their medical tradition, mice are considered the carriers of an ancient sickness that targets the healthiest and strongest (as does HPV) so they've always done their best to keep rodents out of residences and the food supply. The sickness had struck in 1918 and 1933–1934, both years with high numbers of piñon nuts and mice. Some native elders had even predicted the 1993 outbreak.

SAFETY

The most common form of crime in the Four Corners is theft—don't leave anything valuable in view in your car or hotel room—but assaults and robberies do occur. Crime has increased on public lands in recent years, due to a rise in visitors and a decrease in money for law enforcement, particularly in remote areas such as those patrolled by the BLM. I've traveled around this place alone for years without any trouble, sleeping in my car and camping on public land, but this is something I always try to keep in mind.

As a rule of thumb, don't sleep at highway rest areas, and keep one eye peeled and one ear open when alone in the backcountry, particularly if you're a woman alone. Lock your hotel door and your car as a matter of habit. Don't let fear ruin your trip, just be aware of your surroundings. Dial **911** from any pay phone, for free, in case of emergency. If necessary, contact local police, state police, or the various law enforcement agencies active on the reservations: the Hopi police (928/734-3700) and the Bureau of Indian Affairs (BIA) police (928/738-2233) on the Hopi Reservation, or the Navajo Tribal Police (928/871-6112 or 6113).

Information and Services

Electricity

Homes and businesses in the United States operate on 110–220 volt electricity. Modern outlets have three plugs, including two flat prongs and one round (grounding) prong, but older buildings may only have two-prong plugs. If you're using an expensive piece of electronics such as a laptop computer, you should get a three-to-two-prong adapter that also protects against power surges.

Money

Cash is always the easiest way to pay, but the fraud protection, insurance benefits, and other advantages of **credit cards** make them popular among travelers. Unfortunately, in some smaller towns in the Four Corners, and on large parts of the Native American reservations, some vendors can't accept credit cards. **Travelers checks** are another option, but these can also be somewhat of a problem outside larger towns. They offer the advantage of replacement if they're lost or stolen; American Express and Thomas Cook checks are widely accepted at banks, hotels, and restaurants. Forget about using **personal checks** outside your home state. Foreign visitors should change to U.S. dollars at the earliest opportunity.

On the plus side, almost every town has a bank, service station, or bar with an **ATM** (Automated Teller Machine) where you can withdraw cash from your bank card or credit card, as long as you don't mind paying a small fee every time. The most popular ATM networks are Star, Cirrus, Plus, Visa, American Express, and MasterCard. **Western Union** (800/325-6000, www.westernunion.com) lets you to wire money (for a fee) to any of thousands of locations, as well as by phone and over the Internet. Each state charges a different amount of **sales tax:** Arizona (5.6 percent), Utah (4.75 percent), Colorado (2.9 percent), and New Mexico (5 percent). Not to be outdone, the Navajo Nation started charging a 3 percent sales tax in 2002.

Tipping is customary in restaurants, taxis, and whenever someone totes your bags (airports and hotels). As any former restaurant server will tell you—and there are plenty of us out there—a 15 percent tip on restaurant and bar bills is standard, since waiters make considerably less than minimum wage before tips. Leave 20 percent or more for outstanding service, or if you're just feeling nice. Taxi drivers typically receive 15 percent, and airport porters and bellhops at least $1 per bag.

Park Passes

With admission fees climbing ever higher, it's usually a good idea to buy a **National Parks Pass** if you plan on visiting more than two or three parks. At $50, they quickly pay for themselves, and are good for one year for the occupants of any private vehicle at any NPS facility in the country. Get one at any park or from the **National Parks Foundation** (888/GO-PARKS, 888/467-2757, or 202/238-4200, http://buy.nationalparks.org). You can also buy local **"passports"** for parks in certain areas, including the Southeast Utah Group (Arches, Canyonlands, Hovenweep, and Natural Bridges), and the national monuments near Flagstaff (Hovenweep, Wupatki, and Sunset Crater), both $25. **State park passes** are also available for each state.

Maps

By far the best map of the region is the *Guide to Indian Country* map put out by the Automobile Club of Southern California. It covers everything in this book, plus areas to the east (Albuquerque and Santa Fe) and west (to Kingman, Arizona, and St. George, Utah). It's the one Lieutenant Joe Leaphorn fills with pins in Tony Hillerman's Navajo mysteries, and is indispensable for any long-term exploration of the Four Corners area (John Wesley Powell would have killed for one). You can get it from AAA offices, and at bookstores and gas stations throughout the region.

Time Traveler Maps (800/753-7388, timetraveler@mapz.com, www.mapz.com) puts out a number of excellent maps of the Four Corners, including "The Colorado Plateau Recreational Map and Guide to Public Lands," "A Geographical Dictionary of Navajo Country in the 1930s," "Tony Hillerman's Indian Country Map & Guide," "Diné Bikéyah: Illustrated Navajo Lands Wall Map," and "Image of the Four Corners."

National Geographic's **Trails Illustrated Maps** (800/962-1643, fax 800/626-8676, http://maps.nationalgeographic.com/trails/) makes waterproof, tear-resistant maps to Moab, Arches National Park, Bryce Canyon National Park, Canyonlands National Park, Glen Canyon National Recreation Area and Capitol Reef, Grand Canyon National Park, the Canyons of the Escalante, the San Rafael Swell, and Grand Gulch Plateau (Cedar Mesa) for $10 each. They also offer state maps with travel and historic information on the back for $7 each.

Finally, **Latitude 40 Maps** (303/258-7909, fax 303/258-0540, lat40@indra.com, www.angelfire.com/biz/latitude40/) have created the invaluable "Moab East" and "Moab West" recreational topo maps ($10 each), as well as the "Slickrock Bike Trail" map ($7) and another recreational topo map to southwest Colorado ($10). All are available locally and come with trail information on the reverse.

Time Zones

All four states are in the Mountain Time zone, which is two hours behind Eastern Time (New York), one hour ahead of the Pacific Time (California), and seven hours behind Greenwich Mean Time (London). Sound simple? Not so fast. From April to October, Utah, Colorado, and Mexico advance one hour according to daylight savings time ("spring forward, fall back"). Arizona apparently has enough sunshine, because that state stays on the same time year-round—except for the Navajo Reservation, which *does* participate in daylight savings time. To make things even more confusing, the Hopi Reservation *inside* the Navajo Reservation follows Arizona's lead and ignores daylight savings time. From April to October, then, set your watch forward one hour if you enter Utah, New Mexico, or the Navajo Reservation from Arizona, and when you enter the Hopi Reservation. Set it back an hour entering Arizona, or leaving the Hopi Reservation.

Business Hours

Most businesses, aside from restaurants, are open 9 A.M.–6 P.M. Monday–Saturday, with varying hours (if any) on Sunday. In Utah, many businesses, including restaurants, are closed Sunday. Banks and post offices are typically open for the first half of the day Saturday. The seasonal tourism industry means many businesses close for the winter, or at least significantly reduce their hours. This can also apply in the height of the summer in some locations, when visitation drops from the heat. It's always a good idea to call ahead from October to April to make sure your favorite hotel, restaurant, or trading post hasn't closed up shop for the season.

Communications

Every incorporated town, no matter how small, has a **U.S. post office** (800/275-8777, www.usps.gov) usually open 8:30 A.M.–5 P.M. Monday–Friday and 8:30 A.M.–noon Saturday. The main telephone **area codes** in the Four Corners are 435 (southern Utah), 970 (southwestern Colorado), 505 (most of New Mexico), and 928 (northern Arizona). **Toll-free numbers** start with 800, 888, 877, and

866, and you can get **directory assistance** by calling 411 (local), or 1 + area code + 555-1212 (long-distance). Toll-free information is 800/555-1212. For **emergencies** dial 911. **Pay phones** cost $0.35–0.50 for a short local call, but are becoming more rare with the advent of cell phones. For longer and long-distance calls, it's cheaper to get a prepaid **calling card,** available in many different amounts just about everywhere. Cell phone coverage in the Four Corners can be spotty at best outside cities.

Most medium-to-large cities have their own **newspapers,** which are a good source of information on local events and attitudes. This includes the *Gallup Independent* (www.gallup-independent.com), Moab's *Times-Independent* (www.moabtimes.com), the *Canyon Country Zephyr* (www.canyoncountryzephyr.com), the Farmington *Daily Times* (www.daily-times.com), and the *Arizona Daily Sun,* (www.azdailysun.com), available in Flagstaff. On the reservations look for the *Navajo Times* (www.thenavajotimes.com) and the *Navajo Hopi Observer* (www.navajohopiobserver.com).

Internet cafés are starting to spread across the Four Corners. Many coffee shops, hotels, and hostels offer Internet computers for a fee and wireless Internet access for free, but the most dependable place to hop online is still the public library. Ask nicely and they should put you on the waiting list even if you don't have a library card.

Radio stations always offer an interesting taste of local life, and radio is still an important medium of communication in this wide-open countryside. The Navajo run their own station, KTTN (660 AM), "The Voice of the Navajo Nation," which plays mostly country-and-western music interspersed with chants and announcements in Navajo on pertinent topics like the news, weather, and livestock reports. You'll find Hopi Radio (KUYI, meaning "water" in Hopi) at 88.1 FM. Arizona's only high-school radio station, KGHR (91.5 FM), is run by Navajo students at the Grey Hills Academy. They broadcast an interesting mix of country, classical, rock, and Native American music, plus National Public Radio (NPR) programs.

TIPS FOR TRAVELERS
Cultural Issues
You'll encounter conservative values in the Four Corners, particularly in southern Utah and on the Native American reservations. In this mostly rural region, tradition is highly valued and flashy displays of wealth and liberal (read: California or East-Coast) attitudes can be frowned upon. Gay travelers should avoid overt displays in public. This slower pace of life may be difficult for some visitors to get used to, but do your best—people here are still overwhelmingly friendly and accepting. Polygamy still exists in some corners along the Utah-Arizona border, so some residents of towns there may view visitors with distrust.

A visit to a reservation is really a visit to another country, with the expected concerns of cultural sensitivity and personal conduct. The poverty may be startling and the people fascinating, but try to avoid making a camera lens the first thing anyone sees of you. Photography or any other kind of recording is completely

DRINKING LAWS

Getting a drink is complicated in two parts of the Four Corners. Utah's arcane liquor laws limit brewpubs and taverns to 3.2 percent beer, and supermarkets to "near-beer" as well. Wine and hard liquor are sold at state-run liquor stores and some restaurants, although you'll have to ask your server for a drink – he can't offer you one outright. What you probably call a bar back home, here they call a "private club." Locals pay an annual fee, but visitors can pay $5 or so to enter for an evening. (Technically, this is a "sponsorship" by a current member – if you find out who yours is, buy him or her a drink!). Alcohol is forbidden on both the Navajo and Hopi reservations, but this doesn't stop the proliferation of liquor stores at border towns.

prohibited on the Hopi Reservation, and allowed only in rare circumstances on the Navajo Nation. Native American culture is by tradition reserved and harmonious—the squeaky wheel gets ostracized, not greased—and older people are viewed with respect. Tribal members may seem aloof at first, but give them time to open up, and express a genuine interest in their culture and them as people, and you won't be disappointed.

Travelers with Disabilities

The Four Corners is a rough neighborhood, in the sense that many roads are unpaved, trails are steep and crooked, and many buildings are nonaccessible. Many hotel chains require their facilities to be accessible, but B&Bs (often in old buildings) and restaurants are another story. Always try to call ahead and check. The National Park Service is doing a good job of making its facilities accessible to travelers with disabilities, including most visitors centers and at least a paved trail or two at every location. For more information, check the individual park descriptions on the National Park Service website (www.nps.gov), which list degrees of accessibility, and if you have any more questions contact the park directly and ask to speak to the Accessibility Coordinator. The NPS Golden Access Passport offers free lifetime entrance to visitors who are blind or permanently disabled, as well as a 50 percent discount on federal use fees.

For more information on disabled travel contact **Mobility International USA** (541/343-1284, fax 541/343-6812, www.miusa.org) or the **Society for Accessible Travel & Hospitality** (212/447-7284, fax 212/725-8253, sathtravel@aol.com, www.sath.org), formerly the Society for the Advancement of Travel for the Handicapped.

Traveling with Children

A trip to the Four Corners is one your kids will remember their entire lives, although it's up to you to make sure it's because of the sunrises over Monument Valley, not the hours driving across the desert looking for a bathroom. I can

---

BEST OFFBEAT SPOTS

Kokopelli's Cave (Farmington, NM): A B&B with *serious* Anasazi influences.

Hole 'N the Rock (Moab, UT): An entire home carved out of a sandstone cliff.

Pahreah (Grand Staircase-Escalante National Monument,UT): Real ruins, a fake western town, and amazing scenery.

"The Corner" (Winslow, AZ): Stand in the intersection The Eagles made famous.

Four Corners Monument: Play Twister in four states simultaneously.

Goblin Valley (southern UT): Bizarre stone hoodoos ripe for the scrambling.

Fruita (Capitol Reef National Park, UT): Pick your own fruit in the middle of the desert.

Wigwam Motel (Holbrook, AZ): Stay in a tepee in this classic Route 66 throwback.

---

still recall vividly my own first-grade visit to the Grand Canyon, so I can vouch that the area is as fun for the very young as it is for everyone else.

To start with, there's the fact that most of this place is one big rocky jungle gym. Nothing brings out the kids (or the kid in the rest of us) like scrambling over a pile of stones at the edge of a canyon, or climbing a trail to overlook an ancient ruin. Many hikes, bike rides, raft trips, and backpack routes are family-friendly—even some slot canyons. Wild West history is always a surefire hit, from the old-time melodramas to the trading posts and museums elsewhere. Native cultures are part of that appeal, and include festival dances in the Hopi villages, Navajo-led tours into the Canyon de Chelly, and even a night in an authentic hogan for those so inclined.

A few things are important to keep in mind, especially the harsh climate. Always make sure everyone has sunscreen, appropriate clothing, and enough water (get kids their own water bottles and make a game out of drinking, drinking, drinking) when you wander outside.

Don't overestimate how far little legs can go on long, difficult trails, and be aware that the impressively vertical scenery often lacks safety features like guardrails and warning signs. Last but not least, know that it really can be an hour or more to the next pit stop when you pile in the car.

Local babysitting agencies can be found in the yellow pages or through hotel desks. The **Family Travel Times** (212/477-5524, info@familytraveltimes, www.familytraveltimes.com) publishes articles on vacationing with kids. The most recent one is always free, and to access their catalog costs $49 for two years. Also try the "Travel With Kids" section of the **About.com** website (http://travelwithkids.about.com).

Senior Travelers

Many hotels and attractions offer discounts for seniors—ask when making reservations, or at the gate. The **American Association of Retired Persons** (888/687-2277, www.aarp.org) is the country's largest seniors' organization, with discounts for members ($12.50 pp per year) on hotels, car rentals, air travel, and tours worldwide. **Elderhostel** (877/426-8056, www.elderhostel.org) organizes worldwide "extraordinary learning adventures" for people 55 and over. (One half of a couple is sufficient.) Some trips are pure fun, and others are more service oriented, including recording petroglyphs on the Hopi Reservation and cataloging Anasazi artifacts in a Four Corners museum.

Traveling with Pets

Smaller pets are OK at some hotels and motels (often with a small surcharge), but most B&Bs will say no. Remember that pets must stay in vehicles or on roads in all national parks.

Travel Insurance

A number of agencies offer specialized travelers' insurance in various combinations of health, accident, trip-cancellation and trip-interruption, and lost-luggage protection. Two dependable choices are **Travel Guard International**

(800/826-4919, www.travel-guard.com) and **Access America** (866/807-3982, service@accessamerica.com, www.accessamerica.com).

Volunteering

Chronically underfunded as they are, most national parks and national forests gladly accept volunteers for varying positions and time commitments. Either contact the park's volunteer coordinator, or take a look at the Park Service's **Volunteers-in-Parks** program (www.nps.gov/volunteer). They can sometime provide housing and (very limited) living expenses. The **Student Conservation Association** (603/543-1700, www.thesca.org) can also place volunteers (not just students) in conservation-related positions. I've done two stints with them, and it's always been a great experience.

Tour Companies

Whether you want to go hiking, biking, horseback riding, off-road driving, river rafting, visit a Native American village, or try your hand at archaeology, you can depend on at least one tour company—and probably a few dozen—willing to lend a hand. Local tour operators are included in the various city listings, and not surprisingly are concentrated in the major tourist hubs of Moab, Durango, Page, and Flagstaff. Several nation operations also offer tours of the area, including the Sierra Club, whose Outings program (415/977-5522, national.outings@sierraclub.org, www.sierraclub.org/outings) offers many nature and cultural trips on the Colorado Plateau, from sightseeing to service programs. **Elderhostel** is a similar organization for travelers over 55 (see *Senior Travelers*). Organizations like Monticello's Four Corners School of Outdoor Education are good for learning vacations, and in Moab the **Canyonlands Field Institute** (435/259-7750 or 800/860-5262, fax 435/259-2335, info@canyonlandsfieldinst.org, www.canyonlandsfieldinst.org) has been organizing tours on the Four Corners' ecology, geology, and native cultures since 1984.

Phoenix-based **Detours** (866/438-6877,

info@detoursaz.com, www.detoursaz.com) organizes a wide range of cultural and outdoors tours of the Four Corners. Small groups of 6–10 use comfortable, modified vans to get around, and owner Jeff Slade and their other guide are walking treasure troves of local knowledge. Their roster includes day tours of the Grand Canyon and Sedona and multiday excursions of other national parks, the Navajo Reservation, and Spanish missions. One great option is their "Hillerman Country tour," run with the blessing of the author himself, which lets fans visit sites from the novels and even meet people who appeared in them. **360 Adventures** (480/722-0360 or 888/722-0360, info@360-adventures.com, www. 360-adventures.com) is their adventure-travel branch, offering guided rock climbing, hiking, backpacking, mountain biking, and canyoneering trips throughout the Southwest.

RESOURCES

Suggested Reading

OUTDOORS

Falcon Publishing is the undisputed leader in Western outdoor guidebooks. All of their books have detailed route descriptions, elevation charts, and background information. Other companies are edging in on their territory, though, including Michael Kelsey's self-published line. The Mountain Bike: America series (like Falcon, also part of Globe Pequot) is particularly good, with topographic maps and elevation charts for every ride.

Many of these books are available online or by mail from the **Canyonlands Natural History Association** (435/259-6003 or 800/840-8978, www.cnha.org) or the **Western National Parks Association** (520/622-1999, info@wnpa.org, www.wpna.org), both of which supply books to national park bookstores.

Hiking

Adkinson, Ron. *Best Easy Day Hikes Grand Canyon.* Guilford, CT: Globe Pequot (Falcon Guides), 2005. A smaller version of Adkinson's *Hiking Grand Canyon National Park.*

Adkinson, Ron. *Best Easy Day Hikes Grand Staircase–Escalante & the Glen Canyon Region.* Guilford, CT: Globe Pequot (Falcon Guides), 1998. A pocket-size guide listing 19 hikes on Cedar Mesa, the Escalante, and the Paria Plateau.

Adkinson, Ron. *Hiking Grand Canyon National Park.* Guilford, CT: Globe Pequot (Falcon Guides), 2005. Everything from easy day hikes to extended backpack trips.

Adkinson, Ron. *Hiking Grand Staircase–Escalante & the Glen Canyon Region.* Guilford, CT: Globe Pequot (Falcon Guides), 1998. Fifty-nine meticulous trail descriptions across the monument and its surrounding area, with elevation maps and mileage charts.

Grubbs, Bruce. *Best Easy Day Hikes Flagstaff.* Guilford, CT: Globe Pequot (Falcon Guides), 2001. From half-hour rambles to all-day ventures.

Grubbs, Bruce. *Best Easy Day Hikes Sedona.* Guilford, CT: Globe Pequot (Falcon Guides), 2002. Thirty hikes around the New Age mecca.

Grubbs, Bruce. *Hiking Northern Arizona.* Guilford, CT: Globe Pequot (Falcon Guides), 2001. Includes descriptions of dozens of trails in the mountains and national monuments near Flagstaff.

Hinchman, Sandra. *Hiking the Southwest's Canyon Country.* Seattle, WA: The Mountaineers, 2004. A number of 2–3 week itineraries through the Four Corners region, covering more than 100 hikes. A fun book for planning your next venture.

Laine, Barbara and Don Laine. *Little Known Southwest: Outdoor Destinations Beyond the Parks.* Seattle, WA: The Mountaineers, 2001. Hiking and wildlife viewing tips for 16 national parks and recreation areas, 42 national monuments and other federal lands in Arizona, Colorado, New Mexico, and Utah.

Mitchell, Joe and Mike Coronella. *The Hayduke Trail: A Guide to the Backcountry Hiking Trail on the Colorado Plateau.* Salt Lake City, UT: University of Utah Press, 2005. This 800-mile backcountry trail traverses six national parks and some of the most remote scenery of the Southwest.

Molvar, Erik and Tamara Martin. *Hiking Zion and Bryce Canyon National Parks.* Guilford, CT: Globe Pequot (Falcon Guides), 2005. Covers 56 hikes in the two parks, as well as in Cedar Breaks National Monument and other nearby areas.

Ray, Cosmic. *Favorite Hikes Flagstaff & Sedona.* Fifty of this local author's preferred trails, including Sedona "vortex hikes." Self-published, available locally.

Schneider, Bill. *Best Easy Day Hikes Canyonlands and Arches.* Guilford, CT: Globe Pequot (Falcon Guides), 2005. Details of trails to ruins, rock art, and natural wonders.

Schneider, Bill. *Hiking Canyonlands and Arches National Parks.* Guilford, CT: Globe Pequot (Falcon Guides), 2005. Information on more than 60 trails in these two spectacular parks.

Wilson, Dave. *Hiking Ruins Seldom Seen.* Guilford, CT: Globe Pequot (Falcon Guides), 2000. Cultural background and detailed directions to ruins and rock art throughout the Four Corners states—mostly concentrated in central Arizona, but with some in Southeast Utah.

Michael Kelsey's Guides

You'll find that this line of self-published hiking guidebooks is full of information on front- and backcountry destinations throughout the Four Corners. (Just take the time estimates with a grain of salt—Kelsey practically jogs his trails.) Some are getting out of date, but they're all as comprehensive as they come. The list includes *Boater's Guide to Lake Powell* (2001); *Canyon Hiking Guide to the Colorado Plateau* (1999); *Hiking,* *Biking and Exploring Canyonlands National Park and Vicinity* (1992); *Hiking and Exploring the Paria River* (2004); *Hiking and Exploring Utah's Henry Mountains and Robbers Roost* (1990); *Hiking and Exploring Utah's San Rafael Swell* (1999); and *Technical Slot Canyon Guide to the Colorado Plateau* (2003). They're available at bookstores in the area and from Amazon.com.

Mountain Biking

Alley, Sarah Bennett. *Mountain Biking New Mexico.* Guilford, CT: Globe Pequot (Falcon Guides), 2001. Covers the whole state, including six rides near Farmington and Chaco Canyon.

Beakley, Paul. *Mountain Bike America: Arizona.* Guilford, CT: Globe Pequot, 2001. Includes half a dozen trails near Flagstaff, a few more in the Grand Canyon area, and one near Page.

Bridgers, Lee. *Mountain Bike America: Moab.* Guilford, CT: Globe Pequot, 2000. Fifty rides from easy to punishing, plus superb maps and trail details.

Bridgers, Lee. *Mountain Biking Moab.* Guilford, CT: Globe Pequot (Falcon Guides), 2003. Details of 48 rides in the Moab area.

Crowell, David. *Mountain Biking Moab Pocket Guide.* Guilford, CT: Globe Pequot (Falcon Guides), 2003. A quick guide to 42 rides, small enough to slip into you Camelback.

Grubbs, Bruce. *Mountain Biking Flagstaff & Sedona.* Guilford, CT: Globe Pequot (Falcon Guides), 1999. A pocket-size guide with 25 rides near Flagstaff and 10 more around Sedona, with the typical Falcon attention to detail.

Hurst, Robert. *Mountain Biking Colorado's San Juan Mountains: Durango and Telluride.* Guilford, CT: Globe Pequot (Falcon Guides), 2002. More than 70 mountain bike trails around Durango and in the mountains to the north.

McCoy, Michael. *Mountain Bike! Southern Utah*. Birmingham, AL: Menasha Ridge Press, 2000. About half of the 75 rides in this slim but detailed volume are in Southeast and South-Central Utah.

Peel, John. *Mountain Biking Durango*. Guilford, CT: Globe Pequot (Falcon Guides), 1998. Thirty-nine of the city's best rides, form downtown to lung-busting climbs in the hills.

"Rider Mel." *Rider Mel's Mountain Bike Guide to Moab*. An entertaining, self-published local favorite.

Utesch, Peggy. *Kokopelli's Trail: The Utah–Colorado Mountain Bike Trail System: Route 1, Moab to Loma*. Moab, UT: Canyon Country Publications, 1990. This 80-page guide contains maps and photos of the multiday trip from Colorado to Moab.

Rock Climbing

Bjørnstad, Eric. *Desert Rock: Rock Climbs in the National Parks*. Guilford, CT: Globe Pequot (Falcon Guides), 1996. Routes in Arches, Canyonlands, Capitol Reef, Zion, and the Glen Canyon National Recreation Area.

Bjørnstad, Eric. *Desert Rock II: Wall Street to the San Rafael Swell*. Guilford, CT: Globe Pequot (Falcon Guides), 1997. Covers short crack routes in the San Rafael area as well as some spots near Moab.

Bjørnstad, Eric. *Desert Rock III: Moab to Colorado National Monument*. Guilford, CT: Globe Pequot (Falcon Guides), 1999. Authoritative and detailed, this guide covers more than 500 routes in all the climbing spots near Moab, from the Fisher Towers to the Island in the Sky.

Bjørnstad, Eric. *Desert Rock IV: Remote Areas of the Colorado Plateau*. Guilford, CT: Globe Pequot (Falcon Guides), 2003. Includes the Valley of the Gods and other even more isolated spots.

Burns, Cameron. *Selected Climbs in the Desert Southwest: Colorado and Utah*. Seattle, WA: The Mountaineers, 1999. Access and route info on more than 130 routes in western Colorado and southern Utah.

Macdonald, Dougald and Chris McNamara. *Desert Towers Select*. SuperTopo, 2002. This incredibly detailed guide to 15 tower routes in Arches, Castle Valley, Colorado National Monument, Canyonlands, and Indian Creek is available for download in PDF format for $9.95 from www.supertopo.com, and includes free updates for three years.

Canyoneering

Allen, Steve. *Canyoneering: The San Rafael Swell*. Salt Lake City, UT: University of Utah Press, 2000. The definitive guide to exploring the canyons of South-Central Utah. Incredibly detailed and comprehensive.

Allen, Steve. *Canyoneering 2: Technical Loop Hikes in Southern Utah*. Salt Lake City, UT: University of Utah Press, 2002. Seven week-long routes in South-Central Utah, all covered with Allen's typical thoroughness.

Allen, Steve. *Canyoneering 3: Loop Hikes in Utah's Escalante*. Salt Lake City, UT: University of Utah Press, 1997. Thirty-seven hikes and 14 road descriptions, mostly in the Grand Staircase–Escalante National Monument.

Archaeology

Gardner, A. Dudley and Val Brinkerhoff. *Architecture of the Ancient Ones*. Salt Lake City: Gibbs Smith, 2000. A beautifully photographed book on design of the Anasazi ruins.

Kelen, Leslie. *Sacred Images: A Vision of Native American Rock Art*. Salt Lake City: Gibbs Smith, 1996. More great photos of Anasazi remnants, this time concentrating on their rock art, as well as that of the Frémont and the Ute.

Noble, David Grant. *Ancient Ruins of the Southwest: An Archeological Guide*. Flagstaff,

AZ: Northland Publishing, 2000. Rich with background information, this guide covers the ruins of the Mogollon, Hohokam, Anasazi, Fremont, and other ancient cultures.

Slifer, Dennis. *Guide to Rock Art of the Utah Region*. Santa Fe, NM: Ancient City Press, 2000. Background and locational information on dozens of sites on public land in southern Utah, Colorado, New Mexico, Arizona, and Nevada.

Other Guides

Eddington, Patrick and Susan Makov. *The Trading Post Guidebook*. Flagstaff, AZ: Northland Publishing, 1995. Although somewhat out of date, this beautiful book lists trading posts, galleries, museums, auctions, and individual artists throughout the Four Corners region, and is illustrated with maps and hand-tinted photos.

Kosik, Fran. *Native Roads: The Complete Motoring Guide to the Navajo and Hopi Nations*. Tucson, AZ: Rio Nuevo, 2005. Bursting with fascinating details, this guide takes you down all the major roads on the reservations and many of the not-so-major ones. Don't spend any time on either reservation without this book.

NATURAL HISTORY

The **Western National Parks Association** puts out *Shrubs and Trees of the Southwest Uplands, Flowers of the Southwest Deserts, 50 Common Amphibians and Reptiles of the Southwest, 70 Common Cacti of the Southwest, 50 Common Mammals of the Southwest, 50 Common Reptiles of the Southwest, 100 Desert Wildflowers of the Southwest, 100 Roadside Wildflowers of the Southwest,* and *Flowers of the Southwest Mountains*.

Another good line is the **"The Story Behind the Scenery"** series produced by KC Publications (800/626-9673, kcp@kc-publications.com, www.kcpublications.com). These large-format publications (part book, part glossy magazine) treat the natural and human history of a specific Southwest location. They're a good way to get an overview of an area or topic, and are sold at bookstores and gift shops in parks and major towns. *Arches: The Story Behind the Scenery,* is a good example, and the rest of the Four Corners list includes *Canyonlands, Canyon de Chelly Landforms: Heart of the Colorado Plateau, Capitol Reef, Glen Canyon/Lake Powell, Grand Canyon, Grand Circle Adventure, Monument Valley, Petrified Forest, Mesa Verde,* and *Rainbow Bridge*. KC Publications also produces, in a similar format, *Southwestern Indian Tribes, Southwestern Indian Ceremonials, Southwestern Indian Pottery, Southwestern Indian Weaving, Southwestern Indian Arts and Crafts,* and two volumes subtitled "Voyages of Discovery": *Major John Wesley Powell* and *Mormon Trail*.

Flora and Fauna

Fagan, Damian. *Canyon Country Wildflowers*. Guilford, CT: Globe Pequot (Falcon Guides), 1998. Look up that pretty blossom by color in this photo-rich guide, covering the central Colorado Plateau.

Halfpenny, James. *Scats and Tracks of the Desert Southwest*. Guilford, CT: Globe Pequot (Falcon Guides), 2005. Did a bear or bobcat leave that? Find out with this small but intriguing guide.

Kavanagh, James. *Field Guide to the Grand Canyon*. Blain, WA: Waterford Press, 2001. A folding, plastic-coated sheet with pictures and descriptions of common plants and animals.

Kavanagh, James. *Southwestern Desert Birds* Blain, WA: Waterford Press, 2001. A plastic pocket guide with dozens of illustrations of common species.

Kavanagh, James. *Southwestern Desert Life: An Introduction to Familiar Plants and Animals* Blain, WA: Waterford Press, 2001. A folding, plastic-coated sheet with pictures and descriptions of 150 common species.

MacGowan, Craig. *Mac's Field Guides: Southwest Cacti, Shrubs and Trees.* Seattle, WA: The Mountaineers, 1995. A laminated sheet for easy identification.

MacGowan, Craig. *Mac's Field Guides: Southwest Park/Garden Birds.* Seattle, WA: The Mountaineers. A laminated sheet for easy identification.

Peterson, Roger Tory. *A Field Guide to Western Birds.* Boston: Houghton Mifflin, 1998. "The Birder's Bible" includes full-color paintings and range maps of more than 1,000 birds from 700 species.

Stall, Chris. *Animal Tracks Southwest.* Seattle, WA: The Mountaineers, 1990. More than 40 life-size (or close) tracks of the area's common critters, plus details on each one's behavior.

Stuckey, Maggie and George Palmer. *Western Trees: A Field Guide.* Guilford, CT: Globe Pequot (Falcon Guides), 1998. Identification information on common trees from Colorado to Washington state and Northern California.

Geology

Baars, Donald. *A Traveler's Guide to the Geology of the Colorado Plateau.* Salt Lake City, UT: University of Utah Press, 2002. Organized by route, this guide takes you from the Paradox Basin to the High Plateaus and explains everything you see along the way.

Baars, Donald. *Navajo Country: A Geology and Natural History of the Four Corners Region.* Albuquerque, NM: University of New Mexico Press, 1995. If you've ever giggled at terms like "Shinarump Member," this book will tell you what it really means. An in-depth exploration of the amazing scenery on the reservation and surrounding lands.

Hopkins, Ralph. *Hiking the Southwest's Geology: Four Corners Region.* Seattle, WA: The Mountaineers, 2002. A hiking guide with a geological focus, organized by geologic provinces.

General Guides

Grubbs, Bruce. *Desert Sense: Skills for Camping, Hiking and Biking in Hot, Dry Climates.* Seattle, WA: The Mountaineers, 2005. Techniques for staying safe and happy in the desert.

Tweit, Susan. *The Great Southwest Nature Factbook.* Seattle, WA: Alaska Northwest Books, 1992. Packed with tons of tidbits on the region's plants, animals, and natural features, this book is equally fascinating at home as on the trail.

Williams, David. *A Naturalist's Guide to Canyon Country.* Guilford, CT: Globe Pequot (Falcon Guides), 2002. Covers the geology, flora, and fauna of the canyonlands in one handy volume. If you buy only one natural-history guide, make it this one.

NATIVE CULTURES
Anasazi

Frazier, Kendrick. *People of Chaco.* New York: W. W. Norton & Co., 1999. One of the best single-volume treatments of the ancient culture, its history, and descendants.

Lekson, Stephen. *The Chaco Meridian.* Walnut Creek, CA: Altamira Press, 1999. Explores the implications of the fact that the ruins at Aztec, Chaco, and Paquime, Mexico, are on almost the exact same longitude.

Roberts, David. *In Search of the Old Ones.* New York: Simon and Schuster, 1997. The author's descriptions of his explorations of Anasazi ruins and history reads like a good novel.

Modern Tribes

Fergusson, Erna. *Dancing Gods: Indian Ceremonials of New Mexico and Arizona.* Albuquerque, NM: University of New Mexico Press, 2001. Visiting details and background information on native ceremonies open to the public on the Navajo, Hopi, and Apache reservations and the Zuni and Rio Grande pueblos.

Locke, Raymond. *The Book of the Navajo* Los

Angles, CA: Mankind Publishing, 2002. Addresses the Navajo belief system and other aspects of traditional culture, as well as their history.

Pettit, Jan. *Utes: The Mountain People.* Boulder, CO: Johnson Books, 1990. The full tribal history, with rare historic photographs and extensive cultural detail.

Water, Frank. *Book of the Hopi.* New York: Penguin, 1977. The tribe's historical, spiritual, and cultural history, touching on creation stories, clan migrations, and the ceremonial cycle.

Crafts

Bassman, Theda. *Treasures of the Hopi.* Flagstaff, AZ: Northland Publishing, 1997. Covers all the tribe's major crafts, including jewelry, kachinas, pottery, and baskets.

Bassman, Theda. *Treasures of the Navajo.* Flagstaff, AZ: Northland Publishing, 1997. Covers all the tribe's major crafts, including jewelry, pottery, rugs, and sandpaintings.

Day, Jonathan. *Traditional Hopi Kachinas.* Flagstaff, AZ: Northland Publishing, 2000. Describes and depicts the work of new generation of artisans, and their relationship to older styles of carvers.

Hayes, Allan and John Blom. *Southwestern Pottery: Anasazi to Zuni.* Flagstaff, AZ: Northland Publishing, 1996. A definitive guide to all major indigenous styles of pottery in the Southwest, with photos and interesting historical anecdotes.

Page, Jake. *Field Guide to Southwest Indian Arts and Crafts.* New York: Random House, 1998. Fully illustrated guide to crafts, with descriptions of techniques, cultural history, and information on hundreds of individual artisans.

Wright, Barton. *Hopi Kachinas: The Complete Guide to Collecting Kachina Dolls.* Flagstaff, AZ: Northland Publishing, 1977. A concise but comprehensive manual, with photographs and descriptions of most major kachina figures.

NONFICTION
History

Bergera, Gary (Ed). *On Desert Trails with Everett Ruess.* Salt Lake City, UT: Gibbs Smith, 2000. A selection of Everett's poems and letters, with commentary, photos, and woodcuts.

Clark, H. Jackson. *The Owl in Monument Canyon.* Salt Lake City, UT: University of Utah Press, 1993. Fascinating stories and memories from the author's four decades as a trader on the Navajo reservation during the mid-20th century.

Ellis, Reuben (Ed). *Stories and Stone: Writing the Anasazi Homeland.* Boulder, CO: Pruett Publishing Company, 1996. An anthology of writing about the prehistoric Southwest, with contributions from Barry Lopez, Willa Cather, Robert Frost, Leslie Marmon Silko, and others.

Rusho, W. L. (Ed). *Everett Ruess: A Vagabond for Beauty & Wilderness Journals.* Salt Lake City, UT: Gibbs Smith, 2002. The combined edition of both books about the teenage wanderer, combines his letters and journal entries from his all-too-brief life.

Taylor, Mark. *Sandstone Sunsets: In Search of Everett Ruess.* Salt Lake City, UT: Gibbs Smith, 1997. The story of one man's obsession with one of the Southwest's most enduring mysteries.

Warner, Ted (Ed.) *The Dominguez-Escalante Journal.* Salt Lake City, UT: University of Utah Press, 1995. The story of the incredible 1776 journey in the padres' own words, with annotations and maps.

Land Use, Development, and Water Issues

Farmer, Jared. *Glen Canyon Dammed: Inventing Lake Powell and the Canyon Country.* Tucson, AZ: University of Arizona Press, 1999. Discusses the Glen Canyon Dam and its place in the economy and culture of the Southwest.

Fradkin, Philip. *A River No More: The Colorado River and the West.* Berkeley, CA: University of California Press, 1996. The story of the Colorado River and its tributaries, and their impact on the ranches, towns, and cities of the region.

Fradkin, Philip. *Sagebrush Country: Land and the American West.* Tucson, AZ: University of Arizona Press, 1989. Examines the role of land issues in shaping the history of the West, from the perspectives of settlers, miners, scientists, ranchers, environmentalists, and Native Americans.

Martin, Russell. *A Story That Stands Like a Dam: Glen Canyon and the Struggle for the Soul of the West.* Sale Lake City, UT: University of Utah Press, 1999. The colorful story of the construction of Glen Canyon Dam and the controversy that has arisen in its wake.

Murray, John. *Cinema Southwest.* Flagstaff, AZ: Northland Publishing, 2000. The history of the Southwest as seen through the movie camera's lens. Describes movie locations and biographies of major Western stars.

Porter, Eliot. *The Place No One Knew: Glen Canyon on the Colorado.* Salt Lake City, UT: Gibbs Smith, 2000. The commemorative edition of the classic paean to the canyon that was drowned beneath Lake Powell. Evocative photographs accompanied by writings by Wallace Stegner, Joseph Wood Crutch, and others.

Reisner, Marc. *Cadillac Desert: The American West and Its Disappearing Water.* New York: Penguin Books, 1993. The highly entertaining tale of water use, and misuse, in the West.

Scenery and Photography

Spring, Anselm. *Wild and Beautiful: Grand Staircase–Escalante National Monument.* Salt Lake City, UT: Gibbs Smith, 1998. Striking photographs of the monument's many moods, with an essay by Mark Taylor.

Telford, John and Terry Tempest Williams. *Coyote's Canyon.* Salt Lake City, UT: Gibbs Smith, 1981. Telford's photographs and Williams's prose do a wonderful job of evoking the grandeur of the Four Corners' landscapes.

Other

Abbey, Edward. *Beyond the Wall: Essays from the Outside.* New York: Henry Holt, 1984. A collection of essays on life in the West, in Abbey's trademark cantankerous, reverent style.

Abbey, Edward. *Desert Solitaire.* New York: Ballantine, 1991. The classic story of the author's sojourn at Arches before the crowds arrived. Should be required reading for all visitors.

Abbey, Edward. *The Journey Home: Some Words in Defense of the American West.* New York: E. P. Dutton, 1991. More essays, with a focus on the desert Southwest.

Dunaway, David King and Sarah Spurgeon. *Writing the Southwest.* New York: Penguin, 1995. An excellent introduction to the regional literature, with pieces by Edward Abbey, John Nichols, Barbara Kingsolver, Tony Hillerman, and others, as well as a selected bibliography.

Powell, John Wesley. *The Exploration of the Colorado River and Its Canyons.* Washington, DC: National Geographic, 2002. The exhilarating, firsthand account of one of the most incredible voyages of discovery in American history.

Schlosser, S. E. *Spooky Southwest.* Guilford, CT: Globe Pequot, 2004. More than two dozen folktales of Southwest ghosts and mysteries.

Shoumatoff, Alex. *Legends of the American Desert.* New York: HarperCollins, 1997. Subtitled "Sojourns in the Greater Southwest," this highly readable account covers the many diverging worlds that make up the region, from Mormons to drug traffickers.

Stegner, Wallace. *Beyond the Hundredth Meridian: John Wesley Powell and the Second Opening of the West.* New York: Penguin, 1992. Probably the best account of Powell's life, adventures, and struggles.

Stegner, Wallace. *Mormon Country.* Lincoln, NE: University of Nebraska Press, 1992. Essays on southern Utah, both historical and modern, in the author's gorgeous prose.

FICTION

Tony Hillerman's best-selling series of police mysteries, set on the Navajo Reservation, gives a fascinating glimpse into modern Navajo culture—and they're darn good reading as well. Titles include *A Thief of Time, The First Eagle, Sacred Clowns, The Dark Wind, The Fallen Man, Listening Woman, Skinwalkers, Hunting Badger, Dance Hall of the Dead, Coyote Waits, The Blessing Way, Talking God, People of Darkness, The Ghostway, Skeleton Man, The Sinister Pig,* and *Wailing Wind.*

Two other best-known novels set in the Four Corners are Edward Abbey's rollicking *The Monkey Wrench Gang* (New York: Perennial Classics, 2000) and *Hayduke Lives!* (New York: Little Brown & Co, 1991), both detailing the exploits of a band of eco-saboteurs fighting against the industrialization of the Colorado Plateau. The first (the better of the two) was partly responsible for the creation of Earth First!, the confrontational environmental group.

MAGAZINES AND JOURNALS

A great source of information on the ecosystems of the Southwest is *The Southwestern Naturalist* (www.biosurvey.ou.edu/swan/ swnat.html), a journal published by the **Southwestern Association of Naturalists.** For more on the history, culture, and environments of the Four Corners, check out *Plateau: Land and Peoples of the Colorado Plateau* (928/774-5211, ext. 219, www.musnaz.org/research/publications.htm), offered to members of the Museum of Northern Arizona.

You'll find free copies of *Inside Outside* (970/375-4538, www.insideoutsidemag.com), a tabloid-format magazine covering the sports, recreations, health, fitness, and entertainment options of the Four Corners, available throughout the region.

MAPS

Maps are a critical part of any backcountry venture. The **U.S. Geological Survey** (888/275-8747, http://store.usgs.gov) has been creating topographical maps of the entire country since 1879. At last count they had more than 80,000, including more than 57,000 of the 1:24,000-scale maps better known as 7.5-minute "quads" (quadrangles), perfect for folding up and popping in a backpack or bike rack. You can buy these at many outdoor-gear stores and specialty map stores in the Four Corners, or order them directly from the USGS for $6 each plus a $5 handling fee.

Other good sources include **TopoZone** (978/251-4242, www.topozone.com) and MyTopo (877/587-9004, www.mytopo.com), which let you create and download custom topographic maps based on the USGS line. More Four Corners maps, including the excellent, durable ones made by National Geographic's Trails Illustrated, are listed in the *Information and Services* section.

Internet Resources

Recreation.gov
www.recreation.gov
This government website provides information on federal recreation areas, including many in the Four Corners. It's searchable by state and activity, and has been expanded to include data on state, tribal, and local recreation areas.

DesertUSA
www.desertusa.com
An excellent online resource for information on the deserts of the American Southwest, with everything from cultural history to shopping. It's updated with new articles regularly, and includes maps, wildflower reports, current festivals, and a message board.

Canyons, Cultures, and Environmental Change
www.cpluhna.nau.edu/index.htm
Subtitled "An Introduction to the Land Use History of the Colorado Plateau," this website is full of information of the natural and human history of the Four Corners. It's produced by NASA, the USGS, and Northern Arizona University, so you know it's accurate, covering everything from uranium mining to endangered species.

Outsiders Foundation
http://outsidersfoundation.com/navajo.html
Put out by the Wheelwright Museum of the American Indian, "On the Strength of Their Work" is a documentary about the Hatch Brothers Trading Post in Fruitland, New Mexico, one of the last remaining traditional trading posts in the Four Corners. It's available for download as a Quicktime movie.

Bill Leverton's TravelSW.com
www.travelsw.com
Journalist Bill Leverton's site is packed with articles and information for independent travelers in the Southwest.

Navajo Central
http://navajocentral.org/faq2indx.htm
Computer systems analyst Larry DiLucchio has compiled an extensive collection of information on the Navajo tribe and reservation. Having lived in Chinle for over 15 years, he has assembled an excellent list of questions and answers on daily life on the reservation from an outsider's perspective.

Voices of the Colorado Plateau
http://archive.li.suu.edu/voices
This online archive compiled by Southern Utah University features photographs and oral history recordings of life on the Colorado Plateau. You'll need the Flash player to view the recordings, but it's worth it to be able to hear the voices of native elders and settlers.

Go-Utah.com
www.go-utah.com
More than 10,000 pages of information on the Beehive State, covering 100 cities and towns as well as parks, activities, and lodging. Basically an online travel guide, this rivals many print versions, and even includes an online bookstore.

Notes from the Road
www.notesfromtheroad.com/desert-southwest/desertsouthwest.htm
Intriguing writing and great photography about the Colorado Plateau and many other desert regions in the United States.

Gorp.com
www.gorp.com
The Great Outdoor Resource Page is the place to go for details on anything and everything in outdoor recreation. You can browse by state (Arizona, for example, is at http://gorp.com/gorp/location/az/az.htm) or other destination, as well as activities, and even book trips online—just be ready for plenty of advertisements.

The American Southwest
www.americansouthwest.net

This well-organized site covers the parks and scenic spots of Arizona, California, Colorado, Nevada, New Mexico, Texas, and Utah. Articles feature excellent photography and detailed visiting instructions, and there's a particular good section on slot canyons.

Out West
www.outwestnewspaper.com

Editor/reporter Chuck Woodbury spent much of the period 1987–2000 roving around the American West in his 24-foot motor home. After driving over 200,000 miles, he had logged a million words on the people, places, and things he encountered off (sometimes far off) the beaten path—the best of which are on this website.

Cyberwest Magazine
www.cyberwest.com

An online travel and recreation magazine for the American West, covering topics in the history, culture, and environment.

Index

CAMPING

HIKING

Acknowledgments

I am eternally grateful to everyone who helped update this guide, including Anne Barney (Durango), Dwayne Cassidy (Page), Kathie Curley (Navajo Tourism), Marian DeLay (Moab), Debbie Dusenbery (Farmington), Angela Geissler (Grand Canyon Railway), Jessica Jaret (GoLite), Robbie Levin (Sorrel River Ranch), Jeanie Linn (BLM), Meg Roederer (Flagstaff), Khamsone Sirimanivong (Flagstaff), Tracy Vega (Rio Nuevo Publishers), Steve Ward (Lake Powell Resort), and Bart Wilsey (Farmington Museum).

Thanks to everyone at the NPS who helped with checking over park information, including Russ Bodnar, Judie Chrobak-Cox, Carol Kruse, Linda Martin, Nora McKerry, Cindy Micheli, Char Obergh, Marge Post, Naomi Shibata, and Marti Stebbins.

Special thanks go to Mike Finney (AZ Communications Group), Tony Hillerman, and Jeff Slade (Detours).

This book is dedicated to everyone fighting to protect the beauty, culture, and history of the Colorado Plateau.

MAP SYMBOLS

▧▧▧	Expressway	🄲	Highlight	✈	Airfield	⌁	Golf Course
▬	Primary Road	○	City/Town	✈	Airport	🅟	Parking Area
▬	Secondary Road	◉	State Capital	▲	Mountain	≋	Archaeological Site
- - - -	Unpaved Road	⊛	National Capital	✛	Unique Natural Feature	♦	Church
- - - -	Trail	★	Point of Interest			🛢	Gas Station
··········	Ferry	•	Accommodation	🐾	Waterfall	◠◠	Glacier
─┼─┼─	Railroad	▼	Restaurant/Bar	♠	Park	▦	Mangrove
▤▤	Pedestrian Walkway	■	Other Location	🄣	Trailhead	▱	Reef
▥▥▥	Stairs	Λ	Campground	⛷	Skiing Area	▦	Swamp

CONVERSION TABLES

$$°C = (°F - 32) / 1.8$$
$$°F = (°C \times 1.8) + 32$$

1 inch = 2.54 centimeters (cm)
1 foot = .304 meters (m)
1 yard = 0.914 meters
1 mile = 1.6093 kilometers (km)
1 km = .6214 miles
1 fathom = 1.8288 m
1 chain = 20.1168 m
1 furlong = 201.168 m
1 acre = .4047 hectares
1 sq km = 100 hectares
1 sq mile = 2.59 square km
1 ounce = 28.35 grams
1 pound = .4536 kilograms
1 short ton = .90718 metric ton
1 short ton = 2000 pounds
1 long ton = 1.016 metric tons
1 long ton = 2240 pounds
1 metric ton = 1000 kilograms
1 quart = .94635 liters
1 US gallon = 3.7854 liters
1 Imperial gallon = 4.5459 liters
1 nautical mile = 1.852 km

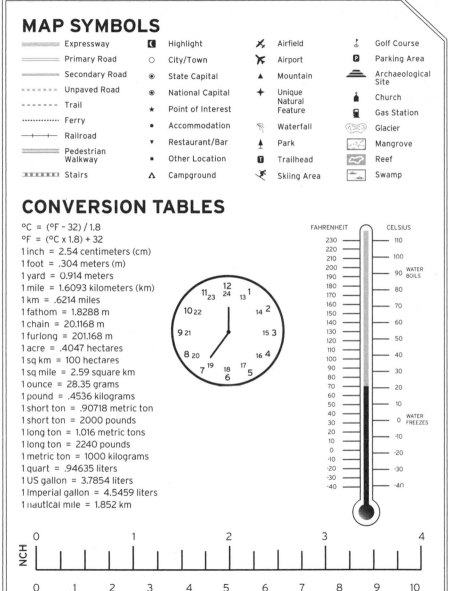

MOON FOUR CORNERS

Avalon Travel Publishing
An Imprint of
Avalon Publishing Group, Inc.

AVALON
publishing group incorporated

1400 65th Street, Suite 250
Emeryville, CA 94608, USA
www.moon.com

Editor: Kay Elliott
Series Manager: Kathryn Ettinger
Acquisitions Manager: Rebecca K. Browning
Copy Editor: Gerardyne Madigan
Graphics Coordinator: Tabitha Lahr
Cover & Interior Design: Gerilyn Attebery
Map Editor: Kat Smith
Cartographers: Kat Bennett, Suzanne Service,
    Kansai Uchida
Cartography Manager: Mike Morgenfeld
Indexer: Judy Hunt

ISBN-10: 1-56691-778-6
ISBN-13: 978-1-56691-778-0
ISSN: 1543-7000

Printing History
1st Edition – 2003
2nd Edition – February 2006
5 4 3 2 1

Front cover photo: Rainbow Bridge, Utah © Tom Till
Title page photo: Horseshoe Tower Ruin, Colorado
    © Russ Bishop

Printed in Canada by Transcontinental.

16.95 3/06

KEEPING CURRENT

If you have a favorite gem you'd like to see included in the next edition, or see anything that needs updating, clarification, or correction, please drop us a line. Send your comments via email to feedback@moon.com, or use the address above.

www.moon.com

For helpful advice on planning a trip, visit www.moon.com for the **TRAVEL PLANNER** and get access to useful travel strategies and valuable information about great places to visit. When you travel with Moon, expect an experience that is uncommon and truly unique.

HANDBOOKS • OUTDOORS • METRO • LIVING ABROAD